Cyrus Lakdawala

Kramnik

move by move

D0860890

EVERYMAN CHESS

www.everymanchess.com

First published in 2012 by Gloucester Publishers Limited, Northburgh House,
10 Northburgh Street, London EC1V 0AT

British Library Cataloguing-in-Publication Data
A catalogue record for this book is available from the British Library.

ISBN: 978 1 85744 991 4

Distributed in North America by The Globe Pequot Press, P.O Box 480,
246 Goose Lane, Guilford, CT 06437-0480.

All other sales enquiries should be directed to Everyman Chess, Northburgh House,
10 Northburgh Street, London EC1V 0AT
tel: 020 7253 7887 fax: 020 7490 3708
email: info@everymanchess.com; website: www.everymanchess.com

Everyman Chess Series
Chief advisor: Byron Jacobs
Commissioning editor: John Emms
Assistant editor: Richard Palliser

Typeset and edited by First Rank Publishing, Brighton.
Cover design by Horatio Monteverde.

About the Author

Cyrus Lakdawala is an International Master, a former National Open and American Open Champion, and a six-time State Champion. He has been teaching chess for over 30 years, and coaches some of the top junior players in the US.

Also by the Author:
Play the London System
A Ferocious Opening Repertoire
The Slav: Move by Move
1...d6: Move by Move
The Caro-Kann: Move by Move
The Four Knights: Move by Move
Capablanca: Move by Move
The Modern Defence: Move by Move

Contents

Foreword 7

Bibliography 8

Introduction 9

1   Kramnik on the Attack 21

2   Kramnik on Defence 83

3   Riding the Dynamic Element 149

4   Exploiting Imbalances 217

5   Accumulating Advantages 269

6   Kramnik on Endings 339

Index of Openings 406

Index of Opponents 407

Foreword

The *Move by Move* format is designed to be interactive, and is based on questions asked by both teachers and students. It aims – as much as possible – to replicate chess lessons. All the way through, readers will be challenged to answer searching questions and to complete exercises, to test their skills in key aspects of the game. It's our firm belief that practising your skills like this is an excellent way to study chess.

Many thanks go to all those who have been kind enough to offer inspiration, advice and assistance in the creation of *Move by Move*. We're really excited by this series and hope that readers will share our enthusiasm.

John Emms
Everyman Chess

Bibliography

1 d4, Volume One, Boris Avrukh (Quality Chess 2008)
1 d4, Volume Two, Boris Avrukh (Quality Chess 2010)
Challenging the Nimzo-Indian, David Vigorito (Quality Chess 2007)
New Ideas in the Four Knights, John Nunn (Batsford 1993)
Play 1 e4 e5!, Nigel Davies (Everyman Chess 2006)
Play the Open Games as Black, John Emms (Gambit 2000)
Starting Out: The Scotch Game, John Emms (Everyman Chess 2006)
The Berlin Wall, John Cox (Quality Chess 2008)
The Caro-Kann: Move by Move, Cyrus Lakdawala (Everyman Chess 2012)
The Four Knights Game, Andrey Obodchuk (New in Chess 2011)
The Nimzo-Indian: Move by Move, John Emms (Everyman Chess 2012)
The Slav: Move by Move, Cyrus Lakdawala (Everyman Chess 2011)

Electronic/Online
Chess Today (with annotations from Ruslan Scherbakov, Maxim Notkin, Alex Baburin, Mikhail Golubev and Andrei Deviatkin)
Chess Publishing (with annotations from John Emms, Ruslan Scherbakov, Glenn Flear, Victor Mikhalevski, Paul Motwani, Luke McShane, Chris Ward, Neil McDonald, Tony Kosten, and Eric Prié)
Chessbase 10 (with annotations by Zoltan Ribli, Konstantin Landa, and Carsten Hansen)
Chesslive database
The Week in Chess

Introduction

The account of a chess player's life is a mosaic of a million moves. In this book we examine the career of one of the all-time great strategists, Vladimir Borisovich Kramnik, 14th World Chess Champion. Born to a sculptor father and a musician mother, Vladimir was destined to become an artist himself, but of the chessboard. He learned chess at the age of five and was quickly recognized as an exceptional talent. At age 16 he went on to win the World Under-18 Championship, a foreshadowing of his future World title reign.

Kramnik's Style
Kramnik plays in a style which sometimes transcends classification. He often starts in super-stodgy, safe lines, but despite his reputation, his games are rarely boring. In essence it is a style without a style. Kramnik is not a standard issue Capablanca- or Ulf Andersson-type positional player. Kramnik's games seem to contain a strange initiative valve, which he controls and may turn on at any given point in a game. His forces, like time, only move in one direction: forward. In essence, he is Botvinnik, but without a safety filter.

Kramnik's Openings/Endings
Kramnik, more than any other world champion, tries to bypass the middlegame entirely by going straight for the ending, relying on his incredible technique to squeeze out wins from otherwise drawish landscapes. Here are some of his instant opening/ending lines in which he specializes:

a) The Berlin Lopez: **1 e4 e5 2 ♘f3 ♘c6 3 ♗b5 ♘f6 4 0-0 ♘xe4 5 d4 ♘d6 6 ♗xc6 dxc6 7 dxe5 ♘f5 8 ♕xd8+ ♔xd8** (see Games 15 and 34).

(see following diagram)

b) The Grünfeld: **1 d4 ♘f6 2 c4 g6 3 ♘c3 d5 4 cxd5 ♘xd5 5 e4 ♘xc3 6 bxc3 ♗g7 7 ♘f3 c5 8 ♗e3 ♕a5 9 ♕d2 ♘c6 10 ♖c1 cxd4 11 cxd4 ♕xd2+ 12 ♔xd2** (see Game 50).

c) An early endgame line from the English: **1 ♘f3 c5 2 c4 ♘f6 3 ♘c3 ♘c6 4 g3 d5 5 d4 cxd4 6 ♘xd4 dxc4 7 ♘xc6 ♕xd1+ 8 ♘xd1 bxc6** (see Game 49).

d) And one from Queen's Gambit Accepted: **1 ♘f3 d5 2 d4 ♘f6 3 c4 c6 4 ♘c3 a6 5 e3 e6 6 ♗d3 dxc4 7 ♗xc4 c5 8 0-0 b5 9 ♗e2 ♗b7 10 dxc5 ♕xd1 11 ♖xd1** (see Game 59).

Of course, Kramnik's career is an unfinished book, since he will most certainly continue to produce many, many new strategic, tactical and theoretical works.

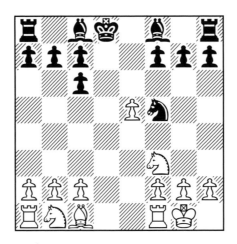

Kramnik's World Championship Matches

Kasparov, London 2000, 8½-6½

Nobody thought he could do it, but he did – and with ease, in one of the most shocking world championship match upsets since Max Euwe took down the alcoholic Alexander Alekhine, who was a mere shell of his real self, back in 1935. Kramnik won the match, not with the white pieces, but with Black. He unearthed the rare (perhaps it is more accurate to say "rare at that time" – now the Berlin Lopez is all the rage!) Berlin Lopez firewall. We saw the frustrated Kasparov unable to tear it down, as Kramnik spread draws like cream cheese generously heaped on a bagel. As White, Kramnik methodically pressured the legend and sailed to plus two, which actually could have been as many as plus four had not Kasparov demonstrated incredible defensive technique with some narrow saves. In hindsight, Kramnik's victory shouldn't have come as such a shock. Previously to the match, Kramnik had lost only one game out his last 100, all against the elite of the chess world. Kasparov graciously called Kramnik's play "pragmatic and tenacious". Thus ended the 15-year reign of a great champion, some consider the greatest of all time.

Leko, Brissago 2004, 7-7

Kramnik, now the reigning World Champion, went in the final game a full point down against his challenger, the unbeatably solid Peter Leko. Kramnik pulled off the impossible. Under unimaginable strain, the white whale exploded to the surface of the water, gusted over captain Leko's ship (taking Leko's leg with him!) and thunderously splashed down again into the endless below. Kramnik took down his challenger in the tension-filled final game to tie the match and retain his world crown – and created a masterpiece as well, almost as a whimsical afterthought! After the game Kramnik said: "I had to give everything, especially at the end, to win against such an opponent. Peter Leko is an incredible defender. For me it was more difficult than my match against Kasparov in the year 2000."

Topalov, Elista 2006, 8½-7½

This was the long awaited unification match between two world champions, ever since Kasparov split from FIDE back in 1993. Before this match, most of my chess friends predicted an easy victory for Topalov (I suspect because they favoured his aggressive style). I suppose the believer always makes the assumption that the robin sings her song in explicit praise of the believer's messiah, when in reality, the robin just likes the sound of her own voice!

Topalov and Kramnik were born to be each other's antagonist. Early on, the players surveyed their new surroundings in a posture of marked defiance. The players circled, strutting about with increasing bravado and swagger, to intimidate and take in the other's measure and gauge power. The infamous *Toiletgate* match was as ugly an episode, filled with intrigue and paranoia, as the first Spassky-Fischer match, with Topalov's camp accusing Kramnik of cheating during the match with the help of a secret, hidden computer in the toilet. (The spoiled kid, not getting what he asked for in his earlier gift, sometimes refuses to unwrap his new present!) Topalov, flinging himself with fervour at his opponent, lost two games early on. Then, with classic Fischer-like paranoia, declared that Kramnik used the toilet suspiciously often. Topa refused to shake Kramnik's hand before each game as well. Perhaps it is in a preyless carnivore's voracious nature to desire to eat everyone else! So the match committee, in somewhat craven fashion, caved under the pressure and ordered the private toilets locked and forced the use of shared toilets (thus tacitly agreeing with camp Topa that Kramnik may indeed be cheating!). King Kram's indignant reaction was similar to when a line judge at Wimbledon calls "out!" when the ball is clearly in, and gets dirty looks from the penalized player. The outraged Kramnik responded by forfeiting a game in protest at the action (just as Fischer did against Spassky for use of the television cameras) and threatened to forfeit the entire match as well. It isn't possible to mingle if nobody shows up at your party!

Despite the forfeit, the match continued, ending in a 6-6 tie (meaning Kramnik actually won without the forfeit!). Then Kramnik once again demonstrated his nerves were second to no other player by winning the rapid tie breaks 2½-1½, sending Topa to bed, despite his sleepy, protested insistence that he be allowed to stay up just a little while longer. Winning is important; winning when you desperately need to win is even more important. For the second World Championship match in a row, Kramnik did just that.

Anand, Bonn 2007, 4½-6½

Everything that could possibly go wrong went awry! Kramnik was finally defeated, mainly due to Anand's superior opening preparation. Kramnik was unable to overcome two early losses, both disastrously as White, in a hotly contested, ultra-sharp line of the Meran Semi-

Slav. He simply misjudged Anand's phenomenal opening preparation, just as Kasparov had against Kramnik himself.

The Misunderstood Champion

A few months ago my friend IM Dionisio Aldama and I were waiting around for the pairings at our weekly Saturday Gambito rapid tournament, and chatting. I told him I had started a book on Kramnik. "I no like Kramnik!" he said calmly. "What!?" I replied, appalled, adding with vehemence, "You would do well to 'Yes like Kramnik!'" Dionisio went on to complain that Kramnik, to him, represented the dull corporate positional interests of the chess world. Of course, nothing can be further than the truth. Just like Capablanca, Kramnik carved out a multitude of dazzling games; yet, for some bizarre reason, neither player is known for his attacking or tactical skills, simply because his strategic abilities eclipse his other talents.

Kramnik's light is difficult to see. One only catches occasional glimpses, as when a sunbeam shines through a slivered opening on a cloudy day. The important thing to remember is that the luminosity is always there, even when we can't easily see it. Observe his hidden power in the following game, which on the surface seems preordained toward a lifeless draw – yet the facts say otherwise.

One other thing: Kramnik was actually slightly off form in this game, and yet managed to put Aronian, ranked number two in the world, through a cruel and secret (secret only to the observers!) interrogation. There are truths we never want revealed: I originally utterly misinterpreted this game as a dull, meaningless draw. Confusion came in powerful waves, as patzer and GM alike booed and hissed on the internet at this game's external worthlessness. Only after the game, when Kramnik and Aronian shed light on the reality, did a glimmer of understanding dawn on the rest of us.

Game 1
V.Kramnik-L.Aronian
Tal Memorial, Moscow 2012
Four Knights Game

1 e4 e5 2 ♘f3 ♘c6 3 ♘c3 ♘f6 4 d4 exd4 5 ♘xd4 ♗b4 6 ♘xc6 bxc6 7 ♗d3 0-0 8 0-0 d5 9 exd5 cxd5

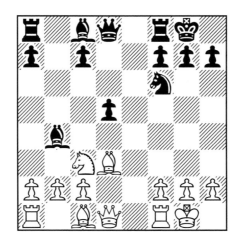

Question: Isn't this kind of a snoozer position?

Answer: Normally, yes! Kramnik revives a relict, long considered harmless to Black. At this point in the game I heard the collective internet groans: "OMG! Another boring 12-move Kramnik draw coming up!" This line of the Scotch Four Knights is considered one of the safest and most equal variations White can play versus 1...e5. After the game Kramnik said: "The computer considers it to be equal, but when you begin to move pieces, it becomes clear that it is easier to play with White."
10 h3!?

Question: What on earth ...? Isn't White's only prayer
for an edge based on the immediate pin with 10 ♗g5 - ?

Answer: Well, according to theory, yes; but keep in mind, Kramnik is the guy who manufactures the theory for the rest of us to purchase and consume! We see Kramnik reach into his grab-bag of exotic opening ideas and yank out an ultra-rare line, considered utterly harmless. Yet he manages to nudge the number two-ranked player in the world to the precipice of defeat with it by hiding his intent, the way a sculptor refuses to reveal his art until its completion. When examined in greater detail, it becomes clear it is an awe-worthy idea, laced with tasteless, odourless poison.
10...♖e8 11 ♕f3!
    A new move and a clear improvement over a girls' under-12 French championship game – a game I am guessing Aronian hadn't exactly dissected with coroner-like precision in his pre-game prep! – 11 ♗g5 c6 12 ♘a4 with a (surprise, surprise!) equal position, L.Susini-L.Kambrath, La Roche sur Yon 2008.
11...c6 12 ♗f4!

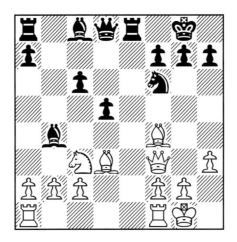

Question: No pin?

Answer: After the game, Kramnik said the position resembled certain Petroff lines – an opening he understands deeply – where Black's equality doesn't materialize so easily. **12...♗d7?!**

The parachute opens properly, but the skydiver lands in a tree and gets tangled, dangling from his harness.

Question: I don't get this move. What is Black's idea?

Answer: Apparently, Kramnik didn't get it either and Aronian didn't explain. In any case, Aronian seems to be getting slightly confused by Kramnik's bizarre opening choices. I would think the normal path to equality would be to eliminate the dark-squared bishops with 12...♗d6 13 ♖fe1 ♗e6 14 ♘e2!, but even then I would rather play White's position. In any case, I will bet Kramnik had some hidden idea here, which may incarnate in some future game of his.

13 a3!

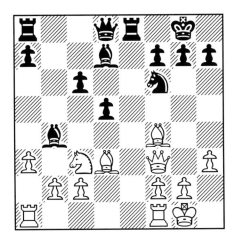

Question: How can this be an exclamation mark move? Kramnik wastes a tempo and wrecks his queenside pawns.

Answer: It's another original strategic idea in the position. Kramnik invites broken queenside pawns in exchange for dark-square control, which haunts Aronian for the remainder of the game. Also, White can play c3-c4 later on, alleviating his structural damage somewhat. Aronian expected 13 ♖fe1 ♖xe1+ 14 ♖xe1 ♕f8 (14...d4 15 a3! doesn't bother White).

13...♗xc3!?

Aronian perhaps overestimates his play on White's weakened queenside pawns. Simply retreating with 13...♗f8 is safer and possibly better.

14 bxc3 ♘e4

Kramnik suggested 14...♕a5!? 15 c4 ♗e6.

15 ♖fe1 ♕f6?!

The queen raises restive eyes upon c3, her beauty marred and fading due to her increasing joylessness. Kramnik felt it was better to take on c3.

16 ♗xe4 dxe4 17 ♕e3!

The witch crooks her fingers and mutters an incantation, as bolts of otherworld energy target the dark squares. Soon White's pieces spew forth in dark-square zeal. "Black's position is already difficult," said Kramnik after the game.

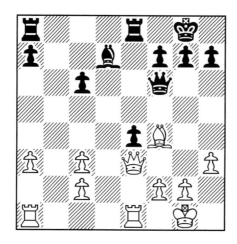

Question: What is so difficult about Black's position?
It looks like he has an easy draw.

Answer: The position is deceptive and there is no easy draw here. Behind the enforced quiescence and behind the lull run multiple, subtle subplots:

1. The balance of power tips toward White, due to the opposite-coloured bishops.

2. Black's bishop, the loser of the brawl, is made plain by the sight of the angry welt over his left eye. The bishop is hemmed in by his e4-pawn, without which he would indeed have an easy draw.

3. On the other hand, a terrifying form emerges from f4, humanoid, yet not quite human. White's bishop reigns prominent.

4. Also, believe it or not, and despite appearances, White has the superior pawn majority, so don't believe your lying eyes!

Conclusion: Suddenly, the once holographic shapes and forms extracted from the nothingness of Kramnik's imagination begin to materialize, solidify and take form in the real world.

17...♗e6 18 ♖ad1

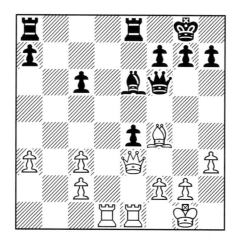

18...♕f5

Both Kramnik and Aronian said the line 18...♗d5!? 19 ♖d4 ♕e6 20 ♖ed1 is difficult for Black.

19 ♖d4 f6

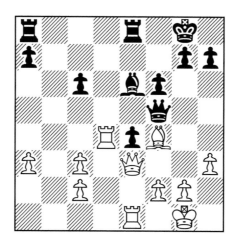

> ***Exercise (planning):*** Aronian just offered his e-pawn
> in order to activate his bishop. Would you take it or not?

Answer: It is better to decline. Kramnik is determined to smother and subdue the black bishop's scope.

20 ♖b1!

Black should probably hold the draw after 20 ♖xe4 ♗f7.

20...♗d5

The bishop's arthritic condition afflicts him with painful joints and a limited range of motion.

21 c4!?

Not bad, but Aronian thought he was close to busted after 21 ♖db4!, when Black senses dark, ethereal forms around him, so terrible, so unnatural, that they should not be. Black can only passively await events and may soon drop his a-pawn, allowing White a dangerous passer.

21...♗f7

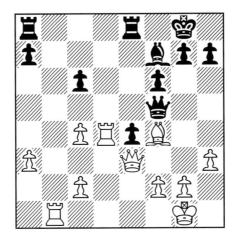

The meek bishop backs off, does what he is told to do and goes where he is told to go. A beaten dog may still follow the cruel master's command. In college, my first job was as an inept hotel clerk. When encountering daily traffic of unruly, spoiled hotel guests, my mouth would obediently respond: "Thank you Sir, for your constructive criticism! Of course, Ma'am! Right away, Ma'am!" As a pressure valve, my chafing mind, suffering from some strange, inward form of Tourette's Syndrome, would add in the dark, silent realm of thought: "Bugger off (anatomically explicit expletives deleted)!"

Black's dreary position reminds me of my similarly uninspiring hotel career. The players agreed that this was the point where Kramnik missed a potential win. White's potential for victory depends on his ability to unearth a unifying, organizing principle.

> *Exercise (critical position/planning):* His choice: a) 22 ♖b7, grab the seventh rank. b) 22 ♖d6, pressure Black's weak c6-pawn. What does your intuition tell you?

22 ♖b7?!

After this inaccuracy, White's game wanes and dims, like a battery-powered light bulb low on energy.

Answer: b) 22 ♖d6! put Black under terrible strain, according to Kramnik and Aronian. For example, 22...♗xc4 23 ♖b7 ♗e6 24 ♖xc6 ♗c8 25 ♖bc7 (the vultures, connoisseurs of human flesh, perch nearby in hope; the rooks corkscrew their way past Black's defences – saving the game won't be easy from here) 25...♗e6 26 ♖c5 ♕g6 27 ♖b5 and finally, *Houdini* reluctantly agrees that Black is under tremendous pressure. White threatens to double rooks on the seventh rank and also to pick off the a-pawn, as the seams in Black's position lose integrity, fray and come apart.

22...♖ad8 23 ♗d6?!

The collective elects the bishop as their leader, hoping he can succeed where they could not. But they picked the wrong leader. White's rooks were the key: 23 ♖d6! still keeps Black under pressure.

23...♖d7!

It feels like Black's position just exhaled in relief. Kramnik may have counted on the trap 23...♗xc4? 24 ♖xc4 ♖xd6 25 ♖xg7+! ♔xg7 26 ♕g3+ with a clear advantage to White.

24 ♖xd7

Kramnik said he missed 24 ♖xe4 ♕xe4! 25 ♕xe4 ♖xe4 26 ♖xd7 a5, when Black should limp to the draw.

24...♕xd7

Now Black should survive.

25 ♗c5 ♕b7 26 ♖xe4

Kramnik thought 26 ♕b3! was his last chance to win.

26...♖xe4 27 ♕xe4 ♕b1+ 28 ♔h2 ♕b8+ 29 g3 ♕a8!?

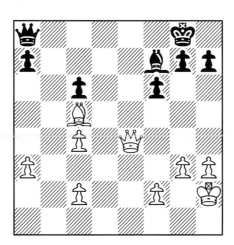

And here Kramnik probably did not see realistic chances to play for a win any longer.

30 ♗d6 ♕e8 31 ♕xe8+

White's queen presses her fists to her mouth in wordless frustration, sullenly acquiescing to share power with her hateful, conniving sister. Exchanging queens is equivalent of a draw offer, but there was nothing better.

31...♗xe8

> ***Question:*** Why are two 2800 players
> playing out an obviously drawn position?

Answer: There was a "no draw before move 40" clause at the Tal Memorial, so the players were forced to endure the meaningless ritual of the remaining moves.

32 ♔g2 ♗g6 33 ♔f3 ♗xc2 34 ♔e3 ♔f7 35 ♔d4 ♔e6 36 ♔c5 ♗d3!

The last accurate move seals the draw.

37 ♗b8 a6 38 h4 h5 39 ♔xc6 ♗xc4 40 ♔c5 ♗b5 ½-½

Dedication

Many thanks to my editor, Grandmaster John Emms, for his unceasing help and support, and to Jonathan Tait for the final edit. Thanks to comma ponderer, Nancy, for her proofreading; and thanks to Timothy for intimidating my computer into cooperation for the duration of the book.

May Kramnik's depth of understanding rub off and increase ours as well.

Chapter One
Kramnik on the Attack

I had the hardest time compiling this chapter, mainly because the cup runneth over from a glut of incredible attacking games – way too many for one chapter, or even one book for that matter. So this chapter is one of the largest in the book, to give Kramnik his attacking due.

Kramnik is not a name which normally comes to mind as associated with the word attack, the way Linda McCartney isn't often associated with her music career. I'm not sure what the reason for this is. (Well, I do know: it's those drawish and often tedious Berlin Lopez and Petroff games he steers into so often, which have a way of soiling his attacking credentials and giving him the reputation of a dullard strategist!) Kramnik creates so many of his attacks by camouflaging true intent. He switches suddenly from strategic build-up, only to cash out mysteriously into a promising attack. He normally earns his attacks the hard way, incrementally, and very rarely attempts a wild leapfrog over the opposing barrier, in Morozevich/Nakamura-style. See how many of his surprised opponents receive discomfiting chastisement in this chapter on their failure to give proper deference to Kramnik's attacking skills.

Game 2
M.Brodsky-V.Kramnik
Kherson 1991
Sicilian Defence

1 e4 c5 2 ♘f3 ♘c6 3 d4 cxd4 4 ♘xd4 ♘f6 5 ♘c3 e5

The young Kramnik produced many brilliant Pelikans. Today's more cautious Kramnik usually goes for the Petroff and Berlin Lopez.

6 ♘db5 d6

Your very odd writer specializes in bizarro un-Pelikan lines like 6...h6 (the Ulfie) and 6...♗c5!? (the Today is a Good Day to Die variation).

7 ♗g5 a6 8 ♘a3 b5 9 ♗xf6

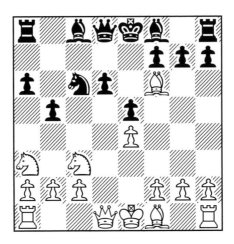

Question: Is this the sharper line?

Answer: Correct. Later in the chapter we look at the more strategically controlled 9 ♘d5 (see Game 7).

9...gxf6 10 ♘d5 f5

Today, the ultra-sharp 10...♗g7 is also played quite often; e.g. 11 ♗d3 ♘e7 12 ♘xe7 ♕xe7 13 c4 f5 14 0-0 0-0 15 ♕h5 ♖b8 16 exf5 e4 17 ♖ae1 ♗b7 18 ♕g4 ♖fe8 19 cxb5 d5 20 bxa6 ♗c6, A.Shirov-Ma.Carlsen, Wijk aan Zee 2010.

Question: Shouldn't Black consider resigning, down three pawns?

Answer: Apparently Black gets full compensation! If you want to avoid such confusion, then be sensible and switch to the Ulfie and the Today is a Good Day to Die lines!

11 ♗d3

Question: Is the sac on b5 line sound for White?

Answer: Probably not at the world class level, but at club level as a surprise weapon – most definitely! Few play the line as White anymore since Kasparov destroyed Shirov with it a decade ago: 11 ♗xb5 axb5 12 ♘xb5 ♖a4! 13 b4?! ♕h4 14 0-0 ♖g8 15 f4 ♔d8!! 16 c3 ♖a6 17 a4 fxe4 18 f5 ♗b7 and White, down a piece, soon found himself under attack as well,

A.Shirov-G.Kasparov, Linares 2002.

11...♗e6 12 ♕h5!?

The hyper-aggressive line. After 12 0-0 ♗xd5 13 exd5 ♘e7 14 c3 ♗g7 15 ♕h5 e4 16 ♗c2 0-0 17 ♖ae1 ♕c8, as in A.Shirov-V.Kramnik, Wijk aan Zee 2003, Black often makes good use of the e5-square.

12...♖g8

12...♗g7 13 0-0 f4 14 c4 scores very well for White, J.R.Koch-G.Kasparov, Evry (simul) 1988.

13 0-0-0!?

White decides to increase his lead in development and hand over g2.

> *Question:* Is the sac justified?

Answer: Justified or not, it is the logical progression from 12 ♕h5, since the tamer 13 g3 ♖g5! 14 ♕d1 (14 ♕xh7?! ♘d4! is risky and probably inferior for White) 14...♗xd5 15 exd5 ♘e7 16 ♘xb5 ♕b6! allows Black to equalize at a minimum, J.Polgar-P.Leko, Budapest 2003.

13...♖xg2 14 f4

14 ♕f3 ♗xd5! 15 ♕xg2 ♗xa2 gave Black loads of compensation for his minor investment in G.Hof-S.Marez, correspondence 2007. The game continued 16 b3?? (a misguided attempt to trap the bishop) 16...♕a5 17 ♔b2 d5! with a decisive attack for Black.

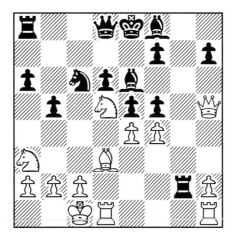

> *Question:* Now that I look at the position again, this looks really dangerous for Black. White has a considerable development lead and pries open the centre to go after the king. Is Black in trouble?

Answer: I admit that if you don't play such positions from either side then the positions which arise feel utterly inscrutable, like the oscillating spray of subatomic particles seen through an electron microscope with the eyes of a non-physicist. In such disorienting landscapes, one gets the feeling there is no sky above and no ground below. White experiences problems as well:

1. Black owns the bishop pair, which grows in strength as the position opens.

2. White's horribly offside knight on a3 remains out of play for some time to come.

3. Matters are not one-sided. Black attacks as well.

4. Black's king is safer than it looks, dead centre of the board, mainly due to his grip on the dark squares.

Conclusion: The position is complex but actually in Black's favour. *Houdini* assesses it -0.71, so clearly the computer isn't intimidated by White's threats.

14...♘d4!

Target: c2.

15 ♘e3?!

Question: Why retreat a centralized piece?

Answer: The knight, capricious as a toddler, changes his mind and unexpectedly retreats. It becomes increasingly clear that White's mysterious plan (or lack of one?) of retreat was jotted down hastily in indecipherable shorthand. Perhaps White intended a double attack: Black's rook and also f5, since White's knight no longer hangs on d5. The trouble is in such open positions of tension, any unforced retreat of an already well-placed piece is generally deemed suspect. After White's last move the effervescence in his position unexpectedly goes flat. The computers think 15 ♔b1 is his best shot to survive.

15...♖f2

Inducing central resolution.

16 exf5?

White clearly underestimates Black's coming initiative. It was high time to eliminate his powerful rook with 16 ♖hf1. One senses that White remains oblivious to danger's creep. A man may look straight at his facial mole each morning in the mirror as he shaves, yet fail to notice the imperceptible, fatal cancerous growth.

16...♗xa2

The bishop lurches, jack-knifing to his right.

17 fxe5

Of course, the attempt to trap the bishop is suicidal for White: 17 b3?? ♕a5 18 ♔b2 d5 and *Houdini* announces a forced mate in ten moves for Black.

17...dxe5 18 ♘xb5

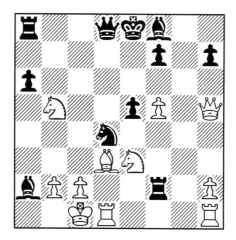

Answer: Power in the hands of the untrained isn't real power. Only the wizard understands
how to recite the incantation properly. Black flows with the chaos rather than attempting
to order it.

18...♗h6!!

Answer: 18...♕b6! 19 ♘xd4 ♗h6! 20 ♖he1 exd4 was also winning.

19 ♖he1

Answer: Black's brutal point is 19 ♕xh6?? ♖xc2+! 20 ♗xc2 (or 20 ♘xc2 ♘b3 mate) 20...♘e2
mate.

19...axb5 20 ♗xb5+ ♔e7 21 ♕h4+

Black's bishop remains stable on h6, as 21 ♕xh6?? is the same song: 21...♖xc2+ 22 ♘xc2
♘b3 mate.

21...f6 22 ♕xf2

White's coffers swell and grow fat, as his king does just the opposite. Black's pieces,
prehistoric creatures of predation, loom terrifyingly with claws extended.

22...♗f7!

Clearance. Threat: ...♖a1+ followed by ...♘xb5+.

23 ♗d3 ♛b6!

White's king has nowhere to run. There is no reasonable defence to ...♖a2.

24 ♗e4 ♖a2! 25 c4

Question: Would 25 c3 be better?

Answer: It fails to help White: 25...♖a1+ 26 ♗b1 ♗a2! mates.

25...♗xc4 26 ♔b1

The king hopes to take cover from the gusts and squalls which blow his way.

26...♛a5

Or 26...♖a1+! 27 ♔xa1 ♛a6+ 28 ♔b1 ♗a2+ 29 ♔c1 ♛c4+ 30 ♔d2 (30 ♗c2 ♘b3 mate) 30...♘b3 mate.

27 ♘d5+

Question: Was there a way out for White?

Answer: White gets mated in all lines, no matter what he does.

27...♗xd5

27...♔f7!, 27...♔f8!, 27...♔d8! and 27...♔d6! all force mate in three moves.

28 ♛xd4

The night moth sees the light inside the house and mindlessly rams the window. Clever, but it fails.

28...♖a1+ 29 ♔c2 ♖xd1! 30 ♛xd1

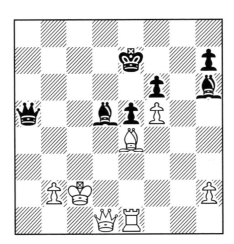

Exercise (combination alert): Black to play and force mate in four moves.

Answer: The ancient vampire, eternally a slave to her own dark cravings, searches the dimly lit streets for a meal.

30...♕a4+! 31 ♔c3 0-1

White walks into a mate in one with 31...♕c4. But after 31 ♔b1 Black mates anyway with 31...♗a2+ 32 ♔a1 ♗b3+ 33 ♔b1 ♕a2. The town submerges in the flood and all that can be seen is the tip of the belfry poking above the water.

> ## Game 3
> ## **V.Kramnik-J.Ehlvest**
> Tal Memorial, Riga 1995
> *Semi-Slav Defence*

1 ♘f3 d5 2 d4 ♘f6 3 c4 c6 4 ♘c3 e6 5 ♗g5 dxc4

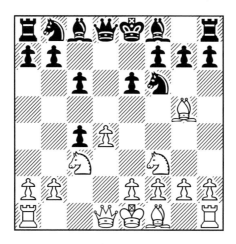

> **Question:** I know the Botvinnik line of the Semi-Slav
> is out of favour right now, but why?

Answer: I was afraid you would ask this question. There are two kinds of players in the chess world: booked-up Semi-Slav guys who know the theory to move 30, and the rest of us who don't! Sometimes there is a good reason a line falls out of favour. But sometimes it falls victim to the vagaries of fashion. A line simply goes out of favour because some titan loses with it to another titan – a fact which has little to no bearing on the average tournament player, for whom it is probably still fully playable and equally confusing to both sides. In essence, the Botvinnik Semi-Slav is an ivory tower line. It seems it is mostly GMs who feel confident enough to deal with the mounds of theory. The rest of us with non-photographic memories tend to shy away from such monumental burdens.

Instead, 5...h6 (the Moscow Variation) is the current darling of the top-level guys; while 5...♘bd7 leads to the Cambridge Springs or old-school Orthodox Queen's Gambit Declined.
6 e4 b5 7 e5 h6 8 ♗h4 g5 9 ♘xg5 hxg5 10 ♗xg5 ♘bd7 11 g3

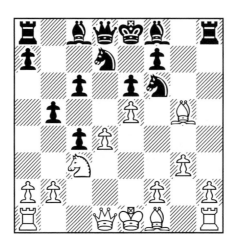

So far so book. 11 exf6 usually just transposes after 11...♗b7 12 g3 c5.
11...♕a5!?

Question: Now this isn't normal, is it?

Answer: Correct. Ehlvest tries to throw Kramnik off with an offbeat line:

a) 11...♖g8!? is another sideline used mainly as an ambush weapon; e.g. 12 h4 ♖xg5 13 hxg5 ♘d5 14 g6 fxg6 15 ♕g4 ♕e7, V.Kramnik-A.Shirov, Monte Carlo (rapid) 2002, looks and feels pretty unclear. Even the computers hedge their bets and declare the position even.

b) 11...♗b7 12 ♗g2 ♕b6 13 exf6 0-0-0 14 0-0 c5 15 d5 b4 16 ♘a4 ♕b5 17 a3, as in H.Nakamura-J.Smeets, Wijk aan Zee 2011, is depressingly enough the tabiya "starting" position of the main line. In Capablanca's day, the game essentially began around move eight. Today, the beginning number usually falls in the late teens, or even later.

12 exf6 ♗a6 13 ♕f3 ♖c8!?

Ehlvest continues to try and lure Kramnik into hidden theoretical backwaters. After the more thematic 13...b4 14 ♘e4 0-0-0 15 b3 cxb3 16 ♗xa6+ ♕xa6 17 ♕xb3 ♕b5 18 ♖c1, Kasparov proved that Black's king position was a matter of great concern for his opponent, G.Kasparov-A.Miles, Basel (5th matchgame) 1986.

14 ♗e2

Question: This looks very odd. Why didn't White follow through and fianchetto with 14 ♗g2 - ?

Answer: In this case White may have trouble castling after 14...b4 15 ♘e4 c3!.

14...b4

Kramnik gave the line 14...c5? 15 d5 ♗b7 16 0-0 b4 17 ♕e3! with a powerful and probably decisive attack.

15 ♘e4 c5 16 d5!!

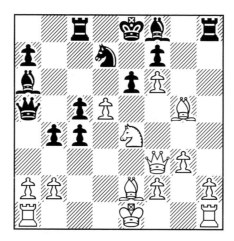

As we see throughout the book, Kramnik displays a finely tuned sense of the grand moment – the perfect time to strike and unlock the beast within. He staggers Ehlvest with a theoretical novelty and a huge improvement over 16 dxc5 ♘xc5 17 ♘xc5 ♗xc5 18 0-0 ♗d4!, when Black looks active and generates counterplay on b2, I.Sokolov-G.Kamsky, Belgrade 1991.

16...exd5 17 ♕f5!

I insist. Please take the knight. There is one set of laws for the poor, and quite another set for the rich and influential. The queen's arc of raw force produces uncomfortable heat on d7.

17...dxe4

Ehlvest bites, seeing that there is no help for him in declining with 17...♗b7 18 ♗g4! ♕a4 19 ♖d1 d4 20 0-0, when White's attack is unstoppable and Black doesn't even have an extra piece to comfort him in his time of grief.

18 0-0-0!

How often do you see White castling queenside in the Botvinnik variation, straight into the teeth of Black's pawn avalanche? White's attack is faster.

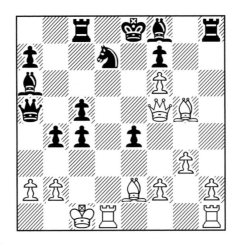

Question: Isn't it kind of crazy for White to castle straight into
a potential attack when he could have castled kingside instead?

Answer: I agree that it takes a kind of confidence level bordering on recklessness to make
such a move. The trouble with castling kingside is that White loses a precious tempo in
placing his rooks on the optimum attacking e1- and d1-squares.

18...♖c7 19 ♗g4!

The bishop swings right with the effortless grace of the hired killer's blade. White continues to cherish and polish d7, as if the square were a diamond.

19...♗b5

Question: Isn't Black's counterattack flaring up after 19...♕xa2 - ?

Answer: Black simply doesn't have the time to get away with it: 20 ♖xd7! ♕a1+ 21 ♔d2!
♕xb2+ 22 ♔e3 ♕c3+ 23 ♔f4 and the lab rat, through habit and practice, effortlessly
weaves his way through the maze. Black runs out of checks, as well as luck, as the bloody
carcass of his king hangs ominously in the slaughterhouse. Looking at variations like this,
we begin to fathom the monumental scale of Kramnik's insight behind 16 d5!!.

20 ♕xe4+ ♔d8 21 ♗xd7!

Stronger than 21 ♖he1, which should win as well.

21...♗xd7

After 21...♖xd7 22 ♗f4!, threatening a deadly check on a8, finishes Black off: 22...♕a6 23
♕a8+ ♕c8 24 ♕xa7 and Black's king has no hope of evading the crossfire.

22 ♖he1

The e8-square is not as well covered as Black would like! Mate on the move is threatened.

22...♗h6

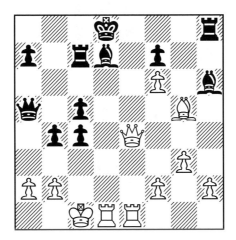

Plans begin as abstractions. Now White's plan of clearing the centre at the cost of a piece reached fruition. Only now can we comprehend the dazzling shock of Kramnik's revelation. It's time to convert and mathematize the position into a calculation.

> ***Exercise (combination alert/calculation):*** White to play and deliver mate in five moves. Take your time and try to work this one out all the way to mate in your mind's eye, without moving the pieces.

Answer: Just play through the remainder of the game.

23 ♕a8+ ♖c8 24 ♖xd7+!

The whip spasms and cracks on d7, and Black's king releases an audible intake of breath as he staggers about.

24...♚xd7 25 ♕d5+ 1-0

The blind king, who pokes and gropes the air with his hands, finally meets his end: 25 ♕d5+ ♚c7 26 ♖e7+ ♚b6 27 ♕b7 mate.

> ## Game 4
> ### G.Kasparov-V.Kramnik
> Dos Hermanas 1996
> *Semi-Slav Defence*

1 d4 d5 2 c4 c6 3 ♘c3 ♘f6 4 ♘f3 e6 5 e3 ♘bd7 6 ♗d3

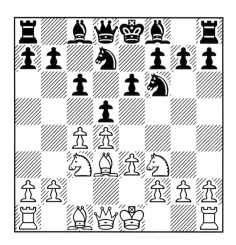

The main line Semi-Slav.

Question: Why is White so willing to lose a tempo with his bishop?

Answer: White does indeed lose a tempo after Black takes on c4, but keep in mind that Black also lost a tempo.

Question: How did Black lose the tempo?

Answer: His ...c5 break is absolutely essential; but Black already expended a tempo on ...c7-c6, so when he plays ...c6-c5, that is the tempo. In the next game we look at 6 ♕c2.
6...dxc4 7 ♗xc4 b5 8 ♗d3 ♗b7
8...a6 is the other main branch.
9 0-0
Or 9 e4 b4 10 ♘a4 c5 11 e5 ♘d5 12 0-0 (12 ♘xc5 and 12 dxc5 are played as well) 12...cxd4 13 ♖e1 g6 14 ♗g5 ♕a5 15 ♘xd4 a6 16 a3 bxa3 17 bxa3 ♗g7 and Black has enough resources to stay level in this sharp position, M.Illescas Cordoba-V.Kramnik, Madrid 1993.
9...a6

Question: A bit slow?

Answer: Yes, but necessary if Black is to engineer his ...c6-c5 break.
10 e4 c5 11 d5

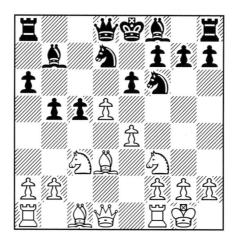

11...c4

Clearing c5 for a bishop or a knight.

> **Question:** Shouldn't Black take on d5, if not
> to win then at least weaken White's d-pawn?

Answer: Black would be opening the game prematurely. For example, 11...exd5 12 exd5 ♗e7 13 ♗xb5 (13 d6! is also strong) 13...axb5 14 d6 ♗xf3 15 dxe7 ♗xd1 and White regains his pawn with an endgame attack: 16 exd8♕+ ♔xd8 (16...♖xd8 17 ♖e1+! ♔f8 18 ♖xd1) 17 ♖xd1 with an edge, V.Malakhatko-M.Lobato Soriano, Coria del Rio 2006.

12 ♗c2 ♕c7 13 ♘d4!?

Very rare. Normally, if White wants to play his knight to d4, he tosses in 13 dxe6 fxe6 before 14 ♘d4.

13...♘c5

13...e5!?, handing the opponent a passed pawn, doesn't make much sense to me but has been played by very strong players; e.g. 14 ♘f5 g6 15 ♘h6 ♘h5 16 g3 ♗c5 17 ♕f3 with an advantage for White, Ma.Carlsen-A.Shirov, Biel 2011.

14 b4

Challenging the knight's cozy position on c5.

14...cxb3 15 axb3 b4 16 ♘a4 ♘cxe4

> **Question:** Isn't Black just opening lines against his own king?

Answer: Kramnik has seen that his good piece activity has the indirect benefit of keeping his king safe.

17 ♗xe4

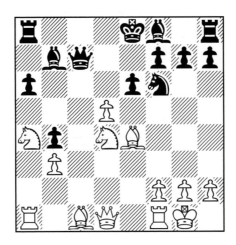

A new idea at the time, but giving up the bishop pair in an open position doesn't look like an improvement. White scores a dismal 22% from nine games with this position in my database. Kasparov attempted to improve on 17 dxe6 ♖d8! 18 exf7+ ♔xf7, Y.Yakovich-M.Sorokin, Calcutta 1991, where Black stood at least equal.

17...♘xe4 18 dxe6 ♗d6 19 exf7+

Kramnik suggests 19 ♗b2!? which gives up h2 with check.

19...♕xf7!

Planning to transfer his queen to assist a kingside attack.

> **Question:** Why not 19...♔xf7 - ? Black can castle
> by hand and he keeps his bead on the h2-square.

Answer: It isn't so easy to castle by hand after 20 ♕h5+! g6 21 ♕h3, when suddenly White is the one issuing the threats.

20 f3 ♕h5 21 g3!?

> **Question:** Is his king any safer after 21 h3 - ?

Answer: White's king is safer, but in this line Black gets to entrench his knight on e4 for good after 21...♕e5 22 f4 ♕f6.

21...0-0?!

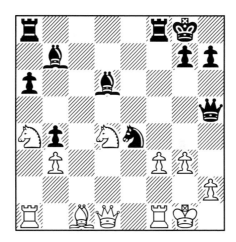

"Fair is foul and foul is fair." A move made on a wish, half a prayer and a grin.

Question: What are you talking about? Every other annotator gave this move at least one exclamation mark!

Answer: Life is rarely how it appears. Black's position radiates a picture of breathtaking beauty, like a tourist brochure. And just like the brochure, the reality of the actual place rarely matches the beauty of the advertisement photo. After this game was played, Kramnik's sac was hailed as pure genius by pundits, but the pronouncement was perhaps a tad premature and didn't hold up under the silicon gaze.

Kramnik actually chose the wrong attacking path – albeit with serious practical chances, since he managed to toss Kasparov into a dark realm which extended the boundaries of conjecture and wild-eyed guesses as to the nature of White's best defensive plan. There is a palpable difference between someone who rings your doorbell and someone who knocks. The doorbell is impersonal, non-threatening; the knock is physical, urgent, passionate and even intimidating. In this position, Kramnik pounds on White's door, bypassing the more polite doorbell entirely.

Correct was 21...♘xg3! 22 hxg3 (22 ♖e1+ ♔f7 doesn't bother Black) 22...0-0 23 ♖a2! ♗xg3 24 ♖g2 and it's anybody's game.

22 fxe4 ♕h3

The gangland queen pin reaches a decision, ordering a hit on White's troublesome king. What she underestimates is just how powerfully protected and well connected White's king really is. As I mentioned earlier, White should win – with perfect play. Kramnik, like all skilled predators, exercises patience. If he waits long enough and remains still, he reasons the prey may wander by eventually. He tosses in a deceptively quiet move after the sac. This move was also lavished with exclams, but I think this reflected emotion more than actual reality. The trouble is White may be winning!

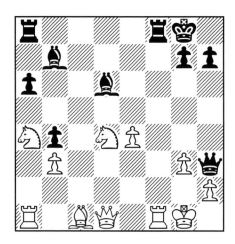

Nevertheless, although the computers all dismiss Kramnik's sac and claim White is winning, we know better. Even if the computer evaluation is correct (and it is!), a human has a devil of a time defending White here. So practical chances shouldn't be dismissed.
23 ♘f3?

The creature attempts to grasp the prize with up-reached fingers but falls short. The defensive task proves even too difficult for a reigning World Champion. White can consolidate with 23 ♕e2! ♖ae8 (or 23...♗xg3 24 ♘f5! ♗e5 25 ♗b2) 24 ♖xf8+ ♗xf8 25 ♗e3 ♗xe4 26 ♕f1, when Black's attack fades.

23...♗xg3!

"By the pricking of my thumbs, something wicked this way comes!" Kramnik smudges the position yet further, like the Kindle reader who turns the electronic pages with greasy fingers.
24 ♘c5?

Kasparov loses his way once more. He had to try 24 ♕e2! again.

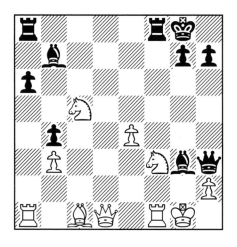

Answer: Destroy the defender of h2. Kramnik refuses to shut off the faucet and end the steady drip of sacrifices.

24...♖xf3! 25 ♖xf3?

Kasparov reels. Instead, Kramnik suggests the better defence 25 ♖a2! ♖xf1+ 26 ♕xf1 ♕xf1+ 27 ♔xf1 ♖c8 28 ♗e3 ♗f4 29 ♘xb7 ♗xe3 30 ♖xa6, when Black has the advantage but White may still hold due to the reduced material.

25...♕xh2+ 26 ♔f1

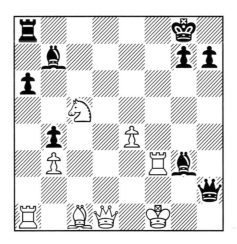

Answer: Enter stage left.

26...♗c6!

A disorienting picture. White is busted, despite his extra rook.

27 ♗g5

Nothing works. For example, 27 ♖a5 ♗c7! regains the rook with a crushing position, since if White retreats with 28 ♖a1 then 28...♗b5+ is much the same as the game.

27...♗b5+ 28 ♘d3 ♖e8!

Threat: ...♖xe4 followed by ...♕h1+.

29 ♖a2

29 ♖c1 ♕h1+ (not now 29...♖xe4? 30 ♖c8+) 30 ♔e2 ♖xe4+ 31 ♔d2 ♕g2+ is also game over, since the rook on c1 blocks the white king's escape route.

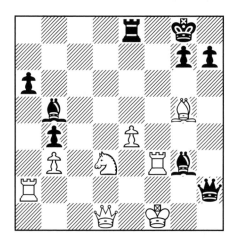

> **Exercise (combination alert):** Kasparov just walked into
> a mate in four moves, which Kramnik also missed!
> Can you do better than two world champions?

29...♕h1+

Winning, but mate is a whole lot better!

Answer: 29...♗xd3+! 30 ♖xd3 ♕h1+ 31 ♔e2 ♕g2+ 32 ♔e3 ♖xe4 mate.

30 ♔e2

In the frigid remains of battle, White's king continues to walk on his own power.

30...♖xe4+ 31 ♔d2

31 ♗e3 ♕g2+ 32 ♖f2 ♕xf2 delivers a mind-blowing mate! The treasonous bishop and knight, having sworn fealty oaths to White's king, suddenly renege on their pledges.

31...♕g2+ 32 ♔c1 ♕xa2 33 ♖xg3 ♕a1+ 34 ♔c2 ♕c3+ 35 ♔b1 ♖d4 0-1

The birds continue to pick over the carcass. At this point, White's king just doesn't give a damn anymore and lays down his weapon in submission.

Rarely does one see a sitting world champion get pushed aside with such disconcerting ease. This game should be viewed as a cautionary tale: not all unsound attacks are destined to fail. If you don't believe me, just ask Mikhail Tal.

Game 5
B.Gelfand-V.Kramnik
European Cup, Berlin 1996
Semi-Slav Defence

1 d4 d5 2 c4 c6 3 ♘c3 ♘f6 4 ♘f3

Gelfand invites a pure Classical Slav.

4...e6

At that time Kramnik played Semi-Slav exclusively. These days he is sometimes willing to chuck the Semi- and enter the Slav with 4...dxc4.

5 e3 ♘bd7 6 ♕c2

This is a curious line since White can play it in drab positional fashion or go psycho.

Question: How can White possibly go psycho in such a controlled position?

Answer: With the Shirov/Shabalov Gambit. Stay tuned!

6...♗d6 7 g4!?

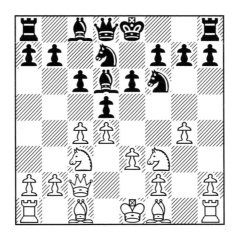

Psycho it is!

7...♗b4!?

Kramnik declines. I have always felt this was Black's best response, mainly influenced by this very game.

Question: Isn't Black's last move wrong on many levels?

Answer: Black does indeed violate principle (intentionally) by moving the same piece twice in the opening. Moreover, it looks like ...♗xc3+ is no real threat since it gives up Black's powerful dark-squared bishop. Still, Black's move makes sense since it inhibits e3-e4 and also gives Black's f6-knight that square should White push with g4-g5. Think of it as a kind of bizarro-world Nimzo-Indian, where Black is down a tempo but White's "free" tempo is the loosening g2-g4.

Question: How is it a "gambit" if Black takes on g4?
Doesn't White win his pawn back immediately on g7?

Answer: Strictly speaking this line isn't really a gambit; it's more of a lashing out. But there is one line which turns it into a gambit:

a) 7...♘xg4 8 ♖g1 ♘xh2 9 ♘xh2 ♗xh2 – There. Now it is a real gambit. But White gets a lot of comp here: 10 ♖xg7 ♘f8 11 ♖g2 ♗d6 12 e4 ♘g6 13 ♗g5 ♗e7 14 ♗xe7 ♕xe7 15 0-0-0 dxe4 16 ♘xe4 and White's open lines and attacking chances give him full compensation for the pawn, A.Morozevich-V.Kramnik, Tal Memorial, Moscow 2008.

b) 7...dxc4 often leads to exceptionally sharp, opposite wing attacks; e.g. 8 ♗xc4 e5 9 g5 ♘d5! 10 ♗d2 (after 10 ♗xd5 cxd5 11 ♘xd5 0-0 Black gets loads of play for the pawn) 10...exd4 11 ♘xd4 0-0 12 ♘e4 ♘e5 13 ♗e2 ♗b4 14 0-0-0, B.Gelfand-A.Shirov, Monte Carlo (blindfold rapid) 2004.

8 ♗d2 ♕e7

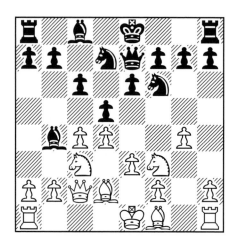

9 a3

Or 9 g5 ♗xc3 10 ♗xc3 ♘e4 11 ♖g1 b6 (Black's bad bishop isn't really so bad here) 12 ♗d3 ♘xc3 13 ♕xc3 dxc4 14 ♗e4 ♗b7 15 ♕xc4 0-0 16 0-0-0 f5 17 gxf6 ♘xf6 18 ♗c2 c5 and Black may already stand a shade better, M.Krasenkow-F.Vallejo Pons, European Championship, Saint Vincent 2000.

9...♗xc3 10 ♗xc3 b6!

10...♘xg4?! gives White exactly what he wants – open lines for the pawn. After 11 ♖g1 f5 12 h3 ♘gf6 13 ♗b4 Black is on the defensive.

11 ♗d3 ♗a6!

It is in Black's best interest to swap off his bishop for one of White's.

12 ♕a4

This may be the spot where White's troubles begin. Instead, after 12 g5! dxc4 13 ♗e2 ♘d5 14 ♗d2 0-0 15 e4 ♘c7 16 ♗xc4 ♗xc4 17 ♕xc4 c5, he remains approximately equal in a complex position.

12...dxc4 13 ♕xa6 cxd3 14 ♕xd3 0-0

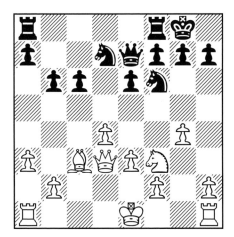

Answer: I don't think so. First, Black's king is a million times safer on the kingside than in the opposite direction. Secondly, Black has access to loads of central counters with ...c6-c5 and ...e6-e5. I feel Black has more than equalized here, since White's king looks easier to pry open should he castle queenside.

15 g5 ♞d5 16 ♗d2

Covering the f4-square so he can play e3-e4 next.

16...f5!?

The computers like the more natural 16...e5!, which gives one pause since machines are beginning to play more human than a human!

17 0-0-0?!

The two kings both ride the subway but in opposite directions. Here we go. It turns into a race, though one in which Black's looks better equipped to open lines more quickly. Gelfand is stirred into action, hoping to escape the morass of his current foul living quarters in which his king wallows. But in doing so he moves into a slum.

Of course White can't blindly open lines with 17 gxf6?? ♛xf6, since this only opens lines against himself, and leaves f3 and f2 loose.

Answer: I believe White's best chance at survival paradoxically lay in castling kingside with 17 ♖c1 c5 18 0-0!.

17...c5 18 ♔b1 b5! 19 ♛xb5!?

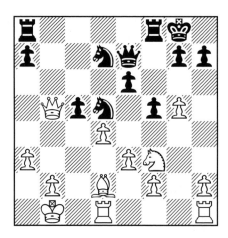

To a hunted man, life is seen mainly through a rear-view mirror.

Question: Isn't it suicide to grab a pawn in front of your king like this?

Answer: In general it is, but in this case if White doesn't take it, Black simply keeps pushing it forward. For example, 19 e4 would be based on the principle "counter in the centre when attacked on the wing"; unfortunately, in this case Black's attack arrives quickly after 19...c4 20 ♕c2 fxe4 21 ♕xe4 c3! 22 ♗xc3 ♘xc3+ 23 bxc3 ♘b6 and White's king is in grave danger. **19...♖ab8 20 ♕a5 ♖b3 21 ♔a2 ♖fb8 22 ♖b1**

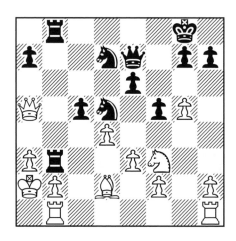

Exercise (planning): Black's position is the usual story. We all realize he has a strong attack, yet there are no obvious ways forward. Look deeply here and try to find entry into White's position.

Answer: 22...e5!

The key to White's collapse lies along the a2-g8 diagonal. Black's queen discovers an unexpected method of entry, as the combustible mixture of hyperactive black pieces, all aimed at the enemy king, soon erupts into a rolling projectile of flame which slowly unfurls on the white king's front lawn.

23 ♖hc1 ♛e6 24 ♔a1 exd4 25 ♖xc5!?

Gelfand places his hopes in a desperate exchange sac, since all other roads lead to a Black victory.

25...♞xc5 26 ♛xc5

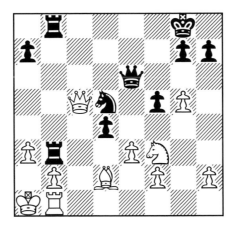

From this moment on, Kramnik's ethereal attackers appear from nowhere with whip-lash quickness, solidify, inflict damage, and then immediately vaporize and dematerialize from conventional space into another dimension.

26...♞c3!! 27 ♞xd4

No choice since 27 bxc3 ♖xb1 mate isn't all that hard to work out!

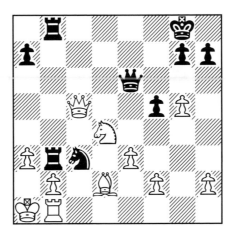

> ***Exercise (combination alert):*** Black began an incredible combination
> with his previous move. It's up to you to find the remainder.

Answer: White's king cover, ancient crumbling parchment, fails to adhere and maintain integrity.

27...♖xb2! 28 ♖xb2

A deathly ill person is willing to consume any necessary medicine, no matter how vile the taste.

28...♕a2+! 0-1

Impossible exclams and double exclams continue to assail White, as the hungry queen punctures the crust of the hot pie with her thumb to get a taste of the sweetness inside. How generous of Kramnik, agreeing to fatten Gelfand's bank account exponentially. White's forces dangle in twisted geometry, every tortured piece exuding the stench of disharmony.

Gelfand resigned here since 29 ♖xa2 ♖b1 is mate.

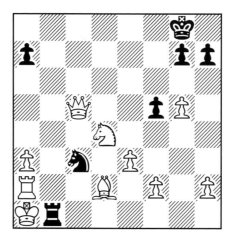

Amazing! I thought such things only happened to Counts and Dukes in Morphy's day.

Game 6
V.Kramnik-J.Polgar
Cap d'Agde (rapid) 2003
Queen's Indian Defence

1 d4 ♘f6 2 c4 e6 3 ♘f3 b6 4 a3

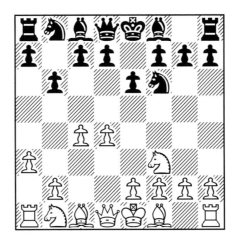

The Petrosian system in the Queen's Indian.

4...♗b7 5 ♘c3 d5

GM John Emms writes: "The most solid way to meet the 4 a3 variation. Black immediately stakes a claim for the centre. Play now more resembles a Queen's Gambit Declined than a Queen's Indian."

> *Question:* All true, but didn't White just get tricked into a line of the QGD where his a2-a3 is rendered a lost tempo?

Answer: Unlikely; a2-a3 is nearly always useful to White, who can later expand with b2-b4.

6 ♕c2

I have never understood the appeal for White of 6 cxd5 ♘xd5 7 ♕c2 ♘xc3 8 bxc3 ♗e7 9 e4 0-0 10 ♗d3 c5 11 0-0 ♕c7.

> *Question:* Doesn't White now lose a tempo since ...c5xd4 is at least a strategic threat?

Answer: Exactly. White must move his queen again with 12 ♕e2, as in H.Nakamura-S.Karjakin, Medias 2011. This is all theory and I don't know a thing about it, but it seems to me like White has landed in a Semi-Tarrasch at least a move down over normal.

Instead, 6 ♗g5, veering toward a QGD-style position, looks a lot more logical. I like White's game at the end of 6...♗e7 7 ♕a4+ c6 8 cxd5 ♘xd5 9 ♗xe7 ♕xe7 10 ♘xd5 exd5 11 e3, A.Karpov-V.Korchnoi, Vienna 1996.

6...c5

> *Question:* Risky for Black to open the game so soon?

Answer: Somewhat, but not really. Black isn't too far behind in development and hopes to open the c-file to exploit White's queen position on c2.

Instead, J.Lautier-A.Karpov, Groningen 1995, went 6...dxc4 7 e4 c5 8 d5!? (White offers a pawn, hoping to exploit his lead in development) 8...exd5 9 exd5 ♗d6 (which Karpov prudently declines) 10 ♗xc4 0-0 11 0-0 h6 12 ♖e1 a6 13 a4 and White's d5-pawn appears more of a strength than a weakness. Still, Black looks like he achieved an acceptable position.

7 cxd5 exd5?

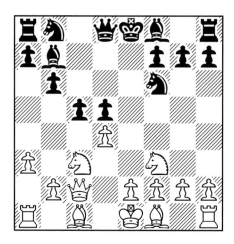

Question: Why the question mark? What could be more natural?

Answer: Natural isn't always so desirable. There are all sorts of "natural" berries and mushrooms in the forest which, if ingested, will kill you in no time! Black now falls seriously behind in development after White's shocking next move.

Better is 7...cxd4 8 ♘xd4 ♘xd5 9 ♘db5! ♘c6 10 ♘xd5 exd5 11 ♗f4 ♖c8, when Black looks just fine, A.Dreev-R.Ponomariov, Moscow (rapid) 2002.

8 e4!

Kramnik blasts the game open to his advantage, splattering Black's position with hot cooking grease.

8...cxd4!

Polgar minimizes her suffering with the most accurate defence.

a) 8...dxe4?! 9 ♗b5+ ♗c6 (9...♘bd7 10 ♘e5 a6 11 ♕b3! ♕e7 12 ♘xd7 ♘xd7 13 ♘d5! also looks rough for Black) 10 ♘e5 ♗xb5 11 ♕b3! ♕e7, A.Ryskin-K.Aseev, Sochi 1993. Now Black is in deep trouble after 12 ♘xb5!.

b) 8...♘xe4? 9 ♘xe4 dxe4 10 ♗b5+ ♗c6 11 ♕xe4+ ♕e7 12 ♘e5! and once again, Black finds himself in deep trouble, I.Zakharevich-A.Derbenev, Voronezh 2005.

9 ♗b5+ ♘bd7

9...♗c6? 10 ♘xd5! is even worse for Black.

10 e5!

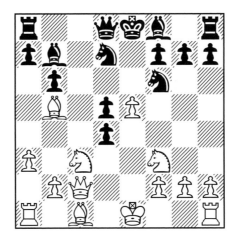

Kramnik one-track-mindedly pries the game open.

10...dxc3!

Once again Polgar finds the narrow path to continued survival after her unfortunate opening. 10...♘e4? leads to immediate disaster after 11 ♘xe4 dxe4 12 e6! fxe6 13 ♘e5.

11 exf6 ♕c7

> *Question:* If Black is suffering, then why not grab a pawn on b2?

Answer: Suicide. That would be like the smallest kid in the class picking a fight with the school bully. There is no chance of survival after 11...cxb2? 12 ♗xb2 gxf6 13 0-0, when Black's pair of extra pawns will be of little comfort to her in her grave.

12 ♕e2+

From this moment on, Polgar's king finds no safe haven across the board.

12...♔d8

Black's uninvited king is greeted with accusatory silence from his comrades.

13 fxg7

The sign of a positional player. Kasparov or Morozevich would probably continue their generosity with 13 0-0!?.

13...♗xg7 14 0-0 ♖e8 15 ♗g5+ f6 16 ♗e3 a6 17 ♗xd7 ♔xd7

Black's king awaits in frozen motion, ready to hightail it and run in any given direction.

18 ♘d4

This knight is destined for great things and seeks, with valedictory ambition, to outdo all the other minor pieces combined.

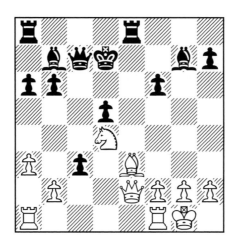

18...♖e4

Preventing ♕g4+.

19 bxc3 ♕e5?!

I am sick and tired of watching horror films and never getting scared. White's attack somehow has the same effect on Polgar, whose queen brazenly abandons defence of the critical b6-square in fatigued exasperation. Now is not the time to try and seize the initiative. Her best shot at survival lay in 19...♖ae8.

20 ♖fb1!

> *Question:* Isn't this the wrong rook?

Answer: Quite the opposite. The other rook remains on duty on a1.

20...b5 21 a4

Now we see why Kramnik left his queen's rook where it was.

21...♗h6 22 axb5 a5

22...♗xe3 23 fxe3 ♖xe3 24 ♕g4+ is of no help to Black.

23 ♕f3

23 b6!, clearing b5 for the queen, looks very powerful.

23...♗xe3 24 fxe3

The immediate queen check on h3 is more accurate, since it may cut Black's a8-rook out of the game.

24...♖g8 25 ♕h3+ ♖eg4

The much hoped-for counterattack yields thin gruel.

26 ♖xa5

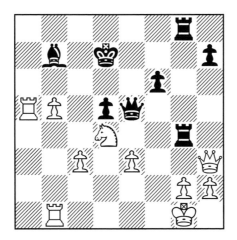

Black's game is a disaster on so many levels:

1. She is down two pawns.

2. White has by far the stronger attack. In fact, Black's counterattack is virtually non-existent, and her king, a leaf in a storm, whirls about without will.

3. White's knight towers over Black's ineffectual remaining minor piece, which remains nothing but a bishop-shaped absence, an empty presence.

26...♔d6 27 ♖a2 ♗c8 28 ♕f3 ♖h4 29 g3 ♖e4 30 b6 ♖xe3

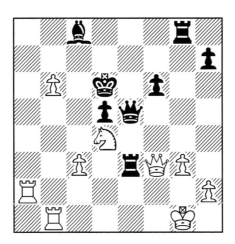

Exercise (combination alert): How can White finish Black off?

Answer: Ignore the threat to his queen.

31 b7! ♖e1+

If Black accepts the queen she gets mated after 31...♗xb7 32 ♖xb7! ♖xf3 33 ♖a6+ ♔c5 34 ♖c6.

32 ♖xe1 ♕xe1+ 33 ♔g2 ♗xb7 34 ♕xf6+ ♔c5

Black's king reminds us of a long-dead relative from a sepia-stained photograph found in the attic.

35 ♖e2 ♕b1 36 ♘e6+ ♔b5 37 ♕f7 ♔a5

It's almost mate. Black's king steps up to the podium, removes a crumpled copy of his resignation speech from his coat pocket, and begins to address the other pieces.

38 ♕c7+! 1-0

The actress on c7 forgets her lines and refuses the offered rook, and instead ad-libs, going for mate: 38...♔a6 39 ♘c5+, when the knight's tentacles prove to have a long reach, as they grope at Black's king and force mate.

Game 7
V.Kramnik-L.Van Wely
Monte Carlo (rapid) 2005
Sicilian Defence

---

1 e4

1 e4 is unusual for Kramnik. He likes to toss it in once in a while to keep his opponents off balance, or if he has something specially prepared for them – as in the case of this game.

1...c5 2 ♘f3 ♘c6 3 d4 cxd4 4 ♘xd4 ♘f6 5 ♘c3 e5 6 ♘db5 d6 7 ♗g5 a6 8 ♘a3 b5 9 ♘d5

Question: Is this version the positional line of the Pelikan?

Answer: Correct. However, this particular game certainly doesn't bear the "positional" label out. The positions tend to be sharper and more forcing after 9 ♗xf6 gxf6 10 ♘d5, which we looked at in the first game of this chapter.

9...♗e7 10 ♗xf6 ♗xf6 11 c3

White prepares re-entry for the offside knight via c2.

11...♗g5

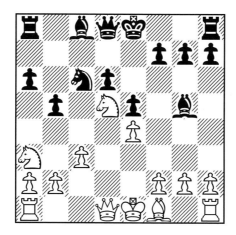

Question: Doesn't White just have a long-term edge with his grip on d5?

Answer: It certainly looks that way, but matters are not so straightforward in the Pelikan. First, White often has trouble finding a practical application of the admittedly wondrous d5-square. Second, Black both controls the bishop pair and also the dark squares.

12 ♘c2 0-0 13 a4

To weaken Black's a-pawn.

13...bxa4 14 ♖xa4 a5 15 ♗c4 ♖b8 16 ♖a2 ♔h8

Black prepares an eventual ...f7-f5 break and gets his king off the diagonal.

17 ♘ce3 g6

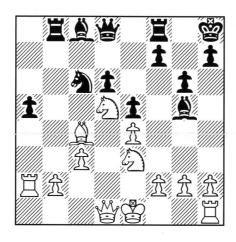

Question: Why is Black willing to weaken his kingside like this?

Answer: He wants to play ...f7-f5 and, on e4xf5, recapture with his g-pawn, which would control e4. Also, Black would then open the g-file for his rook, assuming White castles kingside.

> **Question:** That looks risky. Wouldn't it be better for Black just to eliminate his bad bishop by swapping on e3?

Answer: In theory, yes, but your plan is rather unambitious. Black is also playing for a win and wants to hang on to his bishop. Let's take a look at your plan: 17...♗xe3 18 ♘xe3 ♘e7 19 0-0 f5 20 exf5 ♗xf5 21 b3 ♗e4 22 ♖d2 ♖b6 left White slightly better since he has targets on d6 and a5, though Black's game seems quite defendable, R.Kasimdzhanov-P.Tregubov, Bastia (rapid) 2006.

18 h4!?

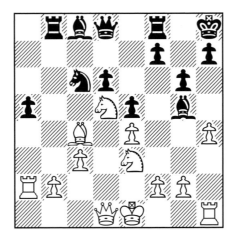

A relatively new idea at the time. White is willing to give up his h-pawn to attack down the h-file. Obviously, castling kingside is a lot safer.

18...♗xh4

Van Wely is up to the challenge.

> **Question:** It looks unbelievably risky to take the h-pawn. Can Black decline?

Answer: The problem with declining is that White is going to engineer h4-h5 anyway, so Black reasons why not grab the pawn? Let's take a look at the declinations:

a) 18...♗xe3?! 19 ♘xe3 f5 20 h5 ♔g7 21 hxg6 hxg6 22 exf5 ♗xf5 23 ♕d2 – advantage White, who has multiple pawn targets to work on, as well as Black's king, I.Denisov-R.Kokshin, Kurgan 2010.

b) 18...♗h6 19 h5 ♔g7 20 ♕d2 ♖h8 21 g3 ♗d7 22 f4, when Black looks like he is on the defensive but may still be okay due to his dark-square control, R.Kasimdzhanov-V.Ivanchuk, Tallinn (rapid) 2006.

19 g3 ♗g5!?

Question: Walking right into the teeth of f2-f4 - ?

Answer: I agree, this is very risky; but I have the feeling Van Wely actually provokes the move. Kramnik, playing Black here, tried 19...♗f6 20 b3 ♗g7 21 f4 exf4 22 gxf4 ♖e8 23 ♕f3 ♔g8 24 ♖ah2 h5, when Pono went for it with 25 ♖xh5!? gxh5 26 ♕xh5 ♖e6 27 ♕h7+ ♔f8 28 ♖g1 ♖g6 29 ♖xg6 fxg6, R.Ponomariov-V.Kramnik, Wijk aan Zee 2005. The game eventually ended in a draw after further adventures.

20 f4

Thematic, but remember: in playing this break White opens the game for Black's bishop pair and also puts his own king at risk.

Instead, F.Amonatov-L.Van Wely, Moscow 2005, continued 20 b3 ♗xe3 21 ♘xe3 f5 22 ♖d2 f4 23 gxf4 exf4 24 ♖xd6 ♕c7 25 ♘f5!? gxf5 26 ♖dh6 ♖b7 27 ♖xh7+ ♕xh7 28 ♖xh7+ ♖xh7 29 ♕d6 ♘e7 and the game soon ended in a chaotic draw. As you can see, Kramnik isn't the only one with experience in the position.

20...exf4 21 gxf4 ♗h4+ 22 ♔f1!

Superior to 22 ♔d2, as in I.Khairullin-V.Kuznetsov, Nojabrsk 2005.

Question: What is Kramnik's idea? His king sits exposed and in danger after Black tosses in ...f7-f5.

Answer: By playing to f1, Kramnik's king doesn't inhibit the swing manoeuvre b2-b3 (or b2-b4) and ♖ah2!.

22...f5!

Both sides play for mate.

23 b4!

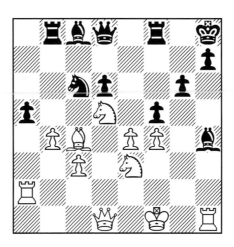

Pushing the b-pawn two squares is more disruptive to Black's defences than the quieter 23 b3, as seen in M.Stangl-S.Kindermann, Altensteig 1987.

23...fxe4!

Van Wely finds the only move and strafes White's king and yet, impossibly, the impregnable wall holds. 23...axb4?? drops a piece after 24 ♖ah2 g5 25 fxg5 fxe4+ 26 ♔e2.

24 ♖ah2

Now Black's bishop at the edge of the world nearly falls off the overhanging crag.

24...g5

Forced. Van Wely strives to slow down White's initiative, or, failing that, to divert it.

25 b5!

The lumpy separate parts congeal into the totality of a clear plan. Now we see why 23 b4! is superior to 23 b3: it chases off Black's knight, which allows White's queen jump to d4.

25...♘e5

All other knight moves lose instantly to ♕d4+.

26 ♕d4

In Kramnik's games, especially as White, one feels a subtle sense of endless expansion, like a sleeper who emerges from a foetal position in his bed, and stretches arms and legs luxuriously as he greets the day.

26...♖b7

Maxim Notkin suggests 26...♕d7!?, but it is unlikely that Black defends after 27 ♔e2! gxf4 28 ♖xh4 fxe3 29 ♘xe3.

27 ♖xh4! gxh4 28 ♔e2!

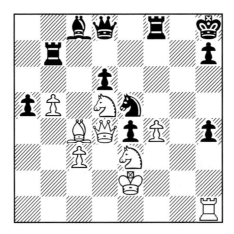

A theoretical novelty (yes, nowadays move 28 is still considered "the opening!") and an improvement over 28 ♔e1 from A.Holmsten-V.Filippov, Polanica Zdroj 1999.

> **Question:** I don't understand the difference between the two moves. What has changed with White's king on e2 rather than on e1?

Answer: Kramnik's move is quite subtle: he pre-empts Black's idea of ...h4-h3 followed by ...♕h4+.

28...♖e8

After 28...h3 29 fxe5 there is no check on h4 anymore! Top-level GM's games are won and lost by such tiny, inconsequential-looking margins these days.

29 fxe5 ♖xe5 30 ♘f4?!

Houdini points out that 30 ♖f1! intending ♘f6! is very powerful for White.

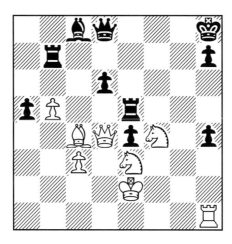

> **Exercise (critical decision):** Kramnik's last move, a single flaw in an otherwise perfect game, allows Van Wely a window to climb through and get back into the game. We have a decision to make. Only one of these moves saves Black: a) 30...♕g5, get active. b) 30...♗d7, counterattack on b5.

30...♕g5?

Answer: The wrong path. The assassin approaches from g5, but White's king's guard spots her in the corner of his eye and stands ready. Now Black's attack manifests in nervous gusts, like the waning of a once powerful storm.

Instead, after 30...♗d7! Black gets back into the game – the point being that d6 isn't really hanging since the ...♗g4+ discovery would win White's queen.

31 ♕xd6!?

Threatening a nasty check on f8.

31...♗g4+?

Black's attack hits bedrock and he finds himself unable to drill further. Understandably, Van Wely gets bogged down in the defensive task and picks one of the many ways Black can go wrong. Here 31...♕xf4? 32 ♕d8+ ♔g7 33 ♕g8+ ♔h6 34 ♖f1! is also curtains, whereas after 31...♖e8! 32 ♕d4+ ♗g7 Black hangs on.

32 ♔e1

Kramnik's equations hold firm against Black's frantic stabs at refutation.

32...♕xf4

This loses, as does 32...♖be7 33 ♘xg4! ♕xg4 34 ♕f6+ ♕g7 35 ♖g1!!.

33 ♕d8+ ♔g7 34 ♕g8+

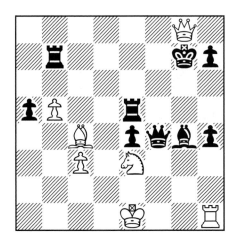

The king and queen, a tongue-tied, shy, courting couple, walk close but not too close.

34...♔h6

34...♔f6 35 ♘xg4+ wins.

35 ♖xh4+

The tarantulas crawl steadily closer to circle their victim.

35...♖h5 1-0

Black's defensive resources (or their lack) feed into themselves in an endless loop, the way a computer infected with a virus acts. Van Wely resigned here, as after 36 ♘xg4+ his king is drawn into the mire with a frantic gurgling sound.

How is it possible to play such a brilliant attacking game without engaging in a single combination (all the combinations are hidden in the notes!)? Only Kramnik can give us the answer.

Game 8
V.Kramnik-L.Bruzon
Turin Olympiad 2006
Queen's Gambit Declined

1 ♘f3 d5 2 d4 ♘f6 3 c4 c6 4 ♘c3 e6 5 ♗g5 ♘bd7 6 e3 ♕a5

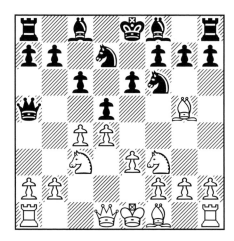

The Cambridge Springs Variation of the Queen's Gambit Declined.

> **Question:** What is Black's idea?

Answer: The Cambridge Springs is quite an ambitious line, since Black hopes to take over the initiative with rapid pressure on c3 after ...♗b4 and ...♘e4, with the added bonus that a knight on e4 simultaneously attacks White's bishop on g5, not to mention Black's queen on a5 also indirectly eyeing the g5-square.

> **Question:** What is the downside to the line?

Answer: Black moves his knight over and over: g8, e4 (or d5), c3. So White may be inclined, as in this game, to sacrifice a pawn for a lead in development.

7 cxd5!

White's highest percentage line and probably superior to 7 ♘d2 ♗b4 8 ♕c2 0-0 or 7 ♗xf6 ♘xf6 8 ♘d2.

7...♘xd5

> **Question:** Why can't Black free his game
> with the natural QGD recapture 7...exd5 - ?

Answer: He can, but Black must be very careful not to end up in a QGD with a totally misplaced queen on a5. One of White's essential strategies in the QGD Exchange is to play for a minority attack and engineer b2-b4. If this is the case, Black may end up losing two tempi. A.Grischuk-M.Godena, European Cup, Saint Vincent 2005, continued 8 ♗d3 ♘e4 9 0-0! ♘xg5 (9...♘xc3 10 ♕d2! regains the piece) 10 ♘xg5 ♘f6 11 h3 and maybe Black is okay, but his queen still looks misplaced on a5.

8 ♕d2

White must deal with the challenge on c3.

> **Question:** Isn't playing the queen to c2 more accurate?

Answer: The trouble with 8 ♕c2? is that after 8...♗b4 9 ♖c1 Black has 9...♕xa2, when White receives no discernable compensation for the pawn.

8...♗b4 9 ♖c1 h6 10 ♗h4

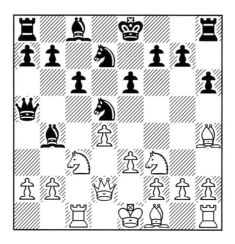

10...0-0

At some point Black must achieve ...c6-c5 or ...e5-e5 or he will stand worse; but the immediate 10...c5 is met by 11 a3! (White is happy to hand over the a3-pawn for the bishop pair and a development lead) 11...♗xc3 12 bxc3 b6 (Shirov isn't interested) 13 c4 ♕xd2+ 14 ♘xd2 ♘e7 15 ♗d3 and White gets a long-term edge due to the bishop pair and stronger centre, V.Kramnik-A.Shirov, Shanghai 2010.

11 a3!

> **Question:** Is White's sac obligatory?

Answer: No, but it is the logical extension of the position, since White hopes to punish Black for violating the principle of moving the same piece more than once in the opening. White can also play in a more mellow fashion with 11 ♗d3 e5 12 0-0, as in A.Moiseenko-B.Esen, Khanty-Mansiysk 2011.

11...♗xc3

Black has no real choice since 11...♗d6 would be an admission that his opening strategy has failed.

12 bxc3 ♕xa3

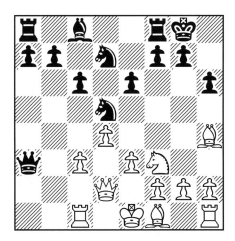

Question: What, specifically, is White's compensation?

Answer: It can be aggregated as follows:

1. Bishop pair;
2. Dark-square control;
3. Central control;
4. Slight development lead;
5. Future kingside attacking chances.

13 e4 ♘e7

Retreating the knight to f6 would be illogical since White may soon gain another tempo on the knight with e4-e5. Instead, after 13...♘5b6 14 ♗d3 ♖e8 15 0-0 e5 16 ♗g3 exd4 17 cxd4 ♘f8 18 ♖fe1 ♗e6 19 ♖a1 ♕e7 20 ♕b2 (Black's queenside pawns are frozen for now, while White has pressure on both wings) 20...♗c4 21 ♗c2 ♗a6 22 ♕c3 ♗c4 23 ♖a5! f6 24 ♘h4! ♗e6 25 ♘f5 ♗xf5 26 ♖xf5 ♖ad8 27 f3, Black found himself under heavy pressure in V.Kramnik-E.Lobron, Frankfurt (rapid) 1995.

14 ♗d3 ♘g6 15 ♗g3 e5!

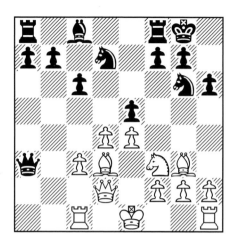

Bruzon is willing to return the pawn to free his remaining bishop and break up Kramnik's imposing centre.

16 0-0

A new move in the position. Kramnik refrains from 16 ♘xe5? ♘dxe5 17 dxe5 ♖d8! (threatening ...♖xd3!, overloading the white queen) 18 0-0 ♕c5! and Black, who has managed to decimate White's centre, will be up a pawn after all.

16...♖e8 17 ♖fe1 ♕a5!?

Bruzon threatens a strategic cheapo with ...e5xd4 but, in so doing, puts his queen out of play. I would have dropped back with 17...♕e7.

18 ♕b2 ♕d8

Black took two moves to retreat his queen to an inferior square, but at least he brought his queen out of harm's way, and also cleared the path for his a-pawn to push forward.

19 ♗b1!

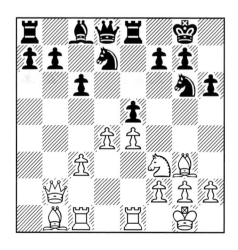

A powerful transference. Kramnik is in no hurry and realizes Black has great difficulty unravelling:

1. If Black is ever forced into ...e5xd4 c3xd4, then White has the attacking plan ♕c2, e4-e5 and h2-h4-h5.

2. The bishop may later be transferred to a2, where it tickles f7 and also blockades Black's passed a-pawn should it manage to run up the board.

19...a5

Black has a hard time moving anything since his knights are stuck defending e5, so he hopes to generate play with his passed a-pawn.

20 ♖cd1 a4!

Ignoring White's "threat" on e5.

21 ♗a2!

A dual-purpose move, as mentioned above. White simultaneously attacks and blockades.

> *Question:* Why can't Kramnik just take on e5?

Answer: He refuses to be party to a hasty pawn grab which falls into Bruzon's strategic trap: 21 dxe5? ♕b6! and Black regains his pawn favourably.

21...♕e7 22 ♕c1

Kramnik waits to see what Black will do.

22...♖a5

He can also just slog forward with 22...b5.

23 ♕d2

Kramnik is in no hurry. He cracks open the cork on the bottle and allows the position to decant for a while.

23...exd4?!

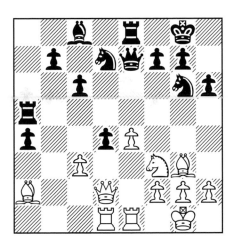

I'm not sure of the motivation behind Black's last move. Was it that the tension was un-bearable to Bruzon, or was it just blind ambition where he wasn't satisfied with equality and played for the win? In any case, Black should do nothing and see how Kramnik planned on making progress.

> *Exercise (planning/critical decision):* Now we have a choice:
> a) Recapture with the pawn, taking control over the centre.
> b) Recapture with the knight, going for piece play and an attack.

Answer: 'b' – the piece play plan puts Black's game under heavy strain.

24 ♘xd4!

Now Kramnik threatens a knight transference to d6 via f5. My old friend, IM Danny Ko-pec, and I predicted this recapture while commenting on the game live on ChessFM, on the Internet Chess Club (although in all likelihood, Danny probably suggested the move and I just passively went along with it, making sure to take equal credit!). The knight threatens to head to d6 via f5.

24...♕c5

Instead, 24...♘de5? is just a loss of several tempi after 25 f4, while 24...♘df8 is met by 25 ♘f5! ♕f6 (the knight can't be touched: 25...♗xf5?? 26 exf5 ♘e5 27 f4 ♕c5+ 28 ♗f2 and Black can resign) 26 ♘d6 ♖d8 27 f4 with e4-e5 next.

25 ♗c7!!

The bishop dances a curlicue pattern on his toes. A scheme grows within Kramnik's mind as he sets a cunning trap...

25...♖a8?

Black's only path to continued survival is to hand over the exchange with 25...♘f6.

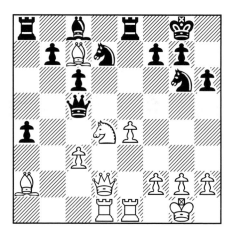

...which Bruzon falls into!

Exercise (combination alert): Kramnik found a way to obliterate the black king's defences. What would you play here?

Answer: I compute, therefore I am. The long-distance bishop strikes with predatory finality. In this inedible soup of murky calculations, endless looping variables and fragmented visions of dark and bright futures, Kramnik extrapolates the essence and unleashes:

26 ♗xf7+! ♔xf7 27 ♕a2+

A fearsome avatar arises in the bishop's absence.

27...♔f8

The only move. Others lose at once:

a) 27...♔e7? 28 ♕e6+ ♔f8 29 ♗d6+ picks off the queen.

b) 27...♔f6? (the startled king zigzags away in an attempt to outrun his pursuers) 28 ♗d8+!! (another reason why White's 25th move deserved two exclams!) 28...♖xd8 (28...♔e5 also walks into a mate in five) 29 ♕e6+ ♔g5 30 ♘f3+ ♔f4 (or 30...♔h5 31 g4 mate) 31 g3+! ♔xf3 (the king falls endlessly into a damned soul's journey to the bowels of hell) 32 ♖d3+ ♕e3 33 ♖exe3 mate.

28 ♘e6+ ♖xe6 29 ♕xe6

Now we see Kramnik's incredibly deep idea behind 25 ♗c7!!. If his bishop still stood on g3, then Black could block on e5 with his g6-knight. But now Black is faced with annihilation from a bishop check on d6, as his scattered defenders bob up and down like trash floating on a polluted river.

29...♘e7

After 29...♕g5 30 ♖xd7! ♗xd7 31 ♗d6+ ♘e7 32 ♕xd7 a3 33 f4 ♕f6 34 e5 ♕f7 35 ♕xb7 Black can't survive the multiple attacking threats.

30 ♖e3!

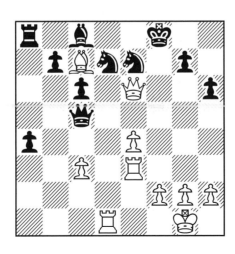

A new attacker is airlifted in. I wonder if Bruzon had only counted on 30 ♗d6?! ♕g5 31 ♖e3 ♘e5, when he is busted but at least continues to resist.

30...♔e8

The d7-knight can't budge a muscle, since 30...♘e5?? 31 ♖d8 is mate!

31 ♖f3

Threatening mate in one.

31...♕h5 32 ♗d6 1-0

The exit wound on d6 reopens, while 32...♕g5 is met by 33 ♖f7, continuing to stroke the dead cat on e7.

Game 9
A.Naiditsch-V.Kramnik
Dortmund 2009
Petroff's Defence

1 e4 e5 2 ♘f3 ♘f6

Opening choices like the Petroff, along with the Berlin Lopez, are one of the reasons so many players falsely accuse Kramnik of being a stodgy positional player.

3 ♘xe5 d6 4 ♘f3 ♘xe4 5 d4 d5 6 ♗d3

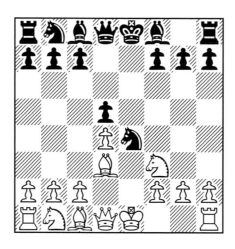

6...♗d6

The previous year, Naiditsch had burned Kramnik through deeper opening preparation in the line 6...♘c6 7 0-0 ♗e7 8 ♖e1 ♗g4 9 c4 ♘f6 10 ♘c3 ♗xf3 11 ♕xf3 ♘xd4 12 ♕d1 ♘e6 13 cxd5 ♘xd5 14 ♗b5+ c6 15 ♘xd5 cxb5 16 ♗f4 ♘xf4 17 ♖xe7+ ♔f8 18 ♖e5 ♕d6, and here Naiditsch had prepared the startling novelty 19 ♕d2!? which confused Kramnik. The game continued 19...♘g6? (19...♕xe5! 20 ♕b4+ ♔e8 21 ♖e1 ♘e2+ 22 ♔f1 ♖c8! 23 f4 ♕xd5 24 ♖xe2+ ♔d7 25 ♖d2 ♖c5! should be okay for Black) 20 ♖ee1! and Black was unable to unravel effectively, A.Naiditsch-V.Kramnik, Dortmund 2008.

7 0-0 0-0 8 c4 c6 9 ♖e1

White also has 9 ♘c3, 9 cxd5 and 9 ♕c2.

9...♗f5 10 c5!?

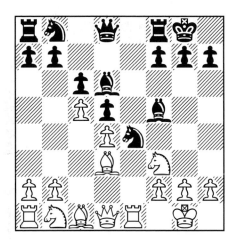

Naiditsch hopes to throw Kramnik off with a little-played line. The move looks like it goes against the natural flow of the position.

> *Question:* Why don't you like 10 c5 - ?

Answer: Although the move does have the plus of gaining queenside space, intuitively it feels like Black is the beneficiary of any release of central tension. The central stability allowed Kramnik later to build up a kingside attack. Better to stick with the main lines: 10 ♘c3, 10 ♕b3 or 10 ♕c2.

> *Question:* What kingside attack? White looks impregnable.

Answer: For now. If you allow an uncontested piece build-up around your king – weakened or not – the attacking side has a nasty way of generating a weak point which didn't previously exist.

10...♗c7 11 ♘c3 ♘d7 12 ♕c2

> *Question:* I don't understand why Kramnik left
> e4 unprotected. Why didn't White win a pawn?

Answer: The pawn is held tactically. After 12 ♘xe4?! dxe4 13 ♗xe4 ♗xe4 14 ♖xe4 Black exploits the pin with 14...♘xc5!, when White has exchanged too many pieces for an isolani position.

12...♖e8 13 ♗e3

> **Question:** Now there is no back rank problem. Why not take on e4?

Answer: 13 ♘xe4 dxe4 14 ♗xe4 is now met by 14...♕e7! 15 ♘g5 ♘f6 16 f3 h6 17 ♗d2 ♘xe4!
18 ♘xe4 (after 18 fxe4? ♗g6! 19 ♘f3 ♗xe4 Black gets the bishop pair and light-square
domination) 18...♕h4 with Ruy Lopez Marshall Attack-like compensation for the pawn,
B.Socko-P.Skatchkov, Cappelle la Grande 2004.

13...h6 14 b4

White gains ground on the queenside.

14...♘df6

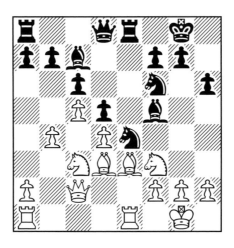

15 h3?!

Eliminating ...♘g4 ideas, but allowing Kramnik a sac target on h3. Naiditsch clearly underestimated the force of Black's coming attack.

> **Question:** Okay, so what do you suggest for White in its place?

Answer: With hindsight White should probably avoid h2-h3 and play something like 15 a4
♕d7 16 ♖ab1, although in that case Black keeps building with 16...♖e6. Perhaps the move
which really deserves the "?!" mark is White's tenth.

15...♕d7! 16 ♘e2!?

He encourages the sac. Baburin suggests 16 ♘d2, but then the sac looks very strong:
16...♗xh3! 17 ♘dxe4 dxe4 18 ♘xe4 ♘d5! 19 gxh3 ♘xb4, when 20 ♕b1? is met by 20...♘xd3
21 ♕xd3 ♕xh3 with a winning attack. Now one feels that tingle of disquiet felt just before
a thunderstorm erupts.

16...♗xh3!

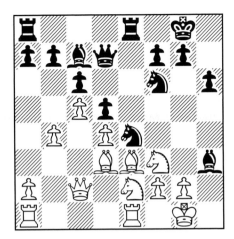

The bishop solemnly places his hand upon the h-pawn's head and recites a benediction. The moment has arrived, as Black intensifies the heat from low burn to high.

17 ♘e5!

In a war without meaning, the soldier's primary mission is self-preservation. White's king views the cheeky bishop's lunge with open-mouthed incredulity. After the initial shock, White gathers himself in a final attempt to stabilize his quickly degenerating situation. Naiditsch probably counted on this tricky zwischenzug, but Black's chances remain superior.

Immediate acceptance loses: 17 gxh3? ♕xh3, when Black's attack grows out of control.

17...♗xe5 18 dxe5 ♖xe5 19 f3 ♖ae8! 20 ♗f4

Or 20 fxe4 ♗xg2! 21 ♔xg2 ♖h5 22 ♘g3 ♕h3+ 23 ♔g1 ♕xg3+ 24 ♕g2 ♕xg2+ 25 ♔xg2 ♘xe4 – advantage Black, who gets four healthy pawns for the piece.

20...♖h5!

Such strong attacks tend to generate simultaneous waves of euphoria and panic, since the attacking side is often left with multiple pieces hanging. Kramnik's move looks more accurate than 20...♗xg2!? 21 ♔xg2 ♘g5 22 ♖h1 ♘xf3 23 ♗xe5 ♘xe5 24 ♗f5, when White's forces let forth a ragged cheer since the invading party has been repelled for now.

21 fxe4?

He had no choice but to play 21 ♘d4! ♖h4!, when Black's attack rages on.

After this text the once luxurious White position transforms into a slum, stark in its squalor. White's king soon crinkles like a photograph on fire.

21...dxe4 22 ♗c4

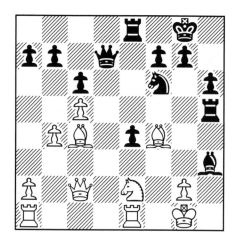

Answer: **22...♗xg2!**

The pawn cover, far from providing safety, becomes the white king's death shroud as
the bishop strips away the final vestiges of defensive barrier.

23 ♘g3

The bishop can't be touched: 23 ♔xg2?? ♕h3+ 24 ♔g1 ♕h1+ 25 ♔f2 ♕f3+ 26 ♔g1 ♖h1
mate.

23...♗f3! 24 ♕b3

Nor is there hope for White after 24 ♘xh5 ♘xh5 25 ♕h2 ♕g4+ 26 ♔f2 ♘xf4. *Houdini*
has Black up by a whopping +12.34!

24...♖h4

24...♕h3! is even more crushing.

25 ♗d6 ♕h3!

The malicious fallen angel plummets from the heavens above the stratosphere, determined to harm the world. The f7-pawn is meaningless.

26 ♗xf7+ ♔h7 27 ♕b2

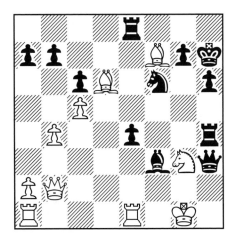

Exercise (combination alert): Kramnik's prosaic next move
leads to mate in five moves and prompts White's resignation.
But look closer. Kramnik missed a mate in three moves.
Can you find the quicker mate a world champion overlooked?

Answer: Kramnik missed a dazzling finish with 27...♕xg3+! 28 ♗xg3 ♖h1+ 29 ♔f2 ♘g4
mate. White's king spasms like the involuntary twitching of a newly dead accident victim.
Instead, the game concluded:

27...♘g4 0-1

The aftermath leaves only bloody water as the sharks have their fill.

Game 10
A.Shirov-V.Kramnik
Wijk aan Zee 2011
Scotch Game

1 e4 e5 2 ♘f3 ♘c6 3 d4

I remember everyone asking why Kasparov never switched from the Berlin Lopez to the
Scotch in his world championship match against Kramnik. Games like this prove that
Kramnik was heavily armed for Scotch as well.

3...exd4 4 ♘xd4 ♘f6 5 ♘xc6 bxc6 6 e5 ♕e7 7 ♕e2 ♘d5 8 c4 ♘b6

8...♗a6 is the most popular move here. For example, 9 ♘d2 g6 10 b3 ♗g7 11 ♗b2 ♘b4
12 0-0-0!? ♘xa2+ 13 ♔b1 ♘b4 14 ♘e4! 0-0 (14...♗xe5?? loses instantly to 15 ♗xe5! ♕xe5
16 ♘f6+) 15 ♕f3 ♖fe8 16 ♘f6+ ♗xf6 17 exf6 ♕c5 18 h4 offered White compensation for
the pawn, Ma.Carlsen-L.Aronian, Wijk aan Zee 2011.

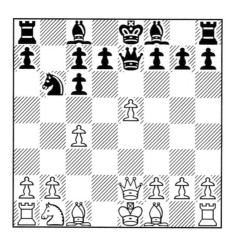

9 ♘c3 ♗b7

Possibly a remnant of match prep against Kasparov. 9...♕e6 is the main line.

10 ♗d2

Deviating from I.Nepomniachtchi-V.Kramnik, Wijk aan Zee 2011 (five rounds earlier in the tournament), which went 10 ♗f4 g6 11 h4 (a novelty) 11...♗g7 12 0-0-0 0-0 13 h5 ♖ae8 14 ♖e1 ♗a6! 15 ♕e4 ♕c5 16 ♗g3 ♗xc4 17 hxg6 fxg6 18 ♘a4! ♘xa4 19 ♕xc4+ ♔h8, when *Houdini* claims that White has full compensation for the pawn.

10...g6!?

Very rare. Black normally castles queenside here.

11 ♘e4

Or 11 0-0-0 ♗g7 12 h4 h6 13 f4 0-0-0 14 ♘e4 c5 with an unclear position, H.Asis Garga-tagli-J.Oms Pallisse, Barcelona 2011.

11...0-0-0

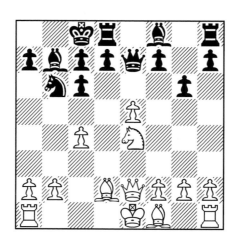

12 a4!?

A new move in the position.

Question: White threatens a4-a5 and, when
Black's knight is sent to a8, then a5-a6, winning a piece.
Shouldn't White's last move be given an exclamation mark?

Answer: I'm not so sure. White does indeed generate serious threats with his last move. But he is also seriously behind in development at this point, and 12 a4 does nothing to alleviate the issue. 12 f4 c5 13 0-0-0 follows a more conventional path, as in R.Alonso-A.Sidenko, correspondence 2011.

12...♗a6

Negating White's threat. Black can also try 12...c5!?, when 13 a5 ♘xc4 14 ♕xc4 d5 regains the piece while retaining a development lead.

13 ♕e3!?

Shirov plays the entire opening oddly, with careful uncertainty, as if each move were some dangerous scientific experiment. He probably didn't like the looks of 13 a5 ♘xc4! 14 ♖a4, when Black can choose between 14...♖e8 and 14...f5!?, either of which sees White's lag in development intersecting with his king-safety woes.

13...♕xe5!

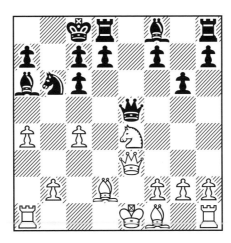

Kramnik boldly sacs a piece to increase his lead in development even further.

Question: Don't you mean sacs a rook?

Answer: No, it's actually just a piece. Play on to see Kramnik's trick.

14 ♗c3 ♗b4!

Kramnik counted on this diversionary tactic. He sacs a minor piece, not a full rook.

15 ♗xb4 ♖he8

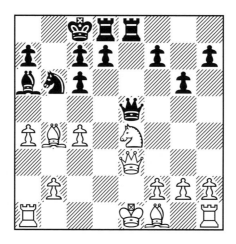

Question: What does Black get for his piece?

Answer: The following:

1. One pawn, plus another one which hangs on c4 if he wants it.

2. A massive lead in development, which may well lead to a powerful attack.

3. A nasty attack on White's e4-knight.

Conclusion: Black has full compensation for the sacrificed material.

16 f3 d5 17 a5 ♘xc4! 18 ♕xa7

After 18 ♗xc4 ♗xc4 19 0-0-0 dxe4 20 ♕xa7 ♗d3! White's king is the one in greater danger.

18...♕xb2!

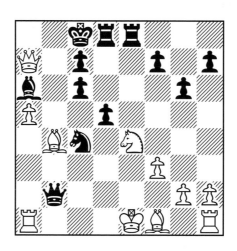

The a6-bishop's mood hardens into open defiance as he refuses to budge.

19 ♕xa6+ ♔d7 20 ♖d1

Or 20 ♗xc4 ♕xa1+ 21 ♔f2 ♕d4+! 22 ♔g3 ♖xe4!, when the rook is untouchable due to a queen check on e3.

20...♕xb4+ 21 ♔f2 ♖xe4! 22 fxe4 ♕c5+ 23 ♔e1

Both f3 and g3 are suicidal squares for the king.

23...♕b4+ 24 ♔f2 ♕c5+ 25 ♔e1

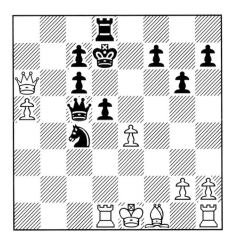

25...♘b2!

Nyet! No draw! The knight pops in and introduces himself to White's rook. There is a Melanie song from *Woodstock* which goes: "I never noticed you before today, I'm ashamed to say."

> *Question:* You gave Kramnik's last move an exclamation mark.
> Yet he is down a rook, has no clear forced win, and still refuses
> to take the draw. Is his decision to play for the win logical?

Answer: I believe so, for the following reasons:

1. Black has a powerful attack despite the reduction of material, since it also means a reduction in White's defenders.

2. White's king is so exposed that it feels like Kramnik can always bail out with perpetual check later on.

3. White's lag in development continues to fester, like mildew and grime on a bathroom tile.

4. White's rook is in grave danger, and if Kramnik picks it off in exchange for his knight, he will only be down a piece for many pawns – which may not even constitute a sacrifice.

26 exd5?!

Shirov, left only with bad choices, picks the worst of the lot. He probably has a better shot of saving himself with:

a) 26 ♕e2 ♘xd1 27 ♕xd1 ♖e8 28 ♗e2 ♕xa5+ 29 ♕d2 ♕a1+ 30 ♕d1 ♕xd1+ 31 ♔xd1 ♖xe4, though White probably won't be able to save himself since Black gets four pawns for the piece.

b) 26 ♗e2 ♘xd1 27 ♗xd1 dxe4 and White's king remains in mortal danger.

26...♕c3+! 27 ♖d2 ♕c1+?

Winning the rook the wrong way. Instead, 27...♖e8+! 28 ♗e2 ♕c1+ 29 ♔f2 ♕xd2 leaves White curiously helpless.

28 ♔e2 ♖e8+ 29 ♔f3 ♕xd2 30 ♕xc6+ ♔d8 31 ♕f6+ ♖e7 32 ♔g4?

Here White has very real chances to save the game with 32 ♗a6!, after which Black's once-powerful initiative slowly dissipates to a trickle, a drip, and may well go dry soon.

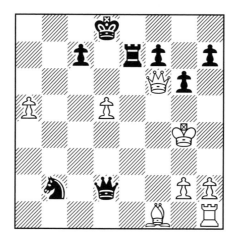

When in the throes of desperation, mixed with low time on the clock, it is only then when radical notions and plans blossom forth from our fevered imaginations. White's king moves here and there with the random gracelessness of a fly in flight.

> **Exercise (planning):** Shirov just blundered in time trouble.
> How can Black reignite his attack?

Answer: Add another attacker to the mix. White now views the approaching knight with wary caution. Inexorably, Black's attackers edge closer, feeding on the white king's fears. With an almost imperceptible ambient glow, Black's power remains intact, despite the recent bruising to his own king's position.

32...♘d1! 33 ♕h8+ ♔d7 34 ♗b5+ c6!

34...♔d6?? walks into 35 ♕d8+ ♔c5 36 ♕xe7+ ♔xb5, when White has at least a draw.

35 ♗xc6+ ♔c7 36 d6+

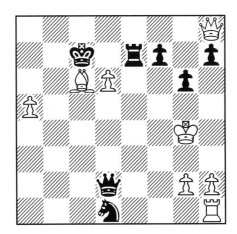

36...♕xd6?!

This is still winning, but Kramnik misses the spectacular 36...♚xc6!! 37 ♕c8+ ♚d5 38 dxe7 f5+ 39 ♚h3 ♕h6+ 40 ♚g3 ♕g5+ 41 ♚f3 ♕g4 mate.

37 ♖xd1 ♕xd1+ 38 ♗f3 h5+ 39 ♚g3 ♕e1+ 40 ♚h3 ♕e6+ 41 ♚h4

Understandably, Shirov realized he had no chance in the technical ending arising after 41 ♚g3 ♕e5+ 42 ♕xe5+ ♖xe5.

41...g5+!

Kramnik tosses a hissing canister of tear gas to disperse the remaining demoralized demonstrators.

42 ♚xg5 ♕g6+ 43 ♚f4

If 43 ♚h4 then 43...♖e4+! wins on the spot.

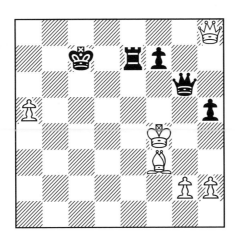

Exercise: Find one powerful move and you force White's resignation.

Answer: 43...f6! 0-1

Such a little move, yet it strikes White a disfiguring blow. Then 44 h4 ♖e8! ends the game; e.g. 45 ♗xh5 (45 ♕xh5 ♖e4+! wins the queen) 45...♖e4+ 46 ♔f3 ♕f5+ (the gathering darkness closes in on White's king as his life gutters out, like a dying candle) 47 ♔g3 ♕f4+ 48 ♔h3 ♕xh4 mate.

Game 11
V.Kramnik-A.Giri
Hoogeveen 2011
King's Indian Defence

1 ♘f3 ♘f6 2 c4 g6 3 ♘c3 ♗g7 4 e4 d6 5 d4 0-0 6 ♗e2 e5 7 0-0 ♘c6 8 d5 ♘e7 9 b4

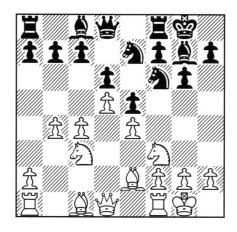

A GM must have incredible self-confidence to allow Kramnik his dreaded Bayonet Attack against the King's Indian.

Question: What is so great about the Bayonet Attack?

Answer: I'm not sure it is the opening. It may be the guy playing the opening! Kasparov utilized the King's Indian as his main weapon for Black versus queen's pawn openings all throughout the 80's and 90's. Then he suddenly abandoned his beloved KID.

Question: Why?

Answer: It is common belief that Kasparov may have lost faith in the opening due to several stinging losses to Kramnik.

Question: So are you saying the line is theoretically shaky for Black?

Answer: Not at all, only hard to play from a practical standpoint. But times may have changed. GM Alex Baburin recently pointed out that Kramnik's score as White, including blitz games, versus Hikaru Nakamura in the King's Indian, is a sorry 1-7 in favour of Naka! The KID goes in and out of favour at the top over the decades for no apparent reason. From time to time paranoia arises that the KID has been refuted by this line or that one! But in reality, there is no – and has never been – any real existential threat to KID.

> **Question:** What is the difference between the
> Bayonet Attack and the ♘e1/♗e3 main line?

Answer: I think in the ♘e1/♗e3 main line, both White and Black's corresponding queenside and kingside attacks tend to accelerate at alarming rates. In the Bayonet Attack, White tends not to apply so much queenside pressure and the same holds for Black on the king-side. The argument tends to take place on common ground, in the centre.

Here is a classic example of what fate can befall White in the ♘e1/♗e3 mainline King's Indian: 9 ♘e1 ♘d7 10 ♗e3 f5 11 f3 f4 12 ♗f2 g5 (White tends to run amok on the queenside, all the while facing annihilation on the kingside) 13 a4 ♘g6 14 ♘d3 ♘f6 15 c5 h5 16 h3 ♖f7 17 c6 a5 18 cxb7 ♗xb7 19 b4 ♗c8 20 bxa5 ♗h6 21 ♘b4 g4 22 ♘c6, V.Korchnoi-G.Kasparov, Amsterdam 1991, when there is good news and bad news: Black is getting crushed on the queenside; unfortunately, White finds himself getting crushed on the other wing!

9...♘h5

Alternatively:

a) 9...a5 is also played quite a lot but has its risks since Black chooses to engage the opponent on White's strong wing: 10 ♗a3 axb4 11 ♗xb4 ♘d7 12 a4 f5 13 ♘g5 ♘c5 14 ♗xc5 dxc5 15 ♗f3 ♖a6 16 a5 ♔h8 17 ♘e6 ♗xe6 18 dxe6 f4 19 ♕xd8 ♖xd8 20 ♖fb1 ♖b8, when Black found himself completely on the defensive on the queenside, V.Kramnik-G.Kasparov, Moscow (blitz, 6th matchgame) 1998.

b) 9...♘e8 10 c5 f5 11 ♘d2 ♘f6 12 a4 g5 13 ♘c4 h6 14 f3 f4 15 ♗a3 ♘g6

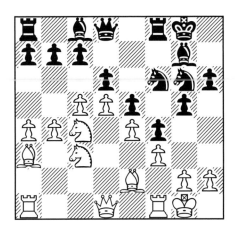

with typical corresponding queenside/kingside attacks, V.Anand-H.Nakamura, London 2011.

Question: What do the computers think about such positions?

Answer: In this case *Houdini* thinks Black is getting his butt kicked and has White up by +1.29! – but in the real world, Black still does okay in such violent storms.

c) 9...♘d7 10 a4 h6 11 ♗a3 f5 12 c5 ♘f6 13 ♘d2 and whose position you prefer probably depends on your style, S.Karjakin-J.Polgar, Moscow (blitz) 2009.

10 g3

Question: Weakening all the light squares around his king?

Answer: Yes, but to gain time by making Black's ...♘h5 look meaningless – although Black, in a sacrificial fury, sometimes moves the knight to f4 later anyway!

10 ♖e1 is what Kramnik used to play in the 90's, before switching recently to the older text move. For example, 10...f5 11 ♘g5 ♘f6 12 ♗f3 c6 13 ♗a3 h6 14 ♘e6 ♗xe6 15 dxe6 fxe4 and Black's central influence counter-balances White's bishop pair, V.Kramnik-A.Grischuk, Moscow (blitz) 2008.

Question: Isn't White going to drop e6 eventually?

Answer: He often does, but in the process Black has had to relinquish his precious light-squared bishop for the knight, which always seems to give White great compensation with the open centre.

10...f5 11 ♘g5 ♘f6

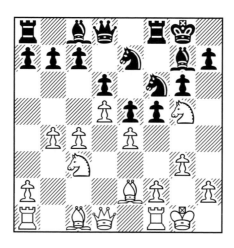

12 ♗f3

A rare line, albeit one which Kramnik plays on occasion, probably designed to throw Giri off his theory. Normally White doesn't mix g2-g3 with ♗f3. Instead, 12 f3 is more usual, and is Van Wely's specialty. The database is permeated with his games from this position. For example, 12...f4 13 b5 h6 14 ♘e6 ♗xe6 15 dxe6 fxg3 16 hxg3 ♕c8 17 ♘d5 ♕xe6 18 ♘xc7 ♕h3 19 ♖f2, L.Van Wely-T.Radjabov, Dresden Olympiad 2008, when *Houdini* thinks chances are even after 19...♖ac8.

12...c6 13 ♗a3

Kramnik had originally prepared a theoretical novelty here, which he plays against Grischuk in Chapter Four (see Game 38). Kramnik said he intended 13 ♗g2! but got his analysis mixed up! Welcome to my world! I do this constantly.

13...cxd5 14 exd5!?

Recapturing with the e-pawn on d5 is almost unheard of in the Bayonet Attack.

Question: Why did Kramnik play that way?

Answer: This may be home prep or an over-the-board impulse buy. In any case, by doing so, Kramnik accelerates both sides' respective wing attacks.

14...e4 15 ♗e2

Designed to keep an eye on the c4-, g4- and h5-squares.

15...♘e8 16 ♖c1 h6

Perhaps he should try 16...♘c7!?.

17 ♘e6

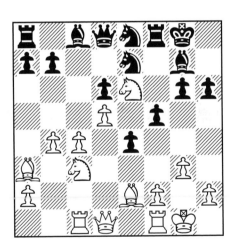

Far from graceful, White's knight pulls an ungainly belly-flop on e6, all in the name of clearing central lines. White never retreats in such Bayonet positions, even when it means giving up a pawn.

17...♗xe6 18 dxe6 ♘c7?!

Black wants to shed himself of the encumbrance on e6 as quickly as possible, but he chooses the wrong way. From this point on, Kramnik makes it look like a forced win for White. Giri had to try the unnatural 18...♕c8.

19 b5!

Target: d6. Kramnik returns to his construction project anew.

19...♗e5 20 ♕b3! ♔g7

20...♘xe6 21 ♖fd1 ♘d4 is met by 22 ♖xd4 ♗xd4 23 c5+ d5 (23...♔g7 would actually transpose to the game) 24 ♘xd5! ♘xd5 25 ♖d1 and Black, a full rook up, is busted!

21 ♖fd1 ♘xe6

White doesn't care. He had always planned on abandoning the e6-foundling on Black's doorstep. 21...b6 fails to halt White's main intention 22 c5!.

22 c5

No sooner had Black sutured the wound on e6, another one opens on d6, oozing blood.

22...♘d4

Losing, as do all other tries; e.g. 22...♕d7 23 cxd6 ♘c8 24 ♘xe4! fxe4 25 ♗g4 ♖f5 26 ♖d5! ♗f6 27 ♖xf5 gxf5 28 ♗xf5 ♔f7 29 ♖c7 and mates.

23 ♖xd4! ♗xd4 24 cxd6

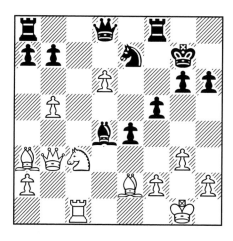

White's central initiative has gotten out of control. *Houdini* assesses this as +2.75 – dead lost for Black, whose pieces utterly lack coordination.

24...♘g8 25 ♘d5

No matter how much Black squirms, the intractable knight refuses to budge one iota for the remainder of the game.

25...♔h8

25...♖c8 loses instantly to 26 ♖c7+! ♔h8 27 ♗b2!.

26 ♖c7 ♗e5 27 ♗b2!?

Intuitively, Kramnik decides to remove Black's best king's defender. 27 ♖e7! ♗g7 28 ♘f4 ♖f6 29 ♖xb7 was stronger.

27...♕xd6 28 ♖xb7 g5 29 b6! a5

29...axb6?? 30 ♖xb6 disconnects Black's queen from his bishop. But now Black must worry about White's deeply passed b-pawn.

30 ♗h5!

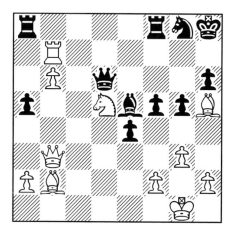

The bishop dances a baroque quadrille to join the party. The number of hostiles swell as attackers seep through the porous defensive perimeter.

30...♖ab8 31 ♖a7

The rooks pass each other with mutual nods, followed by mutters of recognition.

31...♗xb2

And now the bishop says hello in polite, demure greeting to his more powerful brother on b2. It seems the tired sheriff on e5 wants to resign his post but has trouble removing his badge. Black is almost out of moves. A sample line if Black refrains from swapping bishops: 31...♖a8 32 ♗f7! ♘f6 33 ♗a3 ♕b8 34 ♖xa8 ♕xa8 35 b7 ♕b8 36 ♗xf8 ♕xf8 37 ♘xf6 wins.

32 ♕xb2+ ♘f6

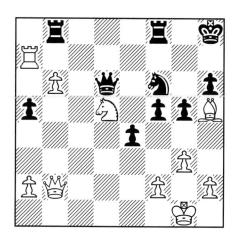

> ***Exercise (combination alert):*** Black's troubles continue
> to collect in a slow drip. White to play and win.

Answer: Interference.

33 ♗f7!

The bishop sweeps away Black's remaining piece cohesion, as his forces begin to desert his king in every direction.

33...♔g7 34 ♖d7!

Kramnik mercilessly assails his opponent with a spattering of threats, all with a unifying theme: play for mate.

34...♕c6

Or 34...♕xd7 35 ♕xf6+ ♔h7 36 ♕g6+ ♔h8 37 ♕xh6 mate.

35 ♗e6+! 1-0

All attacking potentials intersect, as the discovered check leeches whatever blood and life-force that remained in the black king's arteries.

Black resigned, since 35...♔g6 36 ♘e7+ forks king and queen, while 35...♔h8 36 ♘xf6 ♕xe6 (the queen wills herself to avert her eyes and look away from the carnage on h7) 37 ♖h7 is mate.

Chapter Two
Kramnik on Defence

In situations under pressure, it is often better to do than to think. Our survival instinct protects us with greater urgency than the analytical mind, with all its computations and vacillations. In this chapter Kramnik does just that. His style of defence is different from most, since he displays a visceral aversion to any form of passivity – even if his position is passive! Instead, he opts for revitalized, armed resistance.

Kramnik has a way of weaponizing perseverance. When facing multiple threats, his key to survival is to prioritize, identifying the most to least fatal threats and dealing with them in that order.

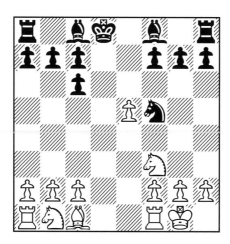

If a position is to be inscribed on Kramnik's gravestone, it will be this one. The Berlin Lopez opening/ending, along with his supernatural defensive skills, earned him the world champi-

onship when he upended the great Garry Kasparov in one of the most shocking upsets since
Euwe defeated the alcohol-impaired Alekhine back in 1935. Kramnik took an offbeat Lopez
line and turned it into a template: how not to lose as Black against 1 e4. In game after game
Kasparov charged head on against the Berlin Wall, only to be stymied each time. Basically
Kasparov burned out all his Whites without a single win by his name. Meanwhile, Kramnik
methodically notched two wins from his own Whites. How is it possible to face a player of
Kasparov's ferocity and genius, and survive the match without a single loss?

> ### Game 12
> ### V.Kramnik-Ju.Hodgson
> ### Groningen 1993
> ### *Slav Defence*

1 ♘f3 d5 2 d4 ♘f6 3 c4 c6 4 ♘c3 dxc4 5 a4 ♗f5 6 ♘e5

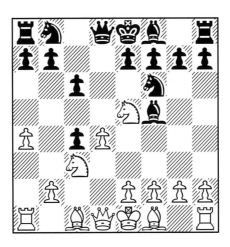

The specialty of the house. Kramnik's success with the 6 ♘e5 Slav greatly helped to
popularize the line.

> **Question:** What is White's main line?

Answer: 6 e3 is still played more often, but as a long-time Slav guy I am convinced 6 ♘e5 is
tougher to deal with.

> **Question:** What is the main difference between the two variations?

Answer: White in both versions seeks to advance e4, but goes about it in different ways. In
the 6 e3 lines, White often plays ♕e2 and then e3-e4, while after 6 ♘e5, White plays for f2-

f3 and e2-e4, or sometimes even g2-g3, ♗g2 and later on e2-e4.

6...e6

Other ideas are 6...♘a6!? (I try and revive this funky line in *The Slav: Move by Move*) and 6...♘bd7 7 ♘xc4 ♕c7 (or 7...♘b6, which I advocate my Slav book) 8 g3 e5 9 dxe5 ♘xe5 10 ♗f4 ♘fd7.

7 f3 ♗b4

The piece sac seen in the game was all the rage for Black back in the 90's, until Kramnik removed some of the fun from it.

On the other hand, I don't believe 7...c5 equalizes: 8 e4 ♗g6 (8...cxd4 9 exf5 ♗b4 10 ♗xc4 dxc3 is also played, E.AlekseevWang Yue, Nizhnij Novgorod 2007) 9 ♗e3 cxd4 10 ♕xd4 ♕xd4 11 ♗xd4 ♘fd7 12 ♘xd7 ♘xd7 13 ♗xc4 is an unpleasant ending for Black due to his out-of-play bishop on g6, V.Topalov-V.Anand, World Championship (3rd, 5th and 8th matchgames) Sofia 2010.

8 e4 ♗xe4

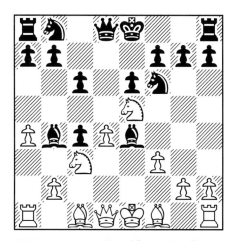

Question: Can Black refuse to sac?

Answer: He just gets a lame Slav if he backs off. Black scores a dismal 24% after 8...♗g6?! 9 ♗xc4 ♘bd7 10 ♘xg6 hxg6, as in A.Shirov-Z.Lozano Garnes, Andorra (simul) 2001. White has both the bishop pair and total control over the centre.

9 fxe4 ♘xe4 10 ♗d2 ♕xd4 11 ♘xe4 ♕xe4+ 12 ♕e2 ♗xd2+ 13 ♔xd2 ♕d5+ 14 ♔c2

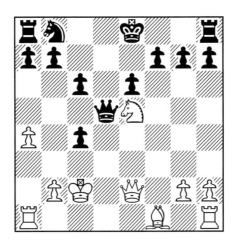

All book. We reach the tabiya position of the sac. Kramnik may have proved through his games that the verdict is an edge for White.

> **Question:** So is the line unplayable now?

Answer: I still think it's very playable, especially at a non-professional level. White's position, despite his extra piece, is hard to play with his king bouncing around the centre.

14...♘a6

The hole on b4 beckons.

15 ♘xc4 ♔e7!?

Much more common is to castle on either wing:

a) 15...0-0 16 ♕e5 ♖ab8 17 a5 f6 18 ♕xd5 cxd5 19 ♘e3 ♖bc8+ 20 ♔b1 ♘c5 21 ♖a3, when I would rather play White but maybe Black has enough for the piece, V.Anand-A.Khalifman, FIDE World Championship, New Delhi 2000.

b) 15...0-0-0 16 ♕e3 ♘c5 17 ♗e2! ♕xg2?! (Black should probably fight the temptation and decline) 18 ♖hg1 ♕xh2 19 ♖xg7 ♖d4!? 20 ♕xd4! ♕xe2+ 21 ♘d2 ♖d8 22 ♕xc5! ♖xd2+ 23 ♔b3 ♖xb2+ 24 ♔a3 and it's still tricky, but Black doesn't have quite enough for the rook, V.Kramnik-A.Shirov, Dortmund 1996.

16 ♕e5

> **Question:** Why not gain a tempo with 16 ♖d1 - ?

Answer: White falls behind in development after 16...♕f5+ 17 ♔c3 ♖hd8.

16...♖hd8 17 ♗e2

White would love to get queens off the board, but not at the cost of improving Black's structure.

17...f6 18 ♕e3

Question: White's king looks like it is in
greater danger. Why not swap queens?

Answer: Black's attack is not as intimidating as it first appears. GM Scherbakov writes: "This is a standard approach for similar positions. White often puts his queen on e5 to decrease Black's possible initiative with a queen swap, but if the situation requires he can retreat his queen and play the middlegame. It is usually White who chooses if the queens stay on because a good endgame for Black usually appears when the c-pawn takes on d5 to create a strong pawn chain." Kramnik also claims that the ending is approximately equal after 18 ♕xd5 cxd5.

18...♘b4+?!

If a small creature moves erratically or suddenly in the forest, it endangers itself by attracting a predator's attention.

Question: What predator? Why the dubious mark
for such a natural attacking move?

Answer: The predator turns out to be White's king! In a few moves Kramnik proves that Black's knight is somewhat wobbly and unstable on b4. Just watch. Instead, Kramnik gives 18...♕f5+ 19 ♔c3 ♘c7 20 ♕g3 ♘d5+ 21 ♔b3 and claims just an edge for White.

19 ♔b3!

Confidently walking into a pin.

19...a5

Black realizes that 19...b5? works out in White's favour after 20 axb5 cxb5 21 ♔xb4! bxc4 22 ♗xc4.

20 ♖ad1 ♕f5 21 ♕c3!

Kramnik concocts machinations designed to undermine and destabilize Black's knight with ♘xa5!.

21...b5?!

Hodgson feeds his attack's voracious appetite with more fuel. In doing so, he overestimates Black's chances. He should stay calm and play 21...♘d5.

22 ♘xa5!

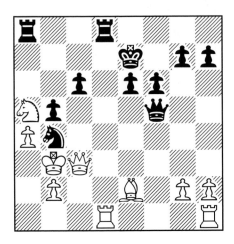

White's knight vacates his spot and decides to sell his life dearly to those who seek his death. Kramnik is unafraid of Black's coming attacking chances, despite the opening of lines. Soon, Black's much anticipated counterplay against White's king, so seemingly real, turns out to be counterfeit.

> **Question:** Isn't White's king in serious danger?

Answer: White's fears are greatly diffused through the filter of the bodyguards who flank him. His king on b3 rests snugly as a marsupial's baby in her pouch.

22...c5

Kramnik gives the line 22...bxa4+ 23 ♔xb4 ♖db8+ (White has no worries after 23...♕xa5+ 24 ♔a3) 24 ♔a3 ♖b3+ 25 ♘xb3 axb3+ 26 ♔xb3 ♖b8+ 27 ♔a2 ♖a8+ 28 ♕a3+ ♖xa3+ 29 ♔xa3, when White gets too much for the queen.

23 ♗xb5!

Kramnik returns the piece but, in doing so, utterly dislocates Black's harmony.

23...♖xa5

Certainly not 23...♖xd1?? 24 ♖xd1 ♖xa5 25 ♖d7+ ♔f8 26 ♕g3!, winning on the spot due to the crushing double attacks on g7 and b8.

24 ♖hf1 ♕h5

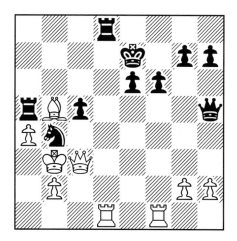

> **Exercise (planning/combination alert):** How can
> White force a winning endgame?

Answer: Deflection. The assailant pops out of a shadowed niche in the alley and pulls a weapon in the dark. Black's queen covering c5 has no choice but to go to e5 and allow a rancid ending.

25 g4!

Forcing the queen swap. Black's attack proved to be illusion, an empty container, devoid of substance.

25...♛e5

Those on the margins of society strive to move toward the centre. The black queen's face creases in confusion and incomprehension at what just transpired. She has no choice but to allow a highly unfavourable swap since 25...♛g5?? is met by the shocking 26 ♖f5!!. The crushing interference shot is an instant game-ender.

26 ♛xe5 fxe5 27 ♖xd8 ♚xd8 28 ♚c4!

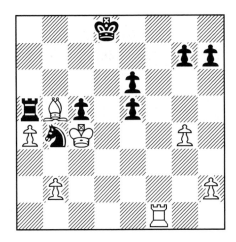

He makes it look so easy. Black drops c5, which gives White two unstoppable queenside passers. White's king emerges from his rubble strewn home unscathed, as he weaves and oscillates like a skilled boxer in the ring.

28...♔e7 29 ♔xc5

The creature casts its terrible shadow upon the queenside.

29...♘d5 30 b4 ♖a8 31 ♗c6 ♖c8 32 b5 e4 1-0

Hodgson resigned, realizing the futility of playing on against those surging queenside pawns.

> ### Game 13
> ### V.Kramnik-G.Kasparov
> Novgorod 1997
> *King's Indian Defence*

1 d4 ♘f6 2 c4 g6 3 ♘c3 ♗g7 4 e4 d6 5 ♘f3 0-0 6 ♗e2 e5 7 0-0 ♘c6 8 d5 ♘e7 9 b4 ♘h5 10 ♖e1

Kramnik played 10 g3 against Giri in the previous chapter (see Game 11) and does so again vs. Grischuk in Chapter Four (see Game 38).

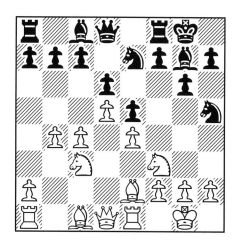

Question: Which line is more popular for White?

Answer: Currently my database contains more 10 ♖e1 games and Kramnik has mostly played this move, but 10 g3 also has its faithful followers. I believe Van Wely plays that line exclusively. In the end it's just a matter of taste which one you pick.

10...♘f4

Kramnik has also faced:

a) 10...f5 11 ♘g5 ♘f6 12 ♗f3 c6 13 ♗a3 h6 14 ♘e6 ♗xe6 15 dxe6 fxe4 16 ♗xe4!? ♘xe4 17 ♘xe4 d5 18 ♘c5 and the usual central confusion arises, V.Kramnik-A.Grischuk, Moscow (blitz) 2008.

b) 10...a5 11 bxa5 f5 12 ♘d2 ♘f6 (12...♘f4 13 ♗f1 ♖xa5 almost transposes to the main game, except that Black has yet to play ...f7-f5) 13 c5!? ♖xa5 (Black didn't like 13...dxc5 14 ♗c4 ♔h8 15 ♘b3 when the queenside is quickly opened) 14 cxd6 cxd6 15 a4 and I prefer White, who again has managed to open his strong wing, V.Kramnik-I.Smirin, Russia vs. World, Moscow (rapid) 2002.

11 ♗f1

11 ♗xf4 is also played but that greatly increases Black's dark-squared power.

11...a5

Question: Isn't Black violating principle
by engaging his opponent on the weak wing?

Answer: He is, but keep in mind that the move also freezes White's pawn chain on the queenside. In general, I agree with you and probably wouldn't play Kasparov's move, but many GMs do, so the idea must have merit.

12 bxa5

Houdini, currently the strongest program on the market, suggests the rather stupid move 12 b5?, closing off his own strong wing after 12...b6!. If they ever come up with a chess program with any measure of strategic finesse, my guess is they could take over the world and enslave humanity.

12...♖xa5 13 ♘d2 c5 14 a4 ♖a6 15 ♖a3 g5!?

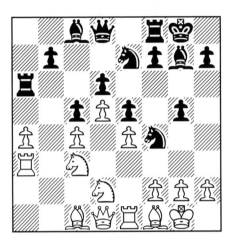

Radical stuff. Kasparov sends in a hired thug to do his dirty work, as he offers Kramnik a pawn in exchange for the light squares.

Question: Is Kasparov's idea sound?

Answer: With the hindsight of Kramnik's almost perfect play, the idea is probably dubious. Keep in mind, it would probably work against a lesser defender. Normal is 15...♘h5 16 ♘b5 ♘f6 17 ♗b2 ♘e8 18 ♘f3 h6 19 g3 f5 20 exf5 ♘xf5 21 ♘d2 with mutual chances, L.Aronian-T.Radjabov, Sofia 2008.

Question: Isn't 15...f5 more thematic for Black
than retreating an already well-posted knight?

Answer: 15...f5 is probably premature in this position. White can play 16 g3 ♘h5 17 exf5 ♘xf5, as in P.Stigar-J.Kristinsson, correspondence 2002. Now if White is brave enough, he can risk 18 g4!? (there is nothing wrong with Stigar's 18 ♘de4) 18...♘h4 19 gxh5 ♕g5+ 20 ♔h1 ♖xf2 21 ♖e2!, when the computers like White, but Black of course gets practical chances.

16 g3! ♘h3+ 17 ♗xh3 ♗xh3 18 ♕h5

Double attack on the bishop and on g5. Kasparov had obviously assessed this position as offering compensation for Black due to his light-square control, which he hoped would be the foundational cause of White's security issues.

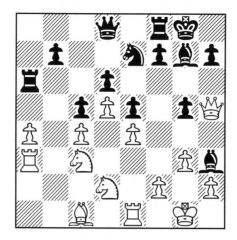

18...♛d7! 19 ♕xg5 h6

Black might have been better off leaving White's queen where it stood and playing 19...f5 immediately.

20 ♕e3

The queen returns quickly with a faint shudder, like a nervous person who accidentally wandered in and out of a dangerous neighbourhood.

20...f5 21 ♕e2 f4 22 ♘b5 ♚h7 23 gxf4!

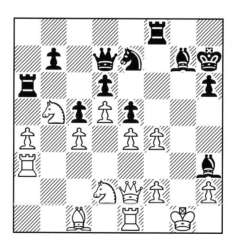

> ***Question:*** Why did White open his own king position?

Answer: I agree that 23 gxf4 is equal parts ambitious and risky – and very powerful. Kramnik wants to attack along the g-file and also allow his a3-rook to participate in the proceedings. In playing his last move, he opens lines for Black as well, and hands over the e5-

square. The course of events confirms his excellent judgment in the decision.

23...exf4 24 ♔h1 ♝g4 25 ♘f3!!

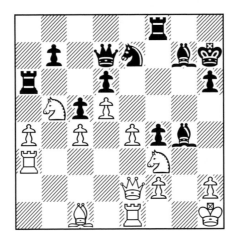

The integrity of White's defensive wall holds firm.

> **Question:** Why walk into a self-pin?

Answer: Somewhere in the universe there must exist a world where poets rule over politicians and military leaders. If so, Kramnik belongs there. Externally, Kramnik's choice looks like a relaxing vacation from common sense. But examining it more deeply, his move is a computer-like decision played solely on its merits, with its exterior ugliness utterly discounted. After the obvious 25 f3 ♝h5 the problem is that White has nothing to do, whereas Black keeps building up with moves like ...♘g6 and ...♘e5. Kramnik didn't see any effective way for Kasparov to exploit the pin, so he self-pinned!

25...♘g6 26 ♖g1

The point: White threatens ♘g5+!.

26...♝xf3+?!

The bishop, a priest in name only, abandons his comrades with heart-wrenching callousness, yet continues to wear the holy robes despite having lost his faith. Instead, 26...♔h8?! 27 ♘c7! ♖b6 28 h3! looks good for White; so, although it goes against Kasparov's character, grovelling with 26...♘h4! may be Black's best shot at survival. After 27 ♘g5+ hxg5 28 ♕xg4 ♕xg4 29 ♖xg4 ♝f6 White still has many technical obstacles to overcome in converting his extra pawn.

27 ♕xf3 ♘e5 28 ♕h5! ♕f7

Unfortunately for Kasparov 28...♘xc4?? fails miserably to 29 ♕g6+ ♔g8 30 ♖h3!.

29 ♕h3!

Not 29 ♕xf7? ♖xf7 30 ♖c3 ♝f8, when White doesn't even manage to keep his extra pawn.

Now White's cocky pieces give one another complicitous smirks, as they eye their vulnerable black counterparts, who feel a palpable sense of unease about the coming storm. Obviously, Kramnik is no longer thinking about defence. White's attacking chances are stronger, so he retains the queens on the board. Suddenly, Black's king shifts uneasily, like the mob boss who knows he is under FBI surveillance.

29...♘xc4 30 ♖f3 ♗e5

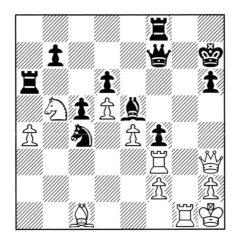

> **Exercise (combination alert):** The attack needs a fresh
> supply of blood. How would you continue for White?

Answer: Overload. White's knight races up the board and into the fight with explosive velocity and zeal.

31 ♘c7!! ♖xa4

Black's queen can't touch the new recruit: 31...♕xc7?? 32 ♕xh6+! (the white queen insists on an ostentatious demonstration of her utter superiority over her sister) 32...♔xh6 33 ♖h3 mate.

32 ♗xf4! 1-0

The bishop tugs free of his tether on f4. Black has no realistic hope of defending after 32...♗xf4 33 ♘e6, so Kasparov resigned.

> ## Game 14
> ### V.Kramnik-V.Akopian
> Dortmund 2000
> *Semi-Slav Defence*

1 ♘f3 d5 2 d4 ♘f6 3 c4 c6 4 ♘c3 e6 5 ♗g5 h6

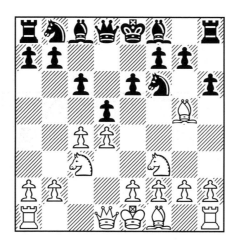

The very popular Moscow variation of the Semi-Slav.

Question: How does it differ from the Botvinnik system?

Answer: In two ways:

1. White isn't *obliged* to enter the wild complications as in the Botvinnik. He can simply take the f6-knight on his next move and steer the game into strategic channels.

2. In the Moscow, White is denied his normal pseudo-sac on g5.

6 ♗h4

Here is an example of the strategic version of the Moscow: 6 ♗xf6 ♕xf6 7 e3 ♘d7 8 ♗e2 ♕d8 9 0-0 ♗e7 10 ♕c2 0-0 11 a3 b6 12 ♖fd1 with a controlled game, V.Kramnik-L.Aronian, Zürich 2012.

6...dxc4 7 e4 g5

As mentioned above, by altering the move order Black denies all g5 sacrificial possibilities to his opponent.

8 ♗g3 b5 9 ♗e2 ♗b7

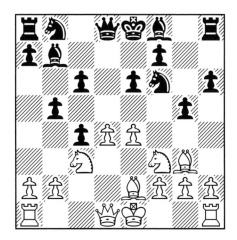

The tabiya position of the Moscow line. I can't help but think that I would lose effortlessly on either side of the board!

Question: What does White exactly get for the pawn?

Answer:
1. Development lead.
2. Strong pawn centre.
3. Loosened pawns in front of Black's king position.

Conclusion: The sum of these factors almost always leads to White having some kind of attacking chances.

Question: Full compensation for White?

Answer: Definitely. Not only does White score a very solid 56%, but the fact that so many top GMs are eager to take on White's position says a lot.

Question: Is it worthwhile breaking up White's centre
with 9...b4 10 ♘a4 ♘xe4, as in K.Sakaev-M.Kobalia,
Russian Championship, St Petersburg 1998?

Answer: I doubt it. Black scores a mere 34% from this position and has only managed to increase his development deficit.

10 h4

Alternatively, White can castle to increase his lead in development and further disrupt Black's structure: 10 0-0 ♘bd7 11 ♘e5 ♗g7 12 ♘xd7 ♘xd7 13 ♗d6 a6 14 a4 b4 15 ♘b1 ♘f6 16 e5 ♘e4 17 ♗xb4 c5 18 ♗a3 cxd4 19 ♗f3 with a standard irrational mess, V.Topalov-

B.Gelfand, Monte Carlo (rapid) 2011.

10...g4 11 ♘e5 h5 12 0-0

Now f2-f3 to open the f-file is in the air.

12...♘bd7

Once again 12...b4?! looks unwise, as after 13 ♘a4 ♘xe4 14 ♗xc4 Black is grievously behind in development.

13 ♕c2 ♘xe5 14 ♗xe5

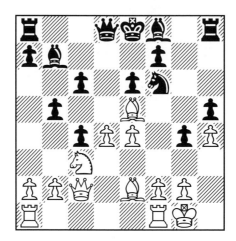

14...♗g7

After 14...♖g8 15 ♖ad1 ♖g6 16 ♗f4 ♗e7 17 g3 a6 18 b3 cxb3 19 axb3 ♗b4 20 ♗d3 ♕xd4 21 ♘a2 e5 22 ♗e3 ♕d6 23 ♗e2 ♕e7 24 ♘xb4 ♕xb4 25 ♗c5 Black stood worse, despite two extra pawns in K.Sakaev-I.Khenkin, European Cup, Belgrade 1999.

15 ♖ad1 0-0 16 ♗g3

Another Sakaev game went 16 b3 cxb3 (better than 16...b4 17 ♘a4 c3 which seals off Black's ...c6-c5 break) 17 axb3 ♘d7 18 ♗d6 ♕xh4 19 ♗xf8 ♖xf8 20 b4 a6, when chances may be dynamically balanced, K.Sakaev-J.Magem Badals, French Team Championship 2005.

16...♘h7!?

The knight crouches low, hoping to remain inconsequential. L.Aronian-V.Anand, World Championship, Mexico City 2007, deviated here with 16...♘d7 17 f3 c5!? 18 dxc5 ♕e7 19 ♔h1 a6 20 a4 ♗c6 21 ♘d5!? exd5 22 exd5 ♗e5 23 f4 ♗g7 24 dxc6 ♘xc5 and White found himself overextended.

17 e5 f5!

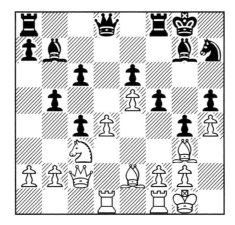

A good decision, fighting back against the cramping effect of the e5-pawn.

18 exf6

This activates Black's pieces but is necessary, as otherwise White relinquishes control over e4.

18...♕xf6 19 f3

I like this thematic move, though Kramnik felt 19 b3 was better.

19...♕f5 20 ♕d2 ♕g6 21 fxg4 hxg4 22 ♕e3 ♖f5

> **Question:** Can't Black gain a tempo with 22...♗h6 - ?

Answer: Not really. After 23 ♗f4 an exchange of bishops only serves to weaken Black's king.

23 ♘e4 c5!

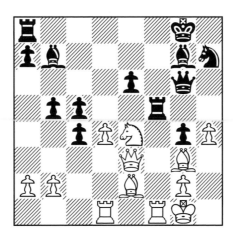

Akopian returns the pawn and hurries to activate his b7-bishop before White smothers it with ♘c5.

24 ♘xc5 ♗d5 25 a4!?

Logical – but a logical plan without factoring in random variables and anomalies ceases to be logical. 25 ♗e5 looks better, as does 25 ♘d7, intending ♘e5.

25...♖af8!

Ignoring White's challenge on b5, Akopian comes up with a remarkable attacking idea.

26 axb5 ♖f3!!

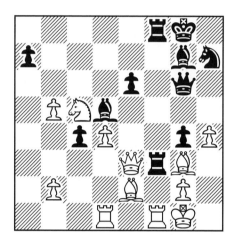

After this startling shot, Black's pieces soar on currents of power, strafing the open files in the direction of White's king. The offered rook, a discarded morsel, isn't so important when Black has in its place the banquet of a king hunt. According to the computers the position is about even. In real life, White's position is far more difficult to handle. Kramnik is thrown onto the defensive where the tiniest slip spells end times for him.

27 gxf3 gxf3

Radioactive dust motes hover over White's kingside, as his seriously exposed king provides a mesmerizing vista of attacking opportunity for Akopian's forces.

28 ♔h2 ♘f6?

Akopian goes astray as the knight agrees to participate with a coy nod. After 28...♗h6! Black gets full compensation for the sacrificed material.

29 ♗xf3! ♗xf3 30 ♕xe6+!

Somehow, Kramnik manages to extract a defensive unity from the broken bits of chaos strewn about. There is something terribly off-putting about an opponent who maintains composure, even after absorbing a punishing blow a few moves earlier. Perhaps Akopian had counted on 30 ♕xf3? ♘g4+ 31 ♔h3 ♖xf3 32 ♖xf3 ♘e3! 33 ♖xe3 ♕f5+! 34 ♔g2 ♕c2+, when White was unlikely to hold the game.

30...♔h8 31 ♖xf3!

Kramnik returns the extra material in exchange for the initiative.

31...♕c2+ 32 ♖f2 ♕xd1 33 ♔g2

To sidestep ...♘g4+ tricks.

33...♕xd4 34 ♕e5!

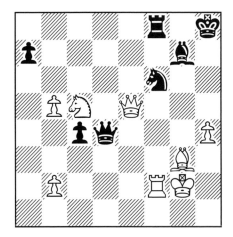

Now White's king breathes a sigh of ease as he realizes he will live to see tomorrow. Kramnik induces a favourable ending and also clears e6 for his knight.

34...♕d5+

Unnerved by the disparity of power on the kingside, Akopian gives way to caution and agrees to swap down into a bad ending. Perhaps he should submit to 34...♕g4 35 ♖f4 ♕g6 36 h5! ♕h6 37 ♘e6, when White's initiative rages on.

35 ♕xd5 ♘xd5 36 ♖xf8+ ♗xf8 37 ♘a4!

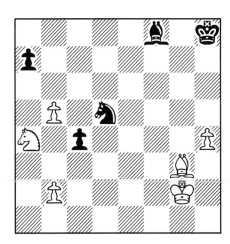

Covering his b2-pawn and preventing simplification with ...c3. Black has problems:

1. a7 and c4 are weak.

2. White's king reaches the centre faster than Black's.

37...♗g7 38 ♔f3 ♘b6

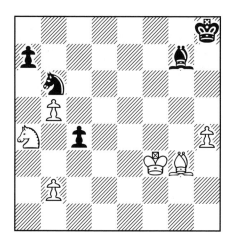

Answer: It is!

39 ♘xb6! axb6 40 ♔e4 ♗xb2 41 ♔d5! 1-0

Playing on would be as futile an exercise as one of those Charles Manson parole hearings. After 41...c3 42 ♗e5+ ♔h7 43 ♔c4! Black drops both queenside pawns (White must only avoid 43 ♔c6?? ♗a1!, when Black holds the draw). The villain (the c3-pawn) always got unhooded at the end of every *Scooby Doo* episode. Black's dazed bishop stares with the wide-open eyes of a person in shock, who looks ahead at nothing at all.

Game 15
G.Kasparov-V.Kramnik
World Championship (3rd matchgame), London 2000
Ruy Lopez

1 e4 e5 2 ♘f3 ♘c6 3 ♗b5 ♘f6 4 0-0 ♘xe4 5 d4 ♘d6 6 ♗xc6 dxc6 7 dxe5 ♘f5 8 ♕xd8+

I don't know if a bad marriage is a better fate than a life spent alone. In one sweeping move, both white and black kings become single men. Black's haughty queen, unpractised in the fine art of humility, now receives her first (and last!) lesson, as she finds herself unceremoniously escorted from the board.

8...♔xd8

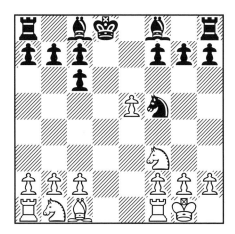

This is one of the most subtle and heavily contested opening/endgame positions on the top-level circuit. Many people, including your writer, believe Kramnik's impossibly deep understanding of this Berlin Lopez ending was the core element which allowed him to defeat Garry Kasparov in their world title match. To this day he continues to weaponize this position against all comers, utilizing his vast experience and profound knowledge in the line. Anand once called Kramnik's understanding of the Berlin Lopez: "simply stunning".

> **Question:** What is the fundamental battle in this ending?

Answer: The battlegrounds:

1. White's healthy kingside pawn majority against Black's crippled queenside majority. If all pieces are magically swept away, White wins the king and pawn ending.

2. Black has the bishop pair in a partially opened position.

3. Black's king lost the right to castle. This can lead to dysfunctional development and king safety issues.

4. White's e-pawn sits on e5, not e4. This means his central light squares, especially f5, have been weakened. Black often erects an irritating blockade on that square.

9 ♘c3 ♗d7

> **Question:** This move looks awfully clumsy. What is the purpose?

Answer: Actually, virtually every Berlin ending line looks unplayably artificial for Black. The reality is that the line is very playable if you understand its secrets. Black plans the cumbersome manoeuvre: ...b7-b6, c8-B-somewhere, ...♔c8 and ...♔b7 which nearly (!) connects his rooks.

> **Question:** How can he get away with this plan?

Answer: I don't know. He just does! The key to the defence is that White, despite his development lead, actually has an incredibly frustrating time gaining entry into Black's position.

Kramnik has also tried:

a) 9...h6 10 ♖d1+ (or 10 h3 ♔e8 11 ♘e4 c5 12 c3 b6 13 ♖e1 ♗e6 14 g4 and, realizing Black had equality at a minimum, a disgusted Kasparov offered a draw, G.Kasparov-V.Kramnik, 13th matchgame, London 2000) 10...♔e8 11 h3 a5 12 ♗f4 ♗e6 13 g4 ♘e7 14 ♘d4 ♘d5 15 ♘ce2 ♗c5 16 ♘xe6 fxe6 17 c4 ♘b6 18 b3 a4 19 ♗d2 ♔f7 20 ♗c3 ♖hd8, when Kasparov was unable to convert, despite his healthier kingside pawn majority, G.Kasparov-V.Kramnik, 9th matchgame, London 2000.

b) 9...♔e8 10 b3 ♗b4 11 ♗b2 ♗xc3! 12 ♗xc3 c5, D.Howell-V.Kramnik, London 2002.

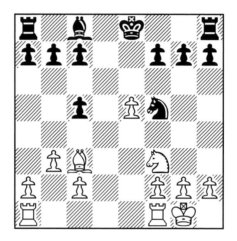

I have used Kramnik's plan from this game myself. Believe it or not, the presence of opposite-coloured bishops greatly favours Black.

Question: How so? White looks better.

Answer: Ah! To find out, skip forward to Chapter Four (Game 34), where we cover this blitz (!) game.

c) 9...♘e7 10 h3 ♘g6 11 ♗g5+ ♔e8 12 ♖ad1 ♗e6 13 ♘d4 ♗c4 14 ♖fe1 ♗b4 15 ♗d2 ♖d8 16 a3 ♗xc3! 17 ♗xc3 ♘f4 18 ♔h2 c5 19 ♘f5 ♖xd1 20 ♖xd1 ♘e6 21 f3 ♗b5 22 ♖d2 h5 23 ♔g3 ♗c6 24 ♔f2 ½-½ V.Anand-V.Kramnik, Moscow (human+computer rapid, 2nd matchgame) 2007.

10 b3

White prepares to fianchetto, securing e5 and aiming the bishop down the long diagonal. 10 h3 and 10 ♖d1 are also commonly played here.

10...h6

To halt both ♘g5 and ♗g5 ideas.

11 ♗b2 ♔c8 12 ♖ad1

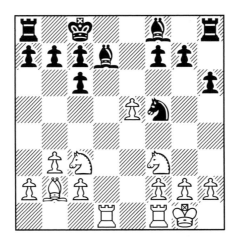

IM Andrew Martin wrote immediately after this game: "He (Kasparov) will have to find a better way to play with White as the match wears on." He didn't! Kasparov had also got depressingly little from 12 h3 b6 13 ♖ad1 ♘e7 14 ♘e2 ♘g6 15 ♘e1 h5 16 ♘d3 c5 17 c4 a5 18 a4 h4 19 ♘c3 ♗e6 20 ♘d5 ♔b7 21 ♘e3 ♖h5! – idea: erect a blockade on f5, nullifying White's pawn majority. Kasparov was unable to make progress and offered a draw in a few moves, G.Kasparov-V.Kramnik, 1st matchgame, London 2000.

12...b6 13 ♘e2

The f4-square is the knight's best post.

13...c5 14 c4 ♗c6 15 ♘f4 ♔b7!

Nigel Davies and Andrew Martin wrote that Black's "position has little appeal but it is very difficult for White to make headway." With hindsight from this match – clearly an understatement!

> *Question:* Why not wreck White's kingside pawns by chopping on f3?

Answer: The move weakens all of Black's light squares, his only trump. After 15...♗xf3 16 gxf3 ♗e7 17 ♘d5 a5 18 a4 ♖d8 19 ♘e3 ♘h4 20 ♖xd8+ ♗xd8 21 f4 White retains some pressure.

16 ♘d5 ♘e7

> *Question:* Retreating a well-placed piece?

Answer: Some chess players consider retreat a pejorative term, synonymous with surrender. Such is not always the case, especially in the Berlin Lopez which is full of slippery retreats on Black's part. First, Black added pressure to the d5-point; secondly, Black's knight wasn't all that stable on f5 since it was vulnerable to g2-g4 ideas.

17 ♖fe1 ♖g8!

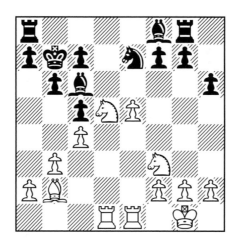

Question: What is the idea behind this mysterious move?

Answer: Dual purpose, grappling with simultaneous and interlocking issues:

1. Black reinforces g7.

2. Black may try and untangle with ...g7-g5 later on, so he gets his rook out of the way from e5-e6 shots. Also, as we see in the game, after ...g7-g5 Black may be able to lift his rook into the game via g6.

18 ♘f4

Clearly Kasparov is at an impasse for a useful plan.

18...g5!

Apparently many of the GMs observing the match were shocked to see this seemingly weakening move. The idea is to active the g8-rook.

19 ♘h5 ♖g6!

And there we have it. Black, in non-conformist fashion, develops his rook through the portal of g6.

20 ♘f6 ♗g7 21 ♖d3 ♗xf3!

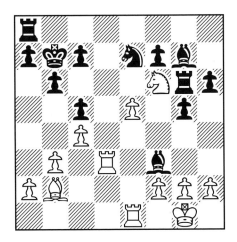

Question: Hey! I suggested ...♗xf3 earlier and you criticized it!
Now Kramnik plays my idea and you give him an exclam! Why?

Answer: Timing and context are everything. A clown at the circus is a comical figure, while a clown in a horror movie is always sinister – in fact, infallibly evil! When you suggested it earlier the moment was not yet right. Kramnik takes now in order to clear c6 for his knight and complete his development.

22 ♖xf3 ♗xf6! 23 exf6 ♘c6

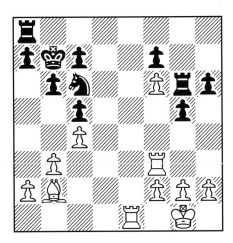

Suddenly White's majority is just as crippled as Black's on the other wing and Kramnik equalizes. The position still remains sharp and unbalanced, due to the bishop versus knight imbalance. And yes, before you ask, I considered placing this game in the *Imbalances* or *Endings* chapters of the book, but it seemed more appropriate in this one since Kramnik's defence was even more impressive.

24 ♖d3 ♖f8 25 ♖e4 ♔c8 26 f4!?

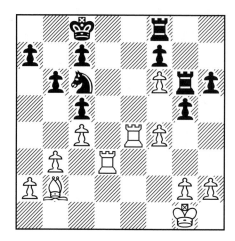

Ambitious. Kasparov reasons: if half an apple is rotten, it threatens to spoil the healthy half of the fruit. He desires his healthy pawn majority back – yet, in playing this move, he greatly increases Black's piece activity.

26...gxf4 27 ♖xf4 ♖e8 28 ♗c3 ♖e2 29 ♖f2 ♖e4 30 ♖h3 a5 31 ♖h5!?

Davies and Martin give this an exclam. I'm not so sure.

> **Question:** What is the purpose of this move?

Answer: I think Kasparov wants to prevent ...♘e5 ideas. He refuses to play 31 a4!? (to prevent Black's next move in the game), as the position grows increasingly unclear after 31...♘d4 32 ♗d2 ♔d7 33 ♖xh6 ♖xh6 34 ♗xh6 ♘xb3, and which imbalance is the greater? The weakness of White's queenside pawns or the power of his passed h-pawn? I don't know the answer. Still, this doesn't looks dissimilar to what White gets in the actual game.

31...a4!

No more crippled queenside pawn majority.

32 bxa4!

During the varied chapters of this long game, Kasparov had always obeyed the law – until now. One could rightfully ask Kasparov just what emotion prompted him to engage in such a blatantly rash action. I am certain his heart began pounding in his throat as he made this brilliant move, which shocked onlookers. He is willing to dance on the cusp of overextension in his attempts to win the game. It soon becomes a race, and who knows who is faster?

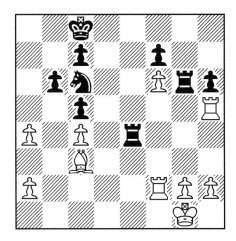

Question: It looks as if Kasparov starts and flinches at threats, real and imagined. Why does White have to take on a4 and mess up all his queenside pawns?

Answer: A person can lose his mind if he thinks too long and too hard about how utterly messed up our world is. The same rule applies on the chessboard if you get caught up in the miseries inherent in your own position. If he omits this move and plays 32 ♗d2 straight away, Black meets it with 32...axb3 33 axb3 ♘d4, and after 34 ♖xh6 ♖xh6 35 ♗xh6 ♘xb3 White gets a similar – but more passive – version of the ending he obtains in the game.

32...♖xc4

White's queenside pawns begin to fall at a calamitous rate.

33 ♗d2

The parties hover over h6, like concerned parents over an injured child. White's point: he picks off h6 and generates a dangerous, passed h-pawn.

33...♖xa4 34 ♖xh6

At last, the hated h-pawn is sent to the next world. Fulfilment of a petty spite brings on such a wonderfully peaceful feeling of contentment, doesn't it?

34...♖g8 35 ♖h7 ♖xa2 36 ♖xf7 ♘e5 37 ♖g7 ♖f8

Three connected passers versus three connected passers! I beg of you: please don't ask me who is faster!

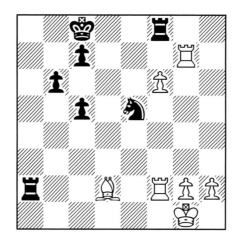

38 h3!?

Still playing for the win. 38 h4 ♘d3 39 ♖e2 ♖xf6 40 ♖ee7 ♖xd2 41 ♖xc7+ is perpetual check.

38...c4 39 ♖e7 ♘d3 40 f7!

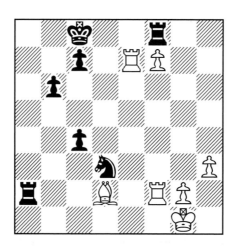

White's forces line up to surf the seductive wave around his f-pawn. It appears that the f-pawn's all-powerful, shimmering luminosity spreads impossibly in every direction, seemingly engulfing the entire board. However, mere appearance is all it really is. Kasparov begins a long, forced sequence which wins a pawn but not the game.

40...♘xf2 41 ♖e8+ ♚d7

Everything is under control.

42 ♖xf8 ♚e7! 43 ♖c8

Unfortunately for White, if he plays 43 ♗h6? he can never move his rook without dropping his beloved f-pawn in the process. Black would then simply begin to push his army of passers, starting with 43...c5. Note that, conversely, White is unable to push his other passers – weird geometry!

43...♔xf7

Whew! The pawn clearly overstayed its welcome. White's f-pawn, always under the presumption that he was the star of the show, now realizes he had been cast merely in a supporting actor's role.

44 ♖xc7+ ♔e6 45 ♗e3!

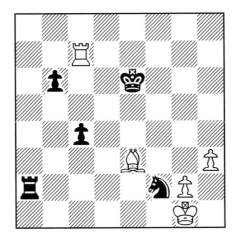

The point: the double attack wins a pawn. However, it fails to alter the balance of power one iota! Black's remaining passer remains a grave danger.

45...♘d1 46 ♗xb6 c3 47 h4

Davies and Martin disliked this move and suggested 47 ♔h2. I played out multiple scenarios against *Houdini* and all were drawn. But White's practical chances do seem better than after the game continuation.

47...♖a6!

Forcing the draw.

48 ♗d4

Or 48 ♗f2 (White's harried bishop looks as out of place as an oil spill on the surface of an otherwise scenic bay) 48...♖a1! (the rook feints in one direction, only to head for another) 49 ♗d4 ♖a4 comes to the same thing. After a short, fitfully fractured sleep, the bishop is awakened and sent on the run again.

48...♖a4! 49 ♗xc3 ♘xc3 50 ♖xc3 ♖xh4 51 ♖f3

Question: Isn't this a win for White? Black's king is cut off.

Answer: It isn't cut off enough. The ending is drawn.

51...♖h5 52 ♔f2

Nor does the immediate 52 g4 work. 52...♖h4 53 ♖f4 ♔e5 draws.

52...♖g5 53 ♖f8

The position is drawn, but a mishap looms, so let's not botch it! We need to work out the king and pawn endings after an exchange of rooks. The key issue is when to exchange.

Exercise (critical decision): Should we go for 53...♖f5+ ?
Or temporize with 53...♔e5 54 ♔f3 and only then
54...♖f5+ ? Be careful. One of the lines loses!

Answer: Know your basic king and pawn endings! Temporize. After a short but pleasant daydream, White is tugged back to the harsh glare of the here-and-now.

53...♔e5! ½-½

Now 54 ♔f3 ♖f5+! 55 ♖xf5+ ♔xf5 is a drawn king and pawn ending; whereas 53...♖f5+?? is a disastrous miscalculation for Black: 54 ♖xf5 ♔xf5 55 ♔f3! ♔g5 56 ♔g3! and the strands of the misadventure thrash Black with the penitent's unforgiving lash – White holds the opposition and wins the game.

Game 16
V.Kramnik-J.Polgar
Sofia 2005
Nimzo-Indian Defence

---

1 d4 ♘f6 2 c4 e6 3 ♘c3 ♗b4 4 ♕c2

Capablanca's line of the Nimzo-Indian. White refuses to allow any damage to his pawn structure and is willing to lose time with the queen – in exchange for the bishop pair – to fulfil this aim.

4...0-0 5 a3

He wants the bishop pair. 5 ♘f3, 5 ♗g5 and 5 e4 are also played here.

5...♗xc3+ 6 ♕xc3

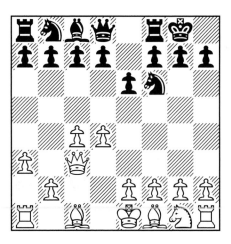

6...b6

Question: What does Black get for
White's bishop pair and space advantage?

Answer: The fundamental compensation in Nimzos for Black is always a development lead.

The text begins Black's most popular set-up here, but other ideas are possible too:

a) 6...d6 7 f3!? c5 8 dxc5 dxc5 9 ♗g5 h6 10 ♗f4 ♘c6 11 ♖d1 ♕a5 12 ♗d2 ♕a4!? 13 e3 was V.Kramnik-V.Ivanchuk, Dresden Olympiad 2008. Kramnik declined to grab a pawn with 13 ♗xh6, as after 13...e5! Black's lead in development grows larger.

> *Question:* Why not gain a tempo on the black queen with 6...♘e4 - ?

Answer: That is a line, but the tempo is probably not running away.

b) 6...♘e4 7 ♕c2 f5 8 ♘h3 b6 9 f3 (this is one problem with an early ...♘e4; White regains the tempo later on) 9...♘f6 10 e3 ♗b7 11 ♗e2 d6 12 0-0 ♕e7 13 b4 a5 14 ♗b2 ♘bd7, Ma.Carlsen-H.Nakamura, Oslo (blitz) 2009, and I prefer White due to the bishop pair and extra space. Still, this is the kind of position most Nimzophiles are okay with as Black.

c) 6...b5!? (offering a pawn to increase his activity) 7 cxb5 c6 8 ♗g5 (wisely declining; after 8 bxc6 ♘xc6 Black gets a ferocious development lead) 8...cxb5 9 e3 ♗b7 10 ♘f3 h6 11 ♗h4 a6 12 ♗d3 d6 13 0-0 ♘bd7 and, despite White's bishop pair, Black can be satisfied with the result of the opening, E.L'Ami-H.Nakamura, Wijk aan Zee 2011.

d) 6...d5 is Morozevich-Kramnik and Carlsen-Kramnik in the next chapter (see Games 29 and 30).

7 ♘f3

We look at 7 ♗g5 in Chapter Four (see Game 32, Kramnik-Adams).

7...♗b7 8 e3

> *Question:* Why would White voluntarily lock in his bishop?

Answer: From b2 White's bishop both aims at Black's king and inhibits ...e6-e5. Of course 8 ♗g5 is also played: 8...d6 9 ♘d2 ♘bd7 10 f3 ♖c8 11 e4 h6 12 ♗h4 c5 13 ♗d3 cxd4 14 ♕xd4 ♘c5 15 ♗e2 e5! and I like Black, who has achieved a kind of Taimanov Sicilian sans bad bishop, Ma.Carlsen-S.Karjakin, Tal Memorial, Moscow 2011.

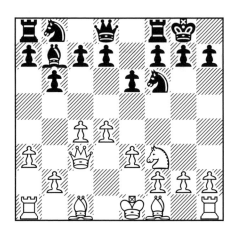

8...d6

> *Question:* Should Black consider taking the second knight on f3?

Answer: I certainly wouldn't. In doing so, Black hands over both bishops, strengthens White's centre and also opens the g-file for an attack: 8...♗xf3?! 9 gxf3 d5 10 ♗d3 c5 11 dxc5 dxc4 12 ♗xc4 bxc5, S.Vranesh Fallin-C.Bourgoin, correspondence 2011. Now White can continue with the plan ♖g1, b2-b3 and ♗b2 with a strong attack brewing against g7. **9 ♗e2 ♘bd7 10 0-0 ♘e4 11 ♕c2 f5 12 b4 ♖f6**

All or nothing. Polgar plays directly for mate.

> *Question:* It looks to me like White is in big trouble. Black builds her king-side attack, while I don't see a central counter for White.

Answer: Please jump ahead to White's next move!

> *Question:* Sorry to keep harping on this point, but how is White okay after an attacking thrust like 12...g5 - ?

Answer: Black is well on his or her way to overextension after 12...g5?. This actually occurred in C.Lakdawala-C.Milton, San Diego (rapid) 2012. White plays exactly as Kramnik did in the main game, but gets a steroidal boost since Black has weakened his own king: 13 d5! (oh what joy! I was actually working on Kramnik-Polgar the very morning I played this game and banged out the move instantly; for once in my life, thanks to Kramnik, I knew exactly what to do in a chess game – a very strange sensation for me!) 13...g4 (consistent and bad, but 13...e5 drops a pawn to 14 ♘e1! g4 15 ♗xg4!) 14 ♘d4 exd5 15 cxd5 ♗xd5 16 ♗c4 and Black's overextended position quickly fell apart.

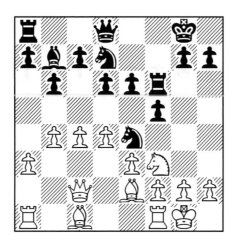

13 d5!

A move which pops up at Black as if written in bright red marker. Principles followed:

1. *Counter in the centre when attacked on the wing.*

2. *Open the game when you have the bishop pair.*

13...♖g6

There are more positional ways to play this but asking a born attacker to alter course is like trying to debate the wind. Polgar has a poor lifetime score against Kramnik and, as we all understand, the desire for revenge is the purest and most sincere of human motivations.

> **Question:** I don't understand Black's last move. First, she can just take the pawn on d5. Secondly, she can bypass. Aren't those both better than what she played?

Answer: Let's look:

a) 13...exd5 14 ♗b2 ♖g6 15 ♖ad1 dxc4 16 ♗xc4+ ♔h8 17 ♗d5! c6, I.Sokolov-S.Kristjansson, Selfoss 2002, when Black's structure begins to creak after 18 ♗f7! ♖h6 19 ♘d4 ♕h4 20 h3.

b) 13...e5 14 ♘h4! (threatening to undermine the e4-knight by taking on f5 next move) 14...g6 15 f3 ♘g5 16 f4 ♘e4 17 ♘f3 and White is ready to undermine the diagonal further with ♗b2 next, Zhao Xue-M.Lushenkov, Moscow 2006.

14 ♘d4! ♕g5!

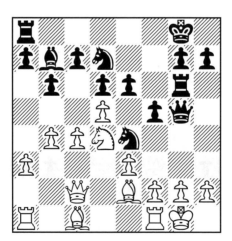

A new move at the time and an improvement. If Black's attack misses then White's central counter will be very tough to deal with. 14...exd5 15 f3 ♕g5 16 ♗d3 looks better for White, S.Matveeva-A.Maric, Serbian Team Championship 2003.

15 g3 exd5?!

Polgar gets distracted from her aim. Black obtained full compensation for the material after 15...♘e5! 16 ♘xe6 ♖xe6 17 dxe6 ♕g6!, clearing the way for ...♘g5, Y.Drozdovskij-A.Grischuk, Odessa (rapid) 2007.

16 cxd5 ♗xd5 17 ♗c4!

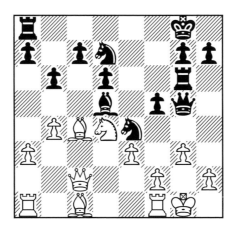

A single slash of the knife isn't enough to pierce Black's tough hide. The bishop strolls by with an air of disapproval, as White simultaneously removes a dangerous black attacker and weakens all the light squares on the queenside.

> **Question:** Why can't White just take on c7 immediately with 17 ♕xc7 - ?

Answer: Black gets dangerous attacking chances after 17...♘e5!, and can keep building with ...♖f8. Even ...♕h4! is in the air.

17...♗xc4 18 ♕xc4+ ♔h8 19 ♕c6!

Picking up a future tempo.

19...♖d8 20 ♕xc7 ♘e5

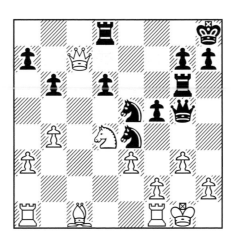

Black's attack continues to bubble on a low boil. She saturates her awareness with valour, preparing to enter the fearful darkness ahead with a piece sac.

Answer: Add a defender from the other side. White can get away with 21 f4, but only if he is happy with a draw.

21 ♖a2!

A powerful defensive move out of thin air. 21 f4 isn't all that winning because of 21...♕xg3+!! 22 hxg3 (after witnessing a trauma, we desperately seek to delete the recurring after-image from our mind's eye) 22...♖xg3+ with perpetual check.

21...♖f8 22 f4!

Now is the time!

22...♕g4!

Black threatens ...♘xg3!.

23 ♕e7!

23 fxe5?? is way too greedy. Black wins with 23...♘xg3 24 ♕c6 ♘xf1+ 25 ♖g2 ♕d1.

23...♖g8

23...♖c8? 24 ♕b7! only benefits White.

24 ♖g2!

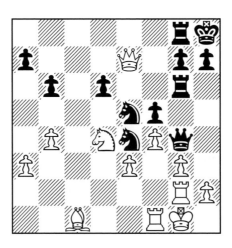

Bolting the door firmly shut to all sacs on g3. Kramnik takes all the fun out of Black's attack.

24...♘d3 25 ♕xa7!

> **Question:** Pawn grabbing while his house is on fire?

Answer: When a nonchalant move like this is made in the midst of what appears to be a storm, we should understand that Polgar's attack has come to an end. There is no good reason to spare the pawn by arbitrarily granting mercy.

25...h5

Throwing everything she has at White, who remains unfazed.

26 ♕a6!

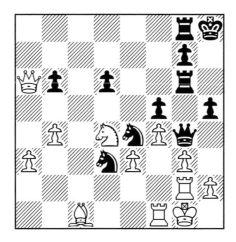

Another deceptively powerful defensive move:

1. White forces a swap of a black attacker.

2. As if alerted by some unspoken signal, White's offside but annoying queen prepares to return to her family with ♕e2 soon.

26...♘xc1 27 ♖xc1 h4 28 ♕e2!

The fat, lazy salmon, exhausted from her swim upstream, decides to flow down river for a while.

28...♕xe2

Polgar finds her rage tempered by self-preservatory instincts. 28...♕h3? 29 ♕h5+ ♖h6 30 ♕xf5 is even worse for Black.

29 ♖xe2 hxg3 30 ♘xf5 gxh2+ 31 ♔h1! ♖g1+ 32 ♖xg1 hxg1♕+ 33 ♔xg1

Time for the technical phase of the game. Recent events conspire to make Black's life in the ending quite intolerable:

1. White is up a pawn.

2. White has the superior structure. In fact, every remaining black pawn is an isolani.

3. White's king has quick access to the centre.

Conclusion: Black is busted.

33...♖a8 34 ♖a2 ♘c3 35 ♖h2+ ♔g8 36 ♖g2 ♔f7 37 ♘xd6+ ♔e6 38 ♘c4 b5 39 ♘a5!

And then there were two... How incredibly annoying for Polgar. Now she is down two pawns.

39...♔f6 40 ♖d2 g5 41 ♖d3 ♘e4 42 fxg5+ ♔xg5 43 ♔g2 ♖f8 44 ♖d5+ ♔g4

Black's game, awash in pain, grows that much more so with each passing move. Now Polgar adopts that very pain as a catalyst to channel a last-ditch effort against Kramnik's king.

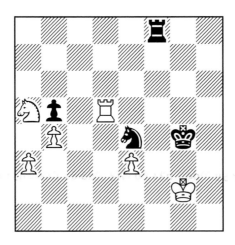

Exercise: Can we get away with taking on b5 or not? Analyze
45 ♖xb5 ♖f2+. Is Black's desperate sac a bluff or not?

Answer: Not!

45 ♖d4!

Kramnik avoids the trap 45 ♖xb5?? which indulges in a bit of presumption by assuming Black's attack was at an end: 45...♖f2+ 46 ♔g1 and within the misery lies the kernel of a deep drawing trap. A shadow of agitation looms over White's defences after 46...♖e2!!. No matter how White squirms, the game ends in a draw.

45...♔f5

The king swallows his annoyance, issues a three-quarters mea culpa and retreats. Instead, 45...♖f2+?? pantomimes the previous trap with a cheap imitation which fails: 46 ♔g1 ♔f3 47 ♖xe4! ♖g2+ 48 ♔f1 ♖f2+ 49 ♔e1 ♖e2+ 50 ♔d1 and White escapes the checks.

46 ♘c6 ♖g8+ 47 ♔f1 ♖a8 48 ♘e7+!

Now watch the hypnotic knight circle which follows.

48...♔e5 49 ♘c6+ ♔f5 50 ♘e7+ ♔e5 51 ♘g6+ ♔f5 52 ♘h4+ ♔e5 53 ♘f3+ ♔f5 54 ♘h4+ ♔e5 55 ♘f3+ ♔f5

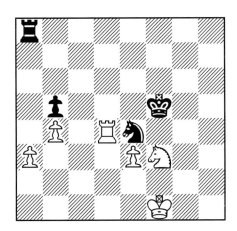

By now, Black's king must feel like he has been caught in a perfect, endless time loop.

56 ♖d5+! ♔f6

56...♔g4 57 ♔g2! ♖xa3 58 ♘e5+ ♔f5 59 ♘c4+ ♔e6 60 ♖xb5 simplifies and wins.

57 ♖d3 ♖h8 58 ♔e2 ♔e7 59 ♘d4 ♖h2+ 60 ♔f3 ♘d6 61 ♖c3 ♖h3+ 62 ♔g4 1-0

After 62...♖h1 63 e4 ♖e1 64 ♘f5+ the knights exchange pleasantries and part on amiable terms. The ensuing rook and pawn ending is hopeless for Black.

Game 17
V.Kramnik-L.Aronian
Yerevan (rapid, 1st matchgame) 2007
Ruy Lopez

1 e4

When Kramnik plays 1 e4, this normally means he is up to something. In this game he braved the scary theoretical winds of Aronian's Marshall Attack.

1...e5 2 ♘f3 ♘c6 3 ♗b5 a6 4 ♗a4 ♘f6 5 0-0 ♗e7 6 ♖e1 b5 7 ♗b3 0-0 8 c3!?

Just before the battle, the night feels unnaturally chilly and still. Acceptance of the gambit takes real courage when taking on the premiere Black-side advocate in his favourite line. Kramnik avoids the parade of declining variations: 8 a4, 8 h3, 8 d4 and 8 d3.

8...d5

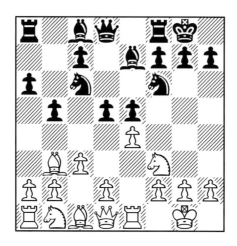

Question: Is the Marshall Attack considered sound?

Answer: Maybe a century from now some computer will refute it, but I doubt it. Ever since Marshall unsuccessfully attempted (in New York, 1918) to ambush Capablanca with his amazing attacking idea, the gambit continues to thrive, remaining alive and well to this day, even at the very top levels.

9 exd5 ♘xd5 10 ♘xe5 ♘xe5 11 ♖xe5 c6 12 d4

The main line.

Question: Is there a way for White to avoid Black's auto-pilot attacking set-up with ...♗d6 and ...♕h4 - ?

Answer: White can avoid that line by playing a quick g2-g3. For example, 12 g3 ♗d6 13 ♖e1 (White has prevented ...♕h4 but not queen infiltration itself) 13...♕d7! and Black's queen enters the kingside anyway, via the h3 backdoor, J.Polgar-P.Svidler, Wijk aan Zee 2005. Black is supposed to get enough play for the pawn in this position.

12...♗d6 13 ♖e1 ♕h4 14 g3 ♕h3 15 ♗e3 ♗g4 16 ♕d3 ♖ae8 17 ♘d2 ♖e6

This is really the main starting position of the Marshall Attack, with nearly 2200 games in the database at the time of this writing.

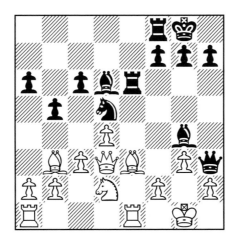

18 ♕f1

Slightly unusual. 18 a4 is played a lot more often; e.g. 18...♕h5 19 axb5 axb5 20 ♕f1 ♗h3 21 ♗d1 ♕f5, P.Leko-V.Kramnik, Monte Carlo (blindfold rapid) 2007. Kramnik went on to win this game. Our hero doesn't always play the Berlin Lopez!

18...♕h5 19 f3!?

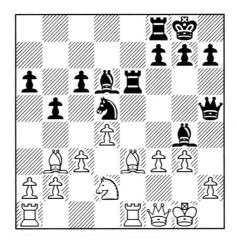

Kramnik's prep.

> ***Question:*** A theoretical novelty?

Answer: Not a novelty, but a rare, backstreet byway – at the time only played in a few obscure email games, probably well under Aronian's radar.

19...♘xe3

> **Question:** Did White just overlook loss of material?

Answer: No, Black's extra piece can't run away. Jump ahead to Kramnik's next move. V.Anand-V.Ivanchuk, Bilbao 2008, deviated here with 19...♖f6 20 ♕e2 ♗xf3 21 ♘xf3 ♖xf3 and Black had no trouble holding; but White might try the computer's suggestion of 20 ♕g2, when *Houdini* claims a slight edge.

20 ♕f2!

The white queen turns out to be the surly, uncooperative co-worker whom everyone in the office loathes, as she pulls a dirty trick to recuperate White's losses. Certainly not 20 fxg4?? ♘xf1 21 gxh5 ♖xe1 22 ♖xe1 ♘xd2, when Black absconds with an extra piece.

20...♘d5

> **Question:** Does the sac on g3 work?

Answer: Not yet. 20...♗xg3? 21 ♕xg3! (White avoids the trap 21 hxg3?? ♖h6! instantly ending the game) 21...♖g6 22 fxg4! ♖xg4 23 ♖xe3 gives White too much material for the queen.

21 fxg4 ♕xg4 22 ♕f3 ♕g5?!

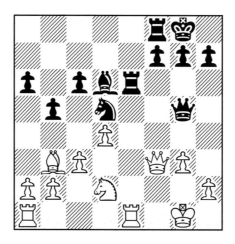

A decision he will come to regret. Aronian downloads his vast Marshall experience into the core mind of the position and still comes up short. He overestimates his attacking chances by taking on an isolani to open the f-file. Soon his strategic deficiencies spread and take root like gangrene. Golubev suggested 22...♕xf3 23 ♘xf3 ♖fe8, but White may still have a tiny pull after 24 ♖xe6 ♖xe6 25 c4!.

23 ♖xe6

23 ♘e4? walks into a pin with 23...♕e7!.

23...fxe6 24 ♘e4!

Andrei Deviatkin says Kramnik played this move instantly, meaning he was still in his home prep!

24...♕g6

No choice. 24...♖xf3?? drops a pawn after 25 ♘xg5, since 25...♖e3? 26 ♔f2 and 25...♖f6? 26 ♘e4 make things even worse.

25 ♕e2! ♘f4!?

Dialogue and negotiation are next to impossible when facing a violence-crazed foe. Aronian fires his rifle into the air, not realizing a weapon is of little use when you lack a concrete target.

> **Question:** It looks like Aronian generated enough piece
> activity to compensate for his inferior structure – correct?

Answer: I don't think so. I will bet Kramnik was still in his home prep.

26 ♕c2 ♘h3+?!

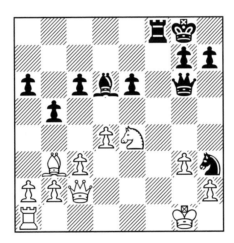

> **Exercise:** A little analytical test for you.
> Should White play his king to g2 or h1?

Answer: 27 ♔g2!

If you said h1, you walked into Aronian's cheapo: 27 ♔h1?? ♕xe4+! with a knight fork on f2.

27...♕g4

The silly 27...♘f4+?? 28 ♔h1 leaves two black pieces hanging.

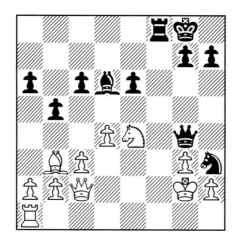

Black's forces indolently float and drift at ease, unsuspecting of the coming explosion. I know you just solved an exercise but there is no time to rest. Here is another one!

> *Exercise (combination alert):* If White plays 28 ♘xd6, Black gets a strong attack for the piece after 28...♘f4+. Instead, Kramnik found (or prepared at home!) an amazing sleight of hand, where he simplifies into a won ending. Take your time. This one is really difficult.

Answer: The e6-pawn burns hot as a whistling tea kettle on the boil.

28 ♗xe6+!! ♕xe6 29 ♕b3!

The deep point: Kramnik takes a swipe at Aronian's attacking dream with a giant warcleaver. No matter how Black squirms, he is down material in the ending.

29...♘f4+ 30 gxf4 ♕xb3

The frustrated black queen sobs to ease the pressure of her tortured psyche, as her dream of attack goes up in a haze of smoke.

31 axb3 ♗xf4 32 ♖xa6 ♖c8

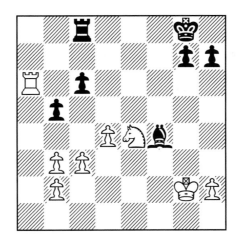

33 ♘c5!

Heading for d3, the knight's best square.

33...♔f7 34 ♘d3!

Curiously, the bishop finds itself out of viable squares on an open board.

34...g5

Question: This looks like capitulation. Why not move the bishop?

Answer: It's not so easy to finesse when the raw materials are a sprawling pile of dysfunction. Black's move is hopeless, as are the alternatives:

a) 34...♗b8 35 ♖b6! ♔e6 36 ♘b4 ♔d7 37 ♖b7+! ♗c7 38 d5 (the protective barrier splinters and cracks open, as White breaches the defensive wall) 38...cxd5 39 ♘xd5 and White wins the king and pawn ending.

b) 34...♗d6 35 d5! and again Black collapses.

35 ♘xf4 gxf4 36 ♔f3 ♔e6 37 ♔xf4

Pawn number two. The rest is easy for a player of Kramnik's calibre.

37...♔d6 38 c4 ♖f8+ 39 ♔e3 ♔c7 40 ♖a7+ ♔b6 41 ♖xh7 ♖f1 42 ♖h6 ♔b7 43 ♖h5

More careful than the immediate 43 d5.

43...♖b1

Or 43...♔b6 44 c5+ ♔b7 45 ♖h7+ ♔a6 46 ♖c7 ♖f6 47 h4 ♔a5 48 ♖d7! ♔b4 49 ♖d6 and wins.

44 ♔d3 bxc4+ 45 ♔c2! 1-0

This nifty zwischenzug does the job. I'm not sure whether Kramnik had this position in his home analysis as well!

Game 18
V.Kramnik-H.Nakamura
Wijk aan Zee 2010
Dutch Defence

1 d4 f5 2 g3 ♘f6 3 ♗g2 g6 4 c4 ♗g7 5 ♘c3 0-0 6 ♘f3 d6 7 0-0 c6

7...♕e8 and 7...♘c6 are the other main lines.

8 ♖b1!?

Kramnik picks an offbeat move, avoiding the main continuations 8 d5, 8 b3 and 8 ♕c2.

8...♘e4

> *Question:* What is the purpose of moving the knight twice in the opening?

Answer: Black threatens to inflict Nimzo-Indian-like damage by taking on c3.

9 ♕c2

> *Question:* Why can't White trade on e4?

Answer: Black does well after 9 ♘xe4 fxe4 10 ♘d2 d5. Maybe White is okay but his game doesn't inspire much confidence; e.g. 11 e3 ♘d7 12 b4 a6 13 ♕b3 e6 14 cxd5 cxd5, Bu Xiangzhi-H.Nakamura, Cap d'Agde (rapid) 2010.

9...♘xc3 10 bxc3!

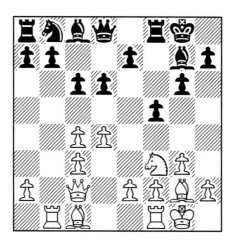

> *Question:* Why the deliberate damage to the structure?

Answer: First, the open b-file compensates somewhat for the structural damage. Second,

10 ♕xc3?! is well met by 10...e5!.

10...e5 11 ♖d1 e4

Multipurpose: Black gains both time and space.

12 ♘g5 h6 13 ♘h3 g5

Question: It looks to me like White has been outplayed
and pushed into a corner – correct?

Answer: I don't think so. White still leads in development, has an open b-file, and is ready to counter in the centre with f2-f3.

14 f3 d5?!

GM Glenn Flear criticized this move, preferring ...♕e7, and wrote: "Nakamura keeps going, with the philosophy that space is important, and the un-doubling of White's pawns less so, but I do feel that this is over-enthusiastic as his centre soon creaks."

Question: Do you agree with Flear's assessment?

Answer: I do. Naka's plan looks like misdirected energy and a depletion of resources. It also violates the principle: *Avoid confrontation when behind in development.*

15 ♘f2 ♔h8 16 cxd5 cxd5 17 c4

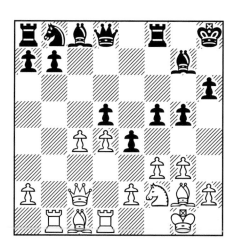

Kramnik sifts the strategic muck, the way a prospector pans for gold, as he prepares to eviscerate Black's enormous pawn-wall, strata by strata. All the same, 17 fxe4 fxe4 18 c4 may be a more accurate move order.

17...e3!?

As always, Naka faithfully does his best to confuse the situation. I doubt Black gets enough compensation after 17...♘c6 18 e3 exf3 19 ♗xf3 f4 20 ♗xd5 fxg3 21 hxg3.

18 ♘d3!

Stronger than 18 ♗xe3!?, which allows Black to take over the initiative with 18...f4 19 ♗c1 ♗f5. Then White can try 20 ♘e4!? dxe4 21 fxe4 and who knows who stands better?
18...♘c6

Question: Doesn't Black get a choking bind after 18...f4 - ?

Answer: Both Kramnik and Nakamura had seen the trick 19 cxd5 ♕xd5 20 gxf4 gxf4?? 21 ♘xf4!, when Black suddenly finds himself dead busted. The clever 21....♗f5 is met by the counter clever 22 ♘g6+!.
19 ♗xe3 ♘xd4

The forces meet in central disharmony – like a pair of unstable liquids, when mixed together, creating a combustible potion.
20 ♗xd4! ♗xd4+ 21 ♔h1

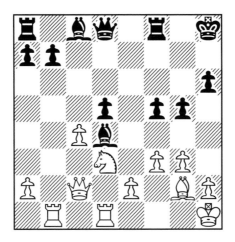

Black finds himself lagging in development. Nakamura comes up with a brilliant solution to his troubles.
21...f4!

The f-pawn approaches, coolly assessing the situation with a lack of urgency possessed only by the supremely confident. Naka is willing to give up a pawn to imprison White's light-squared bishop.
22 ♖b5 ♕f6! 23 ♖xd5 ♗e6?

But now Black goes wrong. After the correct 23....♗e3! he would get full compensation for the pawn.

Question: What is the evaluation then?

Answer: It's difficult to evaluate the probability of success or failure. In such cases intuition is both judge and jury.

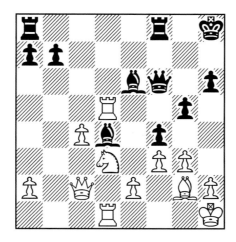

Exercise (combination alert): Black miscalculated on his last move.
White has a forcing sequence which nets him a couple of pawns.

Answer: Discovered attack.

24 ♘xf4! gxf4

Nakamura now understands that 24...♗xd5 fails to 25 ♘g6+ ♔g8 26 ♘xf8 ♗c6 27 ♘e6!, when White cleverly extricates his wayward knight as the apparition appears and disappears.

25 ♖5xd4 fxg3 26 hxg3 ♖g8

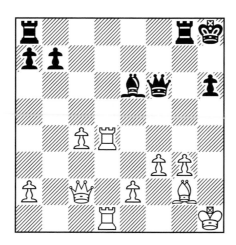

Kramnik managed to bleach the life-force from Black's attack, until it morphed into an anaemic, half-dead creature, incapable of inflicting harm on anyone. We have all been here. With two extra pawns White is now winning, though Black, in desperation mode, will do everything he can to attack or generate counterplay.

27 ♖f4 ♕g5 28 ♖h4

Reminding Black that his king is exposed as well.

28...♖g6 29 ♕c3+ ♔h7 30 f4!

Black's non-attack is smoke in a strong breeze, dissipating before it does any damage. Kramnik activates his bishop and forces simplification.

30...♕xg3

No choice but to swap since 30...♕e7?? walks into 31 ♗e4.

31 ♕xg3 ♖xg3 32 ♗xb7 ♖b8 33 ♗e4+ ♔g7 34 ♔h2!

Taking control of the g-file.

34...♖e3 35 ♖g1+ ♔f7 36 ♗g6+ ♔e7 37 ♗d3 ♖b2

Threatening ...♖xd3.

38 ♖g2 ♖xa2 39 ♖xh6 ♗f7 40 ♖h7 ♔f6

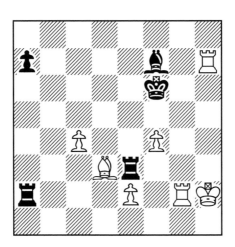

> *Exercise (planning):* Come up with the core of a winning plan for White.

Answer: Push the c-pawn fast and hard. Black's tangled rooks and king are curiously unable to do anything about it. From this point, White continues to nurture his passer through coming tactics, the way a soldier on the battlefield wills himself to carry a wounded buddy, whose weight grows with each step.

41 c5! ♖a4

41...♖a1 42 c6 ♖c1 43 ♖g5! (threatening a deadly rook check on f5) 43...♗e8 44 c7 leaves Black in zugzwang.

42 c6!

The upward trek remains unimpeded and unchallenged.

42...♖xf4 43 c7

The pawn continues to slip by, like rainwater gushing down a storm drain. Note how Black's rooks are indistinguishable in their mutual uselessness in halting the advanced pawn.

43...♖e8

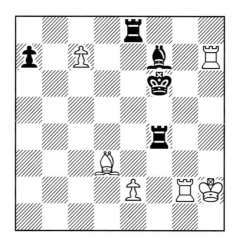

Exercise (combination alert): Find White's simplifying combination.

Answer: The rook mutters an oath and ploughs headlong into the bishop.

44 ♖xf7+! 1-0

Since 44...♔xf7 45 ♗g6+ ♔e7 46 ♗xe8 leaves White a piece up.

Game 19
Ma.Carlsen-V.Kramnik
Wijk aan Zee 2010
Catalan Opening

This was a high stakes game for both parties, who shared the lead with two rounds to go. Neither wanted a draw.

1 d4 ♘f6 2 c4 e6 3 ♘f3 d5 4 g3

Chutzpah! The World's highest rated player issues a challenge to the world's leading Catalan expert!

4...dxc4 5 ♗g2 ♗b4+!?

A fashionable line of the Catalan.

> **Question:** What is the purpose of throwing in the check?

Answer: The main purpose is to lure White's bishop to d2, where it sits awkwardly and temporarily blocks the white queen's protection of d4.

6 ♗d2 a5 7 ♘c3!?

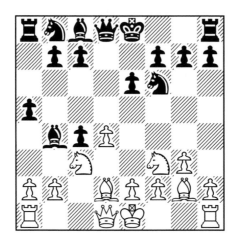

A very unusual line. Clearly, Carlsen prepped the move to try and throw Kramnik off. Perhaps this was a wise choice on Carlsen's part, since Kramnik understands the ins and outs of 7 0-0 better than anyone alive; and 7 ♕c2 ♗xd2+ 8 ♕xd2 c6 9 a4 b5 10 axb5 cxb5 11 ♕g5 0-0 12 ♕xb5 ♗a6 13 ♕a4 was V.Kramnik-V.Topalov, World Championship, Elista 2006, where Kramnik endured a tough defence to steal the first game of his match from his hated rival. In fact, I was going to put this game in this very chapter but, alas, ran out of room in the book!

7...0-0

> **Question:** Why doesn't Black immediately
> attack the d4-pawn with 7...♘c6 - ?

Answer: The move is possible; e.g. 8 a3 ♗xc3 9 bxc3 a4 10 ♗g5 ♖a6 11 0-0 h6 12 ♗xf6 ♕xf6 13 ♘d2 b5 14 ♖b1 ♘a7 15 ♘e4 ♕e7 16 ♘c5 ♖d6 17 f4, when White's bind and central control give him full compensation for the pawn, A.Khalifman-J.Ibarra Jerez, European Championship, Budva 2009.

8 a3

An almost unknown move. 8 0-0 would return to normal paths.

8...♗e7

Taking on c3 gives up the bishop pair and strengthens White's centre, giving him enough for the pawn; e.g. 8...♗xc3 9 bxc3 ♘bd7 10 ♕c2 h6 11 0-0 ♖b8, A.Shimanov-R.Zelcic, Oberwart 2010.

9 ♕a4

White regains his pawn.

9...c6 10 ♕xc4 b5 11 ♕b3!?

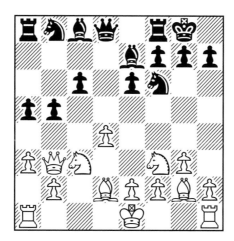

Carlsen's novelty – slightly more logical than 11 ♕d3 which walks into the teeth of Black's bishop after 11...♗a6 12 ♘e4 b4, when 13 ♘xf6+ ♗xf6 14 ♕c2 bxa3 15 ♖xa3 ♗b5 16 ♗c3 was about equal, A.Grischuk-L.Aronian, Nice (rapid) 2010.

11...♗a6 12 ♗g5

> **Question:** Why is White always quick to play ♗g5 and give away
> the bishop pair by swapping on f6 in the Catalan?

Answer: Two reasons:

1. The dark-squared bishop tends to be White's worst piece in open Catalans. There simply is no stable home for it.

2. The key fight is for the c5-square. Generally, Black must achieve the ...c6-c5 break to equalize. By playing ♗g5 and ♗xf6 White aims to deflect a black piece – either e7-bishop or d7-knight – away from c5.

12...♘bd7 13 ♗xf6 gxf6!?

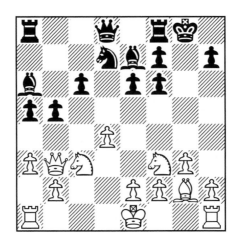

Question: You just said the capture on f6 was to deflect
a black bishop or knight away from the c5-square,
yet here Kramnik recaptures with his g-pawn. Why?

Answer: Kramnik took the nuclear option at a high price. He weakened his king and re-jected:

a) 13...♘xf6? 14 ♘e5! which puts Black under pressure.

b) 13...♗xf6! 14 ♘e4 ♗e7 15 ♖c1 ♕b6 which looks quite okay for Black.

14 ♕c2

Carlsen's queen immediately turns her displeasured gaze toward Black's weakened kingside.

14...b4 15 ♘a4 ♖c8

Kramnik suggested 15...c5, when White still may hold a tiny edge after 16 dxc5 ♖c8 17 axb4 axb4 18 ♕d2.

16 0-0 c5?!

Kramnik mistimes his freeing break.

17 d5!!

The wizard of attack raises his arms. Power begins to crackle and flow, bending and weaving reality's fabric to his will. Carlsen concocts a powerful pawn sac which should have yielded him a decisive attack. The idea is to take control over f5.

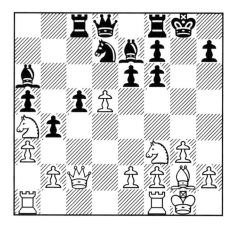

17...exd5 18 &h3?

> ***Question:*** What is so wrong with White's last move?
> It looks very powerful and thematic to me.

Answer: It's hard to pinpoint the specific flaw with the move, but it is inaccurate, and one soon senses an absence in White's attack – of what, I don't know. GM Landa pointed out that after 18 ♖fd1! White's pieces breach the defensive line, leaping over the flimsy barrier with disconcerting ease. For example, 18...d4 19 ♕f5! ♖e8 20 ♘xd4! cxd4 21 ♖xd4 with numerous threats, or 19...&d6 20 axb4 &xe2 21 ♘xd4! cxd4 22 &e4 ♖e8 23 ♕xh7+ ♔f8 24 ♖xd4, once again with a nightmarishly strong attack.

18...&b5

I would have broken the pin immediately with 18...♖c7!?.

19 axb4 axb4 20 ♖fd1 d4 21 &f5 ♘e5!

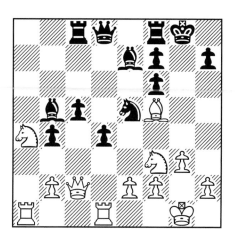

Kramnik, after weighing cost versus benefit, decides the time is right to invest. He wisely offers an exchange to rid himself of White's powerful light-squared bishop.

22 ♗xh7+!?

Carlsen bravely allows the opening of the h-file against his king. The alternative is the greedy 22 ♘xe5 which allows Black to feed his initiative after 22...fxe5 23 ♗xc8 ♕xc8 24 b3 ♕h3.

22...♔g7 23 ♘xe5 fxe5 24 ♗f5 ♖c6!

Here he comes. The rook fulfils both offensive and defensive functions, as it keeps one surreptitious eye on Carlsen's king and the other on his own monarch.

25 ♕e4 ♖h8!

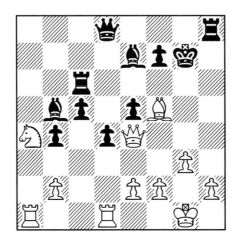

Aggressive defence; Kramnik slathers his Attack/Defence with generous servings of pawns, the way an obese, compulsive eater loads a baked potato with extra butter.

> **Question:** Who is attacking and who defends here?

Answer: Both and both! It feels like both sides are simultaneously being attacked and attacking.

26 ♕xe5+ ♗f6 27 ♕e4 ♖e8!

Kramnik pointed out the line 27...c4? 28 ♕g4+ ♔f8 29 ♗d7!, which is in White's favour.

28 ♕g4+ ♔f8 29 ♗e4 c4!? 30 ♗xc6!?

Wow. It takes guts to grab such an exchange – and also to offer it! Black is down a full exchange and a pawn, but his pieces all breathe fire.

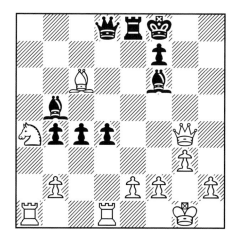

30...♗xc6 31 ♕h5 ♖e5 32 ♕h6+

The funny thing is I think Carlsen is still attacking – or at least thinks he is!

32...♔e7!?

Kramnik's king decides to enter the building, despite the black smoke billowing from the windows.

> **Question:** Why on earth did he play his king
> to the centre rather than to g8?

Answer: I have no idea! Perhaps this is Kramnik's attempt to provoke his hot-headed opponent into something rash?

33 e4!?

Holy mother of Alekhine! As I was saying: "something rash". Carlsen is hell-bent on opening lines against Black's king, whatever the cost. *Houdini* suggests the calmer 33 ♕f4 ♕d5 34 f3 ♖xe2 35 ♖e1, but I still prefer Black's position after 35...d3.

33...d3! 34 ♕e3!?

34 ♖e1! may be White's best move here.

34...♗xe4!? 35 ♘b6??

Houdini gives 35 ♕d2 with an edge to Black. Instead, the knight, having wallowed in self-satisfaction on a4, is rudely yanked from his daydream, back into the merciless waiting arms of reality.

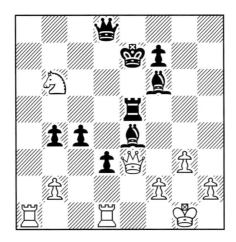

Answer: The bishop, after performing a devotional gesture, shoots to b7, unceremoniously
trapping White's knight. The move probably left Carlsen red-faced and clutching his head.
Carlsen's position is like one of those fairy tales where the magical illusion (of his attack!)
suddenly wears off, as the beautiful young maiden (White's poor queen!) morphs into her
true form – a crone.

35...♗b7!

Black wins the wayward knight.

36 ♕f4 ♕xb6 37 ♕xc4 ♖e2!

Target: f2. The game is over.

38 ♖f1 0-1

Before 38...♗d4 obliterates White.

Game 20
V.Kramnik-L.Aronian
Zürich Chess Challenge 2012
Four Knights Game

1 e4 e5 2 ♘f3 ♘c6 3 ♘c3

In the introduction to this book I bemoaned about people's preconceived notions of

Kramnik. Well, listen to this: Dennis Monokroussos wrote: "Kramnik played 1 e4 for the first time in a long time, but not as a prelude to anything interesting; rather he trotted out the disgustingly dull Scotch Four Knights. (The motto of the Scotch Four Knights player: 'Not everyone is brave enough to play the London System!')." Ouch! I may have to remove him from my Christmas card list. In one efficient sentence Dennis dissed:

1. Kramnik, the subject of this book.
2. The London System and the Four Knights. (Correct – I wrote books on both openings.)

> *Question:* No one argues the London System isn't boring.
> But what is so "disgustingly dull" about the Scotch Four Knights?

Answer: The Scotch Four Knights often leads to forcing lines which make it very difficult for Black (or White for that matter!) to win. So, unfortunately, Monokroussos' criticism of the two opening systems may have been accurate. However, his assessment of Kramnik's style was not!

3...♘f6 4 d4

With his opening choice, Kramnik plunges into the long ago. This is the kind of position people loved to play a century ago.

4...exd4 5 ♘xd4 ♗c5!?

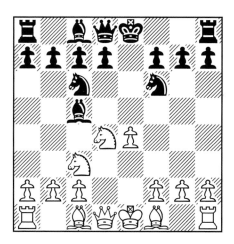

Aronian probably wanted to get away from the forcing positions associated with 5...♗b4 (which he tested out against Kramnik in the Introduction – see Game 1).

6 ♗e3 ♗b6

Time for full disclosure and confession: my very first rated tournament game went: 6...0-0?? 7 ♘xc6 bxc6 8 ♗xc5 1-0 NN-C.Lakdawala, Canadian Open 1972. Not the most auspicious inauguration to a chess career. I didn't even make it to move ten! Now you know why your talentless writer plays "disgustingly dull" lines like the London System!

7 ♕d2

Kramnik prepares long castling. Instead:

a) 7 ♗e2 0-0 8 0-0 ♖e8 9 ♗f3 ♘e5 10 ♗e2 is indeed, "disgustingly dull!" if Black tosses in ...d7-d5 next, P.Bontempi-B.Lalic, Porto San Giorgio 2004.

b) 7 ♘xc6 bxc6 8 e5 ♗xe3 9 fxe3 ♘d5 10 ♘xd5 cxd5 11 ♕xd5 ♕h4+ 12 ♔d1 ♖b8 and Black gets more than enough compensation for the pawn, H.Hoffmann-E.Van den Doel, German League 2006.

7...0-0

Question: Can Black chase the bishop with 7...♘g4 - ?

Answer: After 8 ♗g5 f6 9 ♘xc6, either 9...bxc6 10 ♗h4 or 9...dxc6 10 ♕xd8+ ♔xd8 11 ♗h4, M.Andres Mendez-A.Sorin, Argentine Team Championship 2000, may give White a shade of an edge. However, Black can speculate with 9...♗xf2+! 10 ♕xf2 dxc6; e.g. 11 ♕g3 fxg5 12 h3 ♘h6 and Black looks okay.

8 0-0-0 ♖e8 9 f3

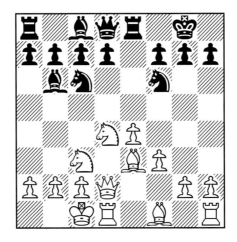

No more ...♘g4.

9...d5!

Principle: *Counter in the centre when attacked on the wing.*

Question: What attack? Isn't 9...d6 okay for Black?

Answer: I doubt it. White, with his extra central space, simply looks faster after 10 g4, B.Reefat-M.Hebden, Dhaka 1995. Now ...d6-d5 is out, since White can toss in g4-g5.

10 exd5!

A new move and an improvement over 10 ♘xc6 bxc6 11 ♗xb6 (GM Victor Mikhalevski suggests 11 g4) 11...axb6 12 ♗c4 ♗e6, when Black stands well, P.Hrvacic-F.Berebora, Split 1998.

10...♘xd5 11 ♗g5!

11 ♘xc6 bxc6 12 ♘xd5 cxd5 13 ♗xb6 axb6 14 ♗b5 ♖f8 is once again equal, since White's a2-pawn hangs at the end.

11...♘xc3!?

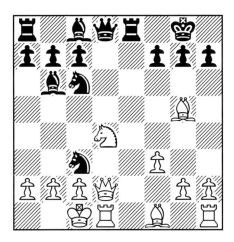

Question: What!?

Answer: Aronian speculates and sacs a tall one, praying the mathematics hold up to scrutiny. Kramnik can do no more than steel himself for the worst and commence preparations for the approaching onslaught.

Question: Is Aronian's queen sac sound?

Answer: Under the glare of the computer's light it isn't. But in the human realm Black gets a ferocious initiative for not too much of an investment, so the answer is yes, the sac is sound!

Aronian may not have liked the looks of 11...♘de7 (or 11...f6!? 12 ♗c4! ♘xd4 13 ♗xf6! gxf6 14 ♘xd5) 12 ♘xc6 ♕xd2+ 13 ♗xd2, R.Kolanek-V.Popov, correspondence 2008, although Black looks fine if he recaptures on c6 with his knight.

12 ♗xd8 ♘xd1 13 ♗xc7!?

Picking off one more pawn. White also distracts Black's dark-squared bishop from e3. The alternative is 13 ♗h4 ♘xd4 14 ♔xd1, when White must still endure a long Black initiative if he is to consolidate.

13...♗xc7!

The correct capture. Aronian seizes control of the dark squares. White's defensive task is easier after 13...♗xd4? 14 ♕xd1.

14 ♘xc6

Kramnik avoids the trap 14 ♕xd1?? ♗f4+! 15 ♔b1 ♘xd4, when White is unable to re-capture the knight due to his loose back rank.

14...♘e3!

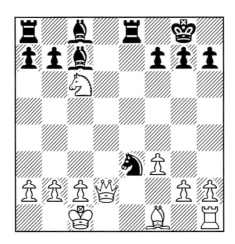

Kramnik's position sits on the brink of disaster:

1. Black's e3-knight is in White's face.

2. White's knight on c6 is loose.

3. Black threatens ...♗f4! with scary consequences.

> *Exercise (critical decision):* What would you play here as White?

Answer: Return some material to cool off Black's raging initiative.

15 ♗b5!

A brilliant move. White transforms one advantage into another. If he tries to hang on to everything with 15 ♘b4?, then after 15...♗f4! 16 ♘d3 ♗h6 17 f4 ♗f5 18 ♔b1 ♖ac8 White can barely move and his position grows increasingly difficult to navigate.

15...bxc6?!

Kramnik's clever point is that the dreaded threat 15...♗f4? doesn't work after 16 ♘e7+! ♔f8 17 g3! ♗h6 18 f4!, when too many recruits in Black's army are left hanging without orders.

Instead, Aronian had a problem-like way to save himself with 15...♗f5! 16 ♘d4 ♗f4! 17 g3 ♘xc2 18 ♕xf4 ♘xd4 19 ♕xd4 ♖ac8+ 20 ♗c4 b5 21 ♔d2 ♖xc4, when Black has sufficient counterplay. But of course this is an inhumanly tricky computer line, to which our species is blind.

16 ♗xc6 ♘c4!

Opening up f4 for his dark-squared bishop. If 16...♗f4?! at once, White plays the non-chalant 17 ♔b1! and Black lacks a useful discovery.

17 ♕d4

Dual purpose:

1. Centralizing the queen.

2. Preventing ...♗f4+ tricks.

But Kramnik thought 17 ♕b4! was more accurate; e.g. 17...♗e6 18 ♗xa8 ♖xa8 19 b3, when White's queen and two pawns are slightly more valuable than Black's three minor pieces.

17...♗e6 18 ♗xa8 ♗b6 19 ♕d3 ♖xa8 20 ♖e1

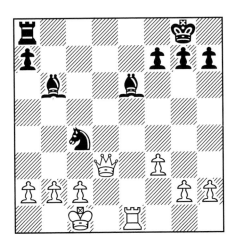

Kramnik finally completes his development.

20...♖d8 21 ♕e4 g5?

Black's activity proves to be an unsavoury stew, as Aronian indiscriminately bungs in whatever ingredients are on hand. It has been my observation that moves like this are only made by patzers or geniuses who short-circuit. Remember Fischer's moronic 29...♗xh2?? in his first match game versus Spassky, which even an 800-rated player would reject. The rest of us in the middle wouldn't even consider such a move. After this rash pawn stab, Aronian experiences great difficulties saving the game.

> *Question:* What could possibly be Aronian's idea behind the move?

Answer: It is difficult to discern meaning when the syntax is off. I have no clue. Ask someone who is a genius! Whatever the idea, it was both brilliant and totally wrong-headed at the same time, if that makes any sense to you! The simple 21...g6 was Black's best chance.

22 c3 ♗c5 23 ♖e2!?

Covering the second rank.

23...h6 24 g3!

Exposing the vulnerability of Aronian's earlier ...g7-g5?!. The intended source of counterplay begins to dovetail into a clear strategic burden. White plans f3-f4 to air out Black's king. Soon Black begins to feel a cloying sense of despair as his forces scatter in disarray.

24...a5 25 f4!

Suddenly Black's pieces begin to destabilize from their once anchored central perches.

25...a4 26 f5 ♗d5 27 ♕d3 ♗b6 28 b3!

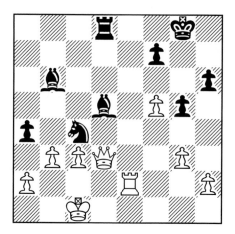

Opening a second front: two queenside passers.

28...axb3 29 axb3 ♘a5

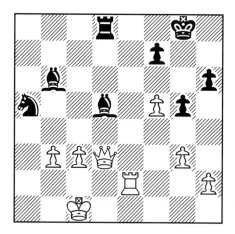

One senses a lack of an organizing cohesiveness in Black's camp, as his pieces dance about, each doing his or her own thing.

> **Exercise (combination alert(s)):** White has two different paths to victory. Both are quite difficult to find. Give it a shot and see what you come up with.

Answer: Deflection/simplification. The black rook's head snaps back as Kramnik engages the taser and the voltage flows.

30 ♖e8+!!

Answer #2: The computer points out that 30 ♕b5!! also wins, but in an insanely more complicated way: 30...♘xb3+ (or 30...♗c7 31 ♖e8+!) 31 ♔c2 ♘c5 (if 31...♗c5 32 ♖e5! or 31...♖d6 32 ♕e8+ ♔h7 33 ♖e6!) 32 ♖e8+ (not 32 ♕xb6+? ♗b3+!) 32...♖xe8 33 ♕xe8+ ♔h7 34 ♕b5 ♗a7 35 ♕a5 and Black loses material.

30...♖xe8

The slippery canned peach slides down Black's gullet, even before he has a chance to chew.

31 ♕xd5

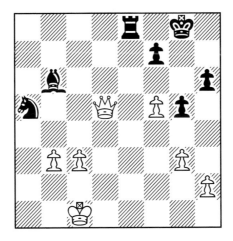

Black is busted:

1. His powerful bishop pair has been disbanded.
2. White's king suddenly looks quite safe.
3. Those two connected passed pawns on the queenside begin to roll.

31...♖d8 32 ♕b5 ♖d6 33 ♔c2 ♔g7?!

33...♗d8 was Black's last chance to put up a defensive wall on the queenside. His only prayer is to sac a piece for both white passers, which won't be so easy since Kramnik will do everything in his power to avoid it.

34 b4 ♘b7 35 c4

A table for two please, with a view of the ocean. The conjoined pawns, an impenetrable knot, begin to roll queenward, leaving Black hopelessly uncoordinated. Kramnik concludes with mercilessly chill finality.

35...♖f6 36 g4!

The deeply entrenched f5-pawn tangles and entwines the activity from Black's game, the way a boa constrictor wraps around its prey.

36...♘d8 37 c5 ♗c7 38 ♕d7!

Black's pieces are in a sorry mess, failing to find kinship amongst themselves.

38...♘c6 39 b5! ♘a7

The knight convulses in its madness.

40 ♕xc7 ♘xb5 41 ♕e5!

Black's forces are a picture of despair:

1. The eternally pinned rook's struggles prove futile, as he lies down in submission in exhausted stupor.

2. The black king's body begins to decompose on g7.

3. The ostracized knight stands away from the group, ill at ease.

The computer, of course, has to ruin our joy by finding the incredibly flashy 41 ♕d7!! ♖c6 42 f6+! which wins even more quickly.

41...♘a7 42 ♔d3 1-0

Black is eternally pinned and hopelessly tied up.

> **Question:** How does White break the blockade on c6?

Answer: It's easier than it looks since Black's rook is frozen on f6. For example, 42...♘c6 43 ♕b2 ♘a7 44 ♔d4! ♘c6+ (Black can't touch the rook) 45 ♔c4 ♘e7 46 ♕a1 ♘c6 47 ♔b5 ♘e7 48 ♕e5 ♘g8 (48...♘c6 49 ♕xf6+! and 48...♘c8 49 ♕c7 both win) 49 c6 and the pawn promotes.

Chapter Three
Riding the Dynamic Element

In my Capablanca book, the chapters were ordered the following way: Attack, Defence, Exploiting Imbalances, Accumulating Advantages, and Endings. When researching Kramnik's games, I found that a percentage of his best games failed to fit snugly into any of the above categories. A new category, the Dynamic Element, needed inclusion.

Boris Spassky explained it in a 2000 interview with Alex Baburin: "Nowadays the dynamic element is more important in chess – players more often sacrifice material to obtain dynamic compensation. Of course, such players were in my generation too..." (Spassky, for example!) "...but fewer players played like that. The game was slower then."

In this chapter we examine how Kramnik seizes and holds onto the initiative. His basic instinct: disrupt and interrupt as he grabs the initiative, often in mysterious ways, or allows a deliberate weakening of his position if allowed initiative as compensation. In this chapter the air over the battlefield buzzes with projectiles, but sails in one direction: toward Kramnik's opponents!

Game 21
V.Kramnik-P.Svidler
Linares 1998
Catalan Opening

1 ♘f3 ♘f6 2 c4 e6 3 g3 d5 4 d4 ♗e7

This was Black's most popular plan at the time the game was played. Today, GMs trend toward the more dynamic line 4...dxc4 5 ♗g2 ♗b4+, as seen in Carlsen-Kramnik from last chapter (Game 19).

5 ♗g2 0-0 6 0-0 dxc4 7 ♕c2

7 ♘e5 is also played here.

Question: What is the difference between
7 ♕a4 and the move Kramnik played in the game?

Answer: 7 ♕a4 simply transposes if Black responds with 7...a6 8 ♕xc4 b5. But it also offers Black the option of playing 7...♗d7, so perhaps the move Kramnik played in the game is the most accurate since it decreases Black's choices in the position. These transpositions can be confusing, but it stands to reason: if a=b+c, then a=c+b as well!

7...a6 8 ♕xc4 b5 9 ♕c2 ♗b7

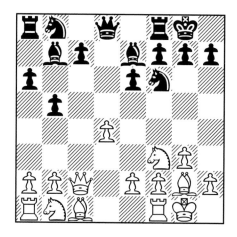

Question: What is the overall theme for both sides?

Answer: ...c7-c5 or not ...c7-c5! If Black achieves his break, he tends to equalize without much sweat. If White manages to bind Black and prevent ...c7-c5, Black is in danger of a squeeze.

10 ♗f4

10 ♗g5 and 10 ♗d2 are also played.

10...♘d5

Question: Doesn't this move gain a tempo?

Answer: Not if White refuses to move his bishop from f4.

Question: But wouldn't Black then get both
the bishop pair and hurt White's pawn structure?

Answer: First, White often deliberately trades off his dark-squared bishop for a black knight in these Catalan structures. Second, by recapturing the knight on f4 with g3xf4, White strengthens his structure, since he now gains a firm grip on e5. Maybe Black's best shot at equality is 10...♘c6!? 11 ♖d1 ♘b4 12 ♕c1 ♖c8, as in V.Korchnoi-V.Kramnik, Dos Hermanas 1999.

11 ♘c3 ♘xf4 12 gxf4

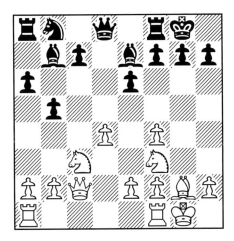

Despite appearances, this structure is actually advantageous to White since he still controls c5 and has increased his grip on e5.

12...♘d7

Answer: It's a trap! 13 dxc5 ♗xc5?? loses to 14 ♘g5 with a deadly double attack on the mating square at h7 and Black's hanging bishop on b7. Note how handy that f4-pawn can be.

13 ♖fd1

Once again discouraging ...c7-c5.

Answer: Not really. White does win the exchange but Black gets two healthy pawns for it, with dynamic equality after 13...♗xg5 14 ♗xb7 ♗xf4 15 ♗xa8 ♕h4 16 ♖fd1 ♕xh2+ 17 ♔f1 ♖xa8 18 ♕e4.

13...♗xf3?!

Answer: The trouble is that White's light-squared bishop is much stronger than Black's dark-squared counterpart. Also, c6 is weak and, in time, the mould and mildew continue to spread on that square.

Better is 13...♕c8 14 ♘e4 c5 15 dxc5 ♘xc5 16 ♘xc5 ♕xc5 17 ♕xc5 ♗xc5 18 ♖ac1 ♖fc8 19 ♘e5 ♗xg2 20 ♔xg2, Z.Ribli-A.Karpov, Amsterdam 1980, though even then White still holds a microbe of an advantage due to his control over c6. In fact, Karpov, in his prime, failed to hold the draw in this game.

14 ♗xf3 ♖b8 15 e3

Sneakier than 15 ♘e4, V.Smyslov-L.Barczay, European Team Championship, Kapfenberg 1970.

15...♘f6

> *Question:* Can't Black power in 15...c5 now?

Answer: It fails tactically to 16 dxc5 ♗xc5 17 ♘e4 ♖c8 18 ♖ac1 ♕e7 19 ♖xd7! ♕xd7 20 ♘xc5 with a winning position for White, whose two minor pieces dominate Black's meagre remainder.

16 ♖ac1

It is becoming increasingly clear that Black is unable to engineer ...c7-c5.

16...♕d6

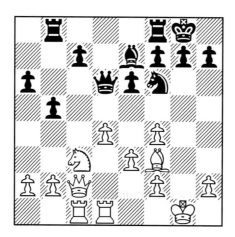

Black wants to cover c6, but in doing so his queen becomes vulnerable on d6. Admittedly the ultra passive 16...♖b6 isn't very tempting.

17 ♘e2!?

Also very tempting was 17 ♘e4 ♘xe4 18 ♗xe4 f5 19 ♗g2 ♗d8 20 ♕b3 (threat: ♖c6) 20...♖b6 21 d5 exd5 22 ♖xd5 ♕e6 23 ♕d3 with strategic domination.

> *Question:* Why would Kramnik reject this line?

Answer: Undoubtedly he wanted to retain knights on the board to reduce Black's drawing power of opposite-coloured bishops. By playing to e2, the knight supports d4 and f4, enabling his next move.

17...♖fc8 18 e4!

Threatening to fork queen and knight next move, and also reminding Black that the structure remains of an unfixed nature.

Question: But doesn't this move loosen
White's once stable central structure?

Answer: It does. Kramnik realizes that Black's game lacks the dynamic factor, and that his position feels and tastes like a mushy bowl of lukewarm gruel. Structure plays only a minor role here since Black's pieces are too passively placed to exploit White's weakening.

18...♕d7

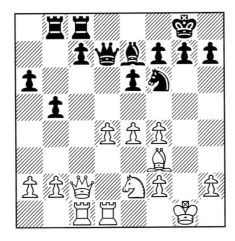

Exercise (planning): White can grab
the initiative if you find the correct plan.

Answer: Strike in the middle, where Black is not ready for a fight.

19 d5!

From this moment on, Kramnik never gives Svidler a moment of peace.

19...exd5

Or 19...♖b6 20 dxe6 ♕xe6 21 e5 ♘e8 22 ♘d4 ♕g6+ 23 ♕xg6 ♖xg6+ 24 ♔f1 c5 25 ♘f5 ♗f8 26 ♖d7 with domination.

20 e5 ♘e8 21 ♖xd5 ♕h3 22 ♗g2 ♕h4

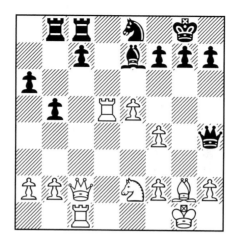

Answer: The conductor points his baton at the knight, singling him out as the soloist. White sacs an f-pawn, in return for accumulating ferocious central piece activity as a dividend.

23 ♘d4!

Now f5 and c6 beckon alluringly.

23...♕xf4 24 ♘c6

The knight turns his head in accusatory glances at the loose b8-rook and Black's hanging bishop on e7.

24...♗h4

The hunting party is destined to return empty handed.

25 ♖cd1!

No thanks. White's knight is worth more than Black's useless b8-rook.

25...♖b6

Black's claustrophobic rook finds another nook to hide from his pursuer.

26 ♖5d4!

Kramnik's forces pirouette across the board with balletic grace. Now White's rooks arrive at the party.

26...♖xc6

Black's rook doubles over in pain but puts on a brave face, raising an arm to signal to the other pieces that he is okay – when in fact, he is anything but okay.

Answer: In such positions the defender is left with the dismal choice: neither or nor. He had to give up some material, since on 26...♕h6 White has 27 ♕f5! ♖a8 28 ♖f4! which wins on the spot.

27 ♗xc6 ♕xe5

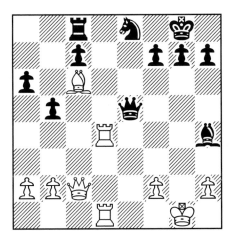

White can't take the loose bishop since Black would respond with ...♕g5+ picking up the rook. But the cheapskate baker who dusts his insipid wares with merely hints of powdered sugar fails much to improve the taste of his product.

> **Exercise (combination alert):** Find one clever in-between move and suddenly the sequence works. How?

Answer: Double attack. White severs the umbilical cord to Black's ...♕g5+ resource. The inclusion of this miniscule addendum is all it takes to push Black over the brink. White's bishop hits Black's c8-rook, but simultaneously covers the g4-square. So suddenly Black's two pieces hang and there is no answer to the threats.

28 ♗d7! ♖d8 29 ♖xh4 1-0

> ## Game 22
> ### V.Kramnik-G.Kasparov
> Zürich (rapid) 2001
> *Queen's Gambit Accepted*

1 d4 ♘f6 2 c4 e6 3 ♘f3 d5 4 ♘c3 dxc4

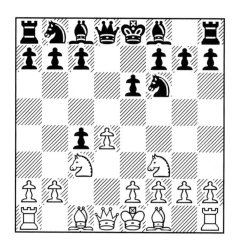

5 e3!?

The players were tied for first and Kramnik was happy to continue sharing the lead with a draw. However, the newly dethroned ex-champ had more ambitious plans. Kramnik backs down from a theoretical challenge and decides to enter a Queen's Gambit Accepted line known to be equal. Perhaps he wasn't ready to challenge Kasparov in the ultra-sharp Vienna line which runs 5 e4 ♗b4 6 ♗g5 c5 7 ♗xc4 cxd4 8 ♘xd4 ♗xc3+ 9 bxc3 ♕a5 10 ♗b5+ ♗d7 11 ♗xf6 gxf6 12 ♕b3, as seen mostly recently in V.Ivanchuk-A.Morozevich, Jurmala (rapid) 2012.

> **Question:** Who stands better here?

Answer: The answer depends on who you ask. An attacking player will say White, while the positional player may prefer Black. Essentially, in the Vienna White's superior piece activity and attacking chances are believed to compensate for his structural deficiencies. Personally, I have never felt comfortable with White, and tend to chicken out like Kramnik and enter the QGA.

5...a6 6 ♗xc4 b5 7 ♗d3 c5

7...♗b7 8 0-0 ♘bd7 9 e4 b4 10 e5 bxc3 11 exf6 ♕xf6 12 bxc3 ♗xf3 13 ♕xf3 ♕xf3 14 gxf3 leads to an unbalanced ending, D.Andreikin-R.Ponomariov, Moscow (blitz) 2010.

8 a4

Principle: *Create confrontation when leading in development.*

8...b4

> **Question:** This leads to a hole on c4. Why not go 8...c4 and
> play for queenside versus central pawn majority?

Answer: In this case Black's majority quickly gets destabilized and broken up after 9 ♗e2 b4

10 ♘b1 ♛c7 11 ♛c2, J.De Souza Mendes-J.Lacerda Guimaraes, Brazilian Championship, Rio de Janeiro 1930.

9 ♘e4 ♘bd7

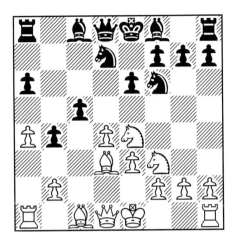

Question: This position looks familiar to me. Why? I don't play the QGA!

Answer: The reason the position looks familiar to you may be that it also arises from the Semi-Slav Meran move order: 1 d4 d5 2 c4 c6 3 ♘f3 ♘f6 4 ♘c3 e6 5 e3 ♘bd7 6 ♗d3 dxc4 7 ♗xc4 b5 8 ♗d3 a6 9 a4 b4 10 ♘e4 c5 reaching an identical position.

10 ♘xf6+ ♘xf6

Question: Should Black consider recapturing with the pawn to utilize the open g-file for the attack?

Answer: The move is very rare but may be playable. The drawback is that Black's king now lacks a safe haven across the board. For example, 10...gxf6 11 0-0 ♗b7 12 ♛e2 ♗d6 13 ♖d1 ♖g8, D.Sanzhaev-V.Shinkevich, Togliatti 2011, when I prefer White after 14 g3, intending e3-e4 next move.

11 0-0 ♗b7 12 dxc5 ♗xc5

Kasparov equalizes with ease, still harbouring ambitions further than a humble draw.

13 ♛e2 ♛d5!? 14 ♖d1 ♛h5 15 h3

Question: Why waste time with 15 h3 - ? Just play 15 e4 instead.

Answer: Kramnik must have feared 15...♘g4. Now the computer line runs 16 ♗b5+! ♚f8 17 ♖d7 axb5 18 ♖xb7 bxa4 19 ♗g5!, claiming that White's fantastic piece activity more than compensates him for his material deficit. So you may be correct!

15...♖d8 16 ♘d4

An admission of opening failure. Kramnik probably rejected 16 b3 fearing 16...♘e4, but White looks slightly better after 17 ♗b2 ♘c3 18 ♗xc3 bxc3 19 ♖ac1 ♗xf3 20 ♕xf3 ♕xf3 21 gxf3 ♗b4 22 ♗xa6. A pawn is a pawn!

16...♕d5?!

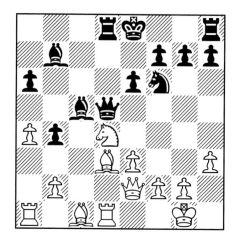

A theoretical novelty, but not a particularly great one. Black's queen moves back and forth in aimless patterns, the way a small child uses meaningless motion to dispel boredom. Kasparov mistakenly avoids the ending after 16...♕xe2! 17 ♗xe2 which may even give Black an edge. White's pieces look quite passive.

17 ♘f3 ♔e7!?

No draw. Once again, Kasparov rejects any overtures for peace negotiations, which can be achieved with 17...♕h5. GM Scherbakov makes an interesting psychological point – White doesn't have to take the draw by repetition: "Yet, it's unclear if White should agree to a draw here – he may gain a slight psychological advantage by refusing the repetition, showing that it is he who is playing for the win." I agree. Even a non-doing implies action.

18 e4!!

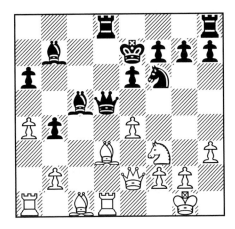

After this startling move, White's initiative swells like a sail in a strong gust.

> *Question:* What? It looks to me as though White just gave up
> a pawn without the slightest trace of compensation.

Answer: I admit the move appears as incongruous as a poet who happens to look like a wrestler. Kramnik, the world champion at the time, tired of playing second fiddle to Kasparov, decides to show the ex-champ that he too can play for the win. White speculates with a deep pawn sacrifice to bring his remaining forces out.

18...♘xe4 19 ♗e3 ♗xe3 20 ♕xe3 ♕c5 21 ♕e1!

Oh no you don't. Queens remain on the board now.

21...♘f6 22 ♖ac1 ♕b6 23 ♘e5

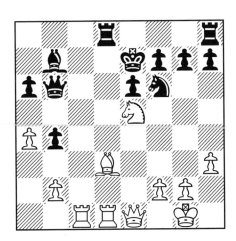

The bats flutter from their cave after sunset. This is the position Kramnik envisioned when he sac'ed the pawn on his 18th move.

Question: What on earth did he get for his sac?
All I see is White down a pawn for nothing.

Answer: There are hidden, ominous signs in the position, as if written by a finger on wet sand. White's compensation:

1. His pieces are suddenly far more active than Black's.
2. White's knight, posted beautifully on e5, eyes both the c4- and c6-squares.
3. Black has trouble developing his h8-rook.

Conclusion: White receives full compensation for the pawn, plus the psychological boost of throwing his ambitious opponent suddenly on the defensive.

23...♖d4?

23...a5 was necessary.

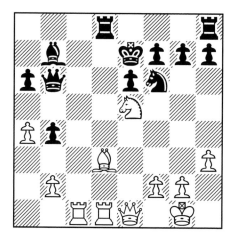

Kasparov finds himself thrown off balance by the sudden psychological shift in the nature of the position and just blunders.

Exercise (combination alert(s)): We have two ways to try to take advantage as White. One is relatively straightforward; the other is incredibly complex. See if you can come up with either answer.

***Answer:* 24 ♗xa6!**

Imaginative and profound. For a long time to come, Kramnik's idea behind the sac remains opaque, hidden behind frosted glass. He decides to double down with an incredibly deep sac. And why not? He holds all four aces and finds himself awash in chips. Kramnik's move would probably get two exclams if he didn't have a simpler, alternative win.

***Answer #2:* 24 ♘c4!** is much simpler and even stronger, when Black must hand over the exchange by taking on c4.

Question: Why give up the exchange? What is wrong with 24...♕c5 - ?

Answer: White has the trick 25 ♘e3! ♕b6 26 ♘f5+, forking.

24...♖xd1

24....♗xa6?? 25 ♘c6+ wins on the spot.

25 ♖xd1 ♗xa6 26 ♕xb4+!

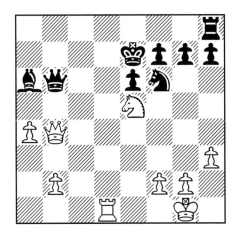

The exclamation mark at the end of a shocking sentence! Quite suddenly, Black's game is enveloped by a tsunami of angry white pieces.

26...♕xb4 27 ♘c6+ ♔f8

The Kasparovs of the world don't walk into 27...♔e8?? 28 ♖d8 mate.

28 ♖d8+! ♘e8 29 ♘xb4

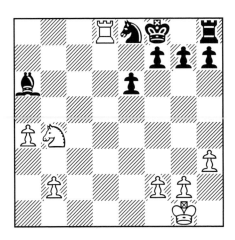

This is the position Kramnik assessed when he played 24 ♗xa6!.

> **Question:** I understand that Black is tied up, but he still
> has a piece for two pawns. Doesn't he stand better?

Answer: White stands better for the following reasons:

1. As you mentioned, Black is badly tied up. His army suffers from an unfair division of labour. Black's overworked bishop is left to do all the heavy lifting while the lazy king, knight and rook do nothing, considering themselves in purely supervisory roles.

2. Black's bishop is attacked but apparently there is no safe haven for it.

3. White's a-pawn is ready to march toward the promotion square.

Conclusion: Black fights for his life.

29...♗e2

The exhausted bishop hopes to outpace his pursuers, but only manages to do so with unsteady, faltering steps. Black has several ways to lose, but line 'c' may be Black's best from a host of unsavoury choices:

a) 29...♗b7? 30 a5 ♔e7 31 ♖b8 ♗d5 32 a6 ♖f8 33 a7 ♘c7 34 ♘xd5+ exd5 35 b4 d4 36 b5 d3 37 ♔f1 ♘a8 38 ♔e1 g6 39 ♖xa8! ♖xa8 40 b6 wins.

b) 29...♔e7? 30 ♘c6+ ♔f6 31 b4 ♗e2 32 b5 and Black is busted.

c) 29...♗c4! 30 a5 ♔e7 31 ♖c8 ♗b5 32 a6 ♗xa6 33 ♘xa6 ♖f8 and Black continues to struggle to hold the draw.

30 f3!

Kramnik correctly rejects the ending after 30 a5 g5 31 a6 ♔g7 32 a7! ♘c7 33 ♖b8 ♗c4 34 b3! ♗xb3 (34...♗e2 35 f3 ♘a8 36 ♔f2 ♗d1 37 ♘a6 wins) 35 ♘a6! ♘xa6 36 ♖xh8 ♗d5 37 a8♕ ♗xa8 38 ♖xa8 ♘c7 and Black holds the draw with a pawn for the exchange, and all the pawns on the same side of the board.

30...h5?!

30...e5 was better.

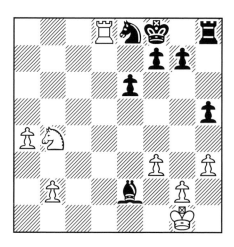

Exercise (combination alert): We are nearly there. One light nudge is all that is required to toss the e2-bishop off the precipice. But how?

Answer: White issues a subsidiary command to his b-pawn: forward!

31 b3! ♖h6 32 ♔f2

White's pieces share a mean-spirited laugh at the e2-bishop's expense, who awaits his fate helplessly as he is trapped on a wide-open board.

32...♖g6 33 ♔xe2

And so the gallant bishop meets an unfortunate end. With the passage of time his very existence may be forgotten by his uncaring comrades.

33...♖xg2+ 34 ♔d3

Black has no chance against the united might of the two connected passed pawns. **34...♖g3 35 a5 ♖xf3+ 36 ♔c4 1-0**

Game 23
Z.Hracek-V.Kramnik
Eurotel Trophy, Prague (rapid) 2002
Ruy Lopez

1 e4 e5 2 ♘f3 ♘c6 3 ♗b5 ♘f6 4 d3

Understandably, Hracek isn't too keen on testing King Kram The First in the Berlin Lopez ending after 4 0-0 ♘xe4 5 d4 ♘d6 6 ♗xc6 dxc6 7 dxe5 ♘f5 8 ♕xd8+ ♔xd8 (seen in Games 15 and 34). I think this is the worst possible way to challenge Kramnik – that is, in a position he understands better than anyone else in the world. If Kasparov banged his head against a wall in their world championship match, it is very likely everyone else will do so as well.

Question: Let's say White is a much lower-rated player who is after a draw. Is there a way for White to vacuum the life out of the position in the Berlin Lopez?

Answer: The following line is White's best shot, if boredom is the ultimate goal: 5 ♖e1 ♘d6 6 ♘xe5 ♗e7 7 ♗f1, as in V.Ivanchuk-L.Aronian, Sao Paulo/Bilbao 2011. This is a very hard position to lose with either side, though it can be done!

4...♗c5

4...d6 5 0-0 ♗e7 (5...g6 is also played here) 6 ♖e1 0-0 7 c3 a6 8 ♗a4 b5 9 ♗c2, V.Ivanchuk-Ma.Carlsen, Medias 2011, is equal, since White's pawn on d3 (rather than on d4) gives him a more passive version of a Closed Lopez.

5 0-0

Or 5 ♗xc6 dxc6 6 ♗e3 (6 ♘xe5?? ♕d4! double attacks and wins: White can regain his lost piece but is completely busted after, for example, 7 ♗e3 ♕xe5 8 d4 ♗b4+ 9 c3 ♕xe4 10 cxb4 ♗g4 11 ♕b3 ♕xg2) 6...♗d6 (Black doesn't want to take on e3 and open the f-file) 7 h3 ♗e6 8 ♘bd2 h6 9 d4 exd4 10 ♘xd4 ♕e7 11 ♕f3 0-0 12 0-0 ♖fe8 13 ♖fe1 ♖ad8 14 c3 ♗c8 and Black equalized, I.Nepomniachtchi-V.Kramnik, Khanty-Mansiysk Olympiad 2010.

5...d6

5...♘d4!? is also played here.

> **Question:** What is the point?

Answer: Early swaps tend to ease Black's defence; e.g. 6 ♘xd4 ♗xd4 7 c3 ♗b6 8 ♘d2 c6 9 ♗a4 0-0 10 ♘c4 ♗c7 11 ♘e3 d5 equalized comfortably in V.Anand-V.Kramnik, Moscow (rapid) 2011.

6 c3 0-0

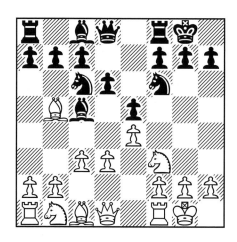

Black reaches a book position virtually a full move up.

> **Question:** How so?

Answer: GM Paul Motwani points out that 7 d4 "would leave White a tempo down compared with the line 1 e4 e5 2 ♘f3 ♘c6 3 ♗b5 ♘f6 4 0-0 ♗c5 5 c3 0-0 6 d4 of the Classical Berlin Defence".

7 ♘bd2 a6 8 ♗xc6!?

Ambitious. White can also opt for the slightly lame d2-d3 Closed Lopez with 8 ♗a4 b5 9 ♗c2, J.Polgar-E.Bacrot, Rishon Le Ziyyon (blitz) 2006.

8...bxc6 9 ♘c4

> **Question:** Why not gain a tempo with 9 d4 - ?

Answer: White's e-pawn may become a cause for concern after 9...exd4 10 cxd4 ♗b6, intending ...♗g4 and ...♖e8. If White pushes it to e5, then he weakens himself on the light squares.

9...h6

Just so he doesn't have to worry about ♗g5.

10 b4

Black has the bishop pair. The principle is: *Exchange one of your opponent's bishops if possible.* So White should consider 10 ♗e3 on this move or the next.

10...♗a7 11 ♕e2

Again, 11 ♗e3 looks best.

11...c5 12 ♘a5

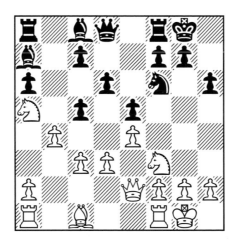

Off on an adventure. Once more White rejects the strategy of swapping off that dark-squared bishop with 12 bxc5 ♗xc5 13 ♗e3.

12...cxb4

> **Question:** Why didn't Kramnik cover the
> c6 invasion square with 12...♗d7 - ?

Answer: It fails tactically to 13 bxc5 ♗xc5 14 ♘b7!, followed by ♘xc5, with damage to Black's pawn structure.

13 cxb4

Hracek yet again spurns the swap of the a7-bishop as if it were a leper. Here 13 ♘c6 ♕d7 14 ♘xa7 ♖xa7 is equal.

13...♗d7 14 ♗d2

Hracek has taken his sweet time about playing (or not playing) ♗e3. It may be late now: 14 ♗e3 c5 15 ♘c4 cxb4 16 ♗xa7 ♖xa7 17 ♘xd6 ♗e6 and I prefer Black, with his queenside pawn majority and nice-looking bishop.

Answer: I don't know! No matter how much our inner voice of common sense begs us to
reconsider, we still sometimes refuse to listen. I suppose the human race, in order to remain healthy, must allow a fraction of the population in opposition to the norm. The sub-
versive will (Hracek's continual refusal to swap off Kramnik's powerful bishop!) may be an
ugly yet necessary ingredient for evolutionary progress.

14...♖b8 15 a3 c5 16 h3 cxb4 17 ♗xb4?

The wrong recapture. Now Kramnik unleashes his pieces in a position pregnant with in-
timation of dark menace.

17...♘h5!

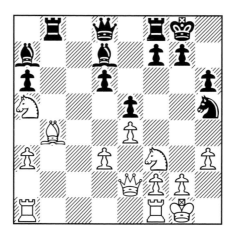

Black's position begins to pulsate with untapped possibility. He threatens to plant his
knight on g3 (which picks off the exchange) or f4 (which accelerates all kinds of attacking
possibilities). From this point until the moment White resigns, every single Black move contains some kind of threat.

18 ♕d2?!

18 ♗xd6 ♕xa5 19 ♘xe5 ♖b5 should be in Black's favour but was still better than what
White got in the game.

18...♕f6!

No rest for White. Black threatens to chop h3 with his bishop.

19 ♔h2 ♘f4

Threat: ...♘xh3. The knight slides to f4 with the easy familiarity of slipping on a favourite t-shirt.

20 ♘g1?

20 ♘c4 ♕g6 21 ♘e1, unpleasant as it appears, was White's last shot at trying to hold
the game.

20...♕g6

Threatening mate in one. Kramnik continues to prod, threaten and probe, asking questions without a question mark at the end – as if he already knows the answer.

21 f3

21 g3 fails to 21...♘xh3! 22 ♘xh3 ♕h5.

21...♗e3!

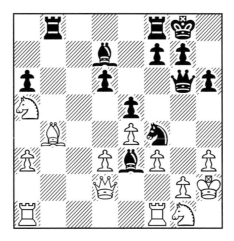

Deflection! It's not an easy thing to disavow a long-cherished but negative philosophy, since in doing so we expose our own past errors for all the world to witness. I am certain Hracek, who had multiple opportunities to eliminate Black's dark-squared bishop earlier in the game, now was racked with regret for his decision to allow the beast to live on.

22 ♕c2

The beleaguered queen gracelessly shuffles sideways, like a crab along the beach, attempting to dodge an incoming wave. Of course White rejects Kramnik's "offer" of the poisoned bishop, the way a pawn broker, with a smirk, declines to buy a cheap piece of jewellery.

22...♖fc8 23 ♘c4

In times of long drought, every farmer – religious or not – pleads to the almighty for rain. White has been dancing around the barrage of Kramnik's threats.

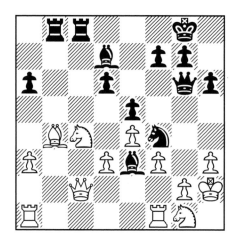

Answer: Having been bullied and beaten up as a child, I can testify from personal experience (and I believe Hracek understands this as well!), that the pain from loss of self-respect exceeds physical pain.

23...d5! 0-1

Answer: 24 exd5 ♗xc4! is overload! The eighth threat in a row. At long last, the urgency of White's plight comes to roost. This time White has no answer since he is unable to recapture, either with queen or pawn, because Black's pinning queen on g6 blocks the line of the d3-pawn's fire, and White's queen is tied down to the mate threat on g2. Now everything fits as it should, like the correct answer to a once-difficult maths problem.

Answer: In such cases the computer efficiently takes care of the tactics. Neither side will hang a queen. So understanding of strategic elements takes precedence. The power of the computer must be guided efficiently, otherwise calculation power fails to have the desired effect. Corporations are capable of replacing one worker with another (or even with a machine) in all job categories but one: the artist, who is unique to himself or herself. In this case it is up to the players to imprint their own individual personality and style on the impersonal – i.e. their computers; non-sentient inert matter which happens to play good chess!

1 ♘f3 d5 2 d4 e6 3 c4 dxc4

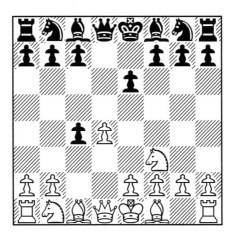

Question: This can't be correct, can it? Black plays
the Queen's Gambit Accepted with ...e7-e6 first?

Answer: It's actually a playable move order.

4 e3

Question: Why hold back when he has the immediate 4 e4 - ?

Answer: Apparently Black is okay there. For example, 4...b5 5 a4 c6 6 axb5 (or 6 b3 ♘f6 7 e5 ♘d5 8 bxc4 bxc4 9 ♗xc4, when White has more space but Black looks okay with his grip on d5, A.Ledger-I.Karkanaque, European Cup, Plovdiv 2010) 6...cxb5 7 b3 ♗b7 8 bxc4 ♗xe4 9 cxb5 and White has a tiny edge at most, F.Vallejo Pons-G.Kasparov, Linares 2005.

4...c5 5 ♗xc4 ♘f6 6 0-0 a6 7 ♗b3

Other lines are 7 a4 and 7 ♕e2, while in Chapter Five we examine Kramnik's handling of the ending after 7 dxc5 (see Game 43).

Question: What is the point of Kramnik's 7 ♗b3 - ?
His bishop isn't even under attack, yet he moves it.

Answer: I think this is actually one of White's more dangerous lines versus the QGA. 7 &b3 is a useful move: the bishop gets out of the way of ...b7-b5 which normally arrives with tempo. White can now meet 7...b5 with 8 a4 b4 (8...c4 9 &c2 is also slightly better for White) 9 ♘bd2 &b7 and then 10 e4!? (a dangerous pawn sac, whichever one Black takes) 10...cxd4 (after 10...♘xe4? 11 ♘xe4 &xe4 12 ♖e1 &d5 13 &g5 Black falls too far behind in development) 11 e5 ♘d5 12 ♘c4, G.Kasparov-J.Piket, Tilburg 1997, when White's e5-pawn gives him attacking chances. He can even regain his sac'ed pawn if he wants it back.

7...cxd4 8 exd4

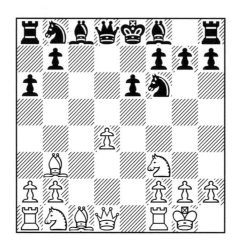

We reach a classical isolani position.

> **Question:** What are the typical strategies of an isolani position?

Answer: The answer requires an entire book! Here is the *CliffsNotes* version:

1. Black seeks exchanges.

2. Black strives to blockade the square in front of the isolani, in this case d5.

3. White avoids exchanges since he normally stands worse in most endings due to his weakened d-pawn and d5-square.

4. White uses the isolani as a central hook for ♘e5 and possibly even a piece later on c5. The pawn gives him a central space advantage which can often be translated into some form of attack.

8...♘c6 9 ♘c3 &e7 10 &g5 0-0 11 ♕d2!?

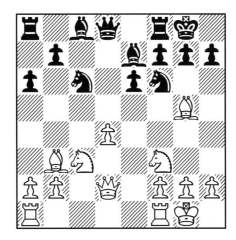

A relatively new idea which has become popular over the last dozen years or so.

Question: Where will White's queen be going from d2?

Answer: Over to the kingside via f4.

Question: What are other set-ups for White?

Answer: There are two other set-ups:

1. a2-a3, ♕d3, ♗c2, and rooks on e1 and d1. White aligns queen and bishop to the h7-battery, which eventually provokes a weakness with ...g7-g6.

2. ♗e3, ♕e2 and rooks on d1, and e1 or c1. White basically holds tight to his isolani and plays more positionally with moves like ♘e5 later on.

11...♘a5

Or 11...♘d5 12 ♘xd5 exd5 13 ♗xe7 ♘xe7 14 ♖fe1 ♕d6 15 ♖ac1 ♗g4 16 ♘e5 ♗f5, P.Leko-A.Karpov, Miskolc (rapid) 2006, and now White gets a developmental edge after 17 ♕f4.

12 ♗c2 b5

Question: Won't 12...♘c4 cause White problems?

Answer: White looks good after 13 ♕e2!. In E.Bacrot-R.Antoniewski, Warsaw (rapid) 2011, Black saw nothing better to do than retreat with 13...♘b6 14 ♕d3 g6 15 ♗b3, when White has a clear advantage.

Question: Isn't White's b-pawn loose in this line?

Answer: It is defended tactically: 13...♘xb2?? 14 ♗c1! – nobody bothered to tell the wayward, trapped knight that White's "sac" of the b-pawn had quotation marks flanking it.

> **Question:** What if Black supports the knight on c4 with 13...b5 - ?

Answer: That also fails to tactics: 14 ♗xf6! gxf6 15 ♕e4 f5 16 ♕xa8 ♕c7 (threatening to trap the queen with ...♗c5 and ...♖a8) 17 ♗e4! fxe4 18 ♕xe4 leaves White up an exchange.

13 ♖ad1 ♘c4

Now he plays the move, but White's queen wants to be chased to the kingside anyway.

14 ♕f4

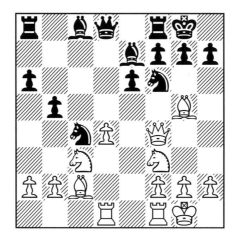

14...♖a7!?

Intending ...♖d7.

> **Question:** Why can't Black chop on b2 this time?

Answer: The b-pawn continues to be protected by strange forces in this line: 14...♘xb2?! 15 ♖b1 ♘c4 16 ♗xf6! (Roberta Flack would agree: the annoying ♕e4! theme, which simultaneously threatens mate on h7 and Black's rook on a8, is killing Anand/comp softly with her song!) 16...gxf6 17 ♕e4 f5 18 ♕xa8 and White's queen isn't going to be trapped since she always receives help with the bailout trick ♘xb5! later on.

15 ♘e5 ♖c7

As a long-time meditator, by now my powers of clairvoyance allow me to read your mind. Black still can't take on b2: 15...♘xb2?? 16 ♘c6 ♘xd1 (16...♕b6? 17 ♘xe7+ ♖xe7 18 ♗xf6 gxf6 19 ♘e4 is crushing) 17 ♖xd1! ♖c7 (or 17...♕c7? 18 ♘xe7+ ♕xe7 19 ♕h4 h6 20 ♘e4) 18 ♘xd8 ♖xc3 19 ♗xh7+! ♔xh7 20 ♘c6! as after 20...♖xc6 21 ♗xf6 ♗xf6 White has that same ♕e4 tactic once again. Black doesn't get enough for the lost queen.

16 ♘xc4 bxc4!

Question: An unnatural recapture?

Answer: Anand and his computer correctly reject the obvious move. They probably fretted over the line 16...♖xc4 17 ♕h4! g6 (or 17...h6 18 ♗xh6! gxh6 19 ♖d3) 18 ♘e4! ♘d5 19 ♗b3 f6 20 ♗h6 f5 21 ♘g5, when White applies strong pressure on the kingside and centre.

17 ♗xf6! ♗xf6 18 d5!

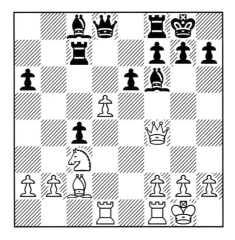

Black's pieces are slightly out of synch and have trouble dealing with this central pawn thrust.

18...e5?!

The lid just won't fit the jar, no matter how much Anand turns it. Cyborg team Anand/comp underestimates the force of White's passed d-pawn. Instead, after 18...exd5! (not 18...♗xc3?! due to the in-between move 19 d6! and White stands better) 19 ♖xd5! ♖d7 20 ♖fd1 ♗xc3 21 ♖xd7 ♗xd7 22 bxc3 ♕c8 Black's pieces are passive but he may well be able to hold the position.

19 ♕f3 ♖b7 20 ♕e4 g6 21 ♕xc4 ♖xb2 22 ♗b3!

Threat: ♘a4!.

22...♗g5 23 d6!

The blue whale slowly rises to the surface to expel stale old air from its lungs and exchange it for fresh reserves.

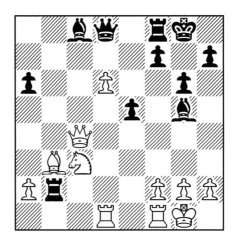

23...♗e6 24 ♕a4

White can also offer the exchange with 24 ♕xa6! since if Black bites with 24...♗g4?! 25 ♘e4! ♗xd1 26 ♖xd1, it is unlikely he can ever shake the death-bind.

24...♗xb3 25 axb3 ♕b6 26 ♕g4!

A double attack: threatening Black's bishop as well as the ♘a4 fork.

26...♗f4

Black's best shot at saving the game may be 26...♖xb3! 27 ♕xg5 ♖xc3 28 ♕xe5 ♖c6 29 ♕e7 ♕d8 30 ♖fe1 – at least White's pawn hasn't yet reached d7 here.

27 ♘d5!

Terminator Kram/comp is/are unlikely to fall for the human cheapo 27 ♘a4? ♕b4! and Black's discovery threat ...♗xh2+ may yet save him/it.

27...♕d8

If Black gets cute with 27...♕xd6?? 28 ♘xf4 ♕b4, White has the counter-cute unpin trick 29 ♘d5!.

28 ♘xf4

Kramnik discards the unnecessary in his position, like ground coffee bean sediment at the bottom of his cup. He deletes the superfluous, while fleshing out the parts of his position which require addition, constantly revising and editing throughout, with the care of a master-crafts-man/machine. It is well known that the most favourable position for a deeply entrenched passed pawn is one in which only the major pieces remain.

28...exf4 29 d7

Nobody enters a life of incarceration of his own free will. The priestess on d8 frowns in disapproval as the d-pawn carelessly parades into the sacred inner precinct of Black's temple with muddy feet. White's monster d-pawn chokes the life out of his opponent's game, until the flow of Black's past counterplay grows sluggish and comes to an absolute standstill.

29...♖xb3 30 ♕xf4 ♖b8 31 ♖fe1 ♕b6

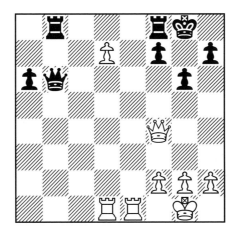

Kramnik has his opponent(s) completely tied up. But now what? A good position and a winning plan are entirely different things.

> ***Exercise (planning):*** A powerful plan remains hidden,
> floating at ease in the amniotic fluid of the position.
> How can White make progress and give it birth?

Answer: Open a second front: to Black's king.

32 h4!

The threat to continue pushing to h6 forces Black to weaken his kingside. Suddenly, Black's king, the neurotic Woody Allen character, exists in a state of chronic infirmity, which in turn eats away at self-assurance as he starts at all sudden noises.

32...h5 33 ♖d6 ♕c5 34 ♕f6 ♕f5

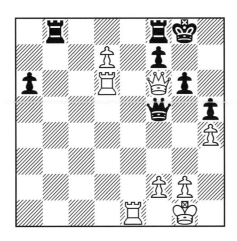

Desperation. Now Black's pawns are dominoes, ready to fall.

> **_Question:_** How will White win if Black remains passive with 34...♖bd8 - ?

Answer: White's ominous build-up allows him to go directly after Black's king: 35 ♖e7! (threatening ♖xf7!) 35...♕c4 36 ♔h2 a5 37 f4! (securing White's king from all perpetual check attempts) 37...a4 38 ♕e5! (threat: ♖xg6+!) 38...♔h7 39 ♕g5! (threatening to take on g6) 39...♕c2 40 ♖f6! (the queen and rooks weave their way in, the way a finger traces a complex route to a destination on a map) 40...♔g7 41 ♕e5 ♔g8 – Have you ever seen the 60's movie *On The Beach*? WWIII breaks out and the U.S. and Soviets exchange a massive barrage of nukes as most of the world is annihilated, with only Australia still standing. Only days remain before the inevitable winds bring radiation, sickness and death to all. Well, Black's king is Australia, awaiting end times. – 42 ♖exf7! (before a cruel action is committed, the cruel idea always precedes it) 42...♖xf7 43 ♕e8+! mates quickly.

35 ♕xf5!

Both Kramnik and his computer easily see through the trap 35 d8♕?? ♖bxd8! 36 ♕xf5 gxf5 which probably allows Black to draw.

35...gxf5 36 ♖xa6

Black's kingside is a dismal picture.

36...♖fd8 37 ♖d6 1-0

Anand/comp resigned since he/they would drop more pawns soon.

Game 25
R.Ponomariov-V.Kramnik
Linares 2003
Sicilian Defence

1 e4 c5 2 ♘f3 ♘c6 3 ♗b5

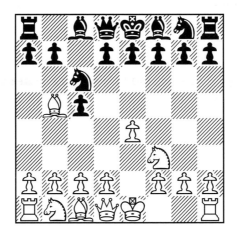

Kramnik has little respect for the Rossolimo Variation, claiming easy equality for Black.

Answer: I'm not so sure this is accurate, since my database has White scoring 57%, slightly over average. There is nothing wrong with the opening and Kramnik's opinion may be biased, due to how well he scores against it – an impressive 62% as Black, according to my database.

Question: What is White's idea behind the Rossolimo?

Answer: It's a safe line which avoids the scary monolith of Open Sicilian theory. Think of it as the Ruy Lopez (or maybe the Exchange Ruy) of the Sicilian. White often exchanges on c6 and takes on the knight versus bishop imbalance, mixed with his slightly superior centre. Or White can play for the Lopez plan c2-c3 and d2-d4.

3...g6

3...e6 and 3...d6 are the other main lines.

4 ♗xc6

Question: Shouldn't he wait until ...a7-a6 to take the knight?

Answer: Then White will be waiting a long time since Black will never play ...a7-a6. Essentially, not swapping on c6 is the c2-c3 plan. In Chapter Five, we see Kramnik's handling of this line against Rozentalis: 4 0-0 ♗g7 5 c3 ♘f6 6 ♖e1 (White can also push his e-pawn) 6...0-0 7 d4 d5! (see Game 42).

4...dxc6 5 h3

Question: Why does White bother to prevent ...♗g4, since
after h2-h3 he would eliminate Black's bishop pair?

Answer: Allowing ...♗g4 get rid of the bishop pair, but it also has a way of sucking some of the vitality out of the position. For example, 5 d3 ♗g7 6 0-0 (last chance for h2-h3) 6...♗g4 7 h3 ♗xf3 8 ♕xf3 ♘f6 9 a4 ♘d7 10 ♘d2 0-0 11 ♕e2 e5 12 b3 ♖e8 13 ♘c4 ♘f8 14 ♗e3 ♘e6 15 a5 ♕c7 16 ♖fd1 and Black equalizes, since he controls both d3-d4 and f2-f4 breaks, I.Smirin-V.Kramnik, Moscow (rapid) 1995.

5...♗g7

Black can even play 5...e5 6 d3 (after 6 ♘xe5?! ♕d4 Black regains the lost pawn and probably stands better already) 6...f6, as in N.Short-V.Ivanchuk, Reggio Emilia 2010/11. Black may have a harder time developing in this set-up but it remains playable for him.

Question: Why?

Answer: In this version Black's knight is deprived of its best square: f6. In the game version Black is able to play the manoeuvre ...♘f6-d7 and use the e5-square if White has not played f2-f4; or continue with ...♘f8-e6, posting the knight on its optimum square.

6 d3 ♘f6 7 ♘c3 ♘d7 8 ♗e3 e5 9 ♕d2

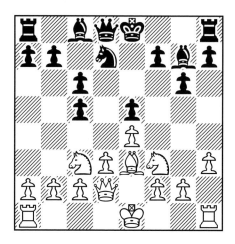

9...h6

Question: Why this move? Now he can't castle.

Answer: Kramnik wants to prevent ♗h6. Also, Black's king is not yet committed to kingside castling, and it gives him the option of a pawn storm later on. He can also allow ♗h6, as in S.Karjakin-Z.Hracek, Khanty-Mansiysk Olympiad 2010: 9...♕e7 10 ♗h6 ♗xh6 11 ♕xh6 f6 12 ♘d2 b6 13 0-0-0 ♗a6 14 g3 0-0-0 15 f4 which looks okay for Black, but White is the only one doing something in this position.

10 0-0

Question: Can White get away with castling opposite wings?

Answer: He can, but remember, Black hasn't committed to castling yet. For example, 10 0-0-0 ♕e7 11 h4 ♘f8 12 h5 g5 13 ♘h2 ♘e6 14 g3 ♗d7 15 ♘e2 b6 16 f4 exf4 17 gxf4 gxf4 18 ♘xf4 ♘g5 19 ♕g2 0-0-0 and White failed to achieve anything from his kingside demonstration, W.Kruszynski-E.Pigusov, Berlin 1994.

10...♕e7 11 a3

Question: What is White's idea behind this move?

Answer: White often plays for b2-b4 in these lines.

Answer: True, but the doubled pawns aren't so bad for Black, as they help him retain a grip on d4. Also, after the structure changes with b2-b4, ...c5xb4, a3xb4, White gets an open a-file to pressure a7.

11...♘f8

Headed for the e6 prime property.

12 b4! ♘e6

Not 12...cxb4? 13 axb4 ♛xb4? 14 ♗xa7!, when Black must lose material because of the discovered attack threat ♗c5!.

13 ♘a4!

Pono hammers away at c5, urging Black to exchange on b4.

13...b6!

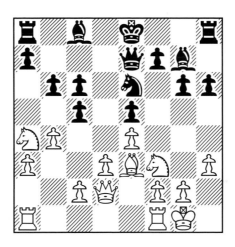

Nyet! Kramnik refuses to comply.

14 ♘h2!?

A novelty, though I'm not so sure it's an improvement.

Answer: He never gets this break in. If this is the case, then why misplace his knight? White's move has another strong feature to it: he is able meet ...f7-f5 with f2-f3, maintaining his centre and not opening the g-file for Black.

14...f5 15 f3 f4 16 ♗f2 h5

Imprisoning White's h2-knight for now.

17 bxc5 b5 18 ♘b2

Now both white knights are poorly placed.

18...g5 19 d4?!

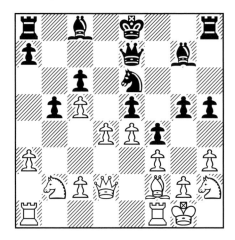

Premature.

> ***Question:*** Why? White follows the principle "counter
> in the centre when attacked on the wing".

Answer: True, but Pono's move looks like an overreaction since he gives away too much to do so. The principles are generalities which work *most* of the time – not 100% of the time. White should go for 19 a4 a6 20 axb5 cxb5 21 c4 ♗b7 22 ♕b4 ♕d7, when Black gets compensation for the pawn.

19...exd4 20 ♘d3 ♘xc5 21 ♘xc5 ♕xc5 22 ♖fd1 ♗e6 23 ♕b4!?

White should now resign himself to an inferior ending after 23 ♗xd4 ♗xd4+ 24 ♕xd4 ♕xd4+ 25 ♖xd4 ♔e7.

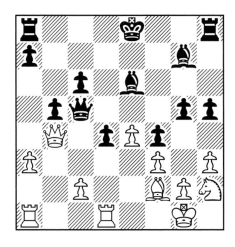

> ***Exercise (critical decision):*** White offers an exchange sac in the line
> 23...♕xb4 24 axb4 d3. If you were Black, would you accept the offer?

Answer: In such situations cool-minded realism trumps a passionate outcry.

23...♕b6!!

Initiative is more important than material. If Black accepts with 23...♕xb4 24 axb4 d3 25 cxd3 ♗xa1 26 ♖xa1 ♖d8 27 d4 ♖h7, he emerges a full exchange up, but conversion of the material advantage will be a chore, despite the computer's gloomy forecast for White. As anyone who has struggled with a weight problem understands, an excess of a thing can be just as detrimental as deprivation.

24 a4

It's too late for 24 ♗xd4? since Black takes over after 24...c5!! 25 ♗xc5 a5! 26 ♗xb6 axb4 27 ♗d4 ♗xd4+ 28 ♖xd4 bxa3.

24...c5! 25 ♕xb5+ ♕xb5 26 axb5 ♔f7

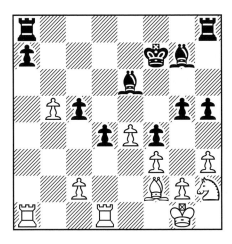

This is the ending Kramnik envisioned when he declined Pono's sac. Black holds clear advantage due to the following factors:

1. Bishop pair.
2. Superior piece activity.
3. Dangerous central pawns.
4. White's humble knight continues to live a life of austere self-deprivation on h2.

27 ♖a5 ♖hb8 28 ♘f1

Heart-warming stuff. At long last, the knight returns. Just as in most Dickens novels, at the end the much-tormented orphan finds himself happily reunited with loving, long-lost relatives, to live happily ever after. This happens here – except for the "happily ever after" part!

28...♗e5 29 ♖da1?

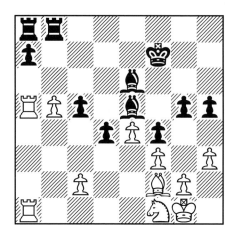

Too late. When my wife, Nancy, and I agree to meet somewhere, the same process repeats every time: I arrive five minutes early; she gets there 15 minutes late. "Sorry I'm late!" she always says, flashing her most charming smile. But I always get an awful feeling she isn't sorry at all, and harbour dark suspicions she may in fact be conducting some mad-scientist-like, twisted psychological experiment in achieving social dominance in marriage!

> **Exercise (combination alert):** White just
> miscalculated. Black to play and win.

Answer: 29...d3! 30 ♖xa7+

And now the shocker which turns White's world upside down and backwards.

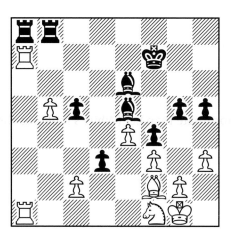

30...♔f6!!

It never occurs to the schizophrenic that the world around him hasn't in fact gone mad. Instead, his own brain simply ceded control to the crazed ramblings of the subconscious mind. Pono probably overlooked this killer zwischenzug. Black gives up a rook but gets a new queen in return.

31 ♖xa8

31 c3 ♖xa7 32 ♖xa7 ♖xb5 is equally hopeless for White.

31...♖xa8 32 ♖xa8

No choice. The dinner left too long on the stove sits in charred ruins and Pono can no longer go back and unburn it.

32...dxc2

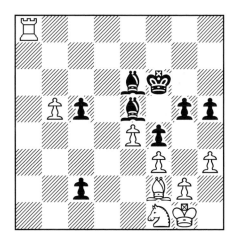

A picture of helplessness. White's extra rook doesn't do him much good.

33 ♖f8+ ♔g6

33...♗f7 34 b6 c1♕ 35 b7 ♕b1 also does the trick.

34 ♖e8 ♔f7 35 ♖f8+ ♔g6 36 ♖e8 ♗c4!

One bishop steps aside for his soon-to-be martyred brother, who willingly sacrifices his life in the blissful knowledge of his own future canonization.

37 ♖xe5 c1♕ 38 ♖xc5 ♕xf1+ 39 ♔h2 ♕xf2 40 ♖xc4

The multi-billionaire heiress, one-percenter black queen laughs in a vulgar display of ostentation at those less fortunate than her (White's rook!), as she lights up her cigar with a hundred dollar bill. The post-apocalypse world looks a lot different. Can there be a grander canyon between the two sides? White's unfortunate rook is the domesticated pet, released into the forest by an uncaring owner, with slim chances of survival. Still, White hopes to quickly adapt to his new, ruthless environment by erecting a rook versus queen fortress.

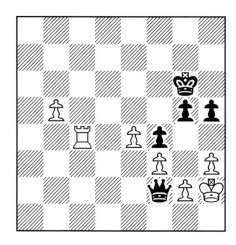

Exercise (combination alert): You can end that dream.
Black to play and force mate.

Answer: Suddenly White's once pristine kingside pawns look like a patch of grass trampled by unruly children on the school playground.

40...g4! 0-1

Since 41 hxg4 hxg4 42 ♖c8 (42 fxg4 f3 mates) 42...♕g3+ 43 ♔g1 ♕e1+ 44 ♔h2 g3+ 45 ♔h3 ♕h1+ 46 ♔g4 (the captain turned off the "fasten seatbelts" sign and passengers may now move about the cabin freely) 46...♕h5+ 47 ♔xf4 ("five, six, seven, eight; open up the pearly gates!" – White's king, in his present state, isn't sure if he is dead or alive) 47...♕g5 is mate.

Game 26
V.Kramnik-A.Naiditsch
Turin Olympiad 2006
English Opening

1 ♘f3

Kramnik's old favourite. Today, he plays 1 d4 more often.

1...♘f6 2 c4 c5 3 g3 d5 4 d4

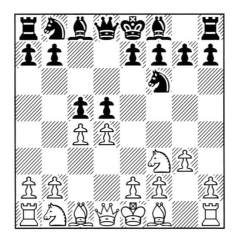

A logical move and I believe White's best shot at an edge against Black's system.

Question: Best on what basis?

Answer: White utilizes his slight lead in development to open the game. Instead, 4 cxd5 ♘xd5 5 ♗g2 ♘c6 6 ♘c3 ♘c7 7 0-0 e5 is a Rubinstein English where Black essentially plays a reversed Maróczy Bind. I have played this position from White's side and can testify that winning isn't easy against Black's space advantage and inherent solidity.

4...cxd4

Kramnik faced 4...dxc4 twice and both times achieved a developmental edge: 5 ♕a4+ ♗d7 6 ♕xc4 ♗c6 7 dxc5 (or later 7 ♗g2!? cxd4 8 0-0 ♕d5 9 ♘a3, V.Kramnik-P.Leko, Frankfurt rapid 2000) 7...♗d5 8 ♕a4+ ♗c6 9 ♕c4 ♗d5 10 ♕c2 e6 11 ♗g2 ♗e4 12 ♕c4 ♗d5 13 ♕h4 ♗xc5 14 ♘c3 ♗c6 15 0-0, V.Kramnik-G.Kasparov, Linares 2000.

5 ♗g2!?

Principle: *Don't be the one to break the central tension.* After 5 cxd5 ♕xd5 6 ♕xd4 ♘c6 7 ♕xd5 ♘xd5 Black has equalized since White must take time out to deal with ...♘b4, Jo.Horvath-M.Palac, Pozega 2000.

5...e6

Question: Doesn't Black get the initiative
after 5...♘c6 6 ♘xd4 e5 7 ♘xc6 bxc6 - ?

Answer: In this case White gets a Grünfeld a full move up – a scary proposition for Black, since an extra tempo asserts itself in such sharp, open positions.

6 0-0 dxc4

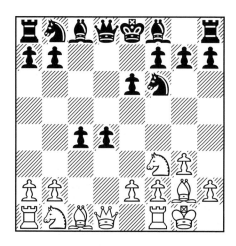

Question: I understand that White has a big development lead.
But at the moment he is down two pawns and is likely
to remain down one. A correct assessment?

Answer: Don't underestimate the dynamic factor – White's massive lead in development. I really don't see a way Black can hang on to either pawn. I would assess this at "+=", a slight edge for White.

7 ♘xd4 ♘d5?

Question: What is the point of the knight move?

Answer: Naiditsch is a GM whose rating nears the towering 2700 mark, but his idea – lord only knows what? – is lost on me too.

Question: What should Black play instead?

Answer: How about developing something – anything? For example, 7...♗c5 8 ♕a4+ ♕d7! 9 ♘b5 0-0 10 ♕xc4 ♕e7 and Black looks okay, L.Polugaevsky-L.Ljubojevic, Amsterdam 1981.

8 ♕a4+ ♘d7

8...♗d7 9 ♕xc4 leaves Black wondering just why he put his knight on d5 in the first place.

9 ♕xc4 ♘7b6 10 ♕b3 ♗d7

10...♗c5 may be wiser, in order to castle soon.

11 ♘c3 ♗c5?!

He has to try 11...♘xc3 12 ♕xc3 ♖c8 13 ♕d3, though Black's position remains uncomfortable, since defence of b7 is a problem.

12 ♘xd5 ♘xd5?

Naiditsch oversteps his boundaries and soon feels the ground crumble beneath his feet. Black's last move is an error, but it's understandable that Naiditsch wants to avoid the technical position 12...♗xd4 13 ♗e3! ♗xe3 14 ♘xe3 ♗c6 15 ♖fd1 ♕c7 16 ♖ac1 0-0 17 ♕a3 ♖fc8 18 ♗xc6 bxc6, when Black can only look forward to a long, difficult defence ahead of him.

13 ♘f5! 0-0

Instead, 13...exf5 14 ♕xd5 drops material, and 13...♕f6 14 ♕xb7 doesn't look like much fun for Black either.

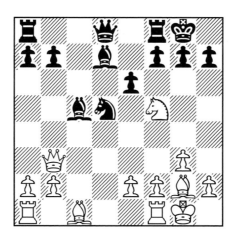

Exercise (combination alert): Kramnik warms up, like a concert pianist who performs imaginary scales in the air before a performance. White has a shot. Do you see it?

Answer: Double attack. Kramnik unexpectedly grabs the g-pawn by the throat, digging away at Black's foundation, the way a shovel scoops up soft soil.

14 ♘xg7! ♘f6!

Black's best practical chance. He tries to trap White's knight.

Question: What double attack? Why can't Black just take the knight?

Answer: After 14...♔xg7? 15 ♗xd5! exd5 16 ♕c3+ the double attack regains the piece with an extra pawn and crushing position to boot.

15 ♗h6

Question: Is White in trouble now? His knight seems to be stuck where it is.

Answer: It may appear that way but looks are deceiving. White's knight slinks down and tries mightily to negate his own presence, like a wanted criminal in a coffee shop who observes a pair of police officers enter for breakfast. Meanwhile, White's obstinate bishop attaches himself firmly to his buddy on g7, the way a clam clamps on to the hull of a sunken ship. Kramnik seems to have worked out the details perfectly.

15...♕e7

15...♘g4? fails to 16 ♘h5! ♘xh6 17 ♕c3!, regaining the piece with the same c5/g7, dirty double attack trick.

16 ♕f3!

Preventing ...♘g4.

16...♗c6 17 ♕f4 ♔h8!

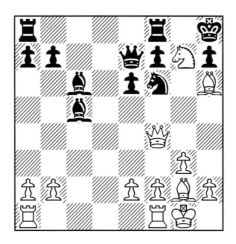

Clearing g8 for his knight. The path from destitution to wealth and power is difficult to cross without treachery or dishonour, but Naiditsch does his very best, defending well after his opening fiasco. He avoids the cheapo 17...♗xg2?? 18 ♘f5! and it's mate or Black's queen.

18 ♗xc6 bxc6 19 ♖ac1 ♗d6 20 ♕h4!

Threat: ♗g5!.

20...♘g8

The knight tries to peer inside but the frosted windows obscure the view. Black's new-found activity isn't exactly a wellspring of initiative gushing forth. I suppose something is better than nothing. In desperately bad positions, free will is but an illusion for the defending side.

21 ♕xe7 ♗xe7

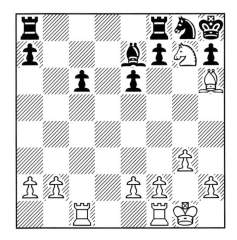

Both white pieces hang, but Kramnik has everything under control.

22 ♘xe6!

Reminding Black that the weak do well not to make demands on the powerful. Kramnik continues to dole out tickets and fines. Everyone hates the parking meter officer, but why? She is just doing her job.

22...♘xh6 23 ♘xf8 ♗xf8 24 ♖xc6

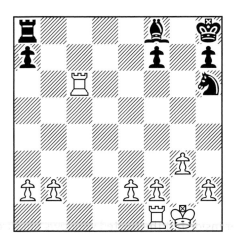

It's not freedom when the tiger breaks free of the net, only to be entangled in another one soon after. A rook and three pawns are too much for Black's puny knight and bishop team.

Question: What is White's plan?

Answer: Multifarious:

1. Black's a-pawn is a target.

2. White can organize attacks along the seventh rank.

3. White owns pawn majorities on both wings and attempts to engage them at some point.

4. White should seek to swap off Black's lone rook, his single prayer for counterplay.

24...♖d8 25 ♖fc1 ♔g7 26 ♖1c2 ♘f5 27 e3 a5 28 ♖a6 ♖d5 29 e4 ♖d1+ 30 ♔g2 ♘d4 31 ♖c7 ♘b5 32 ♖b7!

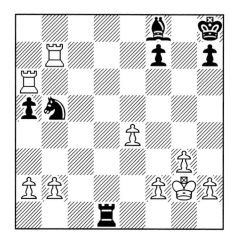

Forcing Black's knight into a deadly pin. Kramnik is an energy vampire, with a nasty habit of soaking up the opponent's extraneous piece activity.

32...♘d6 33 ♖d7! 1-0

White threatens e4-e5, and 33...♔f6 34 f4 or 33...♖e1 34 ♖dxd6 is utterly hopeless for Black.

Game 27
V.Kramnik-E.Alekseev
Tal Memorial, Moscow 2007
Benoni Defence (by transposition)

1 d4 ♘f6 2 c4 e6 3 g3

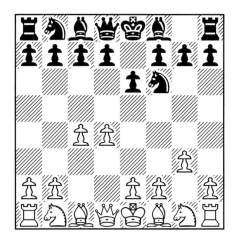

Answer: With this move order White eliminates the Nimzo-Indian and Queen's Indian. Black has a choice of a ...d7-d5 structure, leading to a Catalan, or ...c7-c5 which could turn into a Benoni, or else ...♗b4+ with a Bogo-Indian.

3...c5

Black needs great confidence in his theoretical preparation to challenge Kramnik in his beloved Catalan.

4 d5

Question: White doesn't strictly have to enter a Benoni here does he?

Answer: White can still dodge the Benoni with 4 ♘f3, but Black scores quite well from the following position: 4...cxd4 5 ♘xd4 d5 6 ♗g2 e5 7 ♘f3 d4! 8 0-0 (the naive 8 ♘xe5?? drops a piece to 8...♕a5+) 8...♘c6 9 e3 ♗e7 10 exd4 exd4, when Black gets a kind of favourable Tarrasch Queen's Gambit. The isolated d-pawn probably constitutes a strength more than a weakness, D.Andreikin-E.Tomashevsky, Biel 2010.

4...exd5 5 cxd5 b5!?

Question: Did Black just take advantage of White's failure to play ♘c3 - ?

Answer: Well, he is trying, but matters are not so simple since Black loses time and loosens his position as well. Perhaps he should settle for the mundane 5...d6 6 ♘c3 and just play a standard g3-Benoni.

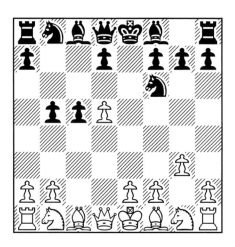

6 e4!?

Question: Giving away an important central pawn?

Answer: The wind unexpectedly changes direction. Kramnik wilfully crosses the line between Benoni dogma to open heresy. This is an old Gennadi Sosonko idea; White gets compensation. Alternatively:

a) 6 ♘d2!? ♘xd5 7 ♗g2 ♘c7 8 ♗xa8 ♘xa8 9 b4!? c4 10 a4 ♗xb4 11 ♕c2 ♗b7 12 ♘gf3 a6 13 axb5 axb5 14 ♕b2 ♕f6 15 ♕xb4 ♕xa1 16 0-0 ♕a6 17 ♗b2 f6 18 ♗a3 was V.Kramnik-L.Aronian, Yerevan (rapid, 5th matchgame) 2007, when White got ferocious compensation for his sacrificed material. GM Alex Baburin speculated that Alekseev may have prepared a variation in this very line for Kramnik, but Kramnik ambushed him first with the old/new Sosonko idea.

b) 6 ♗g2 is the main line; for example, 6...d6 7 b4!? ♘a6 (7...cxb4 8 a3 gives White compensation, G.Agzamov-A.Chernin, USSR Championship, Riga 1985) 8 bxc5 ♘xc5 9 ♘f3 g6 10 0-0 ♗g7 11 ♘d4 0-0 12 ♘c3 a6 13 ♘c6 ♕c7 14 ♗e3 ♗b7 15 ♗d4 ♖fe8 16 a4! bxa4 17 ♗xc5 dxc5 18 ♕xa4 and White's superior structure gave him the better game, G.Kasparov-V.Korchnoi, London (11th matchgame) 1983.

6...♘xe4

Black bites.

7 ♕e2 ♕e7 8 ♗g2 ♘d6!?

More normal is 8...f5, seeking to entrench the knight on e4 for as long as possible; e.g. 9 ♘h3 b4 10 ♗e3 g6 11 ♕c2 d6 12 0-0 ♗g7 13 ♘d2 and White's big development lead gives him clear compensation for the pawn, A.Iljushin-D.Khismatullin, Russian Team Championship 2010.

9 ♗e3 b4?!

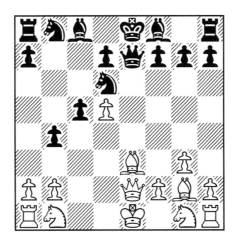

This looks overly ambitious. If Black is destined to suffer, then he needs to be paid for it and should keep his extra pawn with 9...♘a6 10 ♘c3 b4 11 ♘a4 ♗b7 12 ♘h3, although White once again gets decent compensation for the pawn, K.Sasikiran-D.Bocharov, Russian Team Championship 2012.

10 ♗xc5 ♕xe2+ 11 ♘xe2 ♘a6

Black's idea behind returning the pawn: he hopes to gain a tempo on White's bishop. But Kramnik has no plans to retreat.

12 ♗xd6!

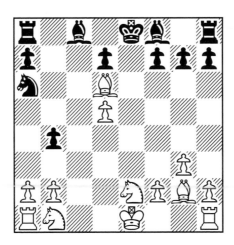

A new idea in the position and I believe an improvement over the original 12 ♗d4 ♘f5 31 0-0 ♗c5, G.Sosonko-F.Olafsson, Wijk aan Zee 1977, which allows Black to hit back at the bishop. Kramnik's move has the appearance of an indefinably odd decision but, interpreted from the context of a broader aerial view, is one that makes perfect sense: White saves time since he didn't back off with his bishop.

12...♗xd6 13 ♘d2

Now it is Black's dark-squared bishop which is exposed, enabling White to gain more time with ♘c4 or ♘e4.

13...♖b8 14 ♘c4 ♗e7 15 d6!

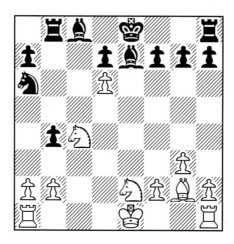

For now, White decides to park his rage on d6, where it continues to fester.

> **Question:** Risky? White's advanced d-pawn may
> become a target if more pieces come off the board.

Answer: The decision is reached, and the consequences are final and far reaching: no middle ground, no limbo, no bardo for White. Heaven or hell is the only possible destination. Kramnik gains more space and clears d5 for his pieces.

15...♗f6 16 ♘f4 ♘c5 17 0-0 ♗a6!?

> **Question:** This looks risky. Shouldn't Black castle first?

Answer: It doesn't really matter since 17...0-0 18 ♘d5 ♗a6 19 ♘xf6+ gxf6 20 ♗d5 transposes to the game.

18 ♘d5!

Power positional play at its very best. Kramnik disdains Black's threat. After a short but tension-dense pause, the hostilities flair up again.

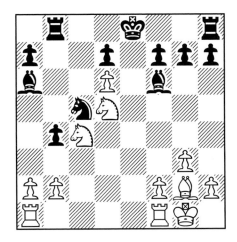

18...0-0

After 18...♗xc4 19 ♘xf6+ gxf6 20 ♖fc1 White regains his piece with structural interest.

19 ♘xf6+ gxf6 20 ♗d5

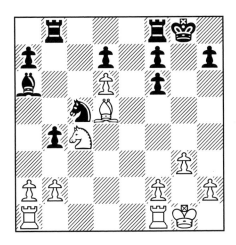

The human move. The computers prefer weird stuff like 20 ♖fd1!? ♗xc4 21 ♖dc1!, although it's not as strong as in the previous note since Black has the extra move ...0-0.

20...♘a4?!

Black goes pawn hunting and loses the initiative for good. Soon, the war he began arrives at his own front yard. Better to stay humble with 20...♖fe8.

21 ♖fc1! ♖fe8

21...♗xc4 22 ♖xc4 ♘xb2 23 ♖g4+! ♔h8 24 ♖b1 ♘d3 25 ♖d4 ♘e5 26 ♖dxb4 favourably regains the pawn.

22 ♘e3!

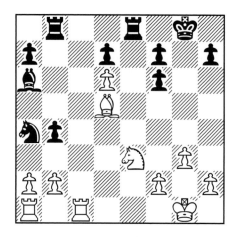

Kramnik offers his b-pawn. For this, he shuts out Black's e8-rook and plans entry via c7.

22...♖b6

22...♘xb2 23 ♖c7 ♖ed8 24 a3! bxa3 25 ♖xa3 also puts Black under tremendous strain.

23 ♖c7 ♖xd6

Removal of the intruder listed high in Black's long list of defensive priorities. Well, it turns out you were right. Kramnik did drop his advanced d-pawn. However, a good servant understands when he is needed and when he is not. The frantic activity of White's forces still give him a winning position.

24 ♖d1!

Threat: ♗xf7+!.

24...♔h8

24...♔f8 drops an exchange to 25 ♘f5 ♘xb2 26 ♘xd6 ♘xd1 27 ♘xe8.

25 ♘f5 ♖b6 26 ♗xf7 ♘xb2 27 ♖dxd7

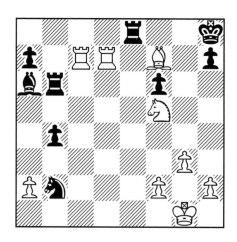

The rooks, in porcine fervour, feed at the trough along the seventh rank. For those with patience, who are willing to wait long enough and place implicit trust in the power of piece activity over mere material, the future becomes the present. Those angry rooks await with arms folded. Just like that, Black is done for. Rather than answering questions, Kramnik asks a new one: how will Black defend his king?

27...♖e1+ 28 ♔g2 ♗f1+ 29 ♔f3 ♗e2+

Alekseev makes a final, frantic lunge at Kramnik's king.

30 ♔f4!

La, la la, la la. White's king daydreams on his pleasant Sunday afternoon stroll in the park.

30...♖b8

30...♘d3+ fails to 31 ♖xd3! with a back rank mate threat.

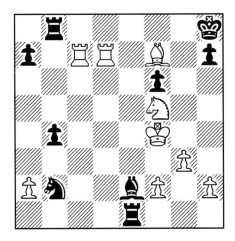

Is it really necessary to fasten your seatbelt if the plane is in a nosedive?

> **Exercise (combination alert):** Black just covered his first rank but it does him no good since White delivers mate in five moves. How?

Answer: Dual purpose: cover d3 and set up unstoppable threats along the seventh rank. The dying black king's lips move as he tries to impart one last statement, yet no sound emerges.

31 ♗c4! 1-0

Game 28
V.Kramnik-V.Topalov
Nice (rapid) 2008
King's Indian Defence

1 d4 ♘f6 2 c4 g6 3 ♘c3 ♗g7 4 e4 d6 5 ♘f3 0-0 6 ♗e2 e5 7 0-0 ♘a6

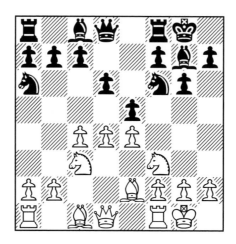

Question: Doesn't this decentralizing move violate principle?

Answer: Yes, but the move is an exception to the normal rule since the post is only temporary. Black's knight has access to all sorts of good squares, such as c5, or even b4 and c7, depending on how White sets up. The idea is to avoid the theoretical monolith stemming from 7...♘c6, from which my database announces nearly 34,000 games. I remember being surprised by 7...♘a6, by a master way back in the 1980's. I thought his move was outrageous and expected to crush him. Unfortunately, I underestimated his opening and went on to lose in confused fashion. So I learned then not to underrate the move.
8 ♗e3
   White's best shot at an edge is to retain the central pawn tension for as long as possible.
8...♘g4 9 ♗g5 ♕e8

Question: An unnatural move?

Answer: This bizarre move is now quite normal in the position. Instead, 9...f6 10 ♗c1 (10 ♗h4 is also played here) 10...♔h8 11 h3 ♘h6 12 dxe5 fxe5 13 ♗e3 ♘f7 14 ♕d2 ♘c5 was A.Karpov-G.Kasparov, World Championship (7th matchgame), New York 1990, when I prefer White slightly after 15 b4 ♘e6 16 ♖fd1.

10 ♖e1 exd4 11 ♘d5

V.Anand-J.Polgar, Leon (human+computer rapid) 2000, saw 11 ♘xd4 ♛e5 12 ♘f3 ♛c5 13 ♗h4 ♘e5 14 ♘xe5 dxe5 15 ♖c1 ♗e6 16 ♘d5 f6 17 a3 c6 18 b4 ♛d4 19 ♛xd4 exd4 20 ♘f4 ♗f7 21 ♗g3 ♖fe8 22 ♗f1 ♖ac8 23 ♘d3 and again I prefer White, who managed to blockade Black's passed d-pawn.

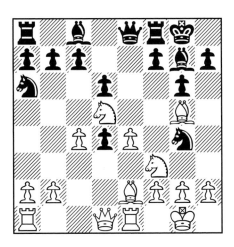

11...d3

It would be a short game if Black played 11...♛xe4?? 12 ♗d3.

12 ♗xd3 c6

> *Question:* Why can't Black take on b2?

Answer: He doesn't have the time. His dark squares grow grievously weak after 12...♗xb2? 13 e5!.

13 ♘e7+ ♚h8 14 ♘xc8

White picks up the bishop pair.

14...♖xc8 15 ♗f1 ♘c5

> *Question:* Can he grab b2 now?

Answer: He can, but Kramnik would undoubtedly give up the exchange for a huge initiative once again with 15...♗xb2 16 ♖b1 ♗c3 17 ♖xb7! ♗xe1 18 ♘xe1!.

16 ♛xd6! ♘xe4

Double attack: Black simultaneously attacks f2 and White's queen. The over-exuberant e4-knight rushes out into the street and looks for someone – anyone – to high five. But he may be celebrating prematurely, since he is pinned.

17 ♛a3 f5

Answer: It is defended tactically. Black drops a piece after 17...♘gxf2? 18 h3! (eliminating the knight's exit route) 18...♕d7 19 ♗h4 ♘xh3+ 20 gxh3 and Black doesn't get enough for the piece.

18 h3 ♘e5 19 ♗f4!

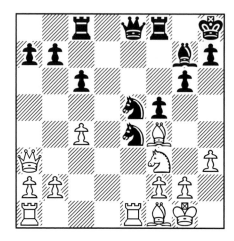

Answer: White stands better for the following reasons:

1. Bishop pair in an open position.

2. The pinned e4-knight gums up the works, like the slow moving supermarket cashier trainee who takes forever with each customer before you in line.

3. a7 is hanging.

4. Black's dream of kingside or central counterplay is an arid desert where life of any sort never takes root.

19...♘d7

Black loses the initiative after this unforced retreat, but good alternatives are hard to find:

a) 19...♘xf3+?? drops a piece to 20 gxf3.

b) 19...b5 20 cxb5 cxb5 21 ♕xa7 ♘c4 22 a4 bxa4 23 ♖xa4 ♘xb2 24 , when White has the initiative and Black's offside knight on b2 is in some danger as well.

c) 19...a6 20 ♖ad1 ♘f7 (what else?) 21 ♕b4 b5 22 ♕a3 and Black remains under strategic pressure.

20 ♕xa7?!

20 ♖ad1! keeps Black twisting in the breeze.

20...♗xb2?!

He decides to ski the slopes, ignoring the prominent avalanche warning sign up ahead. After this move Topa submits to endless defensive drudgery without complaint. He should go for 20...♖a8! 21 ♕xb7 (21 ♕e3 ♗xb2 also looks okay for Black) 21...♘dc5 22 ♕b4 ♖a4! 23 ♕b6 ♖a6 24 ♕c7 ♘e6 25 ♕b7 ♘6c5! with a draw by repetition.

21 ♖ab1 ♗g7 22 ♕xb7 ♘dc5 23 ♕b6 ♖f7 24 ♘g5! ♖b7

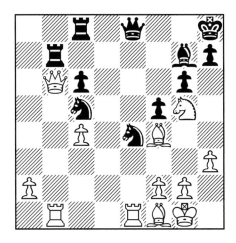

Farmer Topa plucks the withered turnip from his dying field and thinks: "will this drought ever end?" We are at a crossroads: should White sac his queen here by taking on b7? We can decline – reasoning that, just because a novelist writes a revolver into the hands of a character, it need never be fired). Or we can take a chance and sac – thinking that we carry regret for actions not taken when we should have, if only we had the courage.

> **Exercise (critical decision):** Would you sac or not?

Answer: The queen sac is completely sound.

25 ♕xb7!

GM Baburin writes: "One should not call this a sacrifice, as for a queen White will have a rook, bishop and pawn." And a strong initiative, I might add.

25...♘xb7 26 ♖xb7 ♔g8?

26...c5 was called for.

Black's defenders are pilings on an old dock, worn away by the ocean's pounding and by time. There lies a path where White's piece activity grows exponentially.

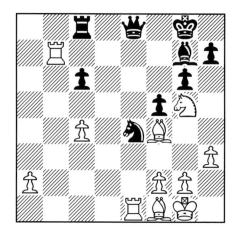

Exercise (planning): Find one powerful move and you open
the spigot, as White's pieces pour out against Black's king.

Answer: Clearance – free the light-squared bishop of his constraints by clearing c4. Black's position collapses quickly with the addition of the new attacker, as Kramnik's vacuum irretrievably sucks all life energy out of Black's game.

27 c5! h6 28 &c4+ &h8

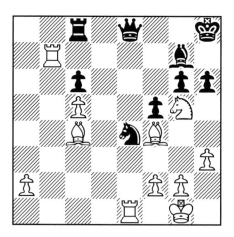

Exercise (combination alert): Sometimes you simply get
an intuition that the disparate elements in one side's
position are subtly out of whack. White has a mind-bending
shot – a shot we all dream about. Do you see it?

Answer: Overload. Neither Black's queen nor bishop can touch White's intruder.

29 ♗e5!! hxg5 30 ♗xg7+ ♚h7 31 ♗f8+! ♚h8 32 ♗e7! ♖b8

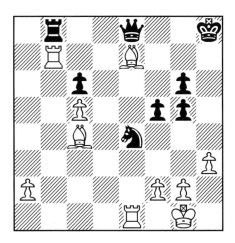

> **Exercise (combination alert):** The black king's corpse, icy to the touch, is ready for the forensic examination to determine cause of death.

Answer: Removal of defender: White clears f6 for his bishop to deliver checkmate.

33 ♖xe4! 1-0

> *Game 29*
> **A.Morozevich-V.Kramnik**
> Tal Memorial, Moscow 2009
> *Nimzo-Indian Defence*

1 d4 ♘f6 2 c4 e6 3 ♘c3 ♗b4

A bold choice, since Morozevich boasts a nearly 70% score with the Capablanca line of the Nimzo-Indian.

4 ♕c2 0-0 5 a3 ♗xc3+ 6 ♕xc3 d5

A painter needs more than just one colour to work the canvas. 6...d5 is a no-nonsense move; Black stakes a claim in the centre. In the previous chapter we looked at 6...b6 (see Game 16).

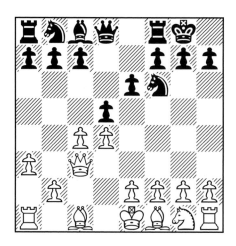

Question: Does White stand better? He has
the bishop pair and Black has a bad remaining bishop.

Answer: Actually, it's quite difficult for White to claim even a small edge. First, Black receives compensation for giving away the bishop with his lead in development. Second, Black's remaining bishop can easily enter the game via a queenside fianchetto.

7 ♘f3

In the next game Carlsen tries 7 e3. Instead, V.Ivanchuk-V.Kramnik, Monte Carlo (rapid) 2011, saw 7 ♗g5 dxc4 8 ♕xc4 b6 9 ♖d1 ♗a6 10 ♕c2 h6 11 ♗h4 ♘bd7 12 e4 ♗xf1 13 ♔xf1 ♕c8 14 ♘e2 ♕b7 15 f3 c5 16 ♔f2 ♖ac8 and Black harmoniously completed his development and equalized.

7...dxc4

Now after White recaptures with the queen, ...b7-b6 and ...♗a6 will soon pick up a tempo. Black can also try 7...♘e4 8 ♕c2 b6 9 g3 ♗a6 10 cxd5 exd5 11 ♗g2 c5 12 dxc5 bxc5 13 0-0, A.Kharlov-L.D.Nisipeanu, FIDE World Championship, Tripoli 2004. White gets the bishop pair and hopes to apply pressure upon Black's hanging pawns, while Black controls more central territory and his pieces remain quite active.

8 ♕xc4

Question: Why can't White postpone capture and
play 8 e3, intending to take on c4 with his bishop.

Answer: Believe it or not, I don't see a single game with your suggestion in my database. I think the reason is that Black can force a favourable Noteboom variation with 8...b5! 9 a4 c6 10 axb5 cxb5 11 b3 a5! 12 bxc4 b4, when Black is ahead in development, compared to the normal Noteboom line.

8...b6

One small change and Black's bad bishop is no longer bad.

9 ♗f4

9 ♗g5 is the safer alternative.

9...♗a6

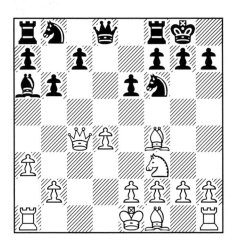

10 ♕c2?!

Moro inexplicably puts his plans on hold, like a bookmark inserted between pages. If I remember my cartoon lore correctly, the main reason Wile E. Coyote failed repeatedly in his dream to trap or kill the roadrunner was overly ornate planning, which always involved complex schematic charts and graphs. It seems to me Moro is guilty of the same transgression here: why attack c7 if not to take it? GM John Emms writes: "Perhaps an important moment from a theoretical point of view. But if White isn't going to take on c7, my feeling is the bishop should be on g5 rather than f4." I suppose an unmade promise can never be broken.

> *Question:* What happens if White does go pawn hunting on c7?

Answer: White falls considerably behind in development and Black gets full compensation; e.g. 10 ♕xc7 ♕d5, Y.Pelletier-E.Bacrot, Basel 2011. Black has also exchanged queens here, but it seems more logical to me to keep queens on the board if you lead in development.

10...♘bd7 11 e4

Others:

a) 11 ♖d1 ♕c8 12 g3 c5 and Black equalized, M.Gurevich-M.Adams, Khanty-Mansiysk 2007.

b) 11 ♗xc7?! doesn't make as much sense since White could have taken the pawn last move; e.g. 11...♕c8 12 ♖c1 ♕b7 13 ♗f4 ♖fc8 and White's development lags dangerously behind, T.Likavsky-A.Delchev, European Cup, Fügen 2006.

11...♗xf1 12 ♔xf1 c5!

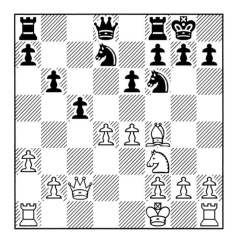

Surprisingly, this rather natural move was a theoretical novelty at the time. It is in Black's best interest to open the position while White's king lags behind in the centre. Kramnik's move is far more potent than 12...♕c8 13 ♖c1 ♕b7 14 ♕c6, V.Calugaru-J.Leroy, correspondence 2007.

13 ♗d6 ♖e8 14 e5

After 14 dxc5?! ♘xc5 15 ♗xc5 ♖c8 16 b4 bxc5 17 b5 c4 White is in deep trouble.

14...♘d5 15 h4!?

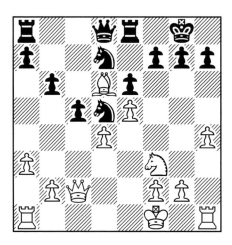

Stylistic preferences aside, Moro continues to fight the currents in opposition to the natural flow. Attacking from a position of inferiority is a sure recipe for failure.

> **Question:** Then what would you suggest?

Answer: Perhaps White should try and complete development with 15 g3.

15...cxd4 16 ♘g5!?

Or 16 ♘xd4 ♘c5 17 ♗xc5 ♖c8 18 b4 bxc5 19 bxc5 ♕c7 20 ♖h3 ♕xe5 and Black clearly stands better since he threatens both the d4-knight and also ...♖xc5!.

16...f5 17 ♕c4

Threat: ♘xe6!.

17...♕c8!

Not 17...♖c8?! 18 ♕xd4 and White threatens ♘xe6! once again.

18 ♕xd4 ♘c5 19 ♖d1

Renewing the ♘xe6! threat. Now Kramnik's knights put on a show and completely take over the game.

19...♘b3! 20 ♕d3 ♘c1!

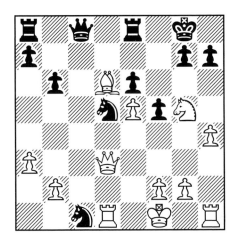

Kramnik extracts the essence of the position and distils poison in a few deadly drops by taking control over e2 and d3.

21 ♕b5?!

This allows the black queen to infiltrate. He had to try 21 ♕f3.

21...♕c2! 22 ♖xd5

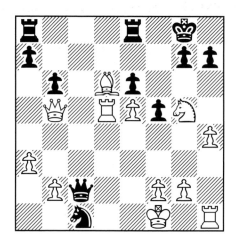

Answer: Kramnik foresaw Moro's last move. Let's do an exercise:

Answer: Zwischenzug/deflection.

22...a6!

This sneaky in-between move throws White's tactic off balance.

23 ♕xb6 ♕c4+ 24 ♔g1 exd5!

Creating a passed d-pawn.

25 g3 h6 26 ♘f3

Answer: It doesn't work but it may be a terrific practical try, since Black must find a series of strong moves to win: 26 ♕b7 hxg5 27 e6 (it looks like Black is in danger – both ♕f7+ and ♗e5 hang in the air – but Black is first) 27...♘e2+! 28 ♔h2 ♖xe6!! 29 ♕xa8+ ♔h7 30 hxg5 ♕e4! (the greedy 30...♖xd6?? fails to 31 ♔g2+ ♔g6 32 ♕e8+) 31 ♕b8 ♕f3 32 ♖f1 ♖g6! (with the terminal threat of ...♖xg5 followed by ...♖h5 mate) 33 ♗f4 ♘xg3!! 34 ♗xg3 ♖xg5 35 ♔g1 f4 and White gets crushed.

26...f4!

White's king is in greater danger than Black's.

27 g4 ♕e4

27...♕e2! (target: f2) was more accurate, when 28 ♔g2 ♘d3 29 ♖f1 ♖ac8 30 g5 ♖c2 is decisive.

28 ♔g2 ♘d3 29 ♕b3 ♕c4 30 ♕b7

30 ♕d1 is also busted after 30...♖ac8 31 ♕d2 ♕e4, though it has the virtue of not allowing Kramnik a killing combination.

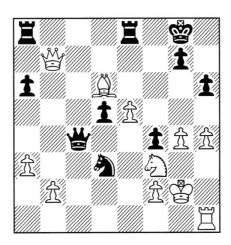

Exercise (combination alert): White's last move wasn't the best.
Find a way for Black's attack to crash through.

Answer: The heartless monarch's tax collector strips the peasants of the few remaining coins they have in their possession. Suddenly White's kingside is nothing more than an abandoned home, with all sense of human warmth vacated as well.

30...♘xf2! 31 ♔xf2 ♕c2+ 32 ♔g1 ♕d1+ 33 ♔f2

33 ♔g2 ♕e2+ is also totally hopeless.

33...♕xh1

White's forlorn king sits alone, reminding us of that Van Gogh self-portrait – the one with the bandaged head just after he cut off his ear.

34 e6

Threat: ♗e5.

34...♖ac8!

A reminder to White that Kramnik's threats take precedence.

35 ♕f7+ ♔h8 36 ♗c5!

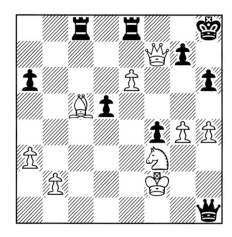

Moro finds a clever interference trick to remain alive. If White insists on attack, he is too slow after 36 ♗e5?? ♖c2+ 37 ♘d2 ♖xd2 mate.

36...♕c1 37 b4 ♕c2+ 38 ♔g1 ♕e2! 39 ♘d4 ♕xg4+ 40 ♔f2

The king arrives on f2, sweating profusely and with laboured breathing.

40...♕xh4+ 41 ♔e2 f3+! 42 ♔xf3

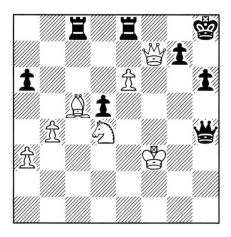

White's king continues to pace his cage aimlessly but safely, for now. The Beatles expressed the king's sentiments when they sang "I get high with a little help from my friends!"

> **Exercise (combination alert):** Magically, Moro managed
> to keep Kramnik's rooks at bay – until now. How can
> Black release one of his rooks into the attack?

Answer: Deflection. The non-spatio-temporal malevolent un-entity, without name or form, arises outside the continuum of space and time on f8, confident in the knowledge that nothing whatsoever in the universe can threaten or harm it. It strikes at White's heart, so that its equally evil twin on c8 is freed from stasis to terrorize the universe.

42...♖f8!! 43 ♗xf8 ♖c3+

A phone call received very late at night is generally the harbinger of bad news.

44 ♔g2 ♕g3+

44...♕h3+ was one move quicker.

45 ♔f1 ♖c1+ 0-1

Due to 46 ♔e2 ♕e1+ 47 ♔f3 ♖c3+ 48 ♔g4 ♕g3+ 49 ♔f5 ♕g5 mate. White's king, a fleeting thing, arrives and passes away, the way a bird hops onto a branch of a tree outside your window, sings her song, and then flies off to who-knows-where, never to be seen or listened to again.

> *Game 30*
> **Ma.Carlsen-V.Kramnik**
> Tal Memorial, Moscow 2012
> *Nimzo-Indian Defence*

1 d4 ♘f6 2 c4 e6 3 ♘c3 ♗b4 4 ♕c2 0-0 5 a3 ♗xc3+ 6 ♕xc3 d5

Just like the previous game, Black plays classically and stakes out a central claim.

7 e3

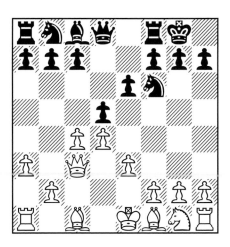

Question: Why lock in the bishop?

Answer: Remember the Kramnik-Polgar Nimzo from last chapter (Game 16)? The bishop is well placed on b2, where it discourages both ...c7-c5 and ...e6-e5 breaks. We looked at 7 ♘f3 in the previous game.

7...b6 8 cxd5?!

After this move White fights for equality, since he allows Black an effective ...♗a6! manoeuvre. Carlsen should stick to his previous play with 8 ♘f3 ♗b7 9 b3!, if he is to have any chance at an edge, Ma.Carlsen-E.Bacrot, Dortmund 2009.

8...exd5

Changing it up from 8...♘xd5 9 ♕c2 ♗a6 10 ♗xa6 ♘xa6 11 e4 ♘e7 12 ♗g5!? (this looks too ambitious; the calmer 12 ♘f3 at least keeps quick castling an option) 12...h6 13 ♗xe7 ♕xe7 14 ♕c6?! e5, when White found himself seriously behind in development, Ma.Carlsen-V.Kramnik, Moscow (rapid) 2011.

9 ♗d3?!

This may be inaccurate too, since it loses a tempo. Better is 9 ♘f3 ♘e4 10 ♕c2, T.Vasilevich-L.Galojan, European Cup, Plovdiv 2010; though even then, I don't much care for White's game.

9...♗a6!

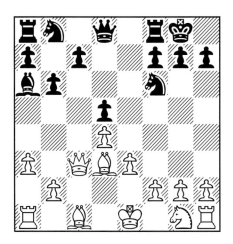

Principle: *When the opponent has the bishop pair, eliminate it.*

> **Question:** Isn't it somewhat redundant to continue
> to repeat the same principles over and over in the book?

Answer: I'm afraid you just opened the door to a lengthy story/explanation. I had a French teacher in seventh grade who repeated everything in a singsong voice, at least twice: "Bonjour! Bonjour! Je m'appelle Monsieur Bernier! Je m'appelle Monsieur Bernier!" At the time I found this annoying. Today, nearly four decades later, I still remember Mr. Bernier's lessons and can still conjugate French verbs like nobody's business! The moral: repetition, annoying though it is, still works!

10 ♗xa6 ♘xa6

Black's lead in development remains intact.

11 ♕d3 ♕c8 12 ♘e2 c5 13 b3 cxd4

> *Question:* Why did Kramnik deliberately take on an isolani?

Answer: To activate his a6-knight via c5. He can also imbalance the game further with 13...c4!? 14 bxc4 dxc4 15 ♕c2 b5, when it's unclear whose supermajority will be the more effective.

14 ♕xd4?!

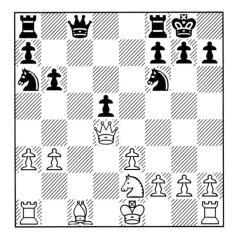

I believe the universe blesses everyone with a special and often hidden talent. My chess superpower is the gifted faculty of a deep understanding of knowing just when to grovel! My intuition tells me White's last move may be misplaced bravery. Carlsen mistakenly takes up the challenge, allowing Black activity in exchange for a superior structure. He hoped to tame, domesticate and leash Black's surging activity flow but soon discovers that such a hope is unlikely on a raw, wild force.

He should consider the safer, duller and, most importantly, equal 14 exd4!, denying Black's pieces c5.

> *Question:* Why not recapture on d4 with his knight?

Answer: Black's development lead allows him tricks: 14 ♘xd4?! ♘c5 15 ♕b5 a6! 16 ♕e2 ♘xb3! wins a pawn.

14...♘c5 15 ♕d1 ♕a6!

The angry goddess looms over the light squares as her probing morphs, taking shape in the form of a caustic agent, whose slow drip erodes the foundations of White's position.

16 ♘f4!?

He was unwilling to fork over a pawn in order to castle and grovel for a draw with 16 0-0 ♘xb3! 17 ♕xb3 ♕xe2 18 ♗b2 ♕c4 19 ♕d1 ♘e4.

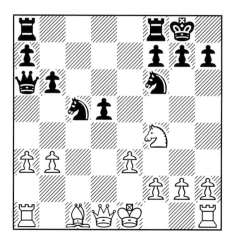

It gets harder and harder to discern a single saving line for White, through the fog of variations and their sidelines. Carlsen's nervous knight refuses to make eye contact with Black's queen, as he reluctantly agrees to leave his king to face the central headwinds.

> **Exercise (planning):** There are multiple paths to try and exploit Black's lead in development. Let's see if you can find one of them.

Answer: Overload. The d-pawn, made brave by alcohol, picks a bar fight with a larger opponent. Principle: *Open the game when ahead in development.* Black's activity spikes exponentially, as his pieces transform into swirling devils of malevolence.

16...d4!

Answer #2: 16...♖fe8! 17 b4 ♘a4 18 ♘e2 d4! 19 ♘xd4 ♕c4! is also very strong.

17 b4!

The entrenched knight must be ejected soon. White hopes to repel the salvo. But how long can he keep it up?

17...dxe3!

17...♖ad8! is strong as well, and would probably transpose to the game position at some point.

18 bxc5

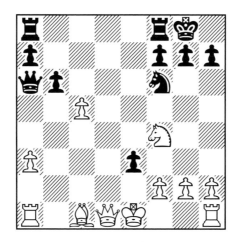

18...♕a5+!

GM Sakaev suggested 18...♖ad8! 19 ♕c2 g5! (Black demands tribute from the conquered territories) 20 ♘h3 ♕a5+ 21 ♔f1 ♕b5+! 22 ♔e1 exf2+ 23 ♔xf2 (the defensive barrier collapses, now hollow as an old skull on the forest floor; White's king, now blistered by fire, continues his useless evasions) 23...♘g4+ 24 ♔g3 ♖d3+! 25 ♔xg4 (White's pieces listen in silent sympathy to their king's pitiful pleas, but are powerless to alter the inevitable execution date) 25...♕d7+! 26 ♔h5 (26 ♔xg5 h6+! also does the job) 26...♕f5! (Black uncloaks his weapon, thrusting its power in the direction of the white king, who continues to flee in a delirium – this in turn forces White to give up his queen) 27 ♕xd3! ♕xd3 28 ♗xg5 h6! 29 ♗f4 ♔h7! 30 ♔h4 ♕d8+ 31 ♔h5 ♕d5+ 32 ♔h4 ♖g8 33 g4 ♕g2 34 ♗g3 f5 35 ♘f2 ♕f3, when Black's queen kisses her forefinger and then tenderly touches the dead white king's lips.

19 ♔f1 ♖ad8 20 ♕c2 ♕b5+ 21 ♔e1

21 ♔g1?? ♕xc5! overloads the back rank and wins.

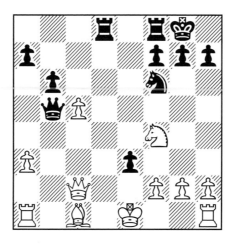

Black is a piece down but also looks like he has a powerful attack. Black can go for it with 21...g5, or he can check on a5 and force perpetual check.

> *Exercise (critical decision):* Would you play for the win or pocket the draw against the number one ranked player in the world?

21...♕a5+

Sometimes the decision to agree to a draw is in itself a blunder. Kramnik underestimates his own latent power.

Answer: He should go for it with 21...g5!, since if White tries to hang on to his extra piece with 22 ♘h3?, he simply transposes to Sakaev's winning line (22...exf2+ 23 ♔xf2 ♘g4+ 24 ♔f3 ♖d3+ etc). Instead, he must grin and bear it, returning the piece with 22 fxe3! gxf4, though his odds of survival don't look so hot here either.

22 ♔f1 ♕b5+ 23 ♔e1 ♕a5+? ½-½

The two most awful words in the chess lexicon: "If only..." Here we see a rare example of Kramnik uncharacteristically underestimating the latent power behind his own attack and initiative. His worst move of the game was in actually agreeing to the draw in a probably winning position, when Carlsen's open wounds congeal and heal as quickly as eggs tossed in a hot frying pan. Clearly, Black should have refused to attend the unilateral disarmament talks. It isn't too late to say "Request denied!" and play 23...g5!, brushing aside the draw offer with polite disinterest.

Chapter Four
Exploiting Imbalances

All the great strategic players are, by default, also masters of exploiting imbalances. Compare the first two games in this chapter. In the first, against Shaked, Kramnik makes it look like a disadvantage to hold the bishop pair versus his knight and bishop; in the second, against Adams, Kramnik pulls off the opposite, making it look like a forced win when he has the bishop pair versus Adams' bishop and knight. Kramnik's infallible strategic intuition lovingly moulds the shape of the position – whatever it is – to suit his and not the opponent's imbalance.

Sometimes Kramnik's decisions look like they could only spring forth from the mind of a genius or someone deemed clinically insane. Just take a look at his infinitely odd decision to surrender the bishop pair to take on the opposite-coloured bishops versus Howell. The pay-off became apparent some twenty moves later!

Somehow the coalition of his opponent's forces always begins to fray at the edges and move out of synch with the requirements of the position, as the freeways of their counterplay get blocked up with extraneous gunk. How do we develop such super-attuned intuition? The only way is to play over (and over) the games of the great strategic giants, until the subtle imprints appear in our minds and such intuition becomes ours as well.

Game 31
T.Shaked-V.Kramnik
Tilburg 1997
Nimzo-Indian Defence

1 d4 ♘f6 2 c4 e6 3 ♘c3 ♗b4 4 e3 0-0 5 ♘e2

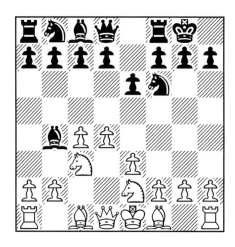

Answer: White wants to play a2-a3 and recapture on c3 with his e2-knight. I agree the move looks a bit clumsy, yet it makes sense if you factor in that e2 isn't necessarily the knight's final destination.

5...d5 6 a3 ♗e7

Black doesn't want to hand over his good bishop without any return, and so agrees to lose a bit of time himself and retreat.

Answer: In essence we now have a QGD, yes, albeit with two strange twists:

1. White is a tempo up on normal QGD lines, but it's not that great a tempo since his free move is a2-a3.

2. White's e2-knight is somewhat misplaced, blocking in his light-squared bishop.

Conclusion: Probably a fair business transaction occurred and the position is in the range of level.

7 cxd5

The main move. Others:

a) 7 ♘f4 c6 8 ♗d3 dxc4 9 ♗xc4 ♘bd7 10 ♕c2 e5, when Black took advantage of the knight's position on f4 and equalized, A.Shirov-V.Kramnik, Dortmund 1998.

b) 7 ♘g3 c5 8 dxc5 dxc4 9 ♕c2 ♕a5 10 ♗xc4 ♕xc5 11 ♗d3 ♘bd7 and I prefer White but it looks close to even, M.Bluvshtein-D.Andreikin, Moscow 2011.

7...♘xd5

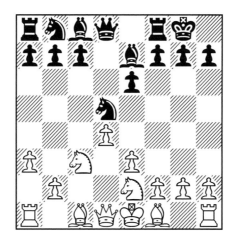

Answer: I guess Kramnik wanted to give the game a QGD Semi-Tarrasch feel. Also, every exchange helps Black free his position. I agree that 7...exd5 is more natural, but it's not necessarily better; e.g. 8 b4 c6 9 ♘g3 b5!? 10 ♗d2 ♘bd7 11 a4 (otherwise Black gets time for ...♘b6 and ...♘c4) 11...♗xb4 12 axb5 c5 13 ♕b3 with mutual chances, F.Caruana-S.Karjakin, Wijk aan Zee 2012.

8 g3

White finds a way to develop his light-squared bishop without moving his e2-knight. 8 ♕c2 and 8 ♗d2 are also played here.

8...♘xc3

GM Chris Ward suggests 8...b6!?, challenging the h1-a8 diagonal; for example, 9 ♗g2 ♗b7 10 0-0 ♘xc3 11 ♘xc3 ♗xg2 12 ♔xg2 c5 and Black looks fine, Z.Gyimesi-P.Lukacs, Budapest 1996.

9 ♘xc3

Answer: In that case 9 bxc3?! ♕d5! is awkward for White, who is forced to move his rook and lose kingside castling rights.

9...c5 10 d5!?

Having lived a safe life of uneventful sameness, White, in a combative mood, soon gets transported to a scary new life of danger. Tal Shaked is a brave man. He faces an opponent nearly 300 points higher rated, yet refuses to grovel (which I would have done in a heartbeat!) with the shameless 10 dxc5, entering the milquetoast ending 10...♕xd1+ 11 ♔xd1 ♗xc5, D.Siedentopf-R.Slobodjan, European Championship, Dresden 2007, when Kramnik would have a devil of a time defeating a lower-rated GM. In this game White, a 2178 rated player, held the draw against his 2525 rated opponent.

10...♗f6!

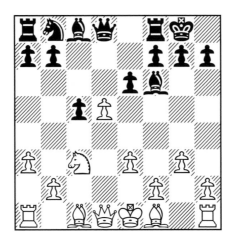

A new move and an improvement over 10...exd5 11 ♘xd5 ♗e6 12 ♗g2, S.Guliev-Y.Balashov, St Petersburg 1994.

> ***Question:*** Why do you feel Kramnik's 10...♗f6! is an improvement?

Answer: Please see Black's next move!

11 ♗g2 ♗xc3+!

The point. Black initiates multiple imbalances:

1. He is willing to give up the bishop pair.
2. Which in turn, inflicted damage to White's structure.
3. We arrive at a kingside pawn majority versus a queenside one for Black.

> ***Question:*** Isn't White's bishop pair a potent force in such an open position?

Answer: This position may be an exception. The uniting of separate powers doesn't necessarily create an even more powerful end product. To prove my point, I call to your attention Sonny and Cher, whose vile warblings disturbed my tranquillity each Sunday evening, all through the late 1960's.

12 bxc3 exd5 13 ♕xd5

I don't like the position White gets in the game. Perhaps he should try something wacky such as 13 ♗xd5!? ♘d7 14 0-0 ♘f6 15 c4!? ♘xd5 16 cxd5, although I get the feeling that Black's bishop outguns his counterpart on White's side.

13...♕e7!

Ensuring that he gains a tempo on the white queen later on with either ...♖d8 or ...♗e6.

The boundary between Kramnik's desire for swaps – which helps him exploit White's pawn weaknesses – and the fulfilment of the desire begin to fade away as he correctly resists the temptation.

14 ♖b1?!

Ward didn't like this move, calling it "a luxury". Kramnik takes advantage of the inaccuracy in just a few moves.

14...♘c6 15 0-0 ♗e6 16 ♕h5 ♖ad8 17 e4

White logically begins to push his kingside pawn majority, hoping to muster an attack with f2-f4 soon.

17...♗a2!

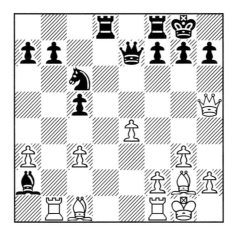

An innocuous-looking yet potent jab, which makes life awkward for White's ambitious rook.

18 ♖a1

> **Question:** Why abandon the file? Doesn't 18 ♖b2 regain the tempo?

Answer: Not after 18...♗c4 19 ♖e1 ♘e5!, when White must suddenly deal with the threat of ...♘d3.

18...♗c4 19 ♖e1 ♘e5

Again, d3 is a big square for the knight.

20 ♗e3 g6! 21 ♕h4!?

The misbehaving nine-year-old, having been banished to the principal's office, slowly begins to turn the doorknob, fully aware of the terror that awaits him on the other side. Shaked probably didn't make such a radical decision lightly.

> **Question:** It looks crazy to purposefully allow
> such structural damage. Why not 21 ♕g5 - ?

Answer: I agree that those ugly pawns now jut out at you like roaches feeding in the sugar jar. White's game lies somewhere in the twilight between uncomfortable and intolerable after the swap; but keep in mind that *Houdini* actually likes Shaked's move. White's queen looks unpleasantly claustrophobic after 21 ♕g5 f6 22 ♕h4 ♗b5!, making rook for the knight on c4.

21...♕xh4 22 gxh4 b6

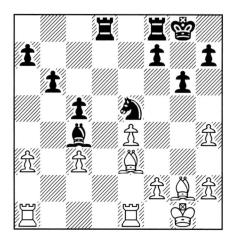

Let's take inventory:

1. The home owner passed away and his garden, previously so meticulously cared for, now lies in abandoned, overgrown ruins. Black seeks to fill the vacuum on the queenside, which calls to him enticingly. White carries the burden of four target isolanis.

2. White's position is riddled with light-square holes, such as on c4 and d3.

3. Black's bishop and knight more than hold their own against White's ineffective bishop pair.

4. More than anything else, the lack of an active plan for White is the undefined absence in his otherwise barely tenable position.

Conclusion: White is in deep trouble.

23 ♗h6 ♖fe8 24 h3 f6 25 ♖ad1 ♗b5 26 ♖xd8

> **Question:** Isn't White guilty of violating the principle
> "Don't be the one to break the tension if you don't need to"?

Answer: White's destiny is to lose control over the d-file whether he stands his ground or not. For example, after 26 ♔h2 ♗a4! White must give way and abandon control over the d-file, since 27 ♖d5?? loses instantly to 27...♖xd5 28 exd5 ♘f3+.

26...♖xd8 27 ♔h2 ♗c6 28 ♔g3 ♖d3+!

Luring White's rook to e3.

29 ♖e3 ♖d1!

Now ...♞c4 is in the air. White has no good way of protecting his a-pawn.

30 ♖e2 ♖a1 31 ♖d2 ♞f7!

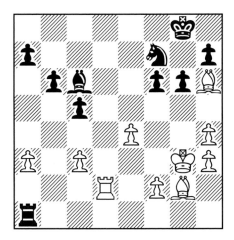

Dual purpose:

1. Black seals all entry points into his position along the d-file.

2. Black gains a tempo and ejects White's dark-squared bishop.

32 ♗e3

The bishop has no choice but to nod in desultory consent and back off.

32...♖xa3

Black, having monetized previous investments, now accrues an extra passed a-pawn, while White continues to nurse further debt via another weakness on c3.

33 ♖c2 ♞e5 34 f3?!

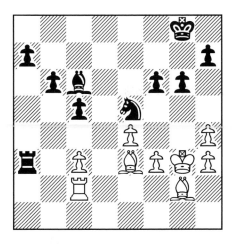

Black views his bounteous position the way a gardener gazes adoringly at her fruits and vegetables, all raised in abundant sunshine and love.

> *Exercise (combination alert):* White just blundered away
> his c3-pawn. Work out the correct sequence to win it.

Answer: Step 1: The bishop angrily pokes the rook in the back with his finger.
34...♗a4! 35 ♖c1 ♘d3! 0-1

Step 2: Not exactly a civil greeting: chase the rook again, this time for good.

> ## Game 32
> ## V.Kramnik-M.Adams
> Linares 1999
> *Nimzo-Indian Defence*

1 d4 ♘f6 2 c4 e6 3 ♘c3 ♗b4 4 ♕c2 0-0 5 a3 ♗xc3+ 6 ♕xc3 b6 7 ♗g5

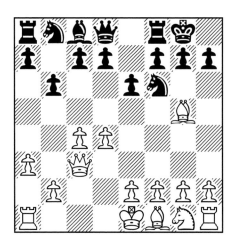

A change of pace from 7 ♘f3 which we looked at in Chapter Two (see Game 16).

> *Question:* What are the differences between pinning and
> keeping the dark-squared bishop inside the pawn chain?

Answer:

1. The pin limits Black's f6-knight.

2. Omitting ♘f3 allows White to play f2-f3, which covers the sensitive e4-square.

3. In the pin line White's bishop and queen on c3 can be vulnerable to future ...♘e4 or ...♘d5 tricks.

4. In the non-pin lines, White's bishop usually ends up on b2, taking direct aim at

Black's king and inhibiting Black's ...e6-e5 break.

Conclusion: One line isn't better or worse than the other. It's simply a matter of style.

7...♗b7 8 f3

Covering the e4-square.

> ***Question:*** What are the main dangers for White here?

Answer: White's main and constant worry in this line of the Nimzo is his lag in development. If the centre opens too quickly, matters may sour quickly.

8...h6 9 ♗h4 d5

At last, Black challenges White's central dominance.

10 e3 ♘bd7 11 cxd5

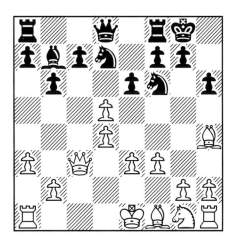

White's main line. He can also maintain the central tension; for example, 11 ♘h3 c5 12 cxd5 cxd4 13 ♕xd4 e5 14 ♕d1 ♗xd5 15 ♗b5 ♗e6 16 ♘f2 ♘c5 17 0-0 ♘b3 18 ♕xd8 ♖axd8 19 ♖ad1 and despite White's bishop pair, Kramnik maintained the balance due to that pesky knight on b3, E.Bareev-V.Kramnik, Novgorod 1997.

11...♘xd5

This leads to an ending where the experts are divided on whether White truly maintains an advantage with the bishop pair.

> ***Question:*** Isn't the pawn recapture tempting
> for Black, now that he has a target on e3?

Answer: That is a riskier option, since e3 isn't as weak as it looks. White can easily defend it with ♗f2 (as well as other pieces); e.g. 11...exd5 12 ♗d3 c5 13 ♗f5 ♕c7 14 ♘h3 g6 15 ♗xd7! ♘xd7 16 0-0 and I prefer White, whose bishop feels more potent than his black counterpart on b7, G.Kasparov-J.Hjartarson, Madrid (rapid) 1988.

12 ♗xd8 ♘xc3 13 ♗h4 ♘d5 14 ♗f2 c5

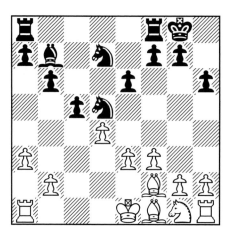

The two sides have mutually contradictory dreams for their imbalances. White just wants to catch up in development and make use of his bishop pair; Black does everything he can to prevent this from happening. The text is Black's main move here, but having studied games from this line, I'm not sure he fully equalizes. White's bishop pair always seems to make Black strain for equality.

> *Question:* Then what line do you suggest for Black?

Answer: It seems to me that the secondary line 14...f5!, which inhibits White's e3-e4 expansion, is Black's best shot and should be promoted as the main line. G.Kasparov-V.Kramnik, Moscow (blitz, 20th matchgame) 1998, continued 15 ♗b5 c6 16 ♗d3 c5 17 ♘e2 ♖ac8 18 0-0 cxd4 19 ♘xd4 ♘e5 20 ♗e2, when Black's activity should ensure equality after 20...♔f7!.
15 ♗b5

No one can fault a move if it develops with tempo.

> *Question:* Isn't 15 e4 even stronger? We gain a tempo there as well.

Answer: That move is also played, but I don't trust it to yield an advantage since White provides a target to open the position on e4.

> *Question:* How so? e4 is a rock.

Answer: Not if Black finds a way to chip away at it with the ...f7-f5 break. For example, 15...♘f4 16 ♗e3 ♘g6 17 ♘e2 and now Kramnik disrupted White's powerful centre with 17...f5!, E.Bareev-V.Kramnik, Wijk aan Zee 2004.
15...♘5f6

Also possible is 15...♖fd8 16 e4 ♘e7 17 ♘e2 ♗c6! 18 ♗a6, G.Kasparov-V.Kramnik, Moscow (blitz, 16th matchgame) 1998. Black is okay after 18...♗a4!, taking control over d1 and clearing c6 for his knight. From the other side, Kasparov achieved a draw with the pawn sac 16...♘c7!? 17 ♗xd7 ♖xd7 18 dxc5 f5! (Black trusts in his massive development lead) 19 cxb6 axb6 and now Kramnik, perhaps wisely, refused to tempt fate and simply returned the material with 20 ♘e2!? fxe4 21 fxe4 ♗xe4 22 0-0 ♖d2 23 ♘c3 ♗b7 24 b4, reaching an equal position, V.Kramnik-G.Kasparov, World Championship (8th matchgame), London 2000.

16 ♘e2 a6 17 ♗a4 cxd4

Adams aims to break up White's central control.

Question: Can Black play for a queenside majority with 17...b5 18 ♗c2 c4 - ?

Answer: That is a possible plan, but White still holds an edge due to his bishop pair. And remember, White owns a majority too.

18 ♘xd4 ♘c5 19 ♗c2 e5?!

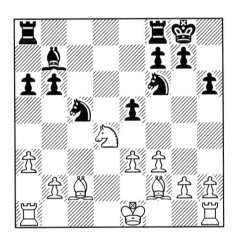

At last, some motion. The spoon stirs the sedentary sugar at the bottom of the cup of tea. Adams, in inversion to the normal requirements of his meek position, decides to bully the white knight by issuing a wordless message, conveyed through his belligerent last move. But in doing so, Black damages his own position by misguidedly attempting to seize the initiative too early, sending White's knight to a towering square. Better to remain humble and only a touch worse after 19...♖ac8.

20 ♘f5 ♖fd8 21 ♗h4! ♘d3+?!

Natural but incorrect. 21...h5 looks like a superior, damage-control move.

22 ♔e2!

Great judgment. Kramnik temporarily gives up a pawn rather than the bishop pair. It isn't really a pawn sac since he wins back two of them in return.

22...♘xb2 23 ♖hb1 ♘c4 24 ♗d3! ♘d6

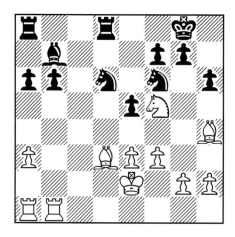

> ***Exercise (combination alert):*** White, down one pawn
> at the moment, has the opportunity to pick up two pawns.

Answer: Overload. One down, one to go.

25 ♘xh6+! ♔f8

The king moves aside, head dipped in fatigue.

26 ♗xf6

Giving up the bishop pair, but inflicting damage in doing so.

26...gxf6 27 ♖xb6

There goes the other one. Not only is Kramnik a pawn up now, he also has Black squirming in a bind. Adams' hope for counterplay, which previously felt so solid and real, turns out to be the apparition of a long-passed memory.

27...♗c8 28 ♖c1 ♗e6 29 ♖cc6 ♔e7 30 e4!

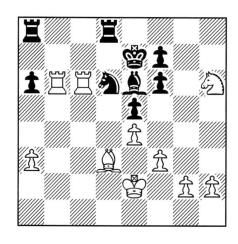

Stronger than 30 ♖xa6 ♖xa6 31 ♖xa6 f5!, when White suddenly experiences difficulties in extricating his wayward knight from h6.

30...♘b5! 31 ♔e3! ♘xa3

So Black regains his lost pawn, but in doing so his knight spends time in the internment camp on a3. Black's forces are badly out of harmony, much like the vague feeling of unease a marathon runner gets when he begins the run with a tiny pebble ensconced in his shoe.

32 ♘f5+ ♔f8

32...♗xf5 33 exf5 ♘b5 34 ♖b7+! ♖d7 (34...♔e8 35 ♗xb5 axb5 36 ♖xf6 is also completely hopeless for Black) 35 ♖xd7+ ♔xd7 36 ♖xa6! wins.

33 ♗xa6

Not only is Black down a pawn again, his knight still lingers in danger on a3.

33...♖d1 34 ♗e2 ♖a1 35 ♖b2! ♖d8

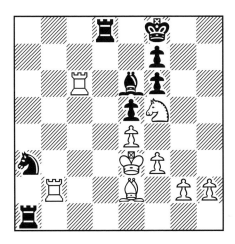

The gears turn a notch forward with a click. Kramnik utilizes another trump: his extra passed h-pawn.

36 h4!

Making good use of the pawn imbalance on the kingside. The h-pawn crawls forward the way a young plant's tendrils move in the direction of sunlight.

36...♘b1

Black's knight and rook, although in close proximity, lack interaction. They are a long-married couple who, through the passage of time, drifted apart and now eat their meals together, yet in complete silence.

37 ♔f2!

Black is nearly in zugzwang.

37...♘d2?

Black's dishevelled knight shuffles out of his hovel, sporting three days of unshaven facial hair growth.

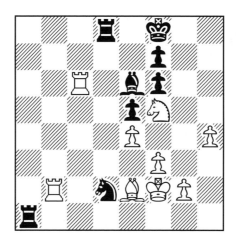

> ***Exercise (combination alert):*** Adams' position was lost in any case,
> but he blundered on his last move. White to play and win material.

Answer: Overload/back rank.

38 ♖d6! 1-0

In a flash of motion, Black spies the silhouette of the assassin on d6. White's rook on d6 strives but fails to hide a tiny smile which suddenly forms on his lips. Meanwhile White's b2-rook glares at the hanging knight on d2 with the stern expression of one of those odd, stone-faced rock gods on Easter Island.

Game 33
V.Kramnik-A.Morozevich
Dortmund 2001
Slav Defence

1 d4 d5 2 c4 c6 3 ♘f3 ♘f6 4 e3 ♗f5

It isn't so easy to equalize with the Reversed London set-up. The Reversed Torre is a better shot at equality, so I normally play the bishop to g4 in this position. For example, 4...♗g4 5 ♘c3 e6 6 ♕b3 ♕b6 7 c5 ♕c7 8 ♗d2!? ♘bd7 9 ♖c1 ♗xf3!? 10 gxf3 e5 11 ♗h3 ♗e7 with a sharp, unbalanced game, R.De Guzman-C.Lakdawala San Francisco (rapid) 2010, though I prefer Black's position since White's structural problems feel like a concern when compared to his bishop pair.

On the other hand, I don't trust 4...e6 5 ♘bd2 c5!? for Black, who tries to take advantage of White's passive move order by going into a Zukertort Colle a full move down.

Question: Is it the end of the world to be down a move in a Colle?

Answer: In my opinion the tempo matters. The Colle and its cousin, the London System, tend to be scapegoated as second rate, milquetoast openings, when in reality, they are not. The normal Colle is a Semi-Slav a move up (in this case two moves up!), so it deserves a lot more respect than it gets in the chess world. For example, after 6 b3 ♘c6 7 ♗b2 cxd4 8 exd4 ♗e7 9 ♖c1 0-0 10 ♗d3 ♗d7 11 0-0 White got a favourable hanging pawns position, mainly since he is a move up on normal, G.Kasparov-Comp Deep Blue, Philadelphia (6th matchgame) 1996.

5 ♘c3 a6!?

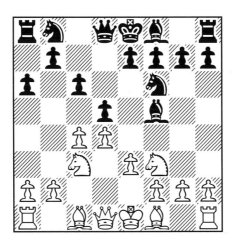

Question: Why ...a7-a6 - ?

Answer: This is called the Chebanenko Slav, a bit of a funky one with Black's bishop on f5 rather than the traditional g4-square. I think Moro's move, although played at the highest levels, is on the cusp of a "?!" mark since it doesn't fit well into his set-up.

Question: What is the usual line here?

Answer: Play usually runs 5...e6 6 ♘h4!, but then White milks an edge due to his possession of the bishop pair; for example, 6...♗g6 7 ♘xg6 hxg6 8 ♗d3 ♘bd7 9 0-0 ♗d6 10 h3 dxc4 11 ♗xc4 0-0 12 ♕c2 ♕e7 13 ♖d1 ♖ac8 14 ♗d2 ♘b6 15 ♗f1 e5 16 dxe5 ♗xe5 17 ♖ac1 and the bishops still gives White a slight but enduring advantage, Ma.Carlsen-B.Gelfand, Wijk aan Zee 2012.

6 ♗d3

> **Question:** Swapping off his good bishop for Black's bad bishop?

Answer: Yes, but keep in mind two points:

1. Black's bad bishop is no longer so bad on f5.

2. White's bad bishop won't be so bad after he achieves e3-e4.

Usually White preserves his light-squared bishop with 6 ♗e2, after which Ma.Carlsen-V.Bologan, Astana 2012, continued 6...h6!? (wasting more time but ensuring that his bishop won't be forced off by ♘h4) 7 ♕b3 ♖a7 (this odd move is actually standard in the Chebanenko) 8 cxd5 cxd5 9 ♗d2 e6 10 ♘e5! ♗d6? (10...♘bd7 was necessary) 11 ♕a4+! and Black's position sours quickly since ♘b5 becomes a big problem. Bologan decided to shank a pawn with 11...♘c6 12 ♘xc6 bxc6 13 ♕xc6+ ♕d7 14 ♕xd7+ ♔xd7 15 ♘a4, but a clean pawn down against the premier technical endgame player in the world is not a good place to be. Needless to say, Bologan was unable to hold the game.

> **Question:** Are you saying you rate Carlsen
> *above* Kramnik, the hero of our book, in the ending?

Answer: Yes, my feeling is Kramnik is the second best endgame player in the world. Please stop asking questions which may adversely affect sales!

6...♗xd3 7 ♕xd3 e6 8 0-0 ♗e7 9 e4

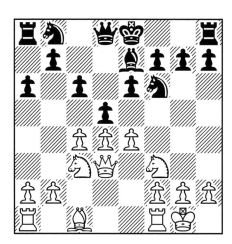

This would be considered quite a harmless line for White, had Black omitted his not terribly useful ...a7-a6 and had swapped it for a developing move. White has a tiny space advantage, though nothing for Black to worry about just yet, who still looks quite solid.

9...0-0!

Other moves:

a) 9...b5 (seeking to resolve the central tension) 10 cxd5 cxd5 11 e5 ♘fd7 12 ♘e2 ♘c6 13

♗d2 ♖c8 14 ♖fc1 ♘b6 15 b3 ♗a3 16 ♖c2 ♘b4 17 ♗xb4 ♗xb4 18 ♖xc8 ♘xc8 19 a4, when White's space, development lead and queenside confrontation gives him an edge, I.Nikolaidis-J.Smeets, European Team Championship, Porto Carras 2011.

b) 9...dxe4 10 ♘xe4 ♘bd7 11 ♗f4 ♘xe4 12 ♕xe4 0-0 13 ♖fd1 ♖e8 14 ♖d3! – from the third rank the rook can harass Black in both directions, and White's greater space again provides a small edge, K.Sakaev-K.Bryzgalin, Taganrog 2011.

10 ♖d1

> *Question:* Why not keep pushing the e-pawn?

Answer: That would suit Black fine. Black doesn't mind a4-e5 at all, since that would fix another pawn on the same colour as White's remaining bishop. Black looks good after 10 e5?! (tossing in 10 cxd5 first just gives Black a nice Advance French position) 10...dxc4! (clearing d5) 11 ♕xc4 ♘d5 with equality.

10...b5 11 c5!

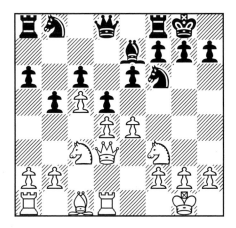

Grabbing more space.

> *Question:* Isn't White in danger of ending up
> with a bad bishop and a hole on d5?

Answer: All true, but this is where Kramnik's remarkable strategic intuition infallibly arrives at the best decision. White correctly judges that his extra space means more than the two potential problems you listed.

11...dxe4

11...b4 12 e5 bxc3 13 exf6 ♗xf6 14 ♕xc3 retains White's advantages.

12 ♘xe4 ♘xe4

After 12...♘d5 13 ♗g5! f6 14 ♗d2 White stands better due to his space and Black's backward e-pawn.

13 ♕xe4 ♕d5?!

Moro bows to reality's appeal and decides to defend an inferior ending, but I think his move is an overreaction.

> **Question:** Why can't Black win a pawn with 13...♗xc5 - ?

Answer: White wins it back after 14 ♘g5! g6 15 ♕h4 h5 16 g4! ♗e7 17 gxh5 ♗xg5 18 ♗xg5 ♕d5 19 hxg6 fxg6 20 ♖d3! and gains a strong attack.

> **Question:** Then do you have a defensive suggestion for Black?

Answer: 13...♘d7! looks best. The c6-pawn isn't really hanging due to tricks on c5. Black can play for ...♖c8 ...♘f6 and ...♘d5, when White should only have the tiniest of edges.

14 ♕xd5 cxd5!?

Moro builds his house, as if casually erected with chance material he found lying around in the vicinity. Now we get a new imbalance: opposite side pawn majorities, with White getting a bonus passed c-pawn. Nevertheless, Moro's decision here isn't an error since 14...exd5 15 ♖e1 ♗f6 16 a4 would keep him on the defensive as well.

15 ♗f4 ♘c6

Moro may have worried about the line 15...♖c8 16 ♗xb8! ♖axb8 and didn't want White to remove a natural blockader of c6.

16 ♘e5!

Principle: *Destroy a passed pawn's blockaders.*

16...♘b8!?

Creative, but it fails to solve Black's difficulties. Perhaps Moro should have gone with the ho hum 16...♘xe5 17 ♗xe5 f6 18 ♗g3 ♔f7, even if White retains pressure here as well. He can lift his rook or rooks to the third rank and also create problems with 19 a4.

17 ♖d3!

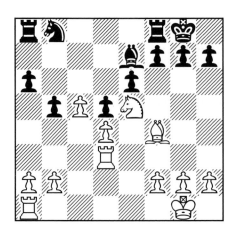

Rooks, like owls, snakes and vampires, are nocturnal creatures. Once it gets dim outside and queens come off the board, they begin to prowl about.

17...♖c8 18 ♖e1 ♗f6

Moro hovers in that mysterious nether-realm between a concrete plan and an incomplete concept. He finds himself awash in too many overlapping pseudo-plans and partial concepts which fail to cohere to a single core element. One senses he can't quite put his finger on how to break free of White's bind. He chases that first, essential, life-giving gasp of air, like a potential drowning victim who manages to break the surface of the water after long, panicked submersion. Here 18...♖a7 may be better, though even then 19 g4! continues to increase White's space and pressure upon Black's game.

19 ♘g4 ♘c6!?

It's understandable that Moro doesn't care for a second humiliating retreat in 19...♗d8, when White can establish a bind with 20 ♗xb8! ♖axb8 21 f4!.

20 ♘xf6+ gxf6

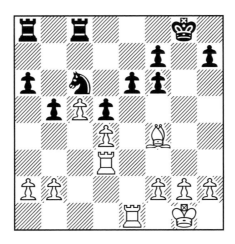

A new imbalance: bishop versus knight.

> **Question:** Isn't the knight a superior piece since
> White's c- and d-pawns are fixed on dark squares?

Answer: White's bishop is superior since it has a target on f6 and the kingside dark squares in general.

21 ♗g3!

Ready to transfer to h4.

21...♔g7 22 ♗h4 ♘e7

22...f5 23 ♖g3+ ♔h6 24 ♗f6 ♖g8 25 ♖xg8 ♖xg8 26 ♖e3! prevents ...♖g6 and leaves Black tied up.

23 g4! ♘g6 24 ♗g3 a5 25 ♗d6 h5!?

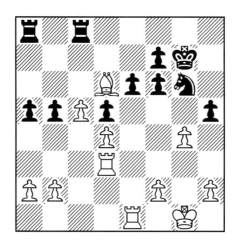

Moro tries to muck things up and cause trouble on the kingside. His aim is to lure White's pawn to h5 and then take control of f5 for his knight.

26 gxh5!

Kramnik has seen deeper.

26...♘h4 27 ♖g3+ ♔h6

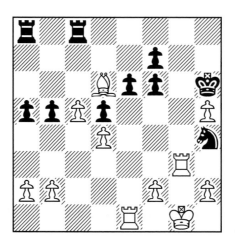

Exercise (critical decision): Evaluate the exchange sac 28 ♗e7 ♘f5 29 ♗xf6 ♘xg3. Would you do it if you were White?

Answer: It works. Black's flow of counterplay suddenly clots after the sacrifice. The power snakes up through the coil until the pent-up energy is released directly on f6.

28 ♗e7!!

Brilliantly evaluated, as the ants get into the fruit bowl. Kramnik walks into the threatened fork but gets a winning position at the end of it. Moro probably had counted on 28 ♖h3 ♖g8+ 29 ♔f1 ♘f5 30 ♗f4+ ♔h7, when Black's counterplay suddenly flares up.

28...♘f5

Black fires his crossbow but the arrow sings over the head of the intended victim.

29 ♗xf6

Kramnik transfers his bishop to f6 as lovingly as a mother who lifts her sleeping infant into the crib.

29...♘xg3

A revolver is a harmless instrument if you have already fired the final bullet.

30 fxg3!

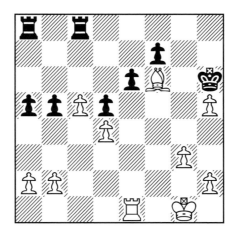

The correct recapture, which ensures a favourable new imbalance: another passed pawn.

30...♖g8 31 ♔g2 ♔xh5 32 h3!

Preventing any ...♖g4 and ...♖e4 ideas.

32...♔g6 33 ♖f1

Black's rooks are utterly useless.

33...♔h7 34 g4

With the simple plan of advancing his kingside pawns. The blacksmith uses the bellows to fan the blaze. His strong arms never tire.

34...b4 35 ♔g3 b3 36 a3

Not so fast, my friend! White of course refuses to open queenside lines for Black's rooks.

36...♖ac8 37 h4 ♖g6 38 h5 1-0

Black's lifeless position – a loathsome sight – looks like a windshield, sticky and splattered with insects after a long drive in the country. Previously, the war was an abstract concept, far off and somehow unreal. Now Black's deprivations increase and commodities grow scarce, as the war comes to his doorstep. Moro decides to lay down his burden and die peacefully, like an old man, after a hard, inconsequential life.

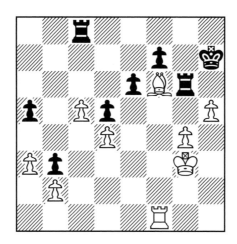

Question: I understand that Black has a terrible, passive position. But how does White win if Black simply remains passive?

Answer: Let's play out a possible scenario: 38...♖gg8 39 g5 a4 40 ♔g4 ♖ce8 41 ♗e5 ♖e7 42 ♖f6! (threatening mate in one) 42...♖g7 43 ♖h6+ ♔g8 44 ♗xg7 ♔xg7 45 ♔f4 is utterly hopeless for Black.

Game 34
D.Howell-V.Kramnik
London (blitz, 1st matchgame) 2002
Ruy Lopez

---

1 e4 e5 2 ♘f3 ♘c6 3 ♗b5 ♘f6 4 0-0 ♘xe4 5 d4 ♘d6 6 ♗xc6 dxc6 7 dxe5 ♘f5 8 ♕xd8+ ♔xd8 9 ♘c3 ♔e8

Challenging cosmic Berlin overlord, King Kram, in his favourite line is an offence normally punishable by death.

Question: Is a blitz game really as worthy as an annotated slow game?

Answer: Actually, believe it or not, blitz and rapid games can be more instructive, since they often exude a clearer flow than games from the torturously slow time controls, which sometimes come off with a disembodied feel of fits and starts. The reason: in rapid and blitz, we don't have enough time to overthink the positions and often pick the simplest (and often best!) moves. This game is one of the clearest examples of how to exploit an imbalance on one colour – and Kramnik manages to accomplish that in just five minutes, proving that a blitz game from a world champion can be more instructive than a slow game played by a lesser player (the rest of humanity!).

Question: Why move the king if White didn't give check?

Answer: It's only a matter of time until White does put a rook on d1, so there is no harm in moving the king early. In this case Black's king remains in the centre, rather than heading for c8 as we saw in Chapter Two (Game 15). On e8 the king helps cover sensitive infiltration points like d7 and f7, but also obstructs Black's development.

10 b3

After 10 h3 h5 11 ♖d1 ♗e7 12 ♗g5 ♗e6 13 b3 h4 14 ♔f1 a5 15 a4 ♖h5! Black equalized, V.Ivanchuk-S.Karjakin, Wijk aan Zee 2012.

10...♗b4 11 ♗b2

Natural, but I don't like it. White's best chance for an edge is to move his knight to e4 or e2.

11...♗xc3!

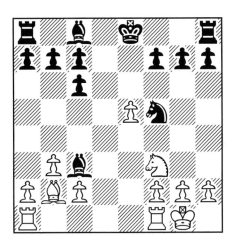

Question: Shouldn't this move be penalized with a "?!" instead?
Black hands over his single trump, the bishop pair.

Answer: True, but he gains something quite hidden: favourable opposite-coloured bishops.

Question: How does this benefit Black?

Answer: White's queenside pawns are placed on light squares, the same colour as Kramnik's remaining bishop. He will later go on to exploit this fact in vivid fashion.

12 ♗xc3 c5

Taking control over d4.

13 ♖ad1 h6

Now his bishop can rest on e6 without harassment.

14 h3 ♗e6 15 ♗b2 b6 16 ♖d2 ♘e7!

Heading for c6, the knight's optimum post.

17 c4

With hindsight, perhaps White should avoid this move which fixes all his pawns on the same colour as Black's remaining bishop – a fact that later haunts Howell.

17...♘c6 18 ♗c3 ♔e7 19 ♖fd1 a5!

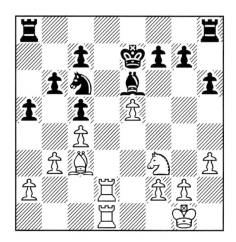

Inducing more fixed pawns on the light squares.

20 a4!?

Forcing an opponent into a disadvantageous negotiation is often the precursor to his future surrender. Now b3 is a perpetual endgame target. Maybe White should have avoided the move, although that would have opened up an entirely new set of problems by allowing ...a5-a4.

20...♖ad8 21 ♖xd8 ♖xd8 22 ♖xd8 ♔xd8 23 ♔f1?!

23 g4! was necessary to keep Black's bishop at bay.

23...♗f5!

Hello there! Black's bishop targets b3 and haunts White for the remainder of the game.

24 ♘e1

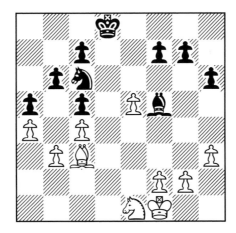

Exercise (planning): Find a good plan which improves Black's position.

Answer: 24...g5!

Artificially isolating e5. Now Black threatens to bring his king to e6 and pick off the pawn.

25 ♔e2 ♔e7 26 ♔e3 ♔e6 27 f4 g4!

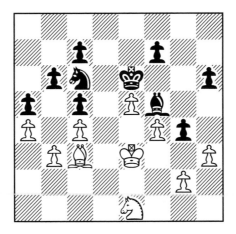

As the two armies collide and mesh, embroiled in a confused ganglion in the middle, Kramnik studiously continues his research on the pathway of converting base metal into gold. Sometimes a tangled geometric form, if rotated at just the right angle, suddenly takes on a clearly identifiable pattern. (Anyone who attempted Rubik's cube as a kid knows exactly what I am talking about.) After this seemingly imperceptible shift, the pattern comes into clear focus and in precise alignment. Understanding dawns as a new imbalance comes to the forefront: Black's king infiltrates the kingside light squares via f5 and White's position grows steadily worse without him seeming to make any meaningful mistakes. Such is Kramnik's magic.

28 hxg4 ♗xg4 29 ♘f3 ♗f5 30 ♘d2 ♘e7 31 ♔f3

Idea: g2-g4.

31...h5

Oh, no you don't!

32 ♘e4 ♗g4+!

This cunning move breaches the defences by aiming straight for White's structural underbelly: b3.

33 ♔f2 ♘f5?!

Safeguarding f7 against ♘g5+, but apparently this isn't necessary. The immediate 33...♗d1 works out well for Black.

34 ♘g5+ ♔e7 35 ♘e4?

He should block the bishop out with 35 ♘f3!, when Black would have a much harder time extracting a win.

35...♗d1! 36 ♘d2 ♔e6 37 ♔e1 ♗c2!

Black's bishop shakes in silent, malicious mirth at White's misfortune, as he harpoons and then tethers White's knight to the defence of b3. No path exists for White's king to expel the unbidden intruder, as Black's bishop holds snug, everlasting vigil on c2.

38 ♔e2 ♘h4 39 g3 ♘g6!

Clearing f5 for king infiltration. White's relief is clearly built upon sand, as a new strategic threat arises.

40 ♔f3 ♗d1+ 41 ♔e4 ♗c2+ 42 ♔f3 ♔f5

Despite temporarily occluded vision, Black's king gropes his way through the maze, nearing the exit to White's side of the board with each step.

43 ♘f1!?

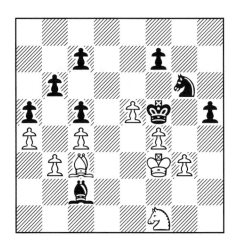

Complete desperation. The knight intercedes but fails to prevent the inevitable. White plunges forward and speculates with this regrouping, not because his "sac" looks so promising, but more because of an absence of reasonable options. His queenside gets dismantled and annihilated no matter which way he plays it. So the young, future-GM Howell reluctantly agrees to the coming ritual mutilation of his queenside as the gateway to adulthood.

Playing the waiting game is also hopeless; for example, 43 ♗b2 ♘f8 44 ♗a1 ♘e6 45 ♗b2 ♗d1+! 46 ♔f2 h4! 47 gxh4 ♔xf4 48 ♗c3 ♗c2 49 h5 ♔g5 and wins.

43...♗d1+!

Zwischenzug! The messianic bishop perseveres. A person is willing to undertake great hardship if he believes he does holy work. Kramnik obviously isn't going to fall for the cheapo 43...♗xb3?? 44 ♘e3+ ♔e6 45 f5+.

44 ♔f2 ♗xb3 45 ♘e3+ ♔e4 46 f5

Or 46 ♘d5 ♔d3 47 ♗a1 ♔xc4 48 ♘xc7 ♘e7 and White can resign.

46...♘xe5

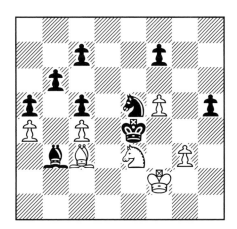

The slaughterhouse gutters clog and overflow with the warm, cloying blood of the newly dead, as White's pawns hang from their hooks in eviscerated ruin. It isn't easy to produce a strategic masterpiece in a five-minute game, yet Kramnik manages to pull it off.

47 ♗xe5 ♔xe5 48 ♘d5 ♗xc4 49 ♘xc7 ♗b3 50 ♘a8 ♗xa4 51 ♘xb6 ♗b5 52 ♔e3 a4 53 ♔d2 ♔xf5 54 ♔c3 ♔g4 55 ♘d5 ♔xg3 56 ♘f6 h4 57 ♘e4+ ♔g2 58 ♘xc5 h3 59 ♘e4 h2 60 ♘d2 h1♕ 61 ♔b4 ♕e1 62 ♔xb5 ♕xd2 63 ♔xa4 f5 0-1

Game 35
V.Kramnik-T.Radjabov
Linares 2003
French Defence

1 e4

As I mentioned earlier in the book, whenever Kramnik opens with 1 e4, he usually has some theoretical ambush ready for his opponent.

1...e6 2 d4 d5 3 ♘c3 ♘f6

The Classical French.

4 e5

4 ♗g5 is also very popular here.

4...♘fd7 5 f4 c5 6 ♘f3 ♘c6 7 ♗e3 cxd4

Radjabov defeated Kasparov earlier in the tournament with 7...a6 but avoided it here, logically anticipating that Kramnik had some dirty prep waiting for him. G.Kasparov-T.Radjabov, Linares 2003, continued 8 ♕d2 b5 9 a3 ♕b6 10 ♘e2!? c4!? (very rare; Black almost never releases the central tension like this in French) 11 g4! (now that the pressure is off his centre, Kasparov launches kingside play) 11...h5 12 gxh5 ♖xh5 13 ♘g3 ♖h8 14 f5! and Kasparov clearly came out of the opening on top, though he lost the game in the end.

8 ♘xd4 ♗c5 9 ♕d2 0-0 10 0-0-0

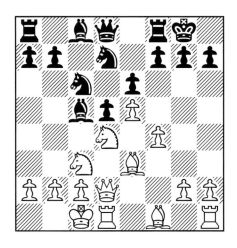

Our first major imbalances:

1. Opposite wing attacks.
2. White's e5-point gives him a space advantage.

> **Question:** It seems to me this is risky for White,
> since he castles into an open c-file. Correct?

Answer: Well, the truth is, it's risky for both sides in any opposite wing castling situation. It's true that Black has the open c-file, but White's extra space is a factor which nourishes all attacks.

10...a6 11 ♕f2!?

A sideline.

Question: What is White's point?

Answer: He wants to play ♗d3, but to do so immediately hangs d4. So he switches his queen to f2 to enable the plan.

11 h4 is the main line; for example, 11...♘xd4 12 ♗xd4 b5 13 ♖h3 b4 14 ♘a4 ♗xd4 15 ♕xd4 f6 16 ♕xb4 fxe5 17 ♕d6 ♕f6 18 f5!! ♕h6+ 19 ♔b1 ♖xf5 20 ♖f3 ♖xf3 21 gxf3 ♕f6 22 ♗h3 ♔f7 23 c4! and White had a powerful initiative for the pawn, G.Kasparov-N.Short, Amsterdam 1994.

11...♘xd4

Black seeks to reduce the pressure through exchanges.

12 ♗xd4 ♕c7 13 ♗d3 b5?!

A natural move but an inaccuracy.

Question: What other move does Black have then?

Answer: GM Neil McDonald suggested 13...♗xd4!, "dragging the white queen to the centre and only after 14 ♕xd4 should he start his counterplay with 14...b5."

14 ♕h4!

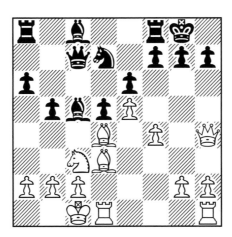

Kramnik immediately takes advantage of Radja's lapse, and forces a weakness around the black king's perimeter.

14...h6

14...f5 15 ♘e2, intending g2-g4, soon opens the g-file.

15 ♘e2 f6

Question: Why does Black voluntarily weaken his kingside?

Answer: He needs counterplay along the f-file. If he refuses to take action, then Kramnik simply pries him open with g2-g4-g5.

16 ♕g4!

Provoking ...f6-f5.

16...♗xd4

Complying with 16...f5 looks quite rough for Black after 17 ♕g6 ♕b6 18 ♗xc5 ♘xc5 19 g4, whose counterplay arrives too slowly.

17 ♘xd4 ♘c5 18 ♕g6!

The prima ballerina scoops up the roses tossed to her on stage by the audience after her performance. Kramnik forces one favourable imbalance or another:

a) Good knight versus bad bishop.

b) Black plays ...f6-f5 and allows the line opening g2-g4!.

18...♘xd3+

Acquiescing to the inferior minor piece. Once again if 18...f5 then 19 g4!.

19 ♖xd3

A new imbalance in White's favour: good knight versus bad bishop.

19...♕c4?

Sending the queen on a fool's errand. The queen reinvents herself in Madonna-like fashion, by taking on the persona of an attacker. Perhaps Black should consider abbreviating the conversation on the queenside and look to his own king.

> **Question:** Why not just take on e5?

Answer: White picks off a pawn after 19...fxe5 20 ♘xe6 ♗xe6 21 ♕xe6+ ♔h7 22 ♕xe5 ♕c4 23 b3 ♕xf4+ 24 ♕xf4 ♖xf4 25 ♖xd5. Instead, 19...♕f7 20 ♕xf7+ ♔xf7 21 ♖e1 may well be Black's best hope, though it isn't a very tempting option against one of the greatest technical players of his generation.

20 ♖hd1!

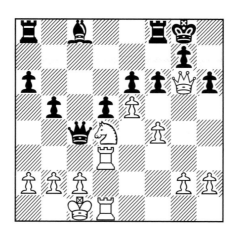

Welcome! Please, be my guest. Come into a2. Black's troop morale suddenly spirals into the gutter, since taking a2 isn't an option after all.

20...♖a7

Question: Okay, I give up. Why didn't Black take
on a2 if he bothered to attack it last move?

Answer: The point is Black shouldn't have attacked it in the first place if he couldn't take it. Here is why: 20...♕xa2? 21 ♖a3! ♕c4 22 ♖c3! ♕a2 23 ♖g3! (not 23 ♖c7? ♕a1+ 24 ♔d2 ♕a5+ and White must mea culpa the rook back with 25 ♖c3) 23...♕a1+ 24 ♔d2 ♕a5+ 25 ♔e2 ♖f7 26 exf6 yields White a powerful attack.

21 ♔b1 ♕c7

An admission that his 19th move was a waste of time.

22 f5!

The joyful, advanced pawns are coins tossed high in the air by a man who just struck it rich.

22...♕b6

Black's horrible non-options:

a) 22...♕xe5 drops an exchange to 23 ♘c6.

b) 22...♕f7 23 ♕xf7+ ♖axf7 24 fxe6 ♖e7 25 exf6 ♖xf6 26 ♖e1 and now, if Black decides to regain his pawn with 26...♗xe6 27 ♖de3 ♔f7, his bishop is glued to e6 in an eternal pin. White can march his king up somehow on the queenside and transpose to a winning king and pawn ending.

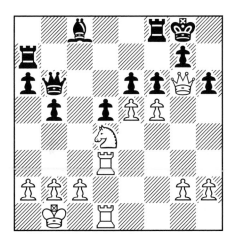

Clearly matters degenerated for Black far worse than a mere bad bishop or space issues. His king now grows fearful of the new, more terrible imbalance: the ominous build-up around him. Find one powerful move and misfortune falls upon Black with stuttering frequency.

Answer: Target h6.

23 ♖h3!

White's attack is now out of control.

23...fxe5 24 ♖xh6! ♖f6

Nor will Black survive 24...exd4 25 ♕h7+ ♔f7 26 f6!.

25 ♕e8+ ♖f8

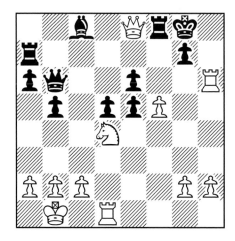

White's pieces flow, each move modelled by the move preceding it. Black's king sits alone, lost in thought, an old man on the park bench reflecting on his life, now oblivious to the passage of time.

Answer: Deflection. The temporary rook sacrifice severs the lonely king's thin thread to life with a razor.

26 ♖h8+!

Black's king is the squash ball; White's attackers are racket and wall.

26...♔xh8 27 ♕xf8+ ♔h7 28 ♘f3!

Game over. The knight reaches g5 as the old black king approaches fate with slow, palsied steps.

28...♕c7 29 fxe6 e4 30 ♘g5+ ♔h6 31 h4 ♔h5

The wobbly king, having indulged in too many drinks at the bar, now eyes the karaoke machine on h5 and tries his hand as a lounge singer.

32 ♕f5

There are a million other wins here.

32...g6 33 g4+ ♔xh4 34 ♖h1+ ♔g3

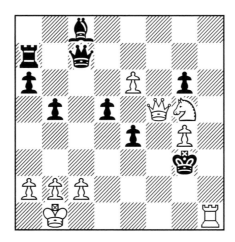

The penitent appears before the magistrate, having already made a de facto admission of guilt from the fact that he sits on g3.

35 ♖g1+ ♔h4 36 ♕f6 1-0

Black's king, licked by searing pain, finally lies down to die, with no more fight left in him.

Game 36
V.Kramnik-V.Anand
Wijk aan Zee 2007
Catalan Opening

---

1 d4 ♘f6 2 c4 e6 3 g3 d5 4 ♗g2 ♗e7 5 ♘f3 0-0 6 0-0 dxc4 7 ♕c2 a6 8 ♕xc4 b5 9 ♕c2 ♗b7 10 ♗d2

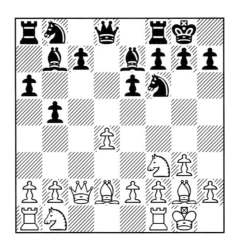

Question: This move seems awfully passive. What is White's point?

Answer: Black always strives for the ...c7-c5 break. If he plays ...♘d7 in preparation, then White plans to slip in the annoying ♗a5!. White's move also accomplishes a couple of other things: he opens up options for b2-b4, with an eternal clamp over Black's ...c7-c5, and also clears c1 for a rook.

10...♖a7

Alternatives are 10...♗e4, 10...♘c6 and 10...♘bd7.

Question: Now I accuse Black of the
same passivity. Why develop the rook to a7?

Answer: There are two ideas behind the move:

1. Black plans to meet ♖c1 with ...♗e4, covering the sensitive c7-point.

2. Black clears a8 for his queen, to exert pressure down the a8-h1 diagonal.

11 ♖c1 ♗e4 12 ♕b3 ♘c6

Preventing ♗a5 but at the obvious cost of blocking the ...c7-c5 break. Instead, B.Gelfand-P.Harikrishna, Bermuda 2005, saw 12...♘bd7 13 ♗a5 ♕b8 14 ♕e3 and again Black has yet to achieve the freeing ...c7-c5.

13 e3 ♕a8!

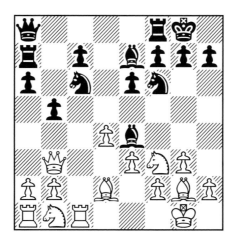

Dual purpose:

1. Black adds force to his control over e4 and the h1-a8 diagonal in general.
2. Black clears the way for ...♖c8.

14 ♕d1

> *Question:* Can White pick off Black's powerful light-squared
> bishop now, or at least chase it away with 14 ♘c3 - ?

Answer: The bishop remains on the long diagonal after the in-between move 14...♘a5 15 ♕d1 ♗b7.

14...♘b8!?

Steinitz and Petrosian would be impressed. The sand-coloured flounder lies on the sea floor on b8, camouflaged and invisible to predators.

> *Question:* Why undevelop?

Answer: Black's knight, having completed its job of provoking e3, now clears the way for the ...c7-c5 break.

15 ♗a5 ♖c8

> *Question:* Is White's last move pointless? Black can repeat the position af-
> ter 15...♘c6.

Answer: It doesn't repeat the position. White would then gain a tempo with 16 ♗e1!, clearing the path for ♘bd2 and ♘b3.

16 a3

Discouraging ...b5-b4.

16...♗d6 17 ♘bd2 ♗d5 18 ♕f1

To unpin his f3-knight, while the queen removes herself from the d-file in case the centre opens.

18...♘bd7 19 b4!

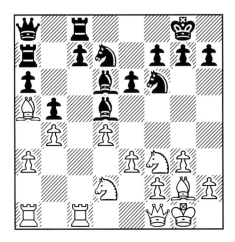

> *Question:* I realize White just slammed the door shut
> on ...c7-c5, possibly for good, but he voluntarily imprisoned
> his own bishop on a5 in the process. Was this wise?

Answer: This is where strategic intuition comes in. Kramnik reasons that the bishop gets self-trapped, yet remains active. As the game goes on, he is proven correct in this decision.

19...e5!?

White clamped down on the c5-break, so Anand goes for the e5-break instead. Unfortunately, it fails to help and possibly even makes Black's position worse, since White soon achieves the superior pawn majority.

> *Question:* What is the alternative?

Answer: To remain passive – but this just isn't in Anand's nature. My son drives his Honda Civic as if it were a Maserati. If I owned a Maserati, I would probably drive it like a Honda Civic! It's difficult to change one's inner nature. We are who we are.

> *Question:* Wouldn't 19...♘b8, intending ...♘c6 next,
> make White pay for his last move?

Answer: In that case Kramnik foresaw the trick 20 ♗b6! ♖b7 21 ♗c5, when White retains a mild bind, while rerouting his formally imprisoned bishop.

20 dxe5 ♗xe5!?

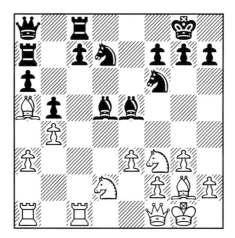

Anand will later regret this risky decision to hand Kramnik the bishop pair. In doing so, two imbalances arise:

1. Two bishops versus bishop and knight.
2. Kingside versus an inferior queenside majority.

> **Question:** Why did he give up the bishop pair? It seems like he has a perfectly good position if he recaptures with the knight.

Answer: Black's position remains somewhat passive at the end of the line 20...♘xe5 21 ♘xe5 ♗xe5 22 ♖a2!. So Anand chose the riskier, but more active route.

21 ♘xe5 ♘xe5

> **Question:** Shouldn't he swap on g2? It follows the principle of eliminating one of the opponent's bishops when he has the bishop pair.

Answer: It follows the principle but is incorrect, since Black gets clamped after 21...♗xg2?! 22 ♕xg2 ♕xg2+ 23 ♔xg2 ♘xe5 24 ♗b6! ♖b7 25 ♗d4 ♘fd7 26 f4, when Black rapidly loses ground and must nurse a chronic ailment on the c-file as well.

22 f3!

Dual purpose:

1. Principle: *Don't allow an exchange of bishops if you own the bishop pair.*
2. White prepares to gain ground by activating his majority with e3-e4.

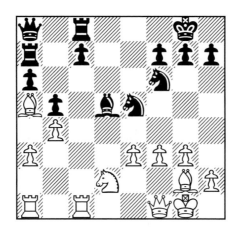

22...♘c4 23 ♘xc4 ♗xc4 24 ♕f2 ♖e8

He still can't break with 24...c5?? due to 25 ♗b6, when White's crafty a5-bishop merely played stupid to catch Black with his guard down.

25 e4

Black's majority remains in stasis due to his inability to engineer ...c7-c5.

25...c6

To allow the sleeping a7-rook into the game. The obvious trouble is that the move is also a big concession, allowing White's once imprisoned bishop to return to society.

26 ♖d1

A new imbalance: White's dark-squared bishop – not so out of play – controls d8, meaning that Black has difficulties challenging the d-file.

26...♖d7 27 ♖xd7 ♘xd7 28 ♖d1 ♕b7 29 ♖d6 f6

Houdini gives 29...f5, but Black looks poorly placed after the simple 30 ♕d4.

30 f4 ♖e6 31 ♖d2 ♖e7 32 ♕d4 ♘f8 33 ♕d8 ♖d7!

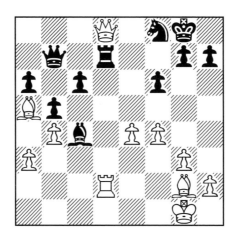

Principle: *When under pressure, ease your pain by forcing exchanges.* Anand defends well, remaining stirred, not shaken. Finally, the armies merge and collide in osmosis at the point where the river meets the ocean, and the fresh and salt water converge.

34 ♖xd7 ♕xd7 35 ♕xd7 ♘xd7 36 e5!

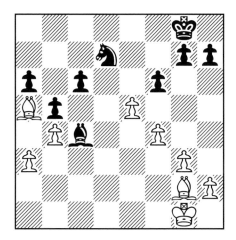

The rich loathe paying taxes even more than the middle class or poor. In this case Kramnik is willing to sac a pawn temporarily in order to activate his light-squared bishop, who suddenly pops out like a paper cut-out doll in a children's book.

White's move may be even stronger than 36 ♗h3 ♘f8 37 ♗c8 ♗d3 38 e5 fxe5 39 fxe5 ♗c4, when White wins a pawn but Black manages to erect a blockade on the light squares.

36...fxe5 37 ♗xc6 ♘f6 38 ♗b7!

Avoiding Anand's trap. Black should draw after 38 fxe5? ♗d5!.

38...exf4 39 gxf4 ♘d5 40 ♔f2 ♘xf4 41 ♔e3 g5

Konstantin Landa suggested the superior 41...♘e2! 42 ♗xa6 (not 42 ♗f3? ♘c3 43 ♔d4 ♘b1 with a probable draw) 42...♔f7, although White still has a shot at winning after 43 ♔d2! intending a3-a4.

42 ♗xa6 ♔f7

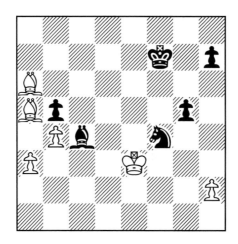

Exercise (combination alert): White to play
and win a pawn:

Answer: Pin. Kramnik methodically continues to debone the chicken on b5.

43 a4!

In a bizarre twist of fate, the players switched pawn majorities! White's tethered bishops suddenly break free, overpowering their overseer on b5 and strangling him with his own whip. Now White's queenside pawn majority, coupled with his bishop pair, is decisive.

43...♔e7 44 ♗xb5 ♗xb5 45 axb5 ♔d7 46 ♔e4

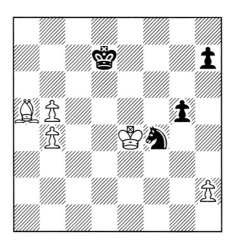

New imbalances:

1. Superior bishop versus ungainly knight.

2. King position for White. Black's kingside pawns are in grave danger. If he can manage to swap off his two for White's one on the kingside, he draws – but he simply can't manage this feat. Kramnik's technique is just scarily good.

46...♘e2

The vagrant knight, despite bleeding from multiple cuts and abrasions received in battle, fights on oblivious to the pain. He continues to loiter just outside the kingside, hoping for a way to eliminate White's h-pawn when there is none to be found.

47 ♗b6 g4 48 ♗f2!

Nyet! Of course Kramnik prevents ...g4-g3.

48...♘c3+ 49 ♔f5 ♘xb5

Anand fights on with noble but, in the end, hopeless valour. The underdog tortoise, unfazed, plods on hoping to catch sight of the rabbit. Unfortunately, in this particular children's story, the rabbit wins the race. Black's knight is no match for White's sweeping bishop, who plays important roles on both sides of the board.

50 ♔xg4 ♔e6 51 ♔g5 ♔f7

Black's king hides in the closet and strives to quiet his ragged breath as he listens for the intruder's footsteps coming from f5.

52 ♔f5!

It's all over. The b-pawn costs Black a knight and, to add insult, White remains with the correct colour h-pawn and bishop.

52...♔e7 53 ♗c5+ 1-0

If Black's king heads queenside, he loses his h-pawn; if he goes the other way he loses his knight.

Game 37
V.Kramnik-P.Leko
Nice (blindfold rapid) 2009
Semi-Slav Defence

It's a bit depressing to reflect upon the fact that Kramnik and Leko play better blind-folded than most IMs do sighted.

1 d4 ♘f6 2 c4 e6 3 ♘f3 d5 4 ♘c3 c6 5 ♗g5 h6 6 ♗h4 dxc4 7 e4 g5 8 ♗g3 b5 9 ♗e2 ♗b7 10 0-0

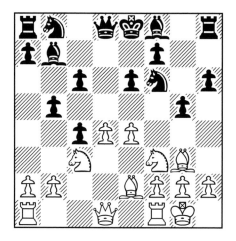

Imbalance number one: White sheds a pawn for a development lead, central control and attacking chances. To players who don't know or play this position, this line of the Semi-Slav may seem like an alien message sent to earth, there only for the government experts to decrypt and interpret. Kramnik deviated from 10 h4 which he played against Akopian in Chapter Two (see Game 14)

10...♘bd7 11 ♘e5

Question: Why does White move the same piece twice in the opening?

Answer: This is White's main line. He clears the way for his f-pawn to move forward and also covers against ...♘h5.

Question: If White leads in development, then shouldn't he
be looking to create trouble in the centre with 11 d5 - ?

Answer: That is a secondary line. Black's position is solid enough to withstand such a direct assault. For example, 11...cxd5 12 exd5 ♘xd5 13 ♘xb5 a6 14 ♘bd4!? (or 14 ♘d6+ ♗xd6 15

♗xd6 ♕b6 16 ♗a3 ♘f4 and Black's pieces are tremendously active, K.Koczo-V.Erdos, Budapest 2004) 14...♗g7 15 ♗xc4 0-0, when Black's control over d5 compensates him for his slightly loose kingside structure, A.Shirov-V.Kramnik, Frankfurt (rapid) 1996.

11...♗g7 12 ♘xd7

Kramnik refuses to speculate with the sharp line 12 ♘xf7!? ♚xf7 13 e5 ♘d5 14 ♘e4 ♚e7 15 ♘d6 ♕b6 16 ♗g4, even if White's attack compensates for his piece investment, V.Topalov-V.Kramnik, Wijk aan Zee 2008.

12...♘xd7 13 ♗d6

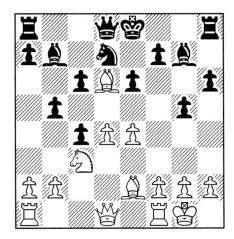

We reach a sharp, theoretically disputed position where, so far, Black has been holding up well.

13...a6

Other moves:

a) 13...♗f8 14 ♗xf8 ♖xf8 15 e5 ♕b6 16 ♘e4 0-0-0 17 ♘d6+ ♚b8 18 b3 c3 19 a4 f6 20 axb5 ♘xe5! is okay for Black, S.Ernst-A.Giri, Dutch Championship, Boxtel 2011.

b) 13...e5?! 14 ♗g4! exd4 15 e5! and e5-e6! is a scary threat. Black seems to be in big trouble; White's attack and initiative are worth more than a piece, E.Najer-V.Shinkevich, Moscow 2010.

14 a4 e5 15 ♖e1!?

Deviating from his previous games in this line:

a) 15 ♗g4 exd4 16 e5! (as mentioned in the previous note, White's attack is ferocious) 16...c5! (Black declines the offer) 17 ♖e1 ♘xe5 18 ♗xe5 0-0 19 ♗xg7 ♚xg7 20 ♘e2 f5 21 ♗h5 f4, when Black's wall of pawns compensated for the piece, V.Kramnik-L.Aronian, Wijk aan Zee 2008.

b) 15 d5 c5 16 b4! ♕b6 17 bxc5 ♘xc5 18 ♗xc5 ♕xc5 19 axb5 axb5 20 ♖xa8+ ♗xa8 21 ♕a1 0-0 22 ♕a5 ♖b8 23 ♖b1 and Black's b-pawn falls, after which he fights for equality, V.Kramnik-S.Karjakin, Nice (blindfold rapid) 2008.

15...♕f6

Double attack on d6 and d4.

16 ♗a3

16 dxe5 ♘xe5 only helps Black, who threatens ...♖d8.

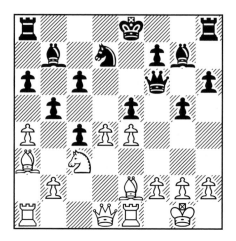

16...♗f8

> *Question:* Can't Black get away with 16...exd4,
> planning to castle queenside?

Answer: I don't think he will make it that far: 17 e5! ♕g6 (17...♘xe5 18 ♕xd4 ♖d8 19 ♕a7 ♖d7 20 ♗g4 wins) 18 e6! and Black is in deep trouble since he can't take the e-pawn either way.

17 ♗g4 ♖d8 18 axb5 axb5 19 ♗xf8 ♔xf8 20 ♗xd7

Imbalance number two: knight versus bishop. In this game White's knight proves to be a better attacker than the bishop is a defender.

20...♖xd7 21 dxe5 ♕e6!

If Black swaps queens with 21...♖xd1 22 exf6 ♖xe1+ 23 ♖xe1, he has a hard time developing his rook.

22 ♕h5 ♕xe5

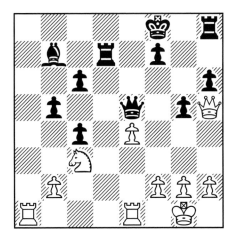

Exercise (planning): Black is up a pawn and looks to be consolidating next move with ...♔g7. We can't let him do that. White utilizes his only trump in the position, his development lead, to launch an attack. Find the attacking plan.

Answer: Open lines and create confrontation while ahead in development. After Kramnik's move the assault is renewed with élan.

23 f4!

Black can't see the enemy yet feels his presence, the way you can't see the fly in the room yet hear the incessant buzzing.

23...♕xf4

Question: Why must Black accept the offer. Why not refuse with 23...♕e7 - ?

Answer: White pries Black open and attacks anyway after 24 e5 gxf4 25 e6 fxe6 26 ♕e5 ♖h7 27 ♘e4!.

24 ♖f1 ♕e5!?

Question: Why does Leko allow Kramnik to double rooks with tempo?

Answer: He wants his queen near his king on e6. Instead, Black may yet hold on after 24...♕c7 25 ♖f6 b4 26 ♖xh6! ♖g8 27 ♘a4, but the odds are against him doing so.

25 ♖f5 ♕e6 26 ♖af1 ♔g7?

Leko may have survived after the correct 26...♖h7!.

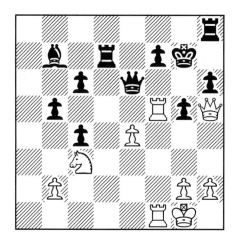

While in public, a wanted criminal must strive to act naturally and avoid undue motion which hints at the furtive.

> ***Exercise (planning):*** Black's last was a mistake which allowed White's attack to take seed and grow. How would you accomplish this feat?

27 ♘e2?

Kramnik brings his knight into the game but the wrong way.

Answer: 27 e5! was correct, after which Black's defences grow lifeless and wither like brown winter's grass. For example, 27...♕g6 (27...c5, hoping to keep the knight out of e4, fails to 28 ♖f6 ♕e8 29 h4! and White reaches his goal through a twisting tunnel of secret conduits hidden in the walls: 29...gxh4 30 ♕g4+ wins) 28 ♕e2 ♖f8 29 ♘e4, when White's attack is out of control.

27...♖f8

The computers like 27...c5.

28 ♘g3

The homing pigeon flies directly to her destination: the kingside light squares e4, f5 and h5. Note the gigantic activity discrepancy:

1. Knight versus a bishop that remains sealed in the air-tight container on b7.

2. White's rooks press hard down the open f-file, while Black's are destined to remain in positions of humble servitude.

28...c5?

28...♕g6 was his last chance.

29 ♖f6!

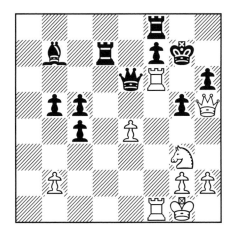

The rooks raise their glasses and toast Black's queen across the table. Good judgment: White's queen and knight team easily run down Black's king.

29...♕xf6 30 ♖xf6 ♔xf6 31 ♕xh6+ ♔e7 32 ♘f5+ ♔e8

The frightened king curls up like a slug.

33 ♘d6+ ♔e7 34 e5

Threatening mate in one.

34...♖g8 35 ♕f6+ ♔f8

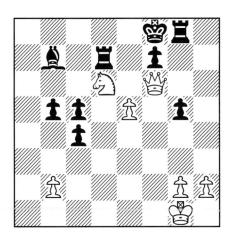

The trembling, purse-snatching, black king runs down the street with the outraged cries of the police and the well-dressed white queen behind him.

> ***Exercise (combination alert):*** One strong
> move and you push Black off the edge. How?

Answer: Pin/overload.

36 e6! 1-0

Police investigators always research the victim's phone records. Who a person associates with tells a lot about them. In this case, Black's king's demise must be directly attributed to the sluggish black rooks, who wilfully shirked community participation.

> ## Game 38
> ## **V.Kramnik-A.Grischuk**
> ## Tal Memorial, Moscow 2012
> ## *King's Indian Defence*

1 ♘f3 ♘f6 2 c4 g6 3 ♘c3 ♗g7 4 e4 d6 5 d4 0-0 6 ♗e2 e5 7 0-0 ♘c6 8 d5 ♘e7 9 b4

The battle begins. The world's leading exponent of the 9 b4 bayonet King's Indian challenges the leading KID player of his time.

9...♘h5 10 g3 f5 11 ♘g5 ♘f6 12 ♗f3 c6 13 ♗g2!

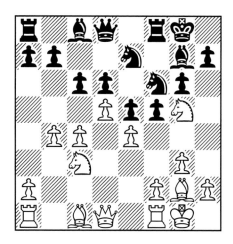

The bishop's gyrations prove to be no more than a nervous twitch. 13 ♗g2 was a new move in this position. The will to train and prepare takes precedence over the will to win over the board. If you recall, Kramnik played 13 ♗a3 in Chapter One (see Game 11). Kramnik confessed that he simply forgot his prep against Giri and had intended his novelty 13 ♗g2! instead. In this game he remembers.

13...h6

> **Question:** What is White's idea?

Answer: Kramnik explained after the game in the press conference: if Black plays 13...cxd5 14 exd5! then ...e5-e4 doesn't arrive with tempo.

14 ♘e6 ♗xe6 15 dxe6

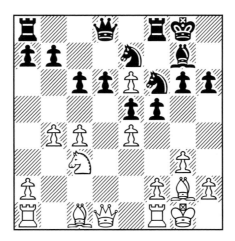

15...♘xe4

> ***Question:*** Can Black try 15...f4 - ?

Answer: White won't take it. Instead, he simply piles on the weak d6-pawn by 16 ♕d3! with a clear advantage.

16 ♘xe4 fxe4

Black is all set for White to recapture on e4. He will then play ...d6-d5 with tempo. But Kramnik's shocking next move throws Grischuk off.

17 b5!

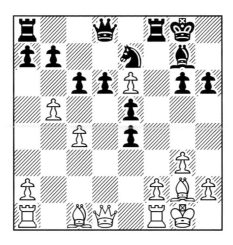

17...♖f6

> *Question:* Why not 17...cxb5 followed by ...d6-d5 when White recaptures?

Answer: White has no intention of recapturing. He continues 18 ♖b1! b6 (18...bxc4? fails to 19 ♖xb7 d5 20 ♖d7 ♕e8 21 ♗a3 ♗f6 22 ♗xe7 ♗xe7 23 ♕xd5) 19 cxb5 d5 20 ♗a3! ♗f6 21 ♕b3!, applying unbelievable pressure upon Black's centre.

> *Question:* What about the plan of planting
> a knight on d4, starting with 17...♘f5 - ?

Answer: Black still looks like he will be under some pressure in the following opposite-coloured bishops position: 18 ♗xe4 ♕e8 19 bxc6 bxc6 20 ♖b1 ♘d4 21 ♗e3 ♖c8 22 ♗xd4 exd4 23 ♖e1!, when White has the superior bishop, and his e-pawn is still alive and well. (23...♕xe6?? 24 ♗d5! wins the queen.)

18 ♗xe4 ♖xe6

> *Question:* Why isn't Black going for 18...d5 - ?

Answer: White ♗a3! theme repeats. For example, 19 cxd5 cxd5 20 ♗a3! ♖xe6 21 ♗xe7 ♖xe7 22 ♗xd5+ ♔h7 23 ♗e4 ♕xd1 24 ♖fxd1 and I don't think Black will hold this ending, despite the opposite-coloured bishops.

19 ♕a4!?

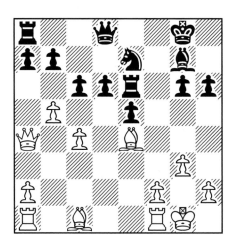

Kramnik said: "White has a strong initiative. It is unpleasant to play with Black."

19...d5 20 ♖d1 ♔h7

GM Mikhail Golubev suggests 20...d4. I'm not a big fan of Black's game after 21 ♗a3, but his suggestion may still be Black's best hope.

21 cxd5 cxd5

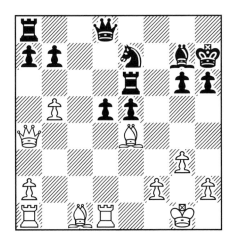

22 ♕b3!

Now d5 has Kramnik's undivided attention. Black's pieces, those outside the law and the dispossessed, gather round but are unable or unwilling to help out in the defence of the d-pawn. Grischuk says he expected 22 ♗a3?! ♕e8 23 ♗xe7 dxe4 24 ♗c5 a6!, when Black generates counterplay.

22...♖b6?

The mad rook isn't listening to anyone but the voices in his head. Challenging White on the queenside is a bit like the CEO of Cadbury Chocolate leading the national fight against tooth decay. Grischuk, not liking the directional course of recent events, hopes to confuse the issue, the way a defence attorney obfuscates when trying to defend an obviously guilty client.

Kramnik thought the text was a decisive error and suggested 22...♕d7, but even then White applies pressure after 23 ♗a3 d4 24 ♖ac1.

23 a4! a6

The puppy bites playfully at the intruder's ankle, which in no way stops or slows him down.

24 ♗a3

Black finds it impossible to flee from the jurisdiction of White's all-powerful bishops, who lay in wait like jealous rivals, plotting and watching an enemy from the shadows.

24...axb5 25 ♗xe7 ♕xe7 26 ♖xd5

Spasibo – thanks! The opposite-coloured bishops and control over e4 spell doom for Black. Kramnik relegates the enemy bishop to languish on the lower levels of the bureaucracy, devoid of influence on the position.

26...b4

Kramnik said 26...♕e6? fails to 27 a5!.

27 a5 ♕f7

The old queen shakes her fist at the defilers of her position with impotent rage. She fails to understand that revolution and overthrow are best left for the young and angry.

28 h4!

Threat: h4-h5. Old domestication fades, by now a dim memory, as the pawn goes feral in search of prey.

28...h5

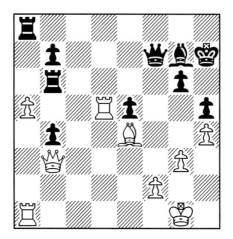

Black's last move was technically a blunder – though (*c'est la vie*) not really since everything else lost as well. One senses a dangerous disturbance coming, even if for the moment it remains hidden.

> *Exercise (combination alert):* How can White punch through the
> final barrier and force aside Black's final remnants of resistance?

Answer: Triple attack. 1) ♕xh5+; 2) a5xb6; and 3) ♖d7.

Kramnik's pieces suddenly well up and burp forth in ferocious activity, like a recently backed up drain spewing forth old ooze, long held prisoner in the pipes.

29 ♕d1! 1-0

Since 29...♖f6 30 ♖d7 ♕e6 31 ♖xb7 is completely hopeless for Black.

Chapter Five
Accumulating Advantages

For the last two decades, my wife Nancy and I, when walking our dogs, go by the house of some odd ex-hippy neighbours. We call them "The Vans", mainly because this family owns six rusted Volkswagen Vans, three bizarrely painted Beatles Yellow Submarine yellow, plus one each white, blue and green as emergency backup vans, just in case something goes wrong with the yellows. For two decades I always announced "Hi!" or raised a friendly arm in greeting. They always ignored us. We may as well have been residents of another dimension, unseen and unheard. For years, Nancy kept inquiring: "Why do you bother saying hello?" My determined response: "Mark my words woman. They *will* love us, whether they want to or not! I will bring them to their knees!" Well, I'm happy to finally report victory for House Lakdawala (under my visionary leadership) in our protracted greeting/non-greeting war. Just last month, father, mother, son and daughter "Van" finally capitulated by waving back at us. The moral: dogged persistence pays off for those with patience.

Kramnik's games in this chapter are reminiscent of our great triumph over "The Vans". Almost imperceptibly, Kramnik chips gradually away, increasing his strategic portfolio with this gain and that, until the accumulated weight forces collapse on opponents who never really feel threatened, until it is too late.

Game 39
V.Kramnik-A.Chumachenko
Gelendzhik 1987
Sicilian Defence

1 e4 c5 2 f4

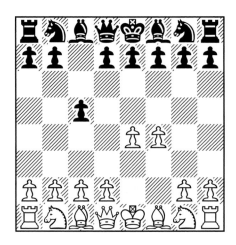

Question: Have we transposed to some kind of Reversed Dutch?

Answer: You can look at it that way. Technically this is an offbeat line of the Grand Prix Sicilian.

2...b6

A passive but playable reaction.

Question: How should Black set up against this line?

Answer: Most of the top players tend to favour the pawn sac 2...d5, intending 3 exd5 ♘f6! 4 ♗b5+ (4 c4 e6 5 dxe6 ♗xe6 6 ♘f3 ♘c6, A.Rosich Valles-G.Kasparov, Barcelona simul 1988, gives Black tremendous play for the bargain price of a pawn: he leads in development and owns a juicy hole on d4) 4...♗d7 5 ♗xd7+ ♕xd7 6 c4 e6 7 ♕e2 ♗d6 8 d3 0-0 9 dxe6 fxe6, when Black's massive development lead, and targets on d4 and f4 offered him excellent compensation, N.Short-G.Kasparov, Paris (rapid) 1990.

3 c4!?

Kramnik wants to get back to a Maróczy Bind-style Sicilian.

3...♗b7

Houdini suggests the inhuman 3...e5!? 4 d3 ♘c6 5 ♘f3 ♗d6, though Black's position strikes me as artificial and overly computery after the simple 6 f5.

4 ♘c3 e6

Question: Can Black goad White forward with 4...♘f6 - ?

Answer: It doesn't look so good for Black after 5 e5! ♘e4?, as White quickly exploits the unwise knight with 6 ♕f3! (GM Paul Motwani gives 6 ♘b1 an exclamation mark but I'm not so sure about it; e.g. 6...e6 7 ♘f3 g5! 8 d3 g4 9 dxe4 gxf3 10 ♕xf3 ♘c6 and Black gets some compensation for the pawn) 6...♘d6 7 ♕h3 ♘c8 8 ♗d3 e6 9 ♘f3 d6 10 0-0, when I don't trust Black's tangled position.

Another option is 4...♘c6 5 ♘f3 ♘d4!? (to mess up White's plans of transposing into an Open Sicilian) 6 d3 e6 7 ♗e3 ♘xf3+ 8 ♕xf3 ♘e7 intending ...♘c6. Now if White insists upon an Open structure, his centre may come under fire after 9 d4!? cxd4 10 ♗xd4 ♘f5 11 ♗f2 ♗b4 12 ♗d3 ♘d6, when ...f7-f5 is in the air.

5 ♘f3 d6 6 d4 cxd4 7 ♘xd4

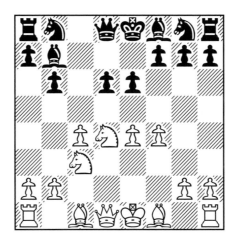

The sight of Kramnik on the white side of an Open Sicilian always strikes one as anomalous. As it happens, I utilize the Kramnik opening game-plan too: I generally open with the "safety first" 1 d4! or 1 ♘f3! in four out of five games, but then cunningly toss in the dubious but fun 1 e4?! (the question mark is an objective evaluation – the exclam is for the excellent practical chances White gets!) in the fifth game just to keep my opponents guessing. The really sad, strange part of it is that my score with 1 e4?! is actually higher than with 1 d4! and 1 ♘f3!. And yet, for some neurotic, Charlie Brown-like reason, I never muster the courage to reverse the ratio, but continue to play 1 e4?! in only 20% of my games! On the other hand, Kramnik recently said that in his heart he wanted to play 1 e4 versus Kasparov in their 2000 World Championship match, but found the theoretical challenge too daunting and played it safe with 1 d4 instead – which as we all know now, worked out just fine!

7...♘f6 8 ♗d3 ♘bd7 9 ♕e2

To cover against ...♘c5.

9...♗e7 10 0-0

Question: Isn't 10 e5 crushing?

Answer: It's too early. Black has 10...dxe5 11 fxe5 ♘c5! and White suddenly finds himself overextended.

10...0-0 11 &h1

Answer: The move is necessary. The trouble is that if White tries to save a tempo and avoid ♔h1, then he has trouble playing for e4-e5 tricks, because this opens the c5-square for Black's dark-squared bishop.

11...♕c7?!

It turns out he never gets time for ...a7-a6 later on, so the queen move leads to a tempo loss. The immediate 11...a6 was required.

12 f5!

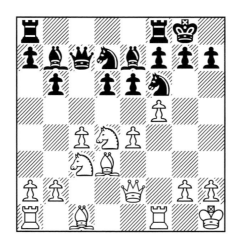

Question: Giving up the e5-square?

Answer: It is committal but strong. White hands over control of e5, correctly judging that his space advantage and attacking chances more than compensate.

12...e5?!

By closing the centre, Black eliminates his source of counterplay as well. It was crucial to maintain the central tension and risk 12...♘c5! 13 fxe6 fxe6 14 ♗c2 ♕d7 15 ♗d2! (15 b4?! ♘cxe4! exploits the back rank) 15...a5 16 ♘db5. I still dislike Black's position, which is under pressure, but it's better than what he got in the game.

13 ♘db5 ♕d8 14 ♘d5! ♘xd5

14...a6 15 ♘bc3 didn't look terribly tempting for Black either, yet might again be more accurate than the game continuation.

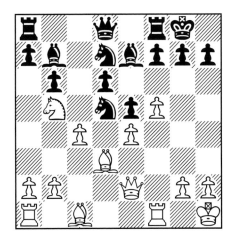

Exercise (planning): Which way should White recapture?
If he takes with his c-pawn he gets a bind. If he captures
with his e-pawn he clears e4 for his pieces.

Answer: Clearing e4 for his knight offers White a potent attack.

15 exd5! a6

Chasing the white knight exactly where it wants to go can't be so great, but I am out of defensive suggestions for Black, who may be strategically lost here, despite the computer's cheerful assessment.

Question: What happens if Black tries to muck things up in
the centre with 15...♘c5 16 ♗c2 a6 17 ♘c3 b5!? - ?

Answer: White simply ignores the provocation and proceeds toward Black's king with 18 ♖f3!, threatening to clear the way by f5-f6! next move, followed by a bishop sac on h7. I played around with the computer in this line and White got a crushing attack each time. Here is one brutal example: 18...♖e8 19 ♖h3 ♘d7 20 f6! ♘xf6 21 ♗xh7+! ♔f8 (or 21...♘xh7 22 ♕h5) 22 ♗f5 ♘g8 23 ♖h8 ♗f6 24 ♗h7 ♔e7 25 c5! dxc5 26 ♗e3 ♖c8 27 ♖d1! and Black gets obliterated.

Question: Why not just play the knight to f6?

Answer: On f6 the knight is vulnerable to g2-g4-g5. Still, I agree that your suggestion may be Black's best survival shot in the position: 15...♘f6! 16 g4! h6 17 ♘c3 ♘h7 18 ♗e3 and although Black lacks counterplay, White's slow build-up toward a kingside break won't be so easy here. He may even decide to switch over to the queenside in search of gains.

16 ♘c3 ♗f6

16...♘c5 17 ♗c2 b5 18 ♖f3! is the same old story.

17 ♗e3!

Planning to eliminate Black's knight if it dares to step to c5.

17...♖c8 18 ♘e4 ♘c5 19 ♗xc5!

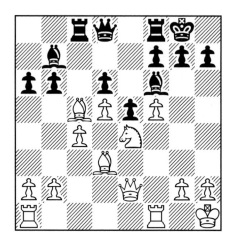

The bishop greets the knight with 99% welcome and 1% ill will. Kramnik's sigil: the formation of an attack, purely achieved through superior strategic build-up. Now White's knight rules from e4 and his pieces work in harmony, at familiar ease, like people in a small town who have known one another their entire lives.

> **Question:** I don't see why. Didn't Kramnik just give away all his dark squares? Black can establish a blockade with ...h7-h6.

Answer: Well, that is exactly what he tried in the game, but Kramnik blew him away anyway! I agree that it requires astonishing strategic prescience to see that he is indeed destined to smash through the dark-squared blockade attempt.

19...bxc5 20 ♕d2!

Here comes g2-g4-g5.

20...♖b8 21 a3!?

The positional player's disease: he gets seduced away from the kingside attack by the promise of safer, queenside speculation. Kramnik contemplates possible queenside manoeuvres with b2-b4, but he probably would be better off omitting such distractions.

21...a5 22 g4!

He changes his mind and returns to the attack.

22...h6

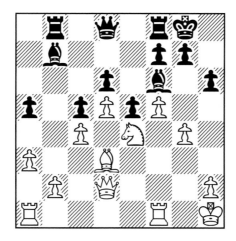

Black believes he speaks the language of evasion and stealth. He erected an iron-clad dark-square blockade. Or did he...? Matters are not so simple. Complex plots and subplots bubble just below the surface of the pot.

> ***Exercise (planning):*** How can White obliterate the
> blockade and smash through on the kingside?

Answer: Deflection. Kramnik gathers fragmentary bits of data and synthesizes his findings into a cohesive plan. His move wins by force – and yet *Houdini*, blissfully ignorant, claims the game is dead equal here.

23 h4!!

The unbeliever isn't swayed by the priest's benediction upon the h4-square. The visual power of such a move has a way of chiselling itself into the recesses of our minds.

23...♗xh4

The bishop tiptoes in but soon finds White's angry queen waiting for him with hands on hips. Have you ever had a dream so disorienting and so alien that you felt it was someone else's? Black's king may be in the throes of just such a dream.

24 f6!

Vlad the Impaler strikes. He squeezes the wet dish-rag and wrings the dirty water out.

24...♗c8

Motwani points out that, if 24...g5, "then White's queen would rapidly find her way to the h7-square after a few preparatory moves such as ♗c2, ♕d3 and ♘xg5". Not to mention plans like ♖f3, ♖h3, ♖xh4 and ♕xh6.

25 ♕h2 ♖b3?

Now he gets slaughtered. He had to try 25...g5! (the correct timing) 26 ♕e2! ♕d7 27 ♖g1

♖e8 28 ♖af1 ♖b3 29 ♘d2! ♖xd3 30 ♕xd3, when White still has some work ahead of him.
26 ♗c2!

Reminding Black that King Kram will have it all his way. Not 26 ♕xh4? ♖xd3, when g4-g5 is unplayable due to ...♖h3+.
26...♖xb2 27 ♕xh4 ♖xc2 28 g5!

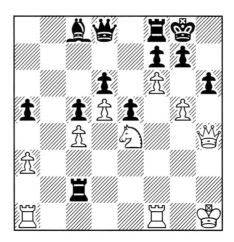

Malicious, vexed spirits circle Black's king. Now Black merely receives an inferior, truncated version of his original intent. No more rook check on h3 in this line.
28...♕d7

Black's queen is one of those annoying people who first announces what she will do rather than go ahead and just do it. For Black, there is good news and bad news. The good news is he saves himself from mate; the bad news: he must play an endgame a rook down, which isn't all that much better than getting mated! In such mathematized positions, it is permissible to declare absolute statements of right and wrong, so I will: Black is done for!
29 fxg7 ♕h3+

29...♔xg7 30 ♕xh6+ mates next move, as Black's king stares at the sky into nothing, with the unblinking eyes of the deceased.
30 ♕xh3 ♗xh3 31 gxf8♕+ ♔xf8 32 ♖f2 1-0

> ## Game 40
> ### Zso.Polgar-V.Kramnik
> World Junior Championship, Guarapuava 1991
> *Sicilian Defence*

1 e4 c5 2 ♘f3 ♘c6 3 d4 cxd4 4 ♘xd4 ♘f6 5 ♘c3 e5 6 ♘db5 d6 7 ♗g5 a6 8 ♘a3 b5 9 ♗xf6

This line tends to produce sharper positions than reached by 9 ♘d5 ♗e7 10 ♗xf6 ♗xf6 which we examined in Chapter One (see Game 7).

9...gxf6 10 ♘d5

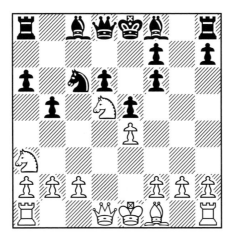

10...f5

It is imperative that Black achieve this freeing move before White has a chance to establish any kind of bind on f5. The main alternative is 10...♗g7, by which Black defers the ...f7-f5 break; for example, 11 ♗d3 ♘e7 12 ♘xe7 ♕xe7 13 0-0 0-0 14 c4 f5 15 ♕f3 ♕b7 16 ♕e2 b4 17 ♘c2 f4 18 b3 ♗e6 looked dynamically balanced, H.Nakamura-T.Radjabov, Wijk aan Zee 2012.

11 ♗d3

The main line. 11 c3, 11 exf5, and even the crazy 11 ♗xb5 are also played here.

11...♗e6

> *Question:* Isn't it more important for Black
> to get castled as quickly as possible?

Answer: Kramnik's move is the best one in the position. He prevents e4xf5 and threatens to plug d5 with a pawn by taking White's knight on that square.

12 c3 ♗g7

> *Question:* If the goal is to take on d5, then why doesn't
> Black get on with it and do so immediately?

Answer: The pesky tactics get in the way. It may be too early to take, since 12...♗xd5?! 13 exd5 ♘e7 14 ♘xb5 wins a pawn – though, oddly enough, Black actually has a pretty respectable score from this position. This may just be a statistical anomaly, or perhaps Black gets some compensation from White's lost time in grabbing the pawn. Nevertheless, I would be happy to grab such a pawn, even with the mediocre stats for White!

13 0-0 ♗xd5

As intended, Kramnik fills the d5-hole in with a white pawn.

14 exd5 ♘e7 15 ♕h5 e4

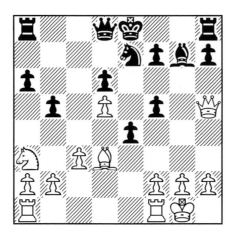

Black opens up the e5-square for his knight or bishop.

16 ♗c2 ♕a5

In a later game Kramnik diverged here with 16...0-0 17 ♖ae1 ♕c8 18 ♗b3 a5!? 19 ♕g5 (if 19 ♘xb5, then 19...a4 20 ♗d1 ♕c5 21 ♗e2 ♘xd5, intending 22 ♕xf5 ♘xc3!) 19...♕b7 20 f3 h6 21 ♕g3 a4 22 ♗c2 b4 23 ♘c4 ♕xd5 24 fxe4 ♕xc4 25 exf5, reaching an unclear mess, A.Shirov-V.Kramnik, Wijk aan Zee 2003.

17 ♖ae1 ♖a7 18 ♔h1

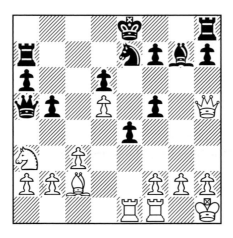

> *Exercise (combination alert):* White is all set to play f2-f3 and go after Black's king. But Black has play too. He can win a pawn here, not so much out of greed, but more to gain a strategic advantage. How?

Answer: Overload. Nothing is sacrosanct to the mind of the heretic. Black gives away his pride and joy to play for the superior minor piece.

18...♗xc3! 19 bxc3 ♕xa3

Kramnik banks on the fact that his knight will be better than White's bishop.

20 ♗b3 ♕b2 21 f3! ♖g8 22 g3 f4! 23 fxe4 fxg3! 24 ♖xf7

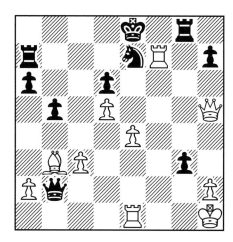

White continues to inflict damaging gashes and striations to Black's king cover, as the loose pawns ooze out like the entrails of a morally wounded gunshot victim. However, appearances deceive. Black is still okay.

24...♔d8

If you can't castle, then run!

25 ♕h6!

White's queen hovers menacingly over d6 and f8 with unspeakable, unspoken threats.

25...♕xc3 26 ♖f8+?

After this move White's position soon manifests as a shredded, besmirched memory of its former glory. Instead, 26 ♕xd6+! leads to perpetual check after 26...♔e8 27 ♖xe7+ ♖xe7 28 ♕b8+ ♔d7 29 ♕b7+ ♔d8.

26...♖xf8 27 ♕xf8+ ♔d7 28 ♖f1 ♕e3!

Forcing the queens off the board. Suddenly, the hostile's numbers dwindle until they lose all semblance of an intimidating force.

29 ♕f4 ♕xf4 30 ♖xf4 gxh2

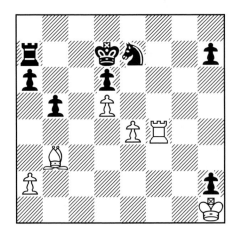

Question: Are Black's advantages enough for a win?

Answer: It won't be easy, but I think so:

1. The knight may reach the powerful e5-square.

2. Black holds ownership of a fast queenside pawn majority.

3. White's king is out of the loop, with no viable land routes and no short cuts to the queenside. He must endure the long sea voyage.

31 ♗d1 ♚c7! 32 ♖f7 ♚b6 33 ♖xh7 ♖c7 34 ♚xh2?!

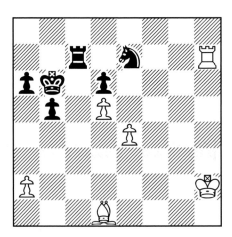

Exercise (combination alert): At long last White re-establishes material equality. Or did she...?

Answer: If you lack sufficient military might to overcome an enemy, then do the next best thing: Strike at the opponent economically.

34...♘xd5!

The beggar dares to break the white rook's gaze, as Black's rook and knight meet, exchange secret passwords, then go their separate ways. After this startling turn of events, the intended prey suddenly turns upon and attacks the stalking predator.

35 ♖xc7?!

White has a better shot at holding the game after 35 ♖h6! ♘c3 36 ♖xd6+ ♖c6! 37 ♖d2 ♘xe4, but would probably still lose, mainly because her king is a million miles away from the action.

35...♘xc7

White is busted:

1. Black is up a pawn.

2. White's king is off somewhere trying to find himself.

3. The a2- and e4-pawns are a coagulate of ugly polyps, both threatened with surgical removal.

4. Black's nimble knight remains the superior minor piece.

36 ♔g3 ♔c5 37 ♔f4 ♔d4 38 ♔f5 b4 39 ♗a4 a5 40 ♗c6 ♔c5 41 ♗d7 ♘b5 42 e5!

So close; Polgar (a non-Judit version!) eliminates one of her weaknesses.

42...dxe5 43 ♔xe5 ♘c3 44 ♗e6

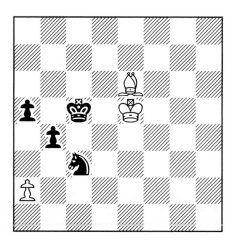

> ***Exercise (combination alert):*** Put White away.

Answer: White's bishop, all alone, is helpless against the two connected passers.

44...♘xa2!

On a breezy autumn day, the tree cherishes its lone, solitary leaf, clinging to life, determined not to join its brethren on the ground cover below.

45 ♗xa2

White's actors recite their lines, but where is the audience? Perhaps it is a poorly attended play?

45...a4 0-1

The pawns swarm the lone bishop like paparazzi giving chase to Kim Kardashian.

Game 41
V.Kramnik-S.Lputian
European Team Championship, Debrecen 1992
Queen's Gambit Declined

---

1 d4 ♘f6 2 c4 e6 3 ♘f3 d5 4 ♘c3 ♗e7 5 ♗f4 0-0 6 e3 c6

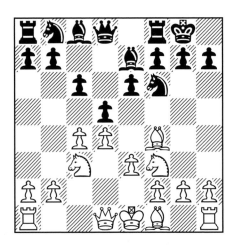

The ultra-passive, ultra-solid, old-school Orthodox Queen's Gambit Declined. I just finished a book on Capablanca, in which there are a load of games from this position.

Question: What do you suggest as a more dynamic option?

Answer: These days most GMs prefer 6...c5. Black willingly takes on an isolani to free his game. The positions can get incredibly sharp, and even opposite wings castling may arise; for example, 7 dxc5 ♗xc5 8 ♕c2 ♘c6 9 a3 ♕a5 10 0-0-0!? ♗e7 11 h4!?, when all hell breaks loose, G.Kasparov-R.Vaganian, Novgorod 1995.

7 ♕c2 ♘bd7 8 h3

To preserve his bishop from ...♘h5.

8...a6 9 ♖d1

Question: What is White waiting for? Why not the more natural ♗d3 - ?

Answer: Then Black would play ...d5xc4, gaining a tempo. Kramnik stalls the bishop development, hoping to outwait Black.

Question: Why did White play his rook to d1 and
not to c1, where it would be on an open file?

Answer: Because d1 is a more subtle square for the rook. It discourages ...c6-c5, since that move would open the rook's gaze on Black's queen on d8.

9...h6 10 a3

Both sides stubbornly wait for the other.

10...dxc4?!

Lputian loses patience and hands Kramnik a tempo. He should stubbornly continue stalling with 10...♖e8!?.

11 ♗xc4 ♘d5

Black seeks freedom through exchanges.

Question: Why not gain the tempo back with 11...b5 - ?

Answer: White stands clearly better after 12 ♗a2 ♗b7 13 e4 ♖e8 14 ♗b1! ♘f8 15 b4!, L.Psakhis-E.Pigusov, Novosibirsk 1993.

12 0-0!

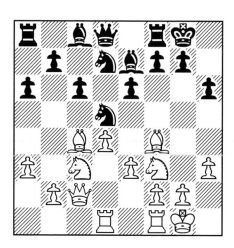

A brilliant strategic decision. What happens if a religion's god gets bored, and packs up and leaves his worshippers? In a new period of adjustment, White must now learn to live without his f4-bishop/god, and his blessings and wrathful curses.

> *Question:* Earlier you said White played h2-h3 to preserve his bishop.
> Now he calmly allows Black to swap off his knight for that same
> bishop, damaging his pawn structure to boot. Why?

Answer: Kramnik's move may seem like an erratic decision or even mad logic, but somehow he makes it work. Let's collect the raw data and build a composite sketch of White's hidden compensation from the transaction:

1. The newly altered structure puts Black in a vice grip on e5.

2. Black's knight was a defender of his king, who just got a little less safe with its departure.

3. White opened the e-file for his rook.

4. Black will have a painfully difficult time activating his pug-ugly light-squared bishop.

I will bet virtually every other GM in the world would have played the standard 12 ♗h2 at this point.

12...♘xf4

Who could resist such temptation? With the advantage of hindsight, maybe 12...♘xc3 should be considered.

13 exf4 ♛c7 14 ♘e5 ♘f6

> *Question:* Why can't Black just break free now with 14...c5 - ?

Answer: Perhaps he should have gone for it. Nevertheless, White's pieces generate tremendous activity after 15 d5! ♘xe5 16 fxe5 ♛xe5 17 ♖fe1 ♛c7 18 dxe6 ♗xe6 19 ♗xe6 fxe6 20 ♖xe6, when the knight is eager to jump onto the d5 (or even e4) square next.

15 ♗a2!

A queen/bishop battery to h7 is in the air.

15...♗d7

The crippled bishop hobbles forward a single square, with nowhere appealing to travel after that.

16 ♗b1 ♗e8?

He has to play something like 16...♖fd8, although Black's position still looks quite miserable after the scary 17 g4!.

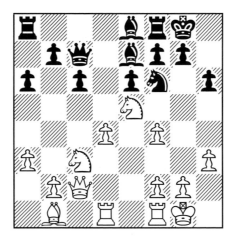

If one member rows off rhythm, the entire boat loses the race.

> *Exercise (combination alert):* Black's last move was an error.
> Kramnik finds an explosive idea, inciting a harsh chain of events
> which sink Black's position. Let's see if you can find it.

Answer: Breaking Black's iron blockade looks to be a vast undertaking, yet through a quirk
of strange geometry, Kramnik impossibly strikes at the most heavily protected sanctuary
on the board: d5.

17 d5!! ℤd8

No choice. Lputian realizes he just wandered into a minefield. He has no chance but to
keep perfectly still, since motion in any direction is fatal: 17...cxd5?? loses on the spot to the
crushing overload shot 18 ♘xd5!, and 17...exd5?? loses the same way.

18 ℤfe1!

Arriving at a new level of sangfroid. It takes staggering self-assurance to play such a
move and not break the tension.

18...♔h8

Black outguns his opponent 4:2 in his coverage of d5 – and yet, unbelievably, he still
can't move a muscle to take it.

19 dxe6 ℤxd1 20 ℤxd1 fxe6 21 ♘e4!

Threatening to remove the sole defender of the mate square, h7. Kramnik gets the all-
clear signal to launch a direct assault on Black's once safe king. The ramifications: White's
last move contradicts and debunks the theory of the black king's absolute safety.

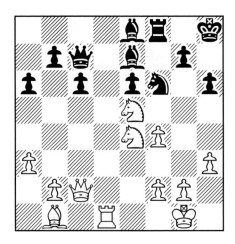

21...g6

Black weakens further to fence in his king, hoping to protect the grazing lamb from the wolf.

22 ♘c5!

Double attack on e6 and g6. White's game flows like a poem. We get the palpable feeling that with each move Black's pieces somehow diminish, while Kramnik's gather power.

22...♗xc5

22...♕c8 23 ♘xg6+! ♗xg6 24 ♕xg6 ♗xc5 25 ♕xh6+ ♔g8 (the escaped prisoner squats in the dark sewer, hoping to elude the guards above) 26 ♕g5+! ♔h8 27 ♕xc5 leaves White two pawns up with a crushing position.

23 ♕xc5 ♖g8

Or 23...♕g7 24 ♖d6 ♗f7 25 ♕a7 and Black collapses.

24 ♗a2!

Dance! Kramnik unexpectedly switches targets.

24...♔g7

The alternatives are just as hopeless: 24...♗f7 25 ♕d6! and the overload trick wins material, while after 24...♘d5 25 ♗xd5! exd5 White exploits a pin with 26 ♖xd5!.

25 ♗xe6 ♖f8

Within the vivid mandala of torment, Black's game reminds us of the Edvard Munch painting of that famously anguished figure clutching his head.

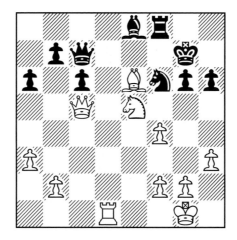

Exercise (combination alert): Black's haunted castle has many entrances but few exits. White can end the game in style. How?

Answer: Interference/zwischenzug. Kramnik's last move seals the stone lid of Black's sarcophagus.

26 ♘d7! 1-0

After 26...♘xd7 (Black is unable to master the compulsion to strangle the smirking d7-knight) 27 ♖xd7+! ♕xd7 (27...♗xd7 28 ♕e7+ mates) 28 ♗xd7 ♗xd7 29 ♕d4+, the remaining corpses are carelessly tossed in a trench, left to rot.

Game 42
E.Rozentalis-V.Kramnik
German League 1994
Sicilian Defence

1 e4 c5 2 ♘f3 ♘c6 3 ♗b5 g6 4 0-0 ♗g7 5 c3

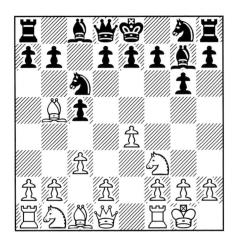

Answer: This is the older handling of Rossolimo. White plays as if in a Closed Lopez, slowly building his centre with c2-c3 and d2-d4.

Answer: A quick ...d7-d5! to challenge White's centre gives Black dynamic equality.

Answer: I think the other line, with an early ♗xc6, is more dangerous. In fact, I actually pre-fer Black's game if we follow theory in the c2-c3 version.
5...♘f6

Answer: That move is also playable. The problem is that the position won't be closed for long once White plays 6 d4! cxd4 7 cxd4 exd4 8 ♗f4, Z.Jovanovic-Z.Kozul, Croatian Champi-onship, Zagreb 2004. This position is supposed to be okay for Black too, but I don't trust it: White's dark-squared bishop will soon land on d6.
6 ♖e1 0-0 7 d4 d5!
    More combative than 7...cxd4 8 cxd4 d5 9 e5 ♘e4 10 ♘c3, G.Kasparov-A.Shirov, Linares 2002, which is also okay for Black.

8 e5

After 8 exd5 ♛xd5 9 c4 ♛d6 10 d5 (10 dxc5 ♛xd1 11 ♖xd1 ♘e4 is at least equal) 10...♘d4! 11 ♘xd4 cxd4 12 ♘d2 (12 ♛xd4? ♘g4! 13 ♛f4 ♛xf4 14 ♗xf4 ♗xb2 wins material) 12...a6 13 ♗a4 b5! 14 ♗b3 ♗b7, Black managed to dismantle White's centre. Channel 4 Viewers-G.Kasparov, London 1993.

8...♘e4 9 h3

Guarding his sensitive d4-point from ...♗g4 and ...♗xf3. The trouble is that the move is really slow.

> **Question:** Does it make sense to take on c6 and damage Black's structure?

Answer: Not at this stage. Black easily dissolves the pawn weakness and keeps the bishop pair after 9 ♗xc6 bxc6 10 ♘bd2 cxd4 11 cxd4 c5!. If White continues 12 ♘xe4?! dxe4 13 ♖xe4 ♗b7, he ends up fighting for equality despite his extra pawn; whereas 12 dxc5 ♘xc5 13 ♘b3 ♘xb3 14 ♛xb3 d4! is equal, A.Grischuk-P.Leko, Dubai (rapid) 2002.

9...♛b6!

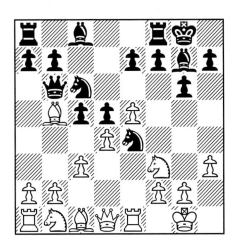

10 ♗a4

It makes no sense to chop on c6 now, giving away the bishop pair and light squares for nothing.

10...♗f5

10...♗e6!? also looks playable, M.Holzhaeuer-A.Engelhart, Illertissen 2005.

11 ♘a3

White finds himself contorting to develop.

11...cxd4 12 cxd4 f6

Chipping away at the white centre. Black can also proceed in Advance French style with something like 12...♖ac8 13 ♘c2 ♗d7 14 ♘e3 e6.

13 ♗b3 ♖ad8 14 exf6

> **Question:** Did White just miss a combination: 14 g4! ♗e6 15 ♖xe4! - ?

Answer: The variation you give is exactly correct, but you are under the assumption that the end position is good for White. It isn't! Black stands clearly better here, because after 15...dxe4 16 ♗xe6+ ♔h8 White must return the piece with an overextended game. If he tries to hang on to his material by 17 ♘h2??, he gets slaughtered after 17...♘xd4 with unanswerable threats.

14...exf6 15 ♘c2!?

Perhaps White has arrived at the stage where he should be looking for equality, say with something like 15 ♘h4 ♕xd4 16 ♕xd4 ♘xd4 17 ♘xf5 gxf5! 18 ♗d1 f4! 19 ♗xf4 f5, when Black's powerful centralization compensates for White's not-so-impressive bishop pair.

15...♖fe8 16 ♗f4

A natural move, but Kramnik quickly turns this piece into a target. Then again, 16 ♘e3 is simply met by 16...♗e6 and White's queenside remains undeveloped.

16...♗e6 17 ♖e2

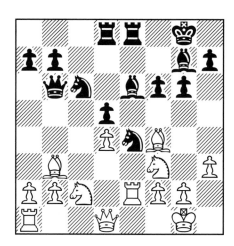

White's opening has been a fiasco, reminiscent of Colin Powell's UN address on the "proof" of Iraq's WMDs. Externally, White looks okay, but this is a deception. Black's threats may seem far off, like dark rain clouds which promise a storm – but not right now. Well, in fact "now" arrived and looks impatient. Black utilizes his trumps: flexible kingside pawns, coupled with pressure on d4 and on the queenside.

17...g5!

Black's serve. White can do nothing but defend for the remainder of the game.

18 ♗h2 f5! 19 ♕e1

White's game sours quickly after 19 ♘e5 f4! (seizing control over e5) 20 ♘xc6 bxc6.

19...♗f7! 20 ♖d1?!

Passive. He had to try and break free of the bind with the risky 20 ♘e3.

20...f4!

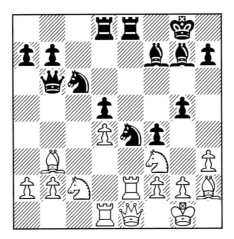

The recipe calls for overnight marinating of that poor guy on h2, who stands out like a beetle in a bowl of vanilla ice cream. The docile, neutered bishop, frosted in place on h2, is unable to take even a single step, and no longer represents a force in the battle for control over e5.

21 g3!

White composes himself and begins to fight back.

> ***Question:*** Risky?

Answer: There is no such thing as risky when on the cusp of busted. Devoid of real choice, White weakens, since he must find a way to activate the h2-bishop.

21...fxg3 22 fxg3 ♖f8 23 ♔g2 ♘a5!

The knight savours her new, elevated social status on a5.

24 ♕b4 ♕xb4 25 ♘xb4 ♘xb3 26 axb3 ♖d6!

Target: b3. Here 26...g4! 27 hxg4 ♗e6 was also strong.

27 ♘d3 ♖b6 28 b4 ♖c8

The sounds of industry and the pounding rhythm of White's machinery grow dim and silent, as his factories are boarded up and closed for good. Black built up multiple strategic trumps:

1. He owns the bishop pair.
2. He controls the light squares.
3. He has a pick of numerous pawn targets, like b4 and d4.
4. He controls the open c-file and his pieces are more active than White's.

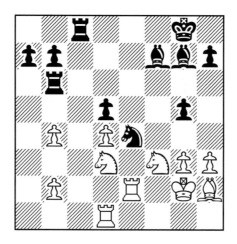

29 ♘fe5 ♗e8!

A move which if not evoking pandemonium from White, then at least the downgraded status of unease. One can see the faint outline of the creature emerging from the forest, moving in the direction of the town. Black's unopposed light-squared bishop looks for fresh feeding grounds on the queenside.

30 g4 ♗a4 31 ♖a1 ♗b5 32 ♖d1

32 ♖xa7?? hangs a piece to 32...♗xe5!.

32...♗f8!

Threat: ...♗xb4.

33 ♖de1 ♗d6!

Once again threatening to take on e5, winning material. I'm beginning to wonder whether this game should have been placed in the *Riding the Dynamic Element* chapter!

34 ♖e3

White's troops await instruction but receive none, since nothing helps at this stage. 34 ♖d1 is met by 34...♗xb4!.

34...♖c2+

Add control over the seventh rank to Black's long list of accumulated advantages.

35 ♔g1

Challenging the second rank is not an option: 35 ♖3e2?? ♖xe2+ 36 ♖xe2 ♗xe5! pulls the same old dirty trick.

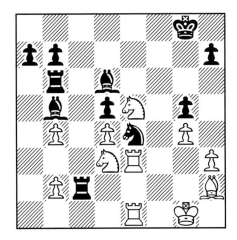

Cornered and with dwindling ammunition, it's only a matter of attrition before White cracks. The queenside topsoil, leeched of all nutrients, is deemed insufficient for plant growth.

> *Exercise (combination alert):* Black to play and win material.

Answer: The pair of wobbly b-pawns marks the spot of the soft underbelly. It is there that Kramnik slowly inserts his blade and twists. Now White must undertake a trail of two steps to try and survive:

Step 1: Pray.

Step 2: I lied. There is no Step 2! Please return to Step 1!

35...♗xd3! 36 ♖xd3 ♖xb2 37 ♖c1 ♖6xb4 0-1

> ## Game 43
> ### V.Kramnik-G.Kasparov
> World Championship (4th matchgame), London 2000
> *Queen's Gambit Accepted*

1 d4 d5 2 c4 dxc4 3 ♘f3 e6 4 e3 c5 5 ♗xc4 a6 6 0-0 ♘f6 7 dxc5

Kramnik dips the blade in poison, so that the tiniest cut induces death.

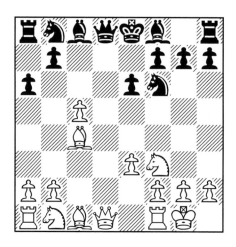

Answer: Not with the white pieces in a match. Memorize the following equation: *subtle does not necessarily equal drawish!* There is a difference between playing for a draw and playing safely for the win. Kramnik, a master of queenless middlegames, steers his tactically all-powerful opponent into purely sedate channels, where Kram's own strategic prowess and endgame skills shine, while Kasparov's strengths diminish.

7...♕xd1 8 ♖xd1 ♗xc5 9 ♘bd2 ♘bd7 10 ♗e2

Getting out of the path of ...b7-b5 and clearing c4 for a knight.

10...b6!?

Answer: Black's main motivation is to avoid weakening a5 and c5. After 11 a4 bxa4 12 ♘c4 ♗b7 13 ♖xa4, Black's a-pawn is slightly weaker than White's b-pawn, A.Grigoryan-K.Grigoryan, Armenian Championship, Yerevan 2012.

Answer: If you don't believe the position is winnable for White, then skip forward to the next chapter and take a look at the final game in the book. Kramnik reaches just such a position and goes on to take down a 2700 player!

11 ♘b3

Probably intended to dodge Kasparov's opening preparation. Kramnik was successful with 11 ♘c4 ♗b7 12 b3 ♔e7 13 ♗b2 ♖hd8 14 ♘e1! (intending ♘d3) 14...b5 15 ♘a5 in

V.Kramnik-A.Karpov, Frankfurt (rapid) 1999, where White achieved a small but nagging edge.

11...♗e7 12 ♘fd4 ♗b7 13 f3!

Denying Black's pieces access to e4 and intending to expand with e3-e4.

13...0-0 14 e4 ♖fc8

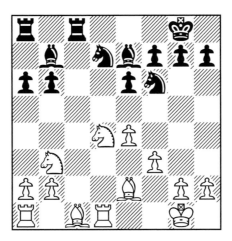

Question: Wouldn't the other rook be a better choice?

Answer: I like Kasparov's move. The fight takes place on the queenside, so he transfers his rooks to that sector. Black also gives himself the option of centralizing his king with ...♚f8.

15 ♗e3 ♚f8 16 ♘d2

Eyeing c4.

16...♘e5 17 ♘4b3!

Multipurpose:

1. White takes control over c5.

2. White clears a path to b6, hoping to provoke the weakening ...b6-b5, which, if played, allows his knight easy access to a5.

17...♖c6 18 ♖ac1 ♖ac8 19 ♖xc6 ♖xc6 20 g4!

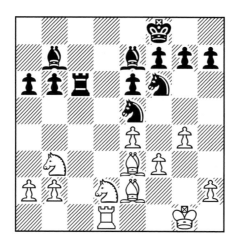

Answer: First, I don't agree that Kramnik played "lamely" in the opening, since he now holds an edge. Second, this isn't necessarily a mating attack as much as a daring expansion plan. Kramnik makes trouble on the other side of the board, having tied Black down somewhat on the queenside. Sometimes a plan of limited ambition (as in White's case) is superior to an overly ambitious one. Who is the more effective thief? The super-villain who schemes to appropriate a nuclear warhead from a military instillation in order to sell it to a terrorist group, or the heroin-addicted street thug who snatches a purse from a little old lady? The latter's chances of success look better.

20...h6

Answer: The trouble is that b2 isn't hanging! Black loses a pawn after 21 ♗xb6 since, if he continues with his plan, he loses material after 21...♖xb2?? 22 ♗d4! ♘xf3+ 23 ♗xf3 ♖xa2, when two pawns for the piece are not enough.

21 h4 ♗c8 22 g5 hxg5 23 hxg5 ♘fd7 24 f4 ♘g6 25 ♘f3!

Ignoring Black's threatened c2 invasion and fighting for control over the key e5- and h4-squares.

25...♖c2?

Understandably, Kasparov, by now itching for counterplay, makes this tempting move – but he should probably refrain and remain passive.

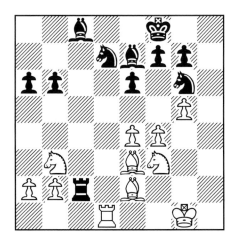

26 ♗xa6! ♗xa6 27 ♖xd7 ♖xb2 28 ♖a7! ♗b5 29 f5!

The millipede extending from e4 to g5 continues to twist and turn.

29...exf5 30 exf5

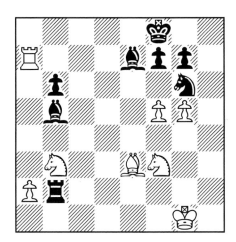

Out of nowhere, Kasparov finds himself in deep trouble. Kramnik promises the black knight heaven, but only if he is good and recites his prayers daily.

30...♖e2

30...♘h8? is met by 31 ♖a8+ ♗e8 32 ♘e5! (threatening a deadly check on d7) 32...♖b1+ 33 ♔f2 ♖d1 34 ♗d4! ♗xg5 35 ♔e2 ♖b1 36 ♗xb6, when Black soon loses a piece.

31 ♘fd4! ♖e1+

31...♖xe3?? 32 ♘xb5 wins a piece, since moving the knight would fail to 33 ♖a8+.

32 ♔f2 ♖f1+ 33 ♔g2! ♘h4+ 34 ♔h3 ♖h1+

Black's anger may be very real, yet this looks like misplaced retribution. Then again, I have no better suggestions. Like a hungry infant, Kasparov's forces continue to suckle at the teat of fictional piece activity, despite dire signs that the imaginary milk fails to nourish.

35 ♔g4 ♗e8 36 ♗f2! ♘g2

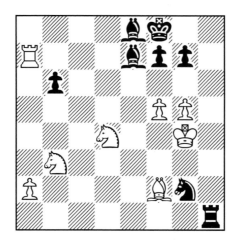

37 ♖a8?!

Kramnik misses an immediate win with 37 f6!! (clearing f5) 37...gxf6 38 ♘f5 ♗b4 39 ♗xb6 and if 39...fxg5? then 40 a3! (running the bishop off the diagonal) 40...♗c3 41 ♗c5+ ♔g8 42 ♖a8 wins.

37...♖f1 38 ♔f3 ♘h4+?

Kasparov loses his way in the heavy fog. The saving grace idea 38...♘f4! may yet save Black. For example, 39 ♘d2 ♖d1 40 ♘c4 ♘d5 41 ♘b5! ♗b4 42 a3 ♔e7 43 ♖a7+ ♔f8 44 axb4 ♗xb5 45 ♘xb6 ♘xb6 46 ♗xb6 and Black may hold the game due to the opposite-coloured bishops, though even here it's not so easy: White's king roams free, while his kingside pawns continue to hem in Black's king.

39 ♔e2 ♖h1

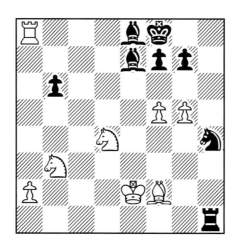

Exercise (combination alert): Black's immobilized machine of pieces jams from rust and lack of use. White can force the win of material. How?

Answer: All of Black's sorrows collect in a pool on e8. He is curiously helpless against ♘c7.

40 ♘b5!

The knight howls into b5 and nothing in the world can stop it from reaching its destination.

40...♗xg5

At this point Kasparov must be thinking: "If this is a dream, then may I please, please wake up!"

41 ♘c7 ♔e7 42 ♘xe8 ♘xf5 43 ♗xb6 ♔d7 44 a4

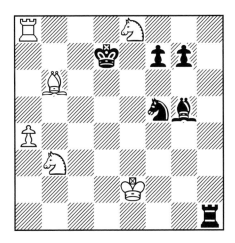

Kramnik accumulates wealth with the voracious acquisition skills of a robber baron. It should be easy now: White is up a piece for one pawn and his passer looks fast to boot. From this point, most players playing Black would be fighting that awful feeling inside when doubt and dread uncoil and you begin to second-guess all your decisions. But not Kasparov, who fights back with the energy of the virtuous, innocently condemned.

44...♖h3 45 ♘c5+ ♔c6 46 a5 ♖e3+ 47 ♔d1 ♖e7 48 ♖c8+ ♔b5 49 ♘e4! ♖xe4 50 ♖c5+ ♔a6 51 ♘c7+ ♔b7 52 ♖xf5 ♗e3!

His best chance. 52...♗f6? is met by 53 ♖b5!, when Black can do nothing about the forward march of the a-pawn.

53 ♗xe3

This allows Kasparov some drawing chances. Perhaps the simple 53 ♘b5! should be preferred.

53...♖xe3 54 ♖xf7?!

The doctor's prescription must fit the illness. All that matters is that White promote his a-pawn. Believe it or not, taking f7 is a waste of time. White should immediately coordinate his forces with 54 ♘d5! ♖a3 55 ♘b4 f6 56 ♔c2 ♔c7 57 a6 ♔b6 58 ♔b2 ♖a4 59 ♔b3 ♖a1 60 ♖d5 ♖b1+ 61 ♔a3 ♖a1+ 62 ♔b2 ♖a4 63 ♔b3 ♖a1 64 ♖d7 ♖b1+ 65 ♔a3 ♖a1+ 66 ♔b2 ♖a4 67 ♔b3 ♖a1 (White gains a tempo every fourth move) 68 ♖b7+ ♔c5 69 ♘a2! and the pawn promotes.

54...♖e5 55 a6+?

Kramnik unwisely dives into the shallow river, without first checking the depth. After this move the position may be drawn. Instead, 55 ♘d5+! ♔a6 56 ♘b4+! ♔b5 57 ♖f4 g5 58 ♖g4 ♖f5 59 a6 consolidates.

55...♔b6 56 ♖xg7

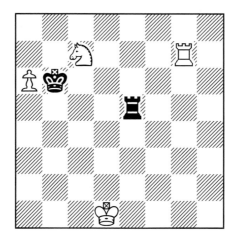

If Black can eliminate White's remaining pawn, the game is drawn. Black can do just that with 56...♖c5. Is this the seed of much needed hope, or does White have some hidden response to deal with the move?

Exercise (critical decision): Would you play 56...♖c5 – or not?

56...♖a5!

Answer: No. It's a trap! 56...♖c5?? loses on the spot to 57 a7! ♔xa7 58 ♘e6+.

57 ♔d2

White can no longer win since his rook, knight and pawn are eternally shackled to each other.

57...♖a1 58 ♔c2 ♖h1?

Which way is North? In desperate, mutual time pressure, the needles of both players' compasses go haywire due to some mysterious magnetic disturbance. After 58...♖a5! White can't make progress, whereas Kasparov just removed his rook from the drawing formation.

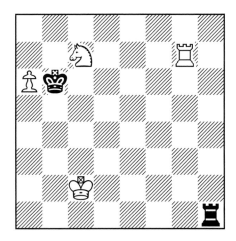

Exercise (combination alert): How can White exploit the error and win?

59 ♔b2?

Swim too close to your drowning enemy and he may pull you under with him. Kramnik blunders right back! In time pressure, accuracy and nuance tend to take a temporary leave of absence.

Answer: The win was his after 59 ♖g8! (this move is as obligatory as a school uniform: White must wear it, like it or not) 59...♖h7 60 ♖b8+! – Kramnik said he saw to this point but thought 60...♔a7?? saved Black. If he had time to calculate one ply further, he would have seen that 61 ♖b7 is mate!

59...♖h8!

Back to a draw again! Nothing can be done against the coming ...♖c8, which forces the win of White's remaining pawn.

60 ♔b3 ♖c8!

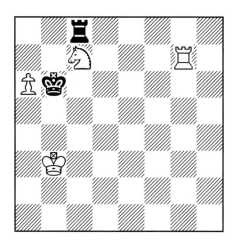

61 a7 ♔xa7

Black eliminates the fossilized remains of an epochs-dead predator, so fearsome when alive, now nothing more than a museum curio for bored school children to examine.

> **Question:** Does White get any practical chances
> with rook and knight versus rook?

Answer: Certainly not at world championship level. In the futile remainder, nothing moves. Even time stands still.

62 ♔b4 ♔b6 63 ♘d5+ ♔a6 64 ♖g6+ ♔b7 65 ♔b5 ♖c1 66 ♖g2 ♔c8 67 ♖g7 ♔d8 68 ♘f6 ♖c7 69 ♖g5 ♖f7 70 ♘d5 ♔d7 71 ♖g6 ♖f1 72 ♔c5 ♖c1+ 73 ♔d4 ♖d1+ 74 ♔e5 ½-½

> *Game 44*
> **P.Leko-V.Kramnik**
> Monte Carlo (rapid) 2002
> *Ruy Lopez*

1 e4 e5 2 ♘f3 ♘c6 3 ♗b5 a6

> **Question:** Doesn't Kramnik always play 3...♘f6 against the Ruy Lopez?

Answer: Not always; but it is a mild surprise for Kramnik to pull the switch from his beloved Berlin Defence.

4 ♗a4 ♘f6 5 0-0 ♗e7 6 ♖e1 b5 7 ♗b3 d6 8 c3 0-0 9 h3 ♘b8

The Breyer Variation. I remember during the first Fischer-Spassky match, my dad and I would go over the games from the *Montreal Gazette*. When we saw Spassky's first Breyer

Lopez, we were totally befuddled – it was like my father and I were lifelong blind people, and Spassky and Fischer were teachers who tried to explain to us the concept of the colour red – and rather naively attributed the bizarre knight retreat to Spassky's fear of Fischer!

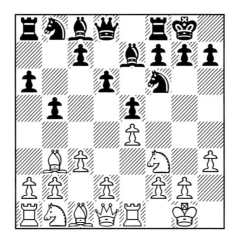

> ***Question:*** I was actually wondering the same thing:
> why does the knight go back home in the Breyer?

Answer: At some point, Black wants to push forward his c-pawn. By retreating the knight to b8, Black accomplishes this task and redeploys it on the flexible d7-square.

> ***Question:*** But two full tempi to accomplish the goal?

Answer: Amazing as it seems, Black has the time to pull it off, since the position remains closed. In closed positions the principle is: *Quality usurps quantity when it comes to development.*

10 d4 ♞bd7 11 ♘bd2 ♝b7

Black must be a bit careful about his move order. For example, the innocent-looking 11...♖e8?? loses to 12 ♗xf7+!, as after 12...♚xf7 13 ♘g5+ ♚g8 14 ♘e6 Black's embarrassed queen has no place to go. Apparently Boris Spassky allowed this trap as Black in his 1993 match against Judit Polgar – and Polgar failed to play 12 ♗xf7+!, so there may be hope for the rest of us!

12 ♝c2

> ***Question:*** Why does the bishop retreat?

Answer: White wants to build up for a kingside attack with the stock manoeuvre ♘f1 and ♘g3, so he first reinforces his e-pawn.

12...♖e8 13 b3

Other moves:

a) 13 a4 ♗f8 14 ♗d3 c6 15 b4 ♖c8 16 axb5 cxb5 17 ♗b2 d5! with huge complications, V.Anand-Ma.Carlsen, London 2010.

b) 13 ♘f1 (in my opinion, White's best chance for an edge) 13...♗f8 14 ♘g3 g6 15 ♗g5 h6 16 ♗d2, J.Polgar-B.Avrukh, Natanya (rapid) 2009. White generally tries to force some kind of kingside pawn concession with ♕c1 next.

13...♗f8

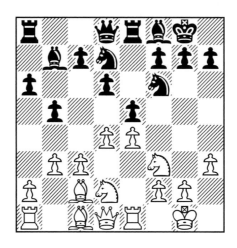

14 d5

The main theoretical move, but I don't trust it.

> **Question:** Why not? White locks down some central space.

Answer: But also allows Black immediate action against White's centre with ...c7-c6.

Instead, retaining central tension with 14 ♗b2 is an alternative; e.g. 14...g6 15 a4 ♗g7 16 ♗d3 c6 17 ♕c2 ♖c8, even if Black still emerges from the opening with a decent position, L.D.Nisipeanu-D.Campora, Decameron 2003.

14...c6 15 c4 ♘b6

Kramnik hits White's chain at its base.

16 ♗d3

A theoretical novelty, but not an earth-shattering one. The map ends here and walking any further means proceeding into uncharted zones. Previously White had played 16 ♗b2 ♘fd7 17 dxc6 ♗xc6 18 cxb5 axb5 19 ♘f1 ♘c5 20 ♘g3 f6!, when Black is ready for the freeing ...d6-d5 break, J.Klovans-E.Geller, USSR Spartakiad, Moscow 1979.

16...♘fd7 17 ♗a3?!

I've had a very difficult time pinpointing just where it is that Leko goes wrong. This may be the point. White later ends up losing two tempi when he retreats back to c1.

Question: What is the alternative? Black will then play a knight to c5.

Answer: Just allow it, but make certain Black can't undermine the centre with a quick ...f7-f5. I think 17 ♘f1 bxc4 18 bxc4 ♘c5 19 ♘e3 is White's best.

17...cxd5 18 cxd5 f5!

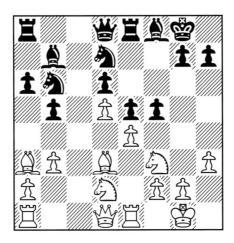

Kramnik continues to corrode White's space plus, even if doing so puts his king at risk.

19 exf5 ♘xd5 20 ♘e4

A sharp position arises, but one which should swing in Black's favour. Black's long-term chances are due to his central majority, while White should be looking toward the enemy king. In the coming moves, Kramnik finds ways to subordinate Leko's dynamic potential so that his static factors dominate. The middle of the board is the black hole factor, which for now lies just outside the influence of White and Black camps – unterritory, for anyone's taking.

20...♘7f6 21 ♘fg5

Going after the sensitive e6-square.

21...♘f4!

We are reminded of the Crosby, Stills, Nash and Young song *Wooden Ships*: "I can see by your coat, my friend, you're from the other side." Unexpectedly, the returns on White's strategic investments begin to slow. Kramnik covers the threatened invasion square, and also eyes both White's powerful light-squared bishop and the potential kingside sac squares g2 and h3.

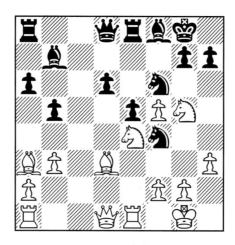

22 ♗c1

Question: This looks passive. Shouldn't White
try to retain his bishop with 22 ♗c2 - ?

Answer: In that case Black takes over the initiative with 22...♘xe4 23 ♗xe4 d5 (two white
pieces are hanging, so his next move is forced) 24 f6 ♕xf6 25 ♘xh7 ♕h4! 26 ♘xf8 dxe4 and
White is busted.

22...♘xd3 23 ♕xd3 ♘xe4

Deflecting White's knight from g5.

24 ♘xe4 d5

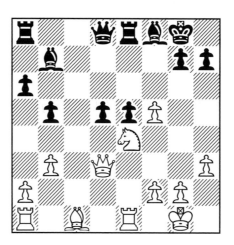

Black's advantages:

1. The bishop pair in an open position.

2. A powerful, rolling pawn centre.

3. The superior pawn structure.

4. Most importantly, the initiative.

25 ♘g3

An admission of failure.

Question: Shouldn't he be heading for the hole on e6?

Answer: After 25 ♘g5? Black can completely destabilize White's position with a powerful series of moves, starting with 25...♕f6 26 ♘e6 e4 27 ♕b1 d4!. Now if White goes for it with 28 ♘c7? he gets crushed by 28...e3!, when 29 fxe3 (29 ♘xe8 ♕g5 is also slaughter) 29...♕c6! wins the knight.

25...e4 26 ♕d2

26 ♕d4 ♗d6! 27 ♗b2 ♗e5 28 ♕d2 d4! breaks the blockade; if White insists on taking on e4, he drops the exchange after 29 ♘xe4 ♗xe4 30 ♖xe4 ♗h2+ 31 ♔xh2 ♖xe4 32 f3 ♖e5 and has to fight for the draw. This line may be White's best though.

26...d4 27 ♗b2 ♗c5 28 ♖ac1 ♗b6 29 ♕f4

Leko fishes for tricks around the black king.

29...♕d5!

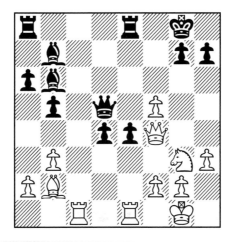

Black's powerful centralization, along with his other advantages, ensure that White's attack will be a non-starter.

30 ♖c2 e3!

If friction took material form, it would look like g2. Kramnik senses the ripe moment for punitive action.

31 fxe3 ♖ac8!

Hoping to deflect the protector of g2.

32 ♖d2

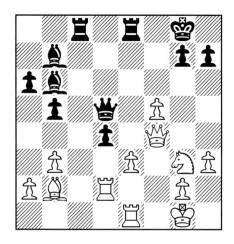

Exercise (combination alert): 32...♗a5 favours Black,
but look around: he has something much stronger.

Answer: Offer a queen instead!

32...♖xe3!! 33 ♖xe3 dxe3 34 ♖e2?

White's rook mistakenly spurns the black queen's tainted love, as the reeling Leko now overlooks Kramnik's next shot. Unpleasant as it was, he had to accept the offer with 34 ♖xd5! e2+ (the mob boss on b6 issues a menacing warning to White's king in a sibilant whisper, just outside the hearing of the other pieces) 35 ♔h2 e1♕ – the point: the double attack on d5, plus the mate threat on g1 force White into 36 ♖d4. This in turn allows Black the shot 36...♗xg2! 37 ♕d2 (not much choice) 37...♕xd2 38 ♖xd2 ♗f3, when the powerful bishop pair offers Black a clear advantage in the ending. Still, this path is much better than the way Leko picked.

34...♖c2!!

Another staggering blow. Black's rook, formally a contented janitor with a 170 IQ, decides to raise his sights and look for a new job at the university. Kramnik's field of unending threats blossom like wildflowers. White's rook, with trembling lips, sounds the alarm, all the while pointing wildly at the intruder on c2. Black's once-hidden but deeply influential bishop on b6 now protrudes like a six-inch nail in the wall.

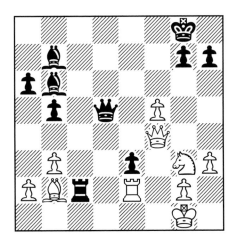

35 ♕g4

The rook is not so hanging: 35 ♖xc2?? is a brain-curdling blunder, since 35...e2+ mates next move. Instead, 35 ♕e5 ♕xe5 36 ♗xe5 ♖xa2! also finishes White off, while 35 ♕b8+ ♔f7 36 ♕h8 ♖xb2! is the same old deflection story.

35...♖xb2!

Clearly White's rook suffers from some type of neurological disorder. There we have it again: the story of the frozen rook, paralyzed in place on e2.

36 f6

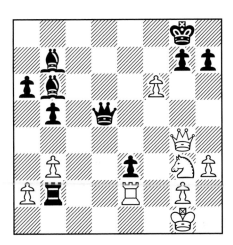

> ***Exercise (combination alert):*** The simple 36...g6 wins. But wait. Black
> also has a breathtaking finish, which Kramnik missed. Can you spot it?

36...g6

The practical move. Kramnik misses the pretty finish.

Answer: White's conventional human weapons are clearly worthless, as the alien-made death ray from d5 incinerates the entire white army in a matter of seconds: 36...♕xg2+!! 37 ♖xg2 e2+ 38 ♔h2 (the pulverized king, now insensate to pain itself, only ponders escape) 38...♗g1+!! (deflection – the cowled monk, having taken a vow of silence, now ignores it and comes to say "hello!") 39 ♔h1 ♗xg2+ 40 ♔xg2 e1♕+ mating.

37 f7+ ♕xf7 0-1

> *Game 45*
> **V.Kramnik-A.Shirov**
> Wijk aan Zee 2007
> *Réti Opening*

1 ♘f3

Kramnik's old favourite first move.

1...♘f6 2 c4 g6 3 ♘c3 d5 4 ♕a4+

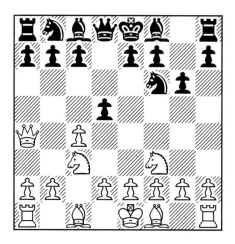

The Neo-Grünfeld.

> **Question:** What is "neo" about it?

Answer: Here 4 d4 just transposes to the Grünfeld proper. In the Neo-Grünfeld, White holds back on d2-d4 and can later play his pawn to d3 with a safer English-like structure.

Another option is 4 cxd5 ♘xd5 5 e4 (5 ♕a4+ and 5 g3 are also played) 5...♘xc3, and now on multiple occasions, when I only needed a draw to win a tournament, I have played the dirty trick 6 dxc3!? ♕xd1+ 7 ♔xd1, when the endgame is next to impossible for Black to win.

4...♗d7 5 ♕b3 dxc4

Question: Can White get away with taking
on b7 to damage Black's pawn structure?

6 ♕xc4

Answer: Database search on 6 ♕xb7: zero games found! The implication is that the line is horrible for White. Let's look: 6...♘c6! (White's wayward queen lacks escape squares) 7 ♘b5 ♘d5 8 ♘bd4 ♘cb4! 9 a3 ♖b8 10 ♕xa7 ♖a8! 11 ♕b7 (after 11 ♕c5? e5 12 ♕xc4 exd4 13 ♘xd4 ♘b6 Black emerges with an extra piece) 11...♗g7 12 ♖b1 c5 13 axb4 ♘xb4! is hopeless for White.

6...♗g7 7 e4 c6

More usual is 7...0-0 8 e5 ♘g4 (after 8...♗e6 9 exf6!? ♗xc4 10 fxg7 ♗xf1 11 gxf8♕+ ♔xf8 12 ♔xf1 ♕d3+ 13 ♔g1 ♘c6 14 h4, I think White's material outweighs Black's bind) 9 d4 ♗e6 10 d5 ♗f5 11 ♗f4 ♘d7 12 ♕e2 f6 with a totally irrational position, yet one senses a White advantage embedded within the chaos, A.Goldin-V.Mikhalevski, Rishon Le Ziyyon 1997/98.

8 d4 b5!?

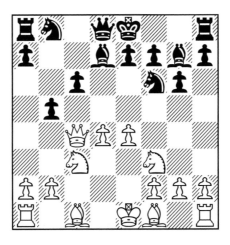

Question: ...b7-b5 is normally associated with
an opening like Semi-Slav, yet here Black makes the
same move in a Grünfeld structure. Is it playable?

Answer: I would say it's playable but inadvisable. Shirov clearly looks to make trouble, pushing random buttons, cranking gears and pulling strange levers, in the hope of igniting the motor of a yet non-existent initiative. I don't see any tangible gain from Black's queenside space, but the weakening involved with his move looks very real.

> **Question:** If you don't like Black's move
> then why don't you give it a "?!" mark?

Answer: I may not like it due to stylistic bias. A man has the right to provoke a drunken bar fight as long as he is willing to face the consequences with the bail bondsman the next day. In a chess game one isn't necessarily obligated to play the absolutely correct move at every turn. Carl Jung once theorized that if a person strove fanatically to reach the perfect good in every life decision, then the "shadow within" – everything negative – also grew in power. I have no idea if this theory is true or not, but Shirov certainly veers far clear of the perfect good in his decision!

9 ♕b3 a5 10 e5 a4 11 ♕d1 ♘d5 12 ♘xd5 cxd5

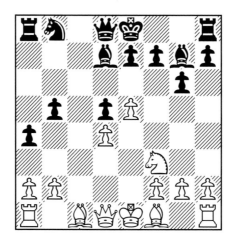

Black's position looks like a slightly inferior Rossolimo Sicilian. White controls more central space, whereas Black's queenside demonstration fails to impress, and c5 remains a potentially occupiable hole for White's pieces.

13 ♗e2 ♘c6 14 0-0 0-0 15 ♗e3 ♘a5 16 b3

Nyet, buddy boy! The knight is denied entry to c4.

16...axb3 17 axb3 ♕b6 18 ♘e1!

It feels like nothing much is happening, but we sense hidden motion in White's game, the way a pregnant woman places her hand on her belly to feel the moving baby. Kramnik immediately zones in on Black's weak point: c5.

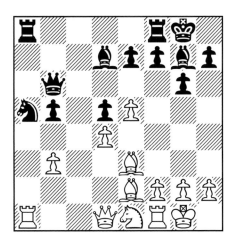

18...b4?!

Lose your equanimity in any given position and you are in danger of adopting a rash course of action.

Question: Why don't you like the move?

Answer: Black's last move is dubious on several counts:
1. Black plugs the hole on b4 with a pawn, rather than a piece.
2. Black does nothing to prevent ♘d3.
3. Black's b-pawn may later turn into a target.

Question: What move do you suggest?

Answer: 18...♘c6 pins White down to his b-pawn and keeps an eye on b4.

19 ♘d3 ♗b5 20 ♘c5 ♘b7 21 ♖xa8 ♖xa8 22 ♗xb5 ♕xb5

22...♘xc5? drops a pawn to 23 dxc5 ♕xb5 24 ♕xd5.

Question: Isn't Black better after the text?
White is now stuck with a bad bishop.

Answer: The position is deceptive and remains in White's favour. His space, control over c5, and the weakness of b4 give him the edge.

23 ♕d3!

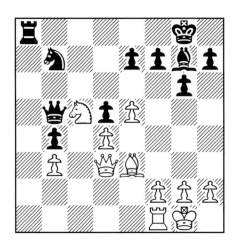

23...♕c6!?

> *Question:* Doesn't swapping queens give Black an easy draw?

Answer: A draw maybe. Easy, no! While your suggestion may well be Black's best shot at a draw, he still struggles in the line 23...♕xd3 24 ♘xd3 ♖a3 25 ♘xb4 e6 26 ♘c6 ♖xb3 27 ♖a1 h6 28 ♖a8+ ♔h7 29 ♔f1. Here Black's knight is awkwardly posted with no easy outs, White owns space and f7 remains weak. White can also try and expand on the kingside. I realize Black may be close to a draw, but keep in mind that "close" doesn't mean a whole lot if you still lose the game.

24 ♘a4!

Blocking the a-file and retaining the superior knight.

24...♘d8 25 ♖c1

White takes control of the only fully open file on the board.

25...♕b7 26 ♕c2 f6 27 f4

One can only stand back and marvel at the ease with which Kramnik accrues territory to glorify his domain.

27...♗h6 28 g3 fxe5

This only ends up helping White. The seed of Black's much desired counterplay is just not discernable.

29 dxe5 ♘e6 30 ♕c6

The c6-square serves as the host body for White's parasitic infestation. Kramnik allowed his opponent to wallow and percolate long enough, and now takes action. The ending will be very difficult for Black to save, due to his numerous pawn weaknesses.

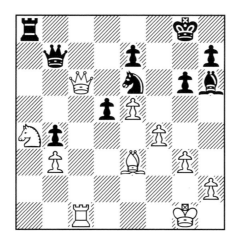

30...♕xc6 31 ♖xc6 ♔f7 32 ♔f2 ♖b8 33 ♔e2 ♗f8

Black's "good" bishop remains a prisoner, entrapped and pickled in brine, while White's not-so-"bad" bishop rules with freedom and ease of movement.

34 ♔d3

Despite a receding hairline, the white king walks with the bouncing steps of a younger man. White continues to find fuel to stoke his engine of pressure, and now a new potential arises: king position. Kramnik effortlessly reconfigures the strategic threads into an intricate lattice of perfect increase.

34...♖b7?? 1-0

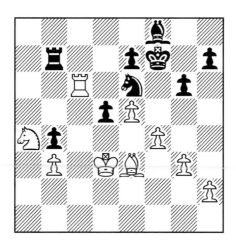

Shirov, now struggling, hopes for some time to regain composure before facing the next wave. Black's rook unknowingly draws closer to the source of dark power, as if to an altar in an ancient, malevolent god's hidden jungle temple. The punitive landscape of the queenside is completely unforgiving if Black takes a single misstep – and he just took a big one!

> ***Exercise (combination alert):*** Shirov cracked in a difficult ending. After
> making his last move he resigned even before Kramnik could reply.
> Do you see the reason for Black's sudden resignation?

Answer: White steals a piece with 35 ♖xe6! (in the inspirational words of Richard Nixon: "I am not a crook!") 35...♔xe6 36 ♘c5+. After the short skirmish, Black's unfortunate rook lies on the bloody ground, unmoving.

> *Game 46*
> **P.Leko-V.Kramnik**
> Nice (rapid) 2008
> *English Opening*

1 c4 e5 2 ♘c3 ♘f6 3 ♘f3 ♘c6 4 g3 d5

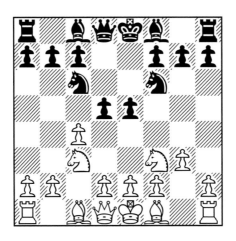

> ***Question:*** Can Black get away with playing against
> a line as sharp as the Dragon a full move down?

Answer: Oddly enough he can, as long as Black himself plays a careful, conservative game and avoids some of the sharper lines in reverse.

5 cxd5 ♘xd5 6 ♗g2 ♘b6

> ***Question:*** Why the unforced knight retreat, rather than
> continue to develop with something solid like 6...♗e7 - ?

Answer: Be careful. This is a well-known Dragon trap in reverse. After 6...♗e7? 7 ♘xe5! ♘xc3 8 ♗xc6+ bxc6 9 dxc3 Black loses a pawn and gets his structure damaged as well.

7 0-0 ♗e7 8 a3 0-0

Question: Shouldn't Black halt White's attempted expansion with 8...a5 - ?

Answer: That is also possible. The other philosophy is to just avoid ...a7-a5, because it gives White something to grasp hold of later on the queenside. The pawn itself may become a target, as in the following game: 9 d3 0-0 10 ♗e3 ♗e6 11 ♖c1 a4!? 12 ♗xb6 cxb6 13 ♘xa4 e4 14 ♘e1 ♘d4 15 ♘c3, when Black has some but perhaps not enough compensation for the pawn, I.Nepomniachtchi-D.Bocharov, Apatity (rapid) 2011.

9 b4 ♗e6

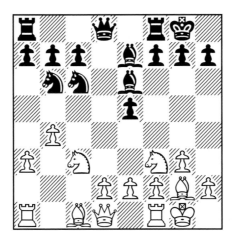

10 ♖b1

Question: Doesn't 10 b5 simply win a pawn?

Answer: You have to keep going with the analysis: 10...♘d4 11 ♘xe5?? ♗b3 12 ♕e1 ♘c2 and it is Black who wins.

10...f6 11 d3 ♘d4 12 ♘d2

Question: Can White just swap away the pesky black knight on d4?

Answer: The trouble then is that Black's new d-pawn cramps White and may even allow Black counterplay on e2. For example, 12 ♘xd4 exd4 13 ♘e4 ♗d5 14 ♗b2 f5 15 ♘d2 ♗xg2 16 ♔xg2 and Black equalized, mainly thanks to the cramping influence of the d4-pawn, D.Navara-V.Topalov, Wijk aan Zee 2012.

12...c6 13 ♘de4 ♗f7!?

So that ♘c5 will not arrive with tempo. Other moves:

a) 13...♖f7 14 ♗d2 ♘d5 15 e3 ♘xc3 16 ♘xc3 ♘f5 17 ♕c2 ♗f8 18 ♖fd1 a5 19 ♘a4 axb4 20 ♗xb4, when White has a tiny queenside edge, due to the potential for a queenside minority attack, L.Aronian-S.Karjakin, Nice (rapid) 2008.

b) 13...♘d5 14 e3 ♘xc3 15 ♘xc3 ♘f5 16 ♕c2 ♖c8 17 ♖d1 ♕d7 18 d4 exd4 19 exd4 ♗d6 20 ♘e4 ♖cd8 21 ♗b2 and again I prefer White, who has access to c5 with his knight, L.Aronian-V.Topalov, Morelia/Linares 2008.

c) 13...♗g4 14 ♗e3 ♘d7 15 ♕d2 ♔h8 16 h3 ♗h5 17 f4 f5 18 ♘g5 h6 19 ♘f3 ♘xf3+ 20 ♗xf3 ♕e8 looks balanced, Kir.Georgiev-A.Kharlov, Yugoslav Team Championship 1996.

14 ♗e3?!

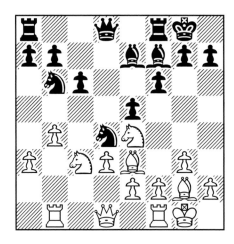

Better to go for 14 ♘c5 and possibly follow with e2-e3, M.Narciso Dublan-J.De la Villa Garcia, Spanish Team Championship 2010. The text is a theoretical novelty, but not a good one. Leko's move surpasses the cusp of dubious and makes little sense.

> **Question:** Why not?

Answer: White's idea must be to take on d4, which only assists Black in multiple ways:

1. Black gets the bishop pair.

2. After the recapture ...e5xd4, Black grabs space, takes control over c3 and makes White's e2-pawn insecure.

14...a5! 15 ♘c5 axb4 16 axb4 ♖a3

Kramnik doesn't play moves like 16...♕c7 if he has more aggressive alternatives.

17 ♘3e4 ♕c7 18 ♗xd4?!

White hopes to refine his idea formed on the 14th move but only succeeds in contaminating it further. Now Black's influence bleeds over to c3. Leko's move is a perfectly logical extension of his novelty, but if this is so, then his novelty wasn't so great! This move just helps Black in the ways mentioned above.

18...exd4

When a low-level underling unexpectedly receives promotion, his former boss always feels resentment upon viewing the enforced equality of his new, sudden colleague. Now Black's once humble e-pawn is destined for a sparkling career.

19 ♗h3!?

> *Question:* What is White's idea behind this strange move?

Answer: I think Leko played it for multiple reasons:

1. White must inhibit ...f6-f5, since if his e4-knight is ejected Black may take over the game with a ...♘d5-c3 infiltration plan.

2. White may also have dreams of ♘c5-e6 later on in the game, but this plan just never comes to fruition.

19...♖fa8!

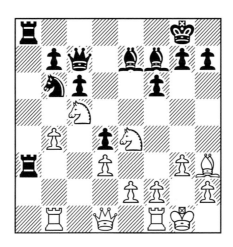

Kramnik correctly assesses that his weak e6-square is in reality not such a concern.

20 ♕c1

> *Question:* Isn't the moment ripe for invasion to e6?

Answer: The knight gets to e6, but I fail to see what he achieves there: 20 ♘e6 ♕e5 21 ♘6c5 (or 21 f4 ♕h5 22 ♘f2 ♘d5) 21...♘d5 is terrible for White since his c3-square remains tender, and I'm not sure just what he is doing.

20...♘d5

The position is ripe for invasion of c3.

21 ♕b2 ♘c3?!

Too soon. Black can build up further with 21...g6!, intending ...f6-f5 and only then ...♘c3.

22 ♘xc3?!

Leko willingly enters dangerous territory, allowing Black a powerful passed c-pawn. White's best defensive hope is to hand over a pawn with 22 ♖a1! ♘xe2+ 23 ♔g2 ♖xa1 24 ♖xa1 ♖xa1 25 ♕xa1, when Black will have a hard time hanging on to his gains.

22...dxc3

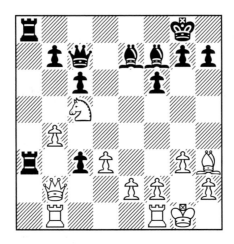

This pawn is destined to be the cause of White's future distress.

23 ♕c2 ♕e5

Intending ...♖a2.

24 ♖fc1 b5

Threatening to take on c5.

25 ♘e4 ♗a2!?

Kramnik resolves to punish the leaders of the insurgency by going after b4. Perhaps he wasn't satisfied with his advantage after 25...♖8a4 26 ♘xc3 ♖xb4.

26 ♖a1 ♗xb4!?

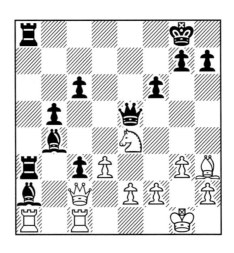

The mysterious stranger on b4 draws hostile stares as he walks into the bar only frequented by locals. Kramnik, in order to hang on to his c3-pawn, allowed Leko a little combination. White must not waste this opportunity.

Answer: Deflection. A merchant views the entire world as potential customers. Leko's payment: two bishops for his rook.

27 Îxa2!

Gain of material is still an afterthought. Raw survival continues to be Leko's prime directive.

27...Îxa2 28 Ëb3+

Double attack.

28...êh8 29 Ëxb4 c2

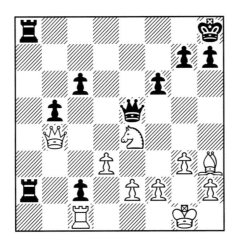

The oracle prophesied that he (c2) was the One! Leko's combination didn't come without a price: Black's deeply embedded pawn now reaches c2, to tie White's forces down.

30 Áf1?

White sounds the retreat, but to where? How can an army retreat when there is no place to back up? Some religions stress their disjointed apartness from non-believers by dressing and acting differently from the societal norm. In this case the bishop comes across as oddly "other" in his strange mannerisms and aloof behaviour on f1. It seems that the effects of the previous combinational communion have had little effect on White's cramped pieces, who continue to feel uncleansed.

Instead, White generates much needed counterplay after the correct 30 êg2! Îb2 31

♕d2 f5 32 ♘g5 ♕f6 33 e4, while 30...♕b2 31 ♕xb2 ♖xb2 32 ♗e6 b4 33 ♔f3 gives White good chances to blockade the black pawns.

30...♕b2!

Kramnik's queen asserts herself. This is her queendom – hers and hers alone!

31 ♕xb2 ♖xb2 32 ♘d2

If 32 d4, then 32...g5! (not yet 32...♖a1?? due to the weakness of the back rank) 33 e3 (33 ♘d2 ♖d8 34 e3 c5! is no better) 33...♖a1!! and Black forces a new queen.

32...c5

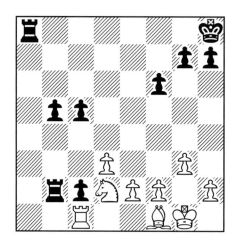

Marching forward in lockstep.

33 f4 c4! 34 ♘f3

34 dxc4?? ♖d8 35 ♘f3 ♖d1 ends the fight.

34...b4!

Kramnik methodically lays tracks toward the final destination: promotion to a new queen.

35 dxc4 ♖d8! 36 ♘e1 b3

Black's queenside passers enter a dark place where monsters are born.

37 ♔f2 ♖d1 38 ♘d3

White's knight tries desperately to self-suture the multiple wounds, despite his own debilitating injury.

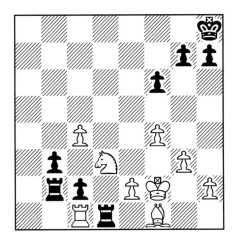

Exercise (combination alert(s)): Find a way to force Black's pawns through the flimsy blockade. There are a million ways to win. See if you can find the flashiest!

Answer: Elimination of a key defender/destruction of a blockade. White's lab experiment goes horribly awry. Black's two passers now transform into something so aberrantly alien that they cease to be human.

38...♖xd3! 0-1

White resigns since ...♖b1 is next. Of course there is absolutely nothing wrong with the equally crushing (but mundane!) 38...♖xc1! 39 ♘xc1 ♖b1, or the just as crushing (and mundane!) 38...♗b1!.

Game 47
V.Kramnik-V.Anand
World Championship (10th matchgame), Bonn 2008
Nimzo-Indian Defence

1 d4 ♘f6 2 c4 e6 3 ♘c3 ♗b4 4 ♘f3 c5 5 g3

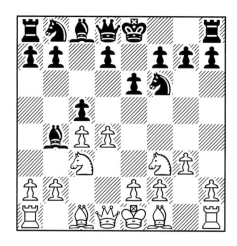

Answer: This is a line of the Nimzo which may transpose to a line of the English Opening. Kasparov favoured this variation for a while, but the current state of theory says Black should equalize.

5...cxd4 6 ♘xd4 0-0 7 ♗g2 d5

Question: Isn't White afraid of those doubled, isolated pawns if Black trades on c3?

Answer: No. After 7...♗xc3+?! 8 bxc3 White gets huge compensation on the dark squares, which Black just gave away, and also pressure along his two open files. A.Miles-D.Velimirovic, Amsterdam 1976, continued 8...♕a5 9 ♕b3 ♘c6 10 0-0 ♖e8 11 ♘b5 d5 12 ♕a3. Now Black, under heavy positional pressure, decided to hand over the exchange with 12...♗d7!? and obtained some counterplay after 13 ♕xa5 ♘xa5 14 ♘c7 ♘xc4, but declining with 13 ♘d6! puts Black under the gun.

8 cxd5 ♘xd5 9 ♕b3

9 ♗d2 was Kasparov's specialty; e.g. 9...♘xc3 10 bxc3 ♗e7 11 ♖b1 e5?! (11...♘d7 prevented White's shot) 12 ♖xb7! exd4 13 ♖b3 ♗e6 14 ♗xa8 ♘a6 15 ♗f3 ♗xb3 16 ♕xb3, when White's bishop pair gave him a clear advantage in the open position, G.Kasparov-V.Anand, Wijk aan Zee (blitz) 1999.

9...♕a5 10 ♗d2 ♘c6 11 ♘xc6 bxc6 12 0-0

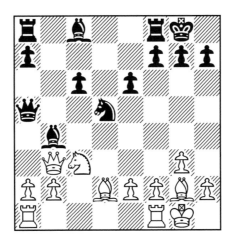

12...♝xc3

> *Question:* Why does Black surrender the bishop pair?

Answer: There is no real choice, since White threatens ♘xd5 followed by ♘e7+ and ♘xc6. The trouble is that Black has no good waiting move; for example, 12...♖b8? 13 ♘xd5 cxd5 14 a3! wins material, S.Atalik-A.Stein, Berkley 2005.

13 bxc3 ♝a6 14 ♖fd1! ♛c5

> *Question:* Why can't Black take on e2? After 14...♝xe2 15 c4 ♝xd1 16 ♖xd1
> ♛b6 17 cxd5 cxd5 he seems to get a lot of material for his two pieces.

Answer: You calculated the line perfectly but may be misassessing. White's bishops are worth more than Black's rook and two pawns.

15 e4 ♝c4

Deviating from a past victory, possibly fearing Kramnik's preparation. Anand won a beautiful game with 15...♘b6 16 ♝e3 ♛h5 17 ♖d6?! ♘c4 18 ♖xc6 ♘xe3 19 ♖xa6? ♖ab8 20 ♛a4 ♖b2! 21 ♖e1.

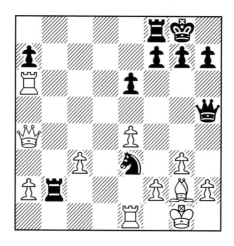

Exercise (combination alert): How did Anand end
the game with a single, mind-bending move?

Answer: Overload/weak back rank: 21...♕e2!! 0-1 E.Bacrot-V.Anand, Bastia (rapid) 2001.
16 ♕a4 ♘b6 17 ♕b4 ♕h5

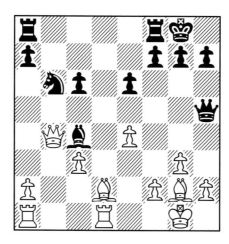

The players reach a well-known position, which is thought to be alright for Black.
17...♕xb4?! 18 cxb4 makes no sense, since it fixes White's pawn weakness.
18 ♖e1!?

Kramnik's new move. Previously White had just developed his c1-bishop:

a) 18 ♗e3 ♗e2 19 ♖d2 ♖ab8 20 ♗xb6 axb6 21 ♕d6 ♗f3 22 ♕xc6 ♗xg2 23 ♔xg2 ♕e5,
when White's extra pawn proved too difficult to convert to a win, G.Kasparov-V.Anand,
Wijk aan Zee 2000.

b) 18 ♗f4 c5 19 ♕b2 ♖ad8 20 ♖xd8 ♖xd8 21 f3 f5!? 22 exf5 ♕xf5 23 ♖e1 ♕d5 24 ♕a3 ♕c6 25 ♕xa7 ♖a8 26 ♕e7 ♘d5 27 ♕d6 ♕xd6 28 ♗xd6 ♘xc3 29 ♗xc5 ♖xa2 and White's bishop pair didn't mean much here, E.Bacrot-Ma.Carlsen, Biel 2008.

18...c5

> *Question:* Can Black play to swap off a pair of bishops
> with 18...♗e2, intending to go to f3 next move?

Answer: White can deny this plan if he responds with 19 h3!, since if Black insists on 19...♗f3??, he loses a piece to the interference shot 20 g4!.

19 ♕a5!

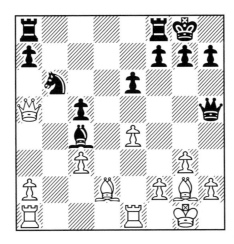

White's queen exerts maximum pressure from a5. Black must watch over both c5 and a7.

19...♖fc8 20 ♗e3 ♗e2!

Dual purpose:

1. Black hopes to swap off a pair of bishops with your above-mentioned plan of ...♗f3.
2. Black clears c4 for his knight.

21 ♗f4!? e5

With his last move Anand's queen loses communication with his queenside pawns. I'm not sure White has much after the correct 21...♗f3! 22 ♕a6 ♗xg2 23 ♔xg2 and only now 23...e5 24 ♗e3 ♕g6 25 f3 ♕e6!, taking control over c4.

22 ♗e3!

The bishop quicksteps in and out. Suddenly, Black's queenside is under assault. Perhaps Anand had only counted on 22 ♗xe5 ♘c4 23 ♕a6 ♕xe5 24 ♖xe2 ♕xc3, when Black looks okay.

22...♗g4!?

Black also stands worse in the line 22...♘c4 23 ♕a6 ♘xe3 24 ♖xe2 ♘xg2 25 ♔xg2, when

White continues to press on the queenside. For example, after 25...♕g6 26 ♕c4 ♖ab8 27 ♖d1 White can use d5 effectively for his rooks.

23 ♕a6!

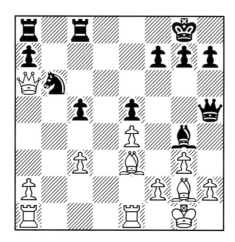

Deceptively powerful. A rule of war: never display your strengths to your enemy if you can help it. Kramnik's position mysteriously continues to creep improvement. Now all who dare to enter the queen's orbit are vacuumed into her black hole of power. Threats soon begin to rain in staccato percussion.

> ***Question:*** Wasn't c5 hanging?

Answer: Black's counterplay flares up after the mercenary grab 23 ♗xc5? ♘c4 24 ♕b5 ♘d2! with all sorts of counterplay on the f3-square.

23...f6?!

Anand's game veers left, with the spasmodic, diagonally agitated motion of a school of fish that just spotted a predator. This logical advance, which prepares the queen's return to the beleaguered queenside via ...♕f7, turns out to be too slow. Instead, Black should stay passive with 23...♗e6 24 ♗f1 ♘d7, when his position is only slightly worse.

24 a4!

The a-pawn soon becomes a force on the queenside.

24...♕f7 25 ♗f1

Black is doing everything according to his plans, but his position gets worse and worse!

25...♗e6 26 ♖ab1

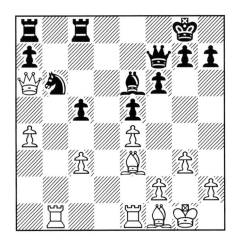

26...c4?

Anand, under heavy positional pressure, inexplicably plugs his one strong square with a pawn – strategic suicide. The trouble is that the intended 26...♗c4?? loses on the spot to 27 ♗xc4 ♕xc4 (nor is 27...♘xc4 28 ♖b7 of any help) 28 ♖xb6!, picking off a full piece. The golem on c4, unable to maintain her form from fading magic, de-solidifies and crumbles in a heap of clay and stone.

> ***Question:*** Well then, what do you suggest?

Answer: Black's position may be unsalvageable. His best may lie in 26...f5 27 a5 f4 28 ♗d2! (even stronger than 28 ♗xf4! which wins a clean pawn) 28...♘d7 29 ♖b7 and White's unrelenting pressure continues.

27 a5

The magma flows down and enfolds the old, the infirm, and the young of the town, who fail to outrun death.

27...♘a4

Black's pieces panic and swell toward the exits. He bids the knight "Godspeed", which is of little comfort to someone on a suicide mission. This knight is destined to lie in its corner, shuddering like a grievously injured animal. 27...♘d7 28 ♖b7 is also totally hopeless.

28 ♖b7 ♕e8

The queenside – which was once a thriving, prosperous city – is now nothing more than a depopulated, uninhabitable (for Black!) wasteland. The stockpiles of food and water dwindle during the long siege, as Black's position swims in an oppressive anaesthesia of drained fatigue.

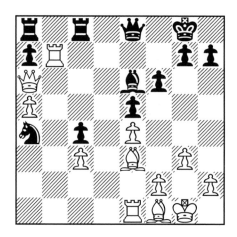

> ***Exercise (planning/combination alert):*** Find one
> powerful move and Black collapses.

Answer: Double attack. The queen seizes power, reinstating herself as the central seat of authority.

29 ♕d6! 1-0

White threatens ♖e7, as well as mortally endangering Black's now stranded knight. For example, 29...♗f7 (the thief flees as the gendarmes approach) 30 ♕b4 (the fallen knight stares at his tormentor in bleak discomfort) 30...♕c6 31 ♖d1! (threat: ♖d6) 31...♖d8 32 ♖xd8+ ♖xd8 33 ♖xa7 h6 34 a6 ♖c8 35 ♕b7 is completely resignable for Black.

> ### Game 48
> ### **V.Kramnik-L.Van Wely**
> Wijk aan Zee 2010
> *King's Indian Defence*

I read that there was a Canadian TV show called *Endgame*, in which the fictional hero, an agoraphobic former Russian World Chess Champion, Arkady Balagan (apparently based on Kasparov's personality!), after witnessing his fiancée being gunned down in front of him – much like Peter Parker (aka Spiderman) and Bruce Wayne (aka Batman) – transferred his rage and profound analytical chess skills to solving unsolvable crimes.

> ***Question:*** That's great, but what does it have
> to do with this game, or Kramnik?

Answer: In one episode Balagan plays an internet blitz game with the white pieces and defeats another GM in brilliant positional style. Apparently, our Kramnik-Van Wely game is the fictional Balagan blitz win on the show!

1 d4 ♘f6 2 c4 g6 3 ♘c3 ♗g7 4 e4 d6 5 ♗e2 0-0 6 ♘f3 e5 7 ♗e3

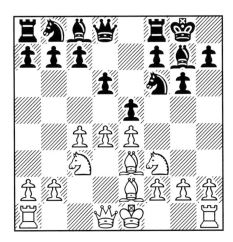

The Gligoric Variation of the King's Indian – and as in all King's Indians, the players' world views contrast sharply in their visions and hope for derivatives.

> **Question:** What is White's idea behind maintaining the tension?

Answer: In such KID situations, Black is normally unable to launch an effective attack on the kingside as long as central tension remains.

7...c6

The main line runs 7...♘g4 8 ♗g5 f6 9 ♗h4 ♘c6 10 d5 ♘e7 11 ♘d2 ♘h6 12 f3 c5 13 ♖b1 with play quite similar to the current game.

8 d5 ♘g4 9 ♗g5 f6 10 ♗h4 c5

Black closes the queenside as much as possible and hopes to take the fight to the kingside.

> **Question:** With the queenside closed, isn't Black better now?

Answer: No; ...c6-c5 fails to close the queenside completely. White eventually plays for b2-b4 and attempts to break in down the b-file.

11 0-0

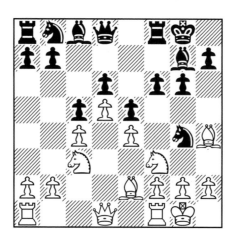

Answer: Agreed. Kramnik obviously has faith in White's defensive chances on the kingside. I would veer toward stalling castling, to keep Black guessing on the whereabouts of my king, with something like 11 ♘d2 h5 12 ♘f1 ♘h6 13 f3 ♘f7 14 ♗d3 ♘a6 15 a3 ♗h6 16 ♕c2 ♔g7 17 ♗f2 ♗d7 18 h4 ♕e7 19 ♘g3, B.Damljanovic-N.Mamedov, Sarajevo 2010.

11...♘h6

The main alternative is 11...h5, when L.Aronian-V.Ivanchuk, Linares 2009, continued 12 ♘e1 ♘h6 13 f3 ♘f7 14 ♖b1 ♗h6 15 ♗f2 ♘a6 16 a3 b6 17 b4 f5 18 exf5 gxf5 19 f4!? ♗xf4 20 ♗xh5 ♗d7 21 ♖b3! and I prefer White's chances, with the rook ready to swing to the kingside.

12 a3

Preparing the b2-b4 break.

12...♘a6?!

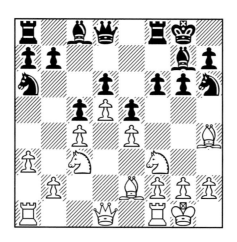

In a vivid transgressing of that which is sacred – "thou shalt not move a knight to the edge of the board!" – Van Wely relegates his piece to an unhappy posting, which Kramnik later exploits, since the wayward knight is unable to participate in Black's usual kingside assault. More natural is 12...♘d7, A.Huzman-E.Miroshnichenko, European Championship, Ohrid 2001.

13 ♘e1

Question: Why retreat the knight?

Answer: Dual purpose:

1. White plans ♘d3 to prepare his b2-b4 break and exert pressure on c5.
2. White clears the way for either f2-f3 or f2-f4.

13...♕e7 14 ♘d3 g5 15 ♗g3 f5 16 f3 f4 17 ♗f2 ♖f6

Van Wely plays directly for mate on the kingside.

18 b4 b6 19 bxc5 bxc5

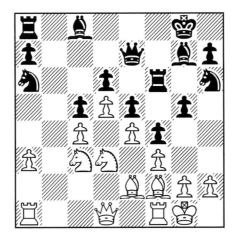

Question: What do you think about the recapture away from the centre with 19...dxc5 - ? I realize Black gives White a passed d-pawn, but has he bought himself time by keeping the queenside closed?

Answer: An interesting idea. That would be a new move in the position. I don't completely trust it but perhaps it's playable. I took White versus *Houdini*: 20 ♘b5 ♖g6 21 h3 ♘f7 22 a4 h5 23 ♗e1! (intending ♘f2; Black must act immediately) 23...g4 24 hxg4 hxg4 25 fxg4 and I prefer White, though an attacker may have faith in Black's kingside chances.

20 ♖b1 ♘f7 21 ♕a4!

Kramnik finds the tender spot in Black's position: c6. He continues to probe and investigate in search of the elusive hidden flaw in Black's camp.

21...♘d8

> ***Question:*** Has Black given up on his kingside assault?

Answer: He had no real choice and pays for his earlier 12...♘a6?! decision. White threat-ened ♕c6 and the a6-knight has no real hope of participation, so Van Wely endeavours to create a fortress on the queenside.

> ***Question:*** Why is ♕c6 a threat? Black can respond
> with ...♘c7, when everything holds together nicely.

Answer: You need to visualize the position just one ply deeper: 21...h5?? (say) 22 ♕c6 ♘c7 23 ♘b5! wins material.

22 ♗b2 h5 23 ♖fb1 ♖g6

The rook regards himself as the leading man in the film, yet lacks an essential some-thing: no charm, no menace, no sex appeal, no screen presence. Black's hoped-for kingside attack never comes to fruition.

24 h3 ♗f6

> ***Question:*** What is he waiting for and why all this
> exquisite nuance? Shouldn't Black go for it with 24...g4 - ?
> Perhaps a thug is required here more than a poet.

Answer: White's defences hold after 25 fxg4 hxg4 26 hxg4 ♗f6 27 ♘b5, because if Black proceeds with his thematic move 27...♗h4?, he walks into a devastating counterattack: 28 ♗xh4 ♕xh4 29 ♘xd6! ♖xd6 30 ♕e8+ ♔h7 31 ♕xe5 ♖h6 32 ♕xf4 and White's king remains remarkably unfazed, whereas Black has no chance against White's central passers.

25 ♔f1!

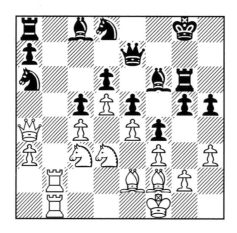

Just in case. Kramnik edges his king closer to the safety of the centre!

25...♕d7

Van Wely has clearly given up playing for mate and simply tries to plug all access squares on the queenside.

> **Question:** Why doesn't Black toss in
> ...g5-g4 at some point and go for mate?

Answer: Sometimes an absence of something – the deliberate not-doing by an opponent – actually provides us with valuable information. In this case, Black's normal kingside attack isn't going to materialize, otherwise Van Wely would indeed have played ...g5-g4 long ago.

26 ♗d1!?

Remarkable sangfroid. I would have jumped at any opportunity to swap queens.

26...g4!?

Van Wely finally urges the reluctant pawn forward one square.

27 fxg4 hxg4 28 hxg4 ♕xa4

Otherwise he can't regain g4.

29 ♗xa4 ♗xg4 30 ♗b5! ♘c7 31 ♗c6!

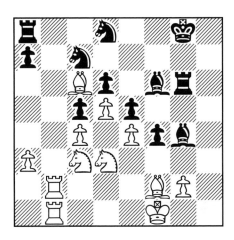

31...♖c8

I doubt Black can hold the game after 31...♘xc6 32 dxc6, because of White's portfolio of advantages:

1. He controls the open b-file with invasion access to b7 and b8.

2. His c6-pawn, far from a weakness, poses an existential threat to Black's survival.

3. White controls the powerful d5-square. When he plants a knight there, Black can't afford to swap and re-establish White's pawn structure.

Conclusion: Black is in deep trouble in the ending.

32 ♖b8

In the words of Trinity, when she and Neo attempt to infiltrate the military installation of the Matrix: "We're in!"

32...♖xb8 33 ♖xb8 ♔h7 34 ♗a4 ♖g7 35 ♗d1!

Offering to swap off Black's best minor piece.

35...♘a6

Question: Why not just retreat the bishop to d7?

Answer: White's position improves after 35...♗d7 36 a4 ♔g6 37 ♘b5! ♘xb5 38 cxb5!, intending ♘b2-c4 and a4-a5, creating a deadly passed pawn.

36 ♖a8

Preventing ...♘c7.

36...♗xd1 37 ♘xd1

Add one more advantage to White's ledger: good bishop versus bad bishop.

37...♖b7 38 ♘c3 ♘c7 39 ♖c8 ♘f7?!

39...♘e8! was a tougher defence to crack.

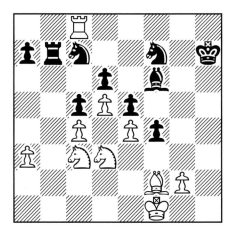

Researchers of the human brain recently discovered a new form of intelligence (and stupidity!) in the form of "risk intelligence". They say people with otherwise high IQs are still capable of making boneheadedly dumb decisions when it comes to taking or avoiding risk (my lifelong problem, except without the high IQ part!). Indulge in too big a risk and you endanger everything; avoid risk altogether and you lose opportunity. Let's test your risk IQ (but I warn you, this test is not so easy!)

Exercise (critical decision): Would you sac a piece for two pawns on c5, or is Black's epidermis too tough for the blunt needle to pierce? If you decide to sac, then with which piece?

Answer: The root tenet of the anarchist: destabilize society, whatever the cost. The bishop sac is totally sound.

40 ♗xc5!

Kramnik pounds and shapes the pawn structure to his liking; whereas after 40 ♘xc5?! dxc5 41 ♗xc5 ♗d8!, Black holds everything together.

40...dxc5 41 ♘xc5

Overloading Black's rook. His next move is forced.

41...♘d6! 42 ♘xb7 ♘xc8 43 c5

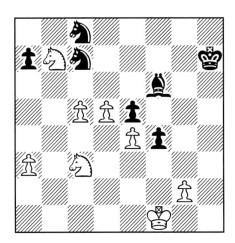

The position Kramnik foresaw when he sac'ed. White's two passers outweigh Black's extra piece.

43...♘a6 44 ♔e2 ♔g6 45 ♔d3?!

Krasenkow frowns upon this move and offers 45 ♘b5! instead. He quotes Shereshevsky: "Centralization of the king in the endgame is almost never wrong. However, it can be ill-timed." Such is the case here.

45...♗e7 46 ♘a4 ♔g5!

Destination: g2. In pioneer days, a man could travel much more quickly by himself than with a large wagon train of settlers. Van Wely makes a race of it.

47 ♔c4

Now d5-d6 is coming. This induces Black's desperado.

47...♗xc5?!

Instead:

a) 47...♔g4? 48 d6 ♘xc5 49 ♔xc5 ♔g3 50 dxe7 ♘xe7 51 ♘b2 ♔xg2 52 ♘d3 f3 53 ♘xe5! f2 54 ♘g4! wins.

b) 47...♘xc5! is Black's best shot; for example, 48 ♘axc5 ♔h4 49 a4! ♔g3 50 ♘d3 ♔xg2 51 ♘xe5 and here Krasenkow's analysis runs 51...♘b6+! 52 ♔b5 (not 52 ♔d4? ♗f6) 52...f3 53 ♘d3 ♘d7! 54 d6 ♗g5 55 ♘e1+ (or 55 ♘bc5 ♘e5!) 55...♔g3 56 ♘xf3 ♔xf3 57 ♔c6 ♘e5+ 58 ♔d5 ♗f4 59 ♘c5 ♘g4! 60 d7 ♗c7 61 ♘b7 ♔f4, when Kramnik's war effort dwindles from lull to complete stagnation. Proof that powerful logic sometimes churns out an incomprehensible conclusion. Whew! Black (barely!) hangs on for the draw. Of course, such lines are only seen through the omniscient eyes of the computers.

48 ♘axc5 ♘xc5 49 ♔xc5 ♔g4 50 d6 ♘b6 51 ♔c6 ♔g3 52 ♘c5!

It becomes quite clear that Kramnik acquired access to alien magic. White is faster by a single tempo. Kramnik worked out the math perfectly, as his knight veers this way and prances that way, obviously late for an appointment. The parties eagerly race toward a head-on collision on freeway f1.

52...♔xg2 53 d7! ♘xd7 54 ♘xd7 f3 55 ♘xe5 f2

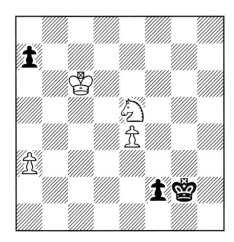

> ***Exercise (combination alert):*** Looks can be deceiving. How do
> we halt Black's queening dream and win the game?

Answer: The sniper draws a bead on his target's forehead in the crosshairs of his rifle. He understands this is his one and only chance. If he misses, the war is over and the other side wins.

56 ♘g4! 1-0

The fork threat on e3 wins the game, no matter which way Black promotes:

a) 56...f1♕ 57 ♘e3+ ♔f3 58 ♘xf1 ♔xe4 59 a4 wins.

b) 56...f1N 57 e5 ♘g3 58 e6 ♘f5 59 ♘e3+! (deflection – heroes are always eager to die gloriously for their cause; here the dark chimera strikes, leaving the stricken town folk to stare in open-mouthed incomprehension) 59...♘xe3 60 e7 promotes.

Chapter Six
Kramnik on Endings

Not since Capablanca has a world champion relied so heavily on his endgame skills as Kramnik. But while the freewheeling Capa basically winged it and just landed in endings, come what may, Kramnik has blurred the traditional boundary of *opening, middlegame and ending* by embracing his bypassed middlegame philosophy one step further. His method is more systematized and home prepared. He is the only world champion who has knowingly schemed to set up a portion of his opening repertoire to circumvent the middlegame completely and plunge immediately into the ending. His opponents – all armed with complex theoretical novelties in the King's Indian on the 27th move and the Sicilian Dragon on the 25th move – are rendered harmless, suddenly transported in disorienting fashion to a drugged, sedate kingdom in which Kramnik rules. It is as if a wizard casts an incantation which stupefies and puts to sleep the invading – and now loitering! – enemy front line.

The following are just a few variations within Kramnik's *no middlegame* arsenal:

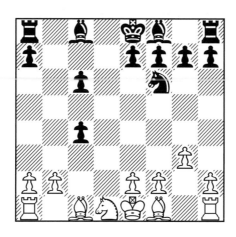

This is his English Opening against Timman from the first game of this chapter. We are only on the eighth move!

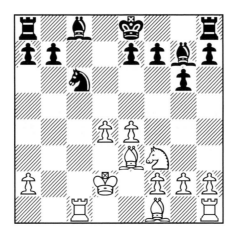

And here we have a Grünfeld versus Van Wely – move 12!

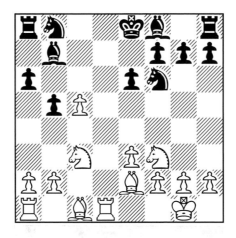

And this is a Queen's Gambit Accepted versus Tomashevsky – the endgame with which Kramnik also tormented Kasparov in their world title match – and it's only move 11!

There is no need to show you another diagram of the starting position of the Berlin Ruy Lopez; the opening/ending which Kramnik weaponized specifically for use against Kasparov; the ending which was responsible for making Kramnik World Champion.

Game 49
V.Kramnik-J.Timman
Wijk aan Zee 1999
English Opening

1 ♘f3 c5 2 c4 ♘f6 3 ♘c3 ♘c6 4 g3 d5 5 d4 cxd4 6 ♘xd4 dxc4 7 ♘xc6 ♛xd1+ 8 ♘xd1 bxc6

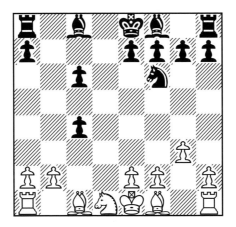

Question: Who do you think stands better in this ending?

Answer: I prefer White due to his structural superiority. Black merely has a temporary extra pawn which White should soon regain.

9 ♗g2 ♘d5 10 ♘e3 e6 11 ♘xc4

White recoups his investment losses while still enjoying the superior pawn structure.

11...♗a6 12 ♘a5!

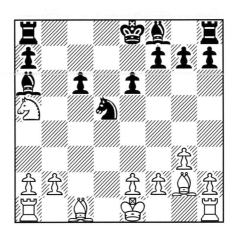

A theoretical novelty (in the opening/ending!?) and an improvement over Kramnik's earlier games (from both sides!) which had seen 12 b3 ♗b4+ 13 ♗d2 ♔e7 14 ♖c1 ♖hc8 (or 14...♖ac8) 15 ♗xb4+ ♘xb4 16 a3 ♘d5, as in V.Kramnik-J.Polgar, Tilburg 1997.

12...♗c5! 13 ♗d2!

Question: Why did White decline the offer of c6?

Answer: The pressure on Black's c-pawn isn't running away. White falls too far behind in development if he indulges in the immediate pawn grab: 13 ♘xc6?! ♖c8 14 ♘e5 0-0 15 ♗e4 ♖fd8 16 ♗d3 ♗xd3 17 ♘xd3 ♘b4!, when White has nothing better than to give back the pawn and suffer a possibly inferior ending.

13...0-0 14 ♖c1

Timman probably felt his strong piece activity and lead in development made up for his weak c6-pawn.

14...♗d4 15 b4!

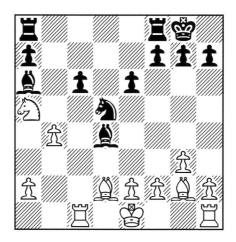

Nailing the weak point to c6.

15...♗b5 16 ♘xc6

Now is the time to take.

16...♗b2 17 ♖c5 ♗xc6 18 ♖xc6 ♖ac8

Question: Is Black just busted? White not only won a pawn, he also picked up the bishop pair.

Answer: White stands better but must still overcome his original problem: a lag in development. Black plans to infiltrate to c2.

19 ♖xc8 ♖xc8 20 ♗xd5!

Question: Doesn't this exchange greatly increase Black's
drawing chances due to the opposite-coloured bishops?

Answer: GM Tony Kosten writes: "A GM touch, swapping one advantage (the powerful light-squared bishop) for another (the IQP)." The swap is the best chance to win and certainly better than 20 0-0?! ♘c3, when White must chop the knight anyway but without the advantage of inflicting Black with an isolani on d5.

Nevertheless, it's hard to believe Kramnik converted this position. It's as if he untethered chess laws from their normal functions and moved them to another dimension where they don't apply.

20...exd5

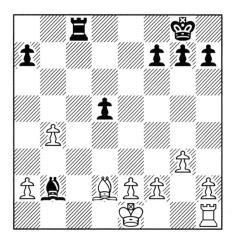

Exercise (planning): White's inactive rook is the umbilicus from which
Black's life-force flows. How to cut the cord and activate White's rook?

Answer: Kramnik refuses to resign himself to the fact that his activity dysfunction is the new status quo.

21 f4!!

Question: This looks like a random move. What is its purpose?

Answer: Dual purpose:
1. White solves the problem of rook development with the manoeuvre ♖f1-f3.
2. White, rather than castling, keeps his king fighting and in the centre.

Answer: Black should draw after 21 0-0 f6 22 ♖d1 ♖c4 23 ♗f4 d4 24 ♗d6 ♔f7 25 ♖d3 ♖c2 26 ♔f1 ♔e6 27 ♗c5 a5! 28 ♗xd4 ♗xd4 29 ♖xd4 ♖xa2 30 bxa5 ♖xa5 with a four versus three rook and pawn ending in which Black has excellent drawing chances.

21...♗a3 22 ♖f1!

The once-shunned mendicant shuffles forward, alms bowl in hand, as he begins his journey toward vindication and redemption.

22...♖c4

Answer: White regains his lost pawn in the following way: 22...♖c2 (the war party is destined to return home empty handed, with nothing to show for their efforts but new scars and new stories) 23 ♖f3 ♖xa2 24 ♖d3, picking up d5 in exchange for a2 and completing his development as well.

23 ♖f3!

The rook spirals into the air, sucked up by the tornado's force.

23...♗xb4 24 ♗xb4 ♖xb4 25 ♖a3

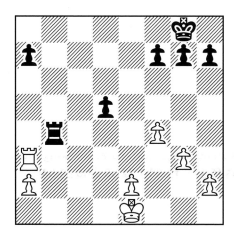

Black regained his lost pawn but not equality. Kramnik foresaw this position when he played 21 f4!!. The indelibly coded instructions in our DNA are essential to the survival of our species: fight or flight?

Answer: The black rook decides now is not the time for sentimentality. He abandons his brother to die on a7 in order to save himself.

25...h5!

Timman correctly followed the golden rule of all rook and pawn endings: *Keep your rook active at all costs, even if it means giving up a pawn.* Instead, after 25...♖b7? 26 ♖a5 ♖d7, White simply walks his king to d4 with a winning position; for example, 27 ♔d2 f6 28 ♔d3 ♔f7 29 ♔d4 ♔e6 30 g4 g6 31 e3 h5 32 h3 hxg4 33 hxg4 ♖b7 34 ♖a6+ ♖b6 35 ♖xa7 and Black won't hold the ending.

26 ♖xa7 ♖b2 27 a4?!

The immediate 27 f5! is more accurate.

27...♖a2?!

Black should play 27...g6! to prevent White's next move, when he has reasonable drawing chances.

28 f5!

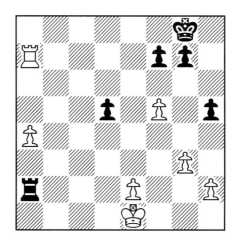

Now he sees it. Black can no longer jump-start his king into the ending.

28...♖a1+ 29 ♔f2 d4 30 a5 f6 31 ♔f3 ♔h7 32 a6 ♔h6 33 h4!

The black king, who moves with the exhausted effort of a man who just woke up, finds himself in limbo – no man's land. Once in, there is no out.

33...g6 34 fxg6 ♔xg6 35 ♖a8 ♖a2 36 ♔f4 ♔f7

36...♔g7 37 a7 ♖a1 38 ♔e4 is also hopeless.

37 a7 ♔g7 38 ♔f5 ♖a5+

Black's rook slashes out into the darkness, striking nothing but the ever-present emptiness.

39 ♔e4 ♖a4 40 ♔d5

The white king strolls alone through the once industrious back streets and lanes, now gone silent and abandoned.

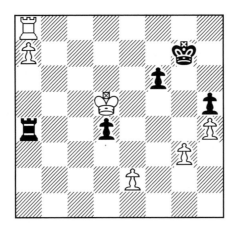

40...♖a1

40...♔h7 fails to alter anything: 41 ♔c5 ♔g7 42 ♔b6 ♖b4+ 43 ♔a5 ♖b2 44 ♖e8 ♖a2+ 45 ♔b6 and the a-pawn soon costs Black a rook.

41 ♔xd4 1-0

Black's broken-down army remains, but without anyone left to issue orders.

Game 50
V.Kramnik-L.Van Wely
Wijk aan Zee 2001
Grünfeld Defence

1 d4 ♘f6 2 c4 g6 3 ♘c3 d5 4 cxd5 ♘xd5 5 e4 ♘xc3 6 bxc3 ♗g7 7 ♘f3 c5 8 ♗e3 ♕a5 9 ♕d2 ♘c6 10 ♖c1 cxd4 11 cxd4 ♕xd2+ 12 ♔xd2

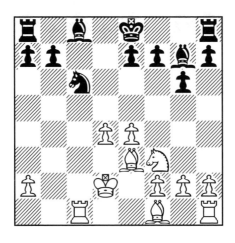

Here we have a classic battle of White's central and kingside majority versus Black's queenside majority.

Question: It seems a bit early for White's king to be roaming around in the middle. Is there danger of a sudden mating attack?

Answer: It's possible, but not likely since White controls the centre, which in turn offers him greater king security.

12...0-0 13 d5 ♖d8 14 ♔e1! ♘a5

The earlier game V.Kramnik-P.Leko, Budapest (rapid, 1st matchgame) 2001, had seen 14...♘e5 15 ♘xe5 ♗xe5 16 f4 ♗d6 17 ♔f2 e5 18 ♗c5!! (a deep pawn sac) 18...♗xc5+ 19 ♖xc5 exf4 20 ♔f3 ♗d7 (Black can't hang on to his early gains with 20...g5?! 21 h4 h6 22 hxg5 hxg5 due to 23 ♖h5 f6 24 e5! when he is in deep trouble) 21 ♗d3 ♖ac8 22 ♖hc1 g5 23 ♖c7 ♖xc7 24 ♖xc7 ♗a4 (24...♗c8 25 ♗c4 continues to exert heavy pressure on Black's position) 25 ♔g4! h6 26 ♖xb7 ♖d7 27 ♖b4 ♗d1+ 28 ♔f5, when Leko was unable to save himself against Kramnik's roaming king and powerful d-pawn.

15 ♗g5

This annoying move is standard operating procedure in such Grünfeld endings.

15...♗d7

No need to defend the pawn just yet.

16 ♗d3 ♖dc8

Perhaps Black should consider the exchange sac, starting with 16...f5! 17 e5 ♗e8 18 d6 exd6 19 ♗xd8 ♖xd8 20 exd6 ♗f8 21 ♔e2 ♗xd6, when his bishop pair and extra pawn should fully compensate him for the slight material deficit.

17 ♔e2 e6 18 ♗e3!

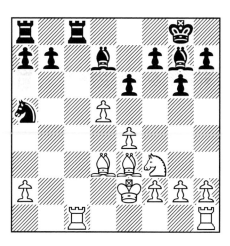

A theoretical novelty, probably prepared (but never used) against Kasparov in their world championship match. GM Neil McDonald points out that Kramnik's move gains a tempo on the line 18 ♗d2 exd5! 19 exd5 (19 ♗xa5? dxe4 regains the piece with clear advantage) 19...♖e8+ 20 ♗e3, V.Chekhov-Wl.Schmidt, Prague 1989.

18...exd5 19 exd5 b6!?

This looks passive, since it cedes temporary control over the c-file. Perhaps it is better to advance the pawn a bit further; i.e. 19...b5 20 ♘d2 a6 with an eye on the c4-square, as in the later game L.Van Wely-E.Sutovsky, Amsterdam 2001.

20 ♗a6! ♖d8 21 ♖hd1 ♗c8 22 ♗xc8 ♖axc8 23 ♖xc8!

Question: Earlier you said White took control over
the c-file, and now he gives it away. Why?

Answer: Kramnik's rather simple plan: promote his d-pawn. So in giving away the c-file he actually misplaces Black's rook, which needs to keep watch over White's soon-to-be surging passer. Compare this game to Kramnik-Anand from Chapter Three (Game 24), where Kramnik was successful with exactly the same plan.

23...♖xc8 24 ♘d4 ♗f8?!

Black's best defensive plan is probably to chop the powerful knight and then bring his king up quickly to help stop the d-pawn; i.e. 24...♗xd4! 25 ♖xd4 f6 and I don't think Black is any worse – as long as he doesn't go psycho with the pawn grab 25...♖c2+? 26 ♔d3 ♖xa2?? 27 d6 ♘b7 28 d7 ♘d8 29 ♗g5 and White wins.

25 ♘b5 a6

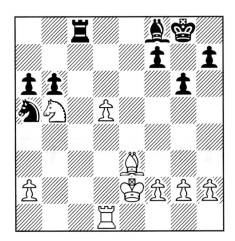

Exercise (combination alert): Black's a-pawn moves with
the urgent panic that follows a collapsing plan. White has
a little tactical trick which improves his position. What is it?

Answer: Ignore the threat to the knight.

26 d6!!

The d-pawn secretes upheaval as he oozes through the pores in Black's position. As all *Star Trek* fans understand, the heavy price one pays in joining the Borg Collective is the leeching of one's individuality, in exchange for absolute efficiency. In this case, every white piece dissolves its own identity to become a mindless servant of the surging d-pawn.

26...♖c2+

> **Question:** Your suggested "combination" comes across as a failed stage effect in a low-budget play. Black gets two pieces for a rook and a pawn, which is not such a bad deal, is it?

Answer: The trouble is that if we keep analyzing, we find the bishop and knight unable to deal with White's soon-to-be-passed a-pawn. For example, 26...axb5? 27 d7 ♖d8 (the exhausted defenders retreat further under the angry gaze of the invading d-pawn) 28 ♗xb6 ♘c6 29 ♗xd8 ♘xd8 30 ♖d5! (dual threats: ♖xb5 and, more importantly, ♖e5! followed by ♖e8) 30...♗g7 31 ♖xb5 ♔f8 32 a4 ♔e7 33 ♔d3!! (to prevent ...♗d4) 33...♔xd7 34 a5 ♔c6 35 a6! ♗d4! 36 ♖b8! (not 36 ♔xd4?? ♔xb5 37 a7 ♘c6+ and Black wins) 36...♘e6 37 ♖b7 ♗b6 38 ♖xf7 ♘c7 39 ♖xh7 ♘xa6 40 ♖h6 ♗xf2 41 ♖xg6+, when White's rook and pawn pair secure the win.

27 ♔d3 ♖xa2?

The emboldened rook inches across to grab a worthless pawn. Instead, he had to focus on halting the threat on the d-file with 27...♖c6! 28 d7 ♗e7 29 ♘c3 ♘b7 30 ♘d5 ♗d8, when Black sweats under the glaring lights of the interrogation, yet refuses to crack.

28 d7

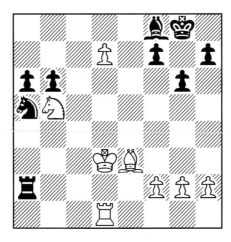

T minus one. Fear and anxiety swell, as the enemy nears. I find the admirably brutish, one-track mindedness of Kramnik's play quite inspiring.

28...♘b7 29 ♘c3 ♖b2 30 ♘d5 ♖b5

Black's rook, as if running in water, finds he can't keep pace with White's d-pawn and is unable to get back in time.

31 ♔c2!

Threat: ♗xb6, taking control over the queening square.

31...♗c5

The bishop intercedes but fails to stop the inevitable.

32 ♗h6!

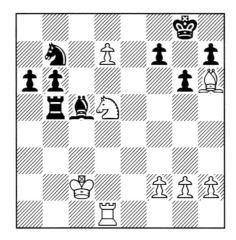

Black's defences, by now stretched, prodded and teased, finally reach their terminus of tolerance and snap, as threats sail out with lazy ease from Kramnik's side and soon detonate along the Southern borders of the board. Nothing can be done about the dual threats of 33 ♘f6+ (followed by 34 d8♕) and 33 ♘c7.

32...f6 33 ♘c7! 1-0

At last, on d8 we see the blooming flower of the coming explosion, which arrives with the careless, oblivious savagery of a baby playing with her blocks.

> ### Game 51
> **V.Topalov-V.Kramnik**
> Dortmund 2001
> *Nimzo-Indian Defence*

1 ♘f3 ♘f6 2 c4 e6 3 ♘c3 ♗b4 4 ♕b3 c5 5 g3 ♘c6 6 a3 ♗a5 7 ♗g2 0-0 8 0-0 d5 9 d3 h6 10 ♗f4 ♖e8 11 ♘a4 b6 12 ♘e5 ♗d7 13 e3 g5 14 ♘xc6 ♗xc6 15 ♗e5 ♘g4 16 ♗c3 ♗xc3 17 ♘xc3 dxc4 18 dxc4 ♗xg2 19 ♔xg2 ♕e7 20 ♘e4 f5 21 h3 ♘e5 22 ♕c3 ♘d7 23 ♘d2 ♖ad8 24 ♖ad1 ♘f6 25 ♘f3 ♖xd1 26 ♖xd1 e5 27 ♕c2 e4 28 ♘g1 ♖d8 29 ♘e2 ♖xd1! 30 ♕xd1 ♕d7 31 ♕xd7 ♘xd7

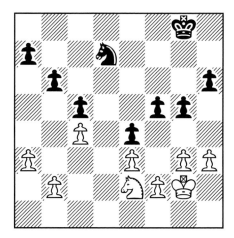

Question: Isn't this a dead draw? The pawn structure is completely level.

Answer: Well, not 100% level. Black still has a space advantage. This in turn gives him a secondary advantage: he can rush his king to the centre while White's king cannot.

Question: But enough to win?

Answer: Enough to hold an edge.

32 b3 ♘e5 33 ♘c3 ♔f7 34 g4!

Topalov immediately undermines Black's centre and, with it, his space advantage.

34...fxg4!

Question: Why didn't Kramnik maintain his space advantage by simply playing 34...♔e6 - ?

Answer: That was an option and he still held an edge there, but instead, Kramnik opts to go for an outside passed pawn, made that much more dangerous since it is a knight ending, which most closely resembles a king and pawn ending.

35 hxg4 ♘xg4 36 ♘xe4 ♔e6

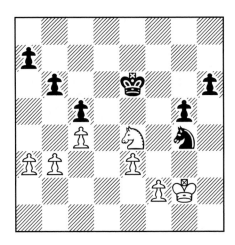

One imperceptible change can turn a loss into a draw or vice versa.

37 ♘c3?
The knight draws his weapon but then notices his hands begin to shake. It's a near-impossible thing to save an addict from craving-infested want. Topalov's instinct toward aggressive counterattack steers him down the wrong path. Soon he realizes the hostile knight's complicity in his downfall is beyond debate. The counterattack attempt is ineffective.

Answer: Instead, he should calmly strengthen his king's position with 37 ♔g3! ♘e5 38 f4 gxf4+ 39 exf4 ♘c6 40 ♔g4 ♘d4 41 b4 cxb4 42 axb4 a5 43 c5 axb4 44 cxb6 and the game is drawn.

37...♘e5! 38 f4 gxf4 39 exf4 ♘c6
Securing a7.

40 ♘b5 h5 41 ♔g3
Moments of stillness can be unnerving. It looks like Black's king position plus outside passed h-pawn may be enough to win. But saying so is just an abstraction.

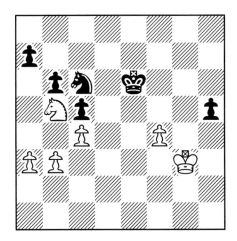

Exercise (planning): Find a concrete plan
for Black to move closer to the goal.

Answer: 41...a5!

The cunning pawn push breaches the defences, as another wave follows, variegated by multidirectional menace:

1. Black evades ♘xa7.

2. Black prevents b3-b4 and fixes a pawn target on b3.

3. Black frees his own knight for ...♘d4 to go after White's pawns.

42 ♘c7+ ♔f5 43 ♘d5 ♘d4 44 ♔h4

The white king finds himself wedged in the corner, propped up through force of will alone. The alternative 44 ♘xb6 ♘xb3 45 ♘d7 h4+! (the authorities haul White's king away, who all the while protests his innocence) 46 ♔xh4 ♔xf4 is similar to the game continuation. Black's king is first in the race toward the queenside pawns.

44...♘xb3 45 ♔xh5 ♘d2 46 ♘xb6 ♔xf4

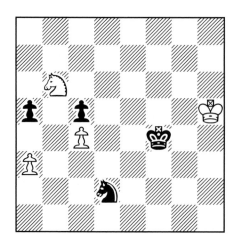

A miniscule alteration has fatal consequences in such delicate endings.

> **Exercise (critical decision):** White can play his knight to a4 or to d7. One of
> them draws; the other loses. Which move does your intuition point to?

47 ♘a4?

The knight, sodden in his own blood, ignores the pain and fear, continuing his hopeless
fight to win a single black pawn. The critical difference is the positioning of the two kings.
White's, now bereft of his former glory, can do no more than watch helplessly as Black's
king overruns the queenside.

Answer: White can save himself with 47 ♘d7!! ♞b3 48 ♔g6 ♔e4 49 ♔f6 ♔d4 50 ♘e5! (not
50 ♘b6? ♞d2) 50...♔c3 (or 50...a4 51 ♘d7! ♔xc4 52 ♘b6+ ♔b5 53 ♘d5 and Black cannot
make progress, while after 52...♔d4! 53 ♘xa4 c4 54 ♔f5! ♞c1 55 ♔f4 ♞d3+ 56 ♔f3 ♞b2 57
♘b6 c3 58 ♔e2, the white king returns just in time) 51 ♔e6 a4 (fixing the target on a3) 52
♔d5 ♔b2 53 ♘d3+ ♔xa3 (this looks lost for White since he can't touch c5, but he now has
an amazing resource) 54 ♔c6!!

(after 54 ♘xc5?? ♘xc5 55 ♔xc5 ♔b3 White loses the queening race) 54...♔a2 55 ♔b5 a3 56 ♔a4! (zugzwang; Black must give way) 56...♘d4 57 ♘xc5 ♔b2 58 ♘d3+ with a draw.

47...♘e4 0-1

Dismissing the threat with brusque efficiency. White's fallen king inclines his head, indicating his willingness to negotiate a surrender. Despite the simplification, White is helpless; for example, 47...♘e4 48 ♘b6 ♔e5 49 ♔g4 ♔d4 50 a4 ♘d6 51 ♔f4 ♘xc4 (shards of rubble fall in pyroclastic flow, as White's pawns begin to crumble) 52 ♘c8 ♘b2 53 ♘a7 (continuing the decaying orbit around Black's pawns in hopeless rotation) 53...♔d5! wins the final white pawn while retaining both of his own.

Game 52
V.Kramnik-M.Krasenkow
Wijk aan Zee 2003
Italian Game

1 e4 e5 2 ♘f3 ♘c6 3 ♗c4 ♗c5 4 c3 ♘f6 5 d3 a6 6 ♗b3 0-0 7 0-0 d5 8 exd5 ♘xd5 9 h3 ♘b6 10 ♖e1 h6 11 ♘bd2 ♕xd3 12 ♘xe5 ♕g3! 13 ♕f3 ♕xf3 14 ♘dxf3

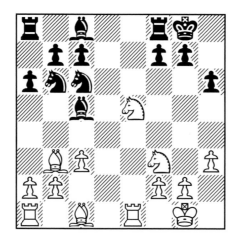

Question: Completely even?

Answer: Believe it or not, Black is in trouble. White's pieces exert pressure on f7 and, strangely enough, there isn't much Black can do about it.

14...♘e7?!

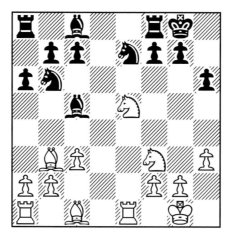

Exercise (combination alert): Black should have traded knights on his last move. Kramnik has a cute trick which exploits the omission. What would you play here?

15 ♘d3

Kramnik goes for the more subtle, positional route. He chooses structure over material gains, which still leaves White in command strategically, but it is much simpler just to pick off a pawn.

Answer: 15 ♘xf7! ♖xf7 16 ♖xe7! (this is the move which is hard to see; White eliminates ...♘d5 blocks) 16...♗xe7 17 ♘e5 ♔f8 18 ♘xf7.

15...♗d6 16 ♗f4!

Eliminating Black's most efficient piece.

16...♘g6!

No choice, since 16...♗xf4? fails to 17 ♘xf4 ♘c6 18 ♘g6! ♖d8 19 ♘e7+! ♔f8 (forced) 20 ♘xc6 bxc6 21 ♘e5 ♗e6 22 ♗xe6 fxe6 23 ♘xc6, when Black is down a pawn, with a train-wreck of a structure.

17 ♗xd6

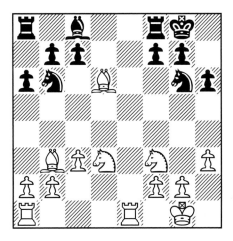

Dual purpose:

1. Black is stuck with a weak, isolated d-pawn.

2. White seizes control over a newly formed hole on d4.

17...cxd6 18 ♖e4!

Black must now watch out for transfers to d4 or b4.

18...a5

Question: Didn't he just create a fresh hole on b5?

Answer: Black did, yet his move looks justified. He desperately needs some activity and correctly allows a slight weakening to get it.

19 ♖d4

Target: d6.

19...♖d8 20 ♖d1 d5 21 ♘c5 ♘e7 22 a4 ♖e8 23 ♖4d2 ♘d7

The annoying, unwelcome guest must be evicted.

24 ♘xd7 ♗xd7

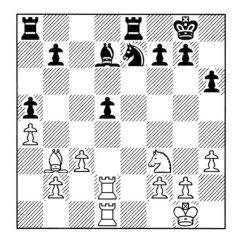

> ***Exercise (combination alert):*** White enjoys a very pleasant
> strategic advantage if he simply plants his knight on d4.
> But look around. White has something even better.

Answer: Pin/seventh rank infiltration.

25 c4! dxc4 26 ♖xd7 cxb3 27 ♖xb7 ♖ab8 28 ♖dd7

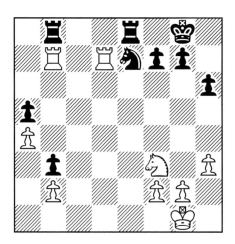

Either b3 or f7 will soon fall.

28...♘c6!?

I would have gone for 28...♖xb7 29 ♖xb7 ♘c6 30 ♖xb3 ♖e4 31 ♖c3 ♘d4 32 ♘xd4 ♖xd4 33 b3 with reasonable drawing chances.

29 ♖xf7 ♖xb7 30 ♖xb7 ♖e4 31 ♖xb3 ♖xa4 32 ♖b6 ♖c4

> ***Question:*** Can't Black get basically the same
> drawish ending if he swaps knights with 32...♘d4 - ?

Answer: In that scenario White won't swap knights.

33 g3 a4 34 h4 ♘d4 35 ♘e5!

The rook and pawn endings are much harder to win.

35...♖c5 36 ♖b8+ ♔h7 37 ♘d7! ♖b5 38 ♖a8 ♘e2+ 39 ♔g2 ♖xb2

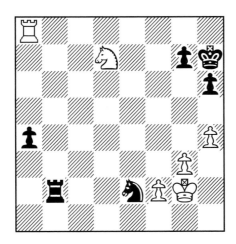

> ***Exercise (planning):*** Of course Kramnik can just take
> on a4 and try his luck in a three versus two ending on
> the kingside. Instead, he set his sights on Krasenkow's king. How?

Answer: Imprison the black king.

40 h5!

The point of White's play. Even with the reduced material Black's king is in trouble.

40...♘c3 41 ♘e5

Threat: ♘g6 and ♖h8 mate!

41...♖b5 42 f4 ♘e4 43 g4!

Renewing the ♘g6 threat.

43...♘f6 44 ♘g6 ♘g8

Black's knight has been forced into indentured servitude on g8.

45 ♘f8+ ♔h8 46 ♘g6+ ♔h7 47 ♔f3!?

White's rook, with immense distaste, only picks up Black's a-pawn (later on) with his fingertips and at arm's length, as if carrying a vomit-soiled rag. Kramnik displays an almost spiritual contempt for all things material, continuing to refuse the offer of a4, which a more crude, worldly player like me would have snatched in a heartbeat! **47...♖b3+ 48 ♔e4 a3 49 ♘f8+ ♔h8 50 ♘g6+ ♔h7 51 g5!**

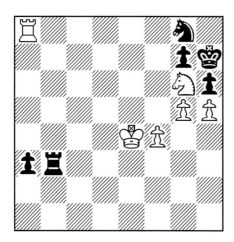

Cutting off f6 for Black's pieces and also adding another attacker into the mix.

> **Question:** But isn't there also the danger of swapping off too many pawns?

Answer: Very correct. Kramnik has factored that in and sees the swap as his only way to play for the win.

51...hxg5 52 fxg5 ♖b4+ 53 ♔f5 ♖b5+ 54 ♔g4 ♖b4+ 55 ♔f5 ♖b5+ 56 ♔g4

> **Question:** Why does Kramnik indulge in all these random, meaningless repetitions?

Answer: They are not so random. It is a standard trick for the superior side to burn moves to gain time on the clock. Also, I think such repetitions inflict subtle psychological damage to the defender, who must dance around to his opponent's irrational whims!

56...♖b4+ 57 ♘f4 a2

57...♖b3?? walks into a mate after 58 g6+ ♔h8 59 ♘e6 ♖b4+ 60 ♔f3 ♖b3+ 61 ♔e4 ♖b4+ 62 ♔d3 ♖b5 63 ♔c4 ♖xh5 64 ♘d8!, when nothing can be done about the coming knight check on f7.

58 ♖xa2

At last. One more item into the paper shredder.

58...♘e7 59 ♖a8 ♘g8 60 ♖a7

Kramnik logically targets g7, missing a study-like win after 60 g6+! ♔h8 61 h6!!, when Black's resistance dissolves as quickly as a teaspoon of sugar in a steaming hot cup of black coffee: 61...gxh6 62 ♖a7 h5+ 63 ♔g5 ♖b5+ 64 ♔h4! ♞f6 65 ♖f7 ♖b6 66 ♔g5 ♞g4 67 ♖f5! ♔g8 68 ♞xh5 ♖b4 69 ♖f7 ♖b6 70 ♖c7! (threat: ♖c8 mate – Black's forces tangle in a cob-webbed landscape of disarray and inefficiency) 70...♖b8 71 ♔xg4 mates in at most seven moves.

60...♔h8 61 ♖a8 ♔h7 62 ♖f8

62 g6+! still wins by transposing to the previous note.

62...♔h8 63 ♔f3 ♖b3+ 64 ♔e4 ♖b4+ 65 ♔e5 ♖b5+ 66 ♞d5?!

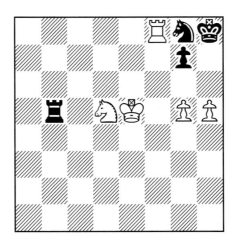

The beginning of an incorrect plan. Kramnik now sees the above idea but in an incor-rect sequence. The addition of this move dilutes White's attack, until it levels off to a mere residue of its original potency.

66...♖a5 67 ♖d8 ♔h7 68 g6+?! ♔h8

He places his king into a storage unit – a hibernation – mainly to conserve his depleted energy stores.

69 h6

This looks like a killing shot, but Krasenkow is ready with an amazing defence.

69...♖a7!!

Krasenkow sets up a devilishly insidious trap, all the while severing the causal link to his present and future suffering. 69...gxh6? 70 ♖d7! is an instant game-ender.

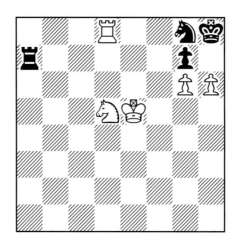

70 ♘e3!

Kramnik deftly sidesteps the trap. 70 h7?? walks into Krasenkow's dirty stalemate scheme: 70...♖e7+ 71 ♔f5 ♖e5+! and draws as the mad rook will not be denied.

70...gxh6 71 ♘f5 ♖a5+??

> *Question:* Aren't both sides making a lot of errors?

Answer: This ending shows how such seemingly simple positions are, in reality, not so simple to work out over the board. Confusion comes in waves so powerful that neither side can be confident enough to parse the core mysteries of the position to perfection. I believe it was the poet Sylvia Plath who once wrote that perfection isn't such a great thing because it is unable to procreate. Here 71...♖a1!, getting ready to bombard White's king with checks, would have saved the game.

72 ♔f4 ♖a4+ 73 ♔f3 ♖a3+ 74 ♔g4 ♖a4+ 75 ♔h5

No more checks.

75...♖a7 76 ♖f8! ♖b7

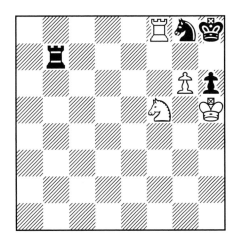

> *Exercise (calculation):* Does 77 ♖f7 work for White?

77 ♔h4?!

Black's fire-stained wall remains erect, a dull reminder of what could have been an in-candescent explosion, if only White had lit the fuse. Luckily for Kramnik, he doesn't throw away his win after this move.

Answer: It works! 77 ♖f7!! ♖xf7 78 gxf7 ♘f6+ 79 ♔g6 ♘d7 80 ♔xh6 ♘f8 81 ♘h4! is zugzwang! The stinging blow knocks Black's king down and sends him sprawling over the pavement and onto his back. The knight swivels right, circumventing all resistance, as White mates next move. The black king finds himself encircled by hostiles with no place to hide or run.

77...♖b4+ 78 ♔g3 ♖b6

78...♖b3+ 79 ♔g4 ♖b4+ 80 ♔h5 ♖b7 returns to the diagram position above, while 80...♖b1 81 ♖f7 ♖h1+ 82 ♘h4! also wins, as White's delegates conspire in illicit congress around Black's king.

79 ♘e7!

In the end, Black was unable to escape the gravitational pull of the vortex on g8.

79...♔g7

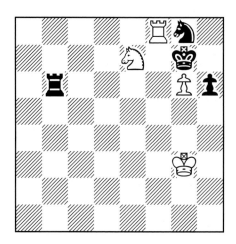

Exercise (combination alert): White can take the g8-knight. Do you see anything better?

Answer: Mate in two moves!

80 ♖f7+! 1-0

Game 53
V.Kramnik-Zhang Zhong
Wijk aan Zee 2004
Nimzo-Indian Defence

1 ♘f3 ♘f6 2 c4 e6 3 ♘c3 ♗b4 4 ♕c2 0-0 5 a3 ♗xc3 6 ♕xc3 b6 7 e3 ♗b7 8 ♗e2 d6 9 0-0 ♘bd7 10 b4 c5 11 ♗b2 ♖e8 12 d4 ♘e4 13 ♕b3 ♖b8 14 ♖ad1 ♕c7 15 ♘d2 ♘ef6 16 ♖c1 a5 17 ♖fd1 e5 18 ♗f1 axb4 19 axb4 h6 20 ♗a1 ♖ec8 21 ♗b2 ♖e8 22 dxc5 dxc5 23 ♘b1! cxb4 24 ♕xb4 ♘c5 25 ♘c3 ♖bd8 26 ♖b1 ♗c6 27 ♗a1 ♖xd1 28 ♖xd1 ♖d8 29 ♘b5 ♗xb5 30 ♗xe5 ♕xe5 31 ♖xd8+ ♗e8 32 ♕xb6 ♕e7 33 ♖c8 ♘fd7 34 ♕c7 ♔f8 35 g3 ♘e6 36 ♕c6 g6 37 ♗h3 f5 38 ♗g2 ♔g7 39 ♗d5 ♘ec5 40 ♕a8 ♗f7 41 ♕a1+ ♕f6 42 ♕a7 ♕a6 43 ♕xa6 ♘xa6

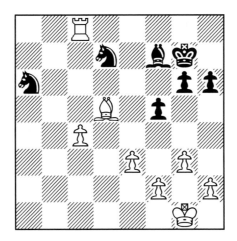

44 f3

Answer: Advantage White. His rook and two pawns outweigh Black's knights.

Question: Why doesn't the knight pair constitute equality?

Answer: Technically, a pair of minor pieces is roughly the equivalent of a rook and two pawns, but not here. Black's main problem is lack of viable targets. White already has a passed c-pawn and he soon begins to move his kingside pawn majority forward to create a second passer.

44...♘ac5 45 ♔f2 ♔f6 46 ♖c6+ ♗e6

Question: Why did Black self-pin?

Answer: He wants to put his king on e5 and so needs to block out White's rook, which prevents this along the sixth rank.

47 ♔e2 ♔e5 48 f4+

Question: Should White be concerned about the newly formed hole on e4?

Answer: No. Black has no real way to exploit it.

48...♔f6 49 ♔d2 ♔e7 50 ♗f3 ♘b3+!?

It's hard to know whether Black should just tuck himself in and wait with 50...♘a4, as after 51 ♔c2 ♘dc5 52 ♖c7+ ♗d7 53 ♗c6! ♘b6 (53...♔d6?? 54 ♖xd7+! wins) 54 ♗xd7 ♘bxd7 55 ♔c3 I don't have great faith in Black's drawing chances.

51 ♔c3 ♘a5!

Black deliberately "falls" for a combination, correctly discerning that the ensuing ending is his best shot to hold the game. Clearly Zhang lacked faith in the integrity of Black's blockading potential after 51...♘bc5.

52 ♖a6

Not 52 ♖c7? ♔d8, when White unceremoniously tosses away his precious c-pawn.

52...♘xc4

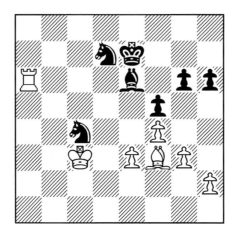

> *Exercise (combination alert):* Here is
> an easy one. White to play and win material.

Answer: Removal of defender.

53 ♖xe6+! ♔xe6 54 ♔xc4

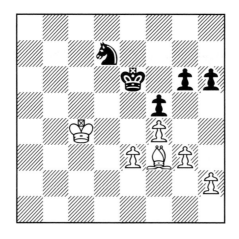

Nevertheless, this isn't going to be simple. Four versus three on the same side, with bishop over knight, is a monumental technical task.

54...g5 55 &d5+ &f6

Question: Why doesn't Black challenge the white's
king entry by posting his king to d6 instead?

Answer: The trouble is that f5 then becomes a source of concern for Black; for example, 55...&d6 56 &d4 ♘f6 57 &b7!, when &c8 is in the air.

56 &c6 ♘f8 57 &d5 ♘g6 58 &d6 ♘e7 59 &b7 ♘g6 60 &f3 ♘f8

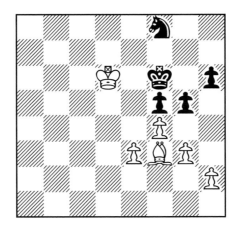

White's bishop is unable to enforce zugzwang by himself. Zhang's defensive plan is just to wait and shuffle his knight back and forth. This in turn forces Kramnik to push forward on the kingside.

61 &d5 ♘g6 62 &c6 ♘f8 63 &d7 ♘g6 64 h3 h5!

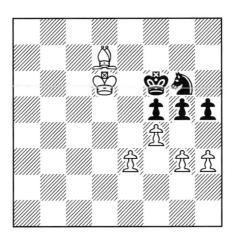

Very alert. At first we see just a ripple of motion from Black, and then comes mass exodus, like bats flushed from the church steeple tower. Zhang goes after both the apex and base of the isosceles triangle on f4 and g3, remaining flexible and seizing his chance to swap more pawns.

Question: Why can't he continue to just shuffle?

Answer: Zugzwang. For example, after 64...♘f8? 65 h4! gxh4 66 gxh4 ♘g6 67 h5, Black loses use of the g6-square and will soon be in zugzwang: 67...♘f8 68 ♗c8 ♘h7 69 ♗e6 ♘f8 70 ♗d5 ♘h7 71 ♔d7! ♔g7 72 ♔e7 ♘f6 73 ♗f3 ♘h7 (73...♘g4 loses ignominiously to 74 e4) 74 ♔e6 and White picks off the second pawn and wins.

65 fxg5+!

Not 65 ♗e8?, when 65...h4! holds the draw.

65...♔xg5 66 h4+! ♔g4

Black's king reaches the limits of his curiosity and decides to peer over White's wall. He defends excellently and should be rewarded with a hard earned draw. White has too few pawns remaining.

Remarkably, Black has another method of holding the game with 66...♔f6, which appears to lose to 67 ♗e8, but watch Black's knight: 67...♘e5 (threat: ...♘c4+ to pick off e3) 68 ♔d5 ♘g4 69 ♔d4 (it looks like the end of the line for Black, but this is an illusion) 69...♘h2! 70 ♗xh5 ♘f1, though Black hasn't yet achieved his goal because of 71 e4! fxe4! (not 71...♘xg3? 72 e5+ ♔g7 73 ♗f3 and wins) 72 g4 with connected passed pawns. But Black is still not dead: 72...♘g3! 73 g5+ ♔f5 74 ♗d1 ♔f4! 75 g6 ♘f5+ 76 ♔c5 ♔e5 77 h5 ♔f6, when nothing stops ...♘h4 and ...♘xg6 with a draw.

67 e4 ♔xg3 68 exf5

The beautiful mystery in the Mona Lisa's smile lies buried in its ambiguity, much like this position.

68...♘h8?

Unnatural and bad. If you thought this was a trick question and chose to get clever by heading into the corner, then I offer a piece of advice. Extremes tend toward the harmful: on the one hand, a person starves to death; on the other, he succumbs to an obesity-related illness. Here decentralization loses, as the combined might of king and bishop overpower their inefficient counterparts.

Answer: Instead, Black achieves a study-like draw with 68...♘f8! 69 f6 (if 69 ♔e7 ♘h7 70 ♔f7 ♔xh4 71 ♔g7 ♘g5 72 f6 then 72...♔g3! 73 ♔h6 ♔f4 holds the draw) 69...♔xh4 70 f7 ♔g5 71 ♔e7 ♘g6+ 72 ♔e8 ♔f6 73 ♗c6 ♔g7 74 ♗e4 ♘f8 75 ♗c2 h4 76 ♗f5! (now Black can't move his knight, so he must toss his final pawn) 76...h3 77 ♗xh3 ♘h7 78 ♔e7 ♘f8 79 ♗f5.

Answer: No! 79...♔h8!.

How annoying. The stalemate saves Black. His knight hopes to attract the white king's attention the way a bored, misbehaving child would get her parent's notice.

69 ♔e7 ♔xh4 70 ♔f6!

The faithful continue to rebuild their f-pawn god's temple, stopping occasionally to rest, kneel and pray. White's last move highlights Black's incorrect decision to send his knight into the corner. From this point on, Kramnik completes the parametric equation with perfect accuracy. The black knight is boxed in and is likely to live out his days within the mathematical prison on the first rank. Each module of White's position sits in perfect harmony, in the creation of a greater whole.

70...♔g4 71 ♔g7 ♔g5 72 f6!

Not 72 ♔xh8?? ♔f6 and draws, as Black simply pushes his h-pawn forward.

72...h4 73 ♗c8 ♔h5! 74 ♗f5!

Kramnik is not going to fall for the cheapo 74 ♔xh8?? ♔g6. Instead, the stern bishop doles out penance, even for the most insignificant infractions.

74...♔g5 75 ♗e6!

Zugzwang!

75...♘g6

Finally, the knight belches forth from the depths, like a bubble of swamp gas rising up and erupting on the surface of slimy, stinking water.

76 f7 ♘f4 77 ♗c8 ♘h5+

77...♘g6 78 ♗d7! ♔h5 79 ♗f5! ends resistance.

78 ♔h7 1-0

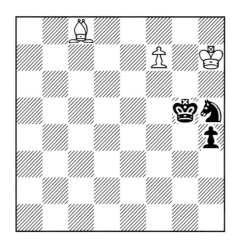

After 78...♘f6+ 79 ♔h8, the knight, alone, out of place and so far from home, is the single black ant living among the colony of hostile red ants. White's bishop and king throw glances laced with poisonous significance the knight's way in silent warning: "Don't come any closer." The mixed-up defenders, tissue paper tossed in a bonfire, have no effect in halting the f-pawn's upcoming promotion.

Game 54
V.Kramnik-P.Leko
World Championship (14th matchgame), Brissago 2004
Caro-Kann Defence

This was the final game of the match, with Kramnik in the most nightmarish scenario imaginable: one point down and having to win to retain the World Championship. And against one of the most solid, difficult to defeat opponents since Emanuel Lasker faced Carl Schlechter. Talk about pressure!

1 e4 c6 2 d4 d5 3 e5 ♗f5 4 h4 h6 5 g4 ♗d7 6 ♘d2 c5 7 dxc5 e6 8 ♘b3 ♗xc5 9 ♘xc5 ♕a5+ 10 c3 ♕xc5 11 ♘f3 ♘e7 12 ♗d3 ♘bc6 13 ♗e3 ♕a5 14 ♕d2 ♘g6 15 ♗d4 ♘xd4 16 cxd4 ♕xd2+

17 ♔xd2

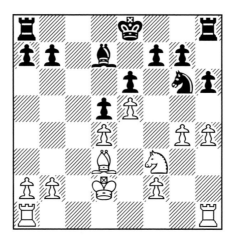

Answer: I don't think so. As a long-time French player, I know a bad French ending when I see one. Not only does White have extra space in the centre and on the kingside, Black must also deal with a bad remaining bishop, hemmed in by his own pawns. Having said that, I must add that such positions are not so easy to win as White.

Answer: Black may be cramped and carry the burden of a bad bishop, but he has no real weaknesses, so White still has a lot of work ahead.

Answer: Most experienced French players would go for something like ...♘e7-c6, ...♔e7 and ...♖ac8, when at least Black connects his rooks to challenge for the c-file.

17...♘f4?!

Threatening *not* to take White's bishop, since that would accentuate Black's remaining bishop's rottenness, versus a rather limber white knight. If that is the case, then we ask: why play the knight to f4?

18 ♖ac1 h5?!

After the game Leko thought he could save the game with 18...♘xd3.

Question: Do you agree with this assessment?

Answer: I don't. It took me decades to figure out that one shouldn't believe in something on the sole basis that you desperately *want* to believe in it. GM Shipov suggested the continuation 19 ♔xd3 ♗b5+ 20 ♔e3 ♔d7 21 h5! ♖ac8 22 ♘h4 ♖xc1 23 ♖xc1 ♖c8 24 ♖xc8 ♔xc8 25 f4! ♔d7 26 f5, claiming good winning chances for White. I agree. White's kingside space and superior minor piece give him every chance to score the full point.

19 ♖hg1! ♗c6

19...♘h3 20 ♖g2 ♘f4 21 ♖g3 doesn't get Black anywhere.

20 gxh5! ♘xh5 21 b4!

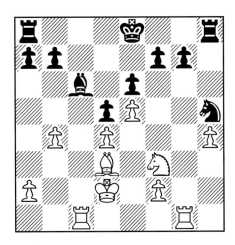

Increasing his spatial gains all across the board.

21...a6 22 a4! ♔d8

Kasparov claimed that Black's best shot to hold the game was to grab a4 with 22...♗xa4 23 ♖c7 ♗b5!, but after 24 ♗b1! Black's position still looks quite grim to me.

23 ♘g5 ♗e8

The tormented soul is consigned to the fires of hell for everlasting eternity.

24 b5 ♘f4

Attacking h4. 24...axb5 25 ♗xb5! also puts Black under enormous strain.

25 b6!

Hey, I said "attacking h4"! Kramnik brushes aside and ignores the flea bite on h4 with dry disdain, as he generates the crushing strategic threat of ♖c7. Black is well on his way toward absolute asphyxiation.

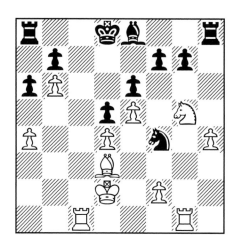

25...♘xd3

Leko wrinkles his nose in disgust at the foul stench permeating from e8, as he acquiesces to bad bishop versus good knight.

26 ♔xd3 ♖c8!

The only move. Not 26...♖xh4? 27 ♖c7 ♖c8 28 ♘xf7+ ♗xf7 29 ♖xf7 and Black can resign.

27 ♖xc8+ ♔xc8 28 ♖c1+ ♗c6

Leko furiously plugs the dyke. The destitute bishop for so long needed a job but was too proud to beg for one. Finally, he achieves gainful employment as a security officer, who prevents rook infiltration to c7. Unfortunately, this is only for show. Black manages to prettify his defences without actually altering them in any meaningful way.

29 ♘xf7 ♖xh4 30 ♘d6+ ♔d8 31 ♖g1!

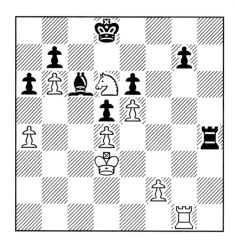

Kramnik faces intractable resistance on the queenside, so he switches to another front.

31...♖h3+ 32 ♔e2 ♖a3

Black's rook politely steps aside, making an "after you" motion with his hands, as he allows White's rook into g7.

Question: This looks like suicide. Why can't
Black just remain passive and cover g7?

Answer: Passive defence loses as well: 32...♖h7 33 a5 ♔d7 34 ♖g3 ♔d8 35 ♖f3! (threatening to infiltrate at f7) 35...g6 36 ♖f6 wins.

33 ♖xg7

The rook mouths a silent "thank you!" as he blows a kiss to the g-pawn from across the room.

33...♖xa4

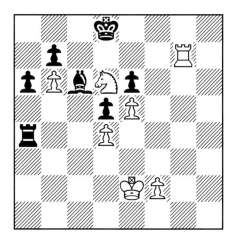

Exercise (planning/combination alert): We all smell a winning idea
here for White, the way a dog senses a near-by bone. But what is it?

Answer: The optimist who dreams of paradise is a fool, since he is already there. White's d-pawn doesn't matter. Instead, he plays for f2-f4-f5!, which frees the path for the e5-pawn to enter the attack.

34 f4!! ♖a2+

After 34...♖xd4? 35 f5! exf5 36 e6 ♖e4+ 37 ♘xe4 dxe4 38 ♖c7!! Black has no reasonable defence to ♖xc6!, which wins the queening race.

35 ♔f3 ♖a3+ 36 ♔g4!

Kramnik's king isn't merely running away from checks, he actively participates in the coming mating attack.

36...♖d3 37 f5!

Anyway, even with check.

37...♖xd4+ 38 ♔g5 exf5 39 ♔f6!

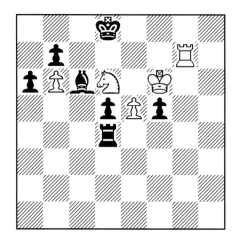

The non-conformist king has a charming way of stressing out the orthodoxy and the powers that be on Black's side. Déjà vu. Do you remember Capablanca's famous rook and pawn ending win against Tartakower at New York 1924? In that game Capa also shunned the capture of an f-pawn, leaving it to shield the king, with (weirdly enough on the same move) 39 ♔f6!.

39...♖g4 40 ♖c7!

White's threats:

1. e5-e6 and e6-e7 (or ♖c8) mate.

2. ♘f7+ and ♖e7 mate.

40...♖h4

Answer: **41 ♘f7+! 1-0**

The knight steps on the back of the black king's cape with blithe disregard for court etiquette, and 41...♔e8 42 ♖c8+ ♔d7 43 ♖d8 is mate.

Game 55
V.Kramnik-V.Topalov
World Championship (4th rapid playoff game), Elista 2006
Semi-Slav Defence

Déjà vu again. Kramnik, under no less pressure than in the previous game, now faced Topalov in a rapid playoff for the world title. Once more he proved that his nerves were stronger than his opponent's.

1 d4 d5 2 c4 c6 3 ♘f3 ♘f6 4 ♘c3 e6 5 e3 ♘bd7 6 ♗d3 dxc4 7 ♗xc4 b5 8 ♗e2 ♗b7 9 0-0 ♗e7 10 e4 b4 11 e5 bxc3 12 exf6 ♗xf6 13 bxc3 c5 14 dxc5 ♘xc5 15 ♗b5+ ♔f8 16 ♕xd8+ ♖xd8

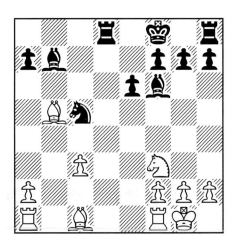

Answer: Believe it or not, Black has yet to equalize, despite his superior structure. White's lead in development matters. Black is uncastled and his h8-rook remains out of the picture for quite a while to come.

17 ♗a3 ♖c8!

More accurate than 17...♗e7?! 18 ♘e5!, when White is ready to invade c6.

18 ♘d4

GM Scherbakov thought 18 ♖ab1!, intending ♗d7!, put more pressure on Black.

18...♗e7 19 ♖fd1?!

Again, perhaps 19 ♖ab1! is better.

19...a6?!

Topalov may have snatched the world title had he found 19...♘e4! 20 ♗b4 ♘xc3 21 ♘xe6+ fxe6 22 ♗xe7+ ♚xe7 23 ♖d7+ ♚f6 24 ♖xb7 ♖b8 25 ♖xb8 ♖xb8 26 ♗c4 ♖b4 27 ♗b3 ♘e2+ 28 ♚f1 ♘d4 29 ♗d1 ♖b2, when it is White who is tied up and fighting for the draw. Perhaps Topalov rejected 19...♘e4 because of 20 ♘xe6+ (??) fxe6 21 ♗xe7+ ♚xe7 22 ♖d7+, but then it is Black who wins after 22...♚f6 23 ♖xb7 ♘d6!.

20 ♗f1

Now White is okay.

20...♘a4!?

Typically, Topalov goes for the target on c3. Perhaps he would have been better served if he played 20...g6 to complete his development.

21 ♖ab1 ♗e4?!

Another inaccuracy gives White the better chances. 21...♗d5! was safer.

22 ♖b3 ♗xa3

Question: Doesn't 22...♗d5 tie White up?

Answer: White has the resource 23 c4!, after which he stands better.

23 ♖xa3 ♘c5 24 ♘b3

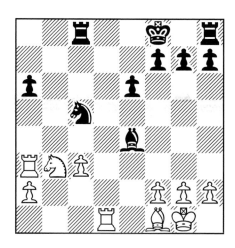

Target: a6.

24...♚e7!

Topalov takes a defiant stance to confront the intruder. He isn't so worried about handing over a6, as he can calmly complete his development and target c3. Instead, 24...♘xb3?! is weak, as after 25 axb3 the c3-pawn isn't hanging due to a rook check on d8.

25 ♖d4 ♗g6 26 c4!

Securing his c-pawn.

26...♖c6?!

Losing time and also his a-pawn. Black holds the draw after 26...♘xb3! 27 axb3 ♖hd8! 28 ♖xd8 ♔xd8! 29 ♖xa6 ♖b8 30 ♖a3 ♗c2.

27 ♘xc5 ♖xc5 28 ♖xa6

The hungry pig, who isn't picky about what he eats, roots around in the soil for grubs.

28...♖b8

Topalov is a natural optimist, and I am willing to bet he liked his position here. Black is ready to generate serious threats along White's first and second ranks. However, Kramnik assessed the ending more accurately, realizing that he can defend against the threats while still retaining his extra material.

29 ♖d1!

It is critical not to allow ...♖b1.

29...♖b2

Everyone in the room goes quiet, as the outlaw enters the saloon.

30 ♖a7+ ♔f6 31 ♖a1!

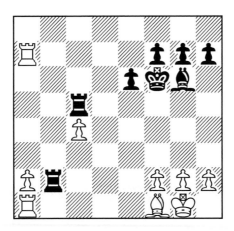

Principle: *Place your rooks behind your passed pawn.* Even as tied up as White is, Black can't make headway, and soon White begins to unravel.

31...♖f5

Inducing a weakness. 31...♗b1 is answered by 32 ♖a3!, intending ♖b3!.

32 f3 ♖e5!

Kramnik plays a dangerous game by allowing Black's pieces to roam about, free from constraint. Black threatens to increase the pressure to stranglehold levels with the manoeuvre ...♗b1! followed by ...♖e1!.

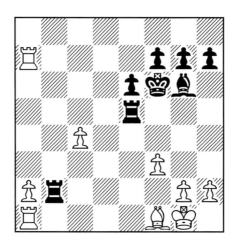

> ***Exercise (planning):*** It's easy to lose one's way within the subterranean catacombs of plans and non-plans. Find a way to disrupt Black's intention.

Answer: **33 ♖a3! ♖c2**

Black takes the slow, careful steps of a trespasser, always keeping an eye out for the occupant. Now if Black blindly proceeds with his plan he loses: 33...♗b1?? 34 ♖b3! ♖xb3 35 axb3, when the pawns hug and exchange handshakes as White's two passed pawns win the game. If instead 33...♗c2 (to stop ♖b3) then 34 ♖c3 ♗a4 35 c5! and White takes over the initiative.

34 ♖b3 ♖a5 35 a4

The ant begins the journey, hoping to scale the mountain. Kramnik managed a Houdini-like (I mean both the escape artist and also the computer!) unravelling. Move by move, Black's options and his former initiative continue to narrow.

35...♔e7

Black's king, like a nervous person who worked late and now enters the darkened parking lot, fumbles with his keys as he scampers to his car. Topa's king rushes to the queenside to assist the hoped-for blockade.

36 ♖b5 ♖a7 37 a5

The once humble a-pawn surges forward.

37...♔d6 38 a6

If only Black could get his bishop in play in time by ...f7-f6 and ...♗e8-c6.

38...♔c7 39 c5

Threat: ♖ab1, followed by ♖b7. The infestation of creepy-crawly white pawns continues unabated.

39...♖c3!

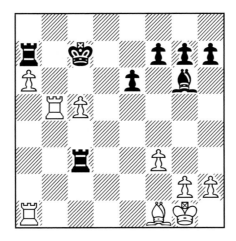

Exercise (planning): White would like to double rooks on the b-file and then play ♖b7+. How can he accomplish this monumental ambition without dropping either of his queenside pawns?

Answer: Overprotect c5.

40 ♖aa5!!

White's rook approaches with insincere nonchalance. Now Black can't deal with the threat of ♖b6!, ♖ab5 and ♖b7+.

♖c1 41 ♖b3!

Oh, no you don't! Kramnik disallows the ...♗d3 cheapo.

41...♔c6 42 ♖b6+ ♔c7 43 ♔f2 ♖c2+ 44 ♔e3 ♖xc5??

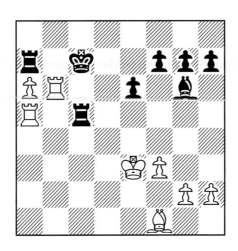

In time pressure, Topa took what he believed to be the short cut to the draw. Unfortunately, it turns out that his trajectory happens to be the long cut.

Answer: Champagne glasses clink in unison, as White's pieces toast their rook for his valour. Meanwhile, the surprised black king erupts in a gargled outcry, remarkably similar to the sound of a recently unclogged drain.

45 ♖b7+! 1-0

After 45...♖xb7 46 ♖xc5+ (zwischenzug) 46...♔b6 47 axb7 White wins a rook.

Game 56
G.Kamsky-V.Kramnik
Baku (rapid) 2010
Benoni Defence

1 d4 ♘f6 2 ♗f4 c5! 3 d5 b5!? 4 a4 ♗b7 5 axb5 ♘xd5 6 ♗g3 g6 7 e4 ♘b6 8 ♘d2?! ♗g7 9 c3 0-0 10 ♘gf3 d6 11 ♗d3 a6 12 0-0 axb5 13 ♖xa8 ♘xa8 14 ♗xb5 ♕b6 15 ♕e2 ♗c6 16 ♗xc6 ♘xc6 17 ♖b1 ♘c7 18 h4 ♖a8 19 ♕c4 ♕b5 20 ♕xb5 ♘xb5

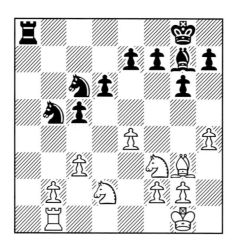

Question: How would you assess this position?

Answer: Advantage Black. The pawn constellation looks quite a bit like a Benko Gambit, but without having given up a pawn.

21 ♗f4

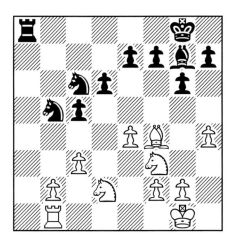

Answer: Swap a wing pawn for a central pawn.

21...f5! 22 g3 ♖a4!

Adding a little nudge to e4.

23 exf5 gxf5

Now Black is ready to roll his central pawns.

24 ♘f1 e5 25 ♗d2 d5?!

Believe it or not, this move may be premature, since Black is unable to stabilize his centre. With hindsight, it was better to play 25...h6 first.

26 ♘e3 ♘e7

Black is about to play ...d5-d4 with a close to winning position. Kamsky, by now saturated with the odd hybrid of despair and desperation, comes up with an amazing idea.

27 c4!!

Kamsky puts two and two together and, oddly enough, comes up with the number five. He gives up a pawn to break up Black's monster centre. I always get nervous whenever I concoct some zany plan, which my logical mind ruthlessly dissects and rejects. But then this dark, insane voice in my head whispers: "Go for it. It will work!" Well, in this instance, Kamsky listened to his dark voice and, for once, the normally loony voice spoke the truth! His idea, crazy as it looks, was absolutely sound and should have saved the game.

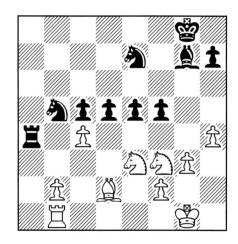

27...dxc4 28 b3!

Suddenly, Kamsky's pieces burst forth in incredible activity.

28...cxb3 29 ♖xb3 ♘d4 30 ♖b8+ ♔f7 31 ♘g5+

White holds the initiative.

31...♔g6 32 ♖b6+ ♗f6

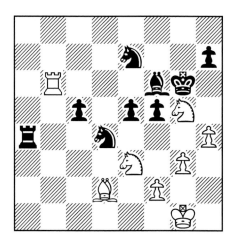

> *Exercise (combination alert/critical decision):* White's pieces savour
> their brand new, elevated social status. Analyze 33 ♘xh7. Does it work?

33 ♔g2?

Kamsky protects against a ghost threat on f3. Now his brilliant idea becomes fragmented.

Answer: He should complete the thought with 33 ♘xh7! ♔xh7 34 ♖xf6 ♘f3+ 35 ♔g2 ♘xd2 36 ♖f7+! – the point; White regains the lost piece.

33...♘ec6 34 ♘d5

GM Eric Prié claims an advantage for White after 34 ♘e6, giving the move two exclams, but *Houdini* says otherwise after 34...h5 and declares the game dead even.

34...♗d8! 35 ♖b1

35 ♖b7 is met by 35...♖a7.

35...h6 36 h5+!?

Kamsky figures he has nothing to lose, since 36 ♘h3 looks quite dismal.

36...♔xh5 37 ♘f7 ♗g5 38 ♗xg5 hxg5 39 ♘d6 g4!

The f3-square is a big one for Black's knight.

40 ♖c1 ♘b4! 41 ♘e3

41 ♖xc5?? ♖a1! leaves White unable to find a reasonable defence to ...♘f3 and ...♖g1 mate.

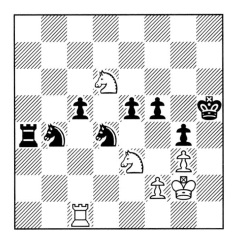

In time pressure, when logic reaches a cul de sac and we lack the leisure to calculate out an exact line, we have no recourse but to take the dreaded "educated guess", which is just a fancy term for eeny meeny miny, mo!

> **Exercise (planning/critical decision):** Black has two ways to play:
> a) 41...♔g6, consolidate.
> b) 41...♖a2, sac f5 and go for f2.
> One of the methods wins. Which one would you play?

41...♔g6?!

Answer: Kramnik uncharacteristically underestimated the dynamic potential of his position. He should go for it with 41...♖a2! 42 ♘dxf5 ♘d3 43 ♖f1 ♘xf5 44 ♘xf5, when White must give up a piece to halt the surging c-pawn after 44...c4 45 ♘e3 c3.

42 ♖xc5?!

42 ♘b7 was his final prayer.

42...♘d3 43 ♖c8

After 43 ♖c3 ♘e1+ 44 ♔h1 ♖a1 45 ♘f1 ♖a7!!, a mysterious figure, a dark mote, appears on the outskirts and soon melts into the horizon. The rook's energy flows radially, reaching every corner of his world. There is no good defence to ...♖h7+.

43...♘e1+

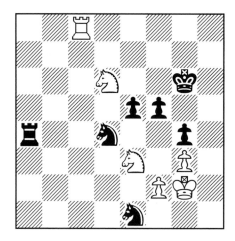

One can only admire the multi-tasking black pieces who, despite their busy schedules, still find the time to hunt vampires after work. Now Black's two knights, rook, and his hook on f3 condemn White's king. In time pressure we just know in our gut that we are on the right track. The details can be put on hold, as long as we head in the correct overall direction.

44 ♔h1 ♖a1

The rook shoots a meaningful glance at White's king and awaits a decision.

45 ♘f1 ♘d3 46 ♔g2 ♖a2

The barbarian horde pounds at the gate of the city and f2 falls. White can resign.

47 ♘e3 ♖xf2+ 48 ♔h1 ♘f3

The impounded king remains locked in the warehouse on h1, hoping to score some much needed Prozac very soon.

49 ♘dxf5

Well, why not?

49...♖h2 mate

White's king claims he isn't crying, citing a lame excuse about just having cut up an onion for the spaghetti sauce.

Game 57
N.Short-V.Kramnik
London 2011
Four Knights Game

1 e4 e5 2 ♘f3 ♘c6 3 ♗b5 ♘f6 4 ♘c3 ♘d4

Kramnik's win in this game can be compared with Capa's, since the theme is identical – exploitation of a hemmed-in bishop: 4...♗b4 5 0-0 0-0 6 ♗xc6 dxc6 7 d3 ♗d6 8 ♗g5 h6 9 ♗h4 c5 10 ♘d5? g5! 11 ♘xf6+ ♕xf6 12 ♗g3 ♗g4 13 h3 ♗xf3 14 ♕xf3 ♕xf3 15 gxf3 f6

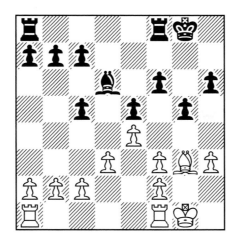

(Short's light-squared bishop in the main game looks even worse than Winter's unfortunate bishop here) 16 ♔g2 a5 17 a4 ♔f7 18 ♖h1 ♔e6 19 h4 ♖fb8 20 hxg5 hxg5 21 b3 c6 22 ♖a2 b5 23 ♖ha1 c4 24 axb5 cxb3 25 cxb3 ♖xb5 26 ♖a4 ♖xb3 27 d4 ♖b5 28 ♖c4 ♖b4 29 ♖xc6 ♖xd4 0-1 W.Winter-J.R.Capablanca, Hastings 1919. I annotate this game in *The Four Knights: Move by Move.*

5 ♘xd4 exd4 6 e5 dxc3 7 exf6 ♕xf6 8 dxc3 ♗c5 9 ♕e2+ ♕e6 10 0-0 0-0 11 ♕f3 d6 12 ♗g5 ♕f5!!

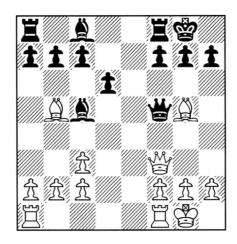

A curving finger beckons White's bishop to e7.

> **Question:** Something is not quite right, like the college student
> who texts his mom to wish her a happy Mother's Day, rather than
> take the effort to call. Did Kramnik just drop a full exchange?

Answer: To a very small child, money is just paper and nothing more. Kramnik sac'ed the exchange – he didn't drop it.

> **Question:** For what compensation? His "sac"
> looks like one part bluster and nine parts bluff.

Answer: Strangely enough, Black gets compensation with the following:

1. White's disfigured, doubled f-pawns and isolated h-pawn.

2. When White takes the exchange on f8, his bishop has trouble returning, since ♗e7 is met by ...f5-f6!, continuing to imprison it (a theme Short was unfortunately unable to evade anyway later in the game!)

3. White's rooks just don't work well in the resulting position.

Conclusion: I think Black stands equal at a minimum after the acceptance.

13 ♗e7!?

The bishop, full of feral insinuation, cautiously approaches e7, though he knows something is wrong. It is too easy. But who could resist? Short gets ambitious and pounces, as his haughty bishop, annoyed by Black's refusal to show deference, decides upon punitive action against Black's f8-rook. Personally, I have grave doubts about the move. In fact, I think White is the one fighting for the draw. A more cowardly-inclined man like me would undoubtedly go for 13 ♕xf5 ♗xf5 14 ♗d3, when the position really is boring and drawish.

13...♕xf3 14 gxf3 a6

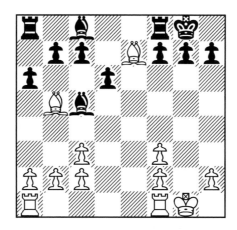

15 ♗a4?!

Nothing is more painful than unrequited love. Short continues to refuse the offer, but immediate acceptance is the most accurate, and the only path to equality: 15 ♗xf8! axb5 16 ♗e7 f6! 17 ♖fe1 ♗d7 18 ♖e2 ♔f7 19 ♖ae1 ♖e8 and how does White make progress? Of course I concede that Black shouldn't have any winning chances in this position either.

15...b5 16 b4?

The losing move. It was his last chance for 16 ♗xf8 bxa4 17 ♗e7 f6 18 ♖fe1 ♗d7 19 ♖e2 ♔f7 20 ♖ae1 ♗b5! 21 ♖e6, when Kramnik could play for the win with 21...♗c6! 22 ♔g2 ♗d5 23 ♖6e2 ♗xa2! as White is totally tied down to his trapped bishop.

16...♖e8! 17 ♖fe1

If 17 bxc5 ♖xe7 18 cxd6 then 18...♖e6 19 ♗b3 ♖g6+ 20 ♔h1 ♗b7!, winning.

17...♗b6 18 ♗b3 ♗b7

Targeting f3.

19 ♔g2

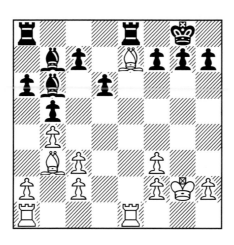

> *Exercise (planning):* Not all deadly shots arrive in sacrificial splendour.
> Find one poisonous move for Black and you essentially end White's hopes.

Answer: Entomb White's light-squared bishop alive.

19...d5!!

The d-pawn pays its respects and tosses a flower into the b3-bishop's grave. One is reminded of the Eagles' song *Hotel California*: "You can check out any time you like, but you can never leave."

> *Question:* But didn't he just free White's e7-bishop?

Answer: He did, but the parole was granted only on condition of exchange for his brother's life on b3. White's light-squared bishop will never see the light of day again.

20 ♗e5 c6!

That's it. Game over. White's b3-bishop ends his existence in Sunny von Bülow fashion, in a coma from which he never arises. White can do nothing but wait and deface Black's impenetrable wall with graffiti.

21 ♖ae1 ♗c7 22 ♖5e2 ♗c8 23 a4

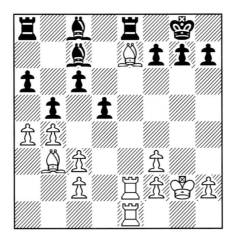

Of course Black isn't going to take. The bishop continues to sit in his corner with the utter disempowerment of a misbehaving school kid, facing down the stern principal's glare.

23...♗d7 24 ♗h4 ♖xe2 25 ♖xe2 ♖e8 26 ♖xe8+ ♗xe8 27 ♗g3 ♗d8

Of course Black declines to straighten out White's broken pawns.

28 ♗e5 f6 29 ♗b8 ♗g6 30 axb5 axb5 31 ♔f1 ♔f7 32 ♔e2 ♔e6 33 ♔e3 ♗b6+ 34 ♔e2 ♗h5 35 ♗a2

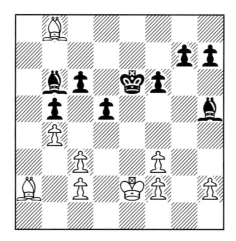

White's unbishop on a2 is dead-weight, a time-traveller caught in an anomalous loop, who materializes in a glimmer and then fades to invisibility once again.

> ***Exercise (planning):*** How can Black exploit this factor
> in concrete fashion to carve out the win?

Answer: Create confrontation and open the kingside, where White remains a piece down in the fight.

35...g5! 36 ♗b3 f5 37 ♗a2 f4 38 ♗b3 ♔f5

Black's king remains completely safe on light squares.

39 ♗d6 g4! 40 ♔f1 g3!?

> ***Question:*** Why not just take on f3?

Answer: Kramnik's move is perhaps simpler. He was probably worried that Short would set up some kind of impenetrable fortress, and wanted to open the kingside. Nevertheless, 40...gxf3 should also win; for example: 41 ♔e1 ♗d8! (targets: c3 and f2) 42 ♗c5 ♗f6 43 ♗d4 (43 ♔d2 ♔g4! and the white h-pawn falls) 43...♗g6! (zugzwang) 44 ♗xf6 ♔xf6 45 ♔d1 ♔g5 46 ♔e1 ♗h4 47 ♔f1 ♗f5! 48 ♔g1 ♗h3! (now White's king is unable to participate in the defence of his queenside) 49 ♗a2 ♔g5 50 ♗b3 ♔f5 51 ♗a2 ♔e4 52 ♗b3 h6 53 ♗a2 d4 54 cxd4 ♔xd4 55 ♗f7 ♗f5! (having done his job on h3, the bishop tells White's king, "You are free to leave.") 56 ♗e8 ♗e4 57 ♔f1 ♔c3 and, finally, Black wins.

41 fxg3 fxg3 42 ♗xg3 ♗xf3 43 ♗a2 ♗e3! 0-1

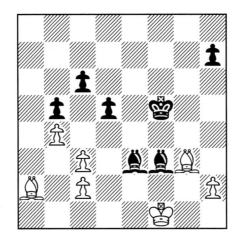

White faces twin enemies. Had Short not resigned here, the game might have finished 44 ♗b3 ♗f4! (eliminating White's only functional piece) 45 ♔f2 ♔e4 (threat: ...♗d2!) 46 ♗xf4 ♔xf4 47 ♗a2 h5 48 ♗b3 ♗e4! (zugzwang to the unfortunate white bishop) 49 ♔e2 ♔g4 50 ♔f2 ♔h3 51 ♔g1 h4 52 ♗a2 (the infirm old man on a2 thinks of all the people in his life he loved, all dead now, and of happier times of youth and freedom) 52...♗xc2 53 ♔h1 ♔g4 54 ♔g2 ♔f4 55 ♔h3 ♔e3 56 ♔xh4 ♔d2 57 ♔g5 ♔xc3 (the scissors easily slice through the paper) 58 h4 ♔xb4 59 h5 ♔a3 and Black wins easily.

Game 58
J.Gustafsson-V.Kramnik
Dortmund 2012
King's Indian Defence

---

1 d4 ♘f6 2 c4 g6 3 ♘c3 ♗g7 4 e4 d6

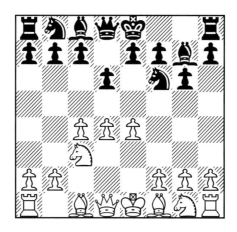

> *Question:* Why is Kramnik playing a King's Indian? I'm not
> sure that I ever remember a game of his on the black side.

Answer: Clearly Kramnik's opening choice is something of a stylistic mongrel. He simply experiments with the KID (though almost certainly with a line prepared). Perhaps what emboldened Kramnik was the fact that his opponent, Gustafsson, is considerably lower rated (at a mere 2629!).

5 ♘f3 0-0 6 ♗e2 e5 7 ♗e3 c6 8 0-0 exd4 9 ♘xd4 ♖e8 10 f3 d5 11 cxd5 ♘xd5 12 ♘xd5 cxd5 13 ♖c1 a5 14 ♕b3 a4 15 ♕xd5 ♕xd5 16 exd5 a3 17 b3 ♘c6 18 ♘c2

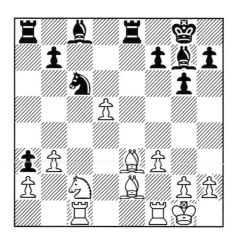

> *Question:* This looks a lot like Kramnik-Van Wely, from earlier
> in this chapter (see Game 50) – only worse, since Black is a
> pawn down this time. Surely Kramnik is in trouble, correct?

Answer: Actually not. His piece activity and pressure down the e-file miraculously compensate for the missing pawn. The overarching narrative of the position is that Black's seemingly unsustainable, temporary initiative is about to flicker out and die, leaving him a pawn down. Let's do an exercise and discuss this further.

> *Exercise (planning/critical decision):* Would you consider giving up the exchange on e3 in incandescent hostility, to give Black's initiative life?

Answer: The exchange sac works, spreading confusion like melting butter on a bagel. The sea rises and falls in violent swells, as cruise-liner passenger Gustafsson finds he is unable to keep his food down, despite the inviting bounty before him on his plate. Initiative plus dark squares are at least worth an exchange. In fact, after the sac, it is White who must find an impossibly difficult path to the draw.

18...♖xe3!!

The deranged rook goes non-linear on White.

> *Question:* Is this sound? I understand that such sacs are standard issue in ...e5xd4 King's Indian lines, but from my experience this sac only occurs when queens remain on the board. In this case, not only have queens come off but Black is down a pawn as well as the exchange.

Answer: As it turns out, the position is something of an anomaly and Kramnik's sac is absolutely sound. His ferocious piece activity, coupled with threats against a2, see to it that he is the only one with chances to win.

19 ♘xe3 ♘b4

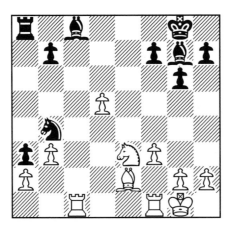

In reality, Black's exchange sac created mild ripples of discrepancy rather than the loud splash he envisioned. White still has a miraculous method of saving himself.

Exercise (critical decision): White repelled the first wave
at heavy cost since a2 falls, as well as his dark squares.
Would you play 20 ♖c4, which covers the sensitive d4-point,
or should White go for a counterattack with 20 ♖c7 instead?

20 ♖c4?

Gustafsson seeks perfection but misses. He logically covers against ....♗d4 by handing over his a-pawn. But now Black's soon-to-be-passed a-pawn grows out of control.
Answer: GM Alejandro Ramirez gave the following forced line as White's narrow pathway to a draw: 20 ♖c7!! (on the surface it looks like this haughty manoeuvre is nothing more than an annoying affectation rather than a tangibly real move of power) 20...♗d4 21 ♖e7! ♘xd5 22 ♖e8+ ♔g7 23 ♔h1! ♘xe3 24 ♖c1 ♘d5 25 ♖cxc8 ♖xc8 26 ♖xc8 ♘c3 27 ♖xc3! ♗xc3 with a dead draw. Ramirez added: "This is the computer line. Good luck finding that."
20...♘xa2 21 ♖a4?

Question: Can White erect a blockade on a1, starting with 21 ♘c2 - ?

Answer: I think your plan is White's last hope of saving the game. After 21...♘c3 22 ♗d3 a2 23 ♖a1 White remains under pressure, but at least the computers don't point out some forced loss.
21...♖xa4 22 bxa4

White's pieces exchange exasperated looks as they see Black's obnoxious, braying bishop approaching d4.
22...♗d4

Kramnik doubles down on his "your-dark-squares-suck!" message. By now the course of the dark-square illness grows irreversible, as the bishop jams a stick into the crocodile's open jaws, rendering the creature on e3 helpless. White's obviously guilty pinned knight squirms under the pitiless gaze of the jury. In comparison, just look at White's useless counterpart on e2, blending into the room, present yet absent, as if old familiar furniture.
23 ♔f2

They say the need for inordinately long periods of sleep is a tell-tale sign of depression. Here, White's king has great difficulty rousing himself out of bed from g1 in order to go to work, defending his pinned e3-knight. White's position has only minutes of life before he succumbs.

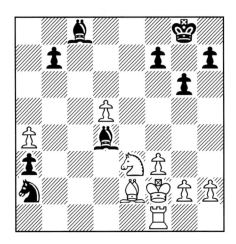

Answer: Double attack: d5 and c2.

23...♘b4! 24 ♖c1 a2!

No need to bother moving the c8-bishop! Kramnik finally punts the pawn forward a single, deadly square. Once again, White's pieces brace themselves as they prepare to endure yet another tediously lengthy sermon from the all-powerful dark-squared cardinal.

25 ♖xc8+ ♔g7 26 ♖c1 ♘xd5!

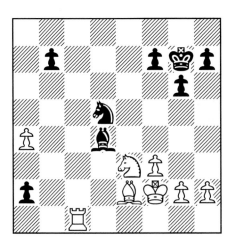

Black's bishop knight and a-pawn synchronize to represent a single mind occupying three separate bodies. Of course the cheapo offer to rush to promotion with 26...a1♕?? 27

⟐xa1 ⟐xa1 28 d6, after which only White can win, is rejected with derision from Black.
27 ⟐d1 ⟐xe3 0-1

1 ⟐f3 d5 2 d4 ⟐f6 3 c4 c6 4 ⟐c3 a6 5 e3 e6 6 ⟐d3 dxc4 7 ⟐xc4 c5 8 0-0 b5 9 ⟐e2 ⟐b7 10 dxc5 ⟐xd1 11 ⟐xd1

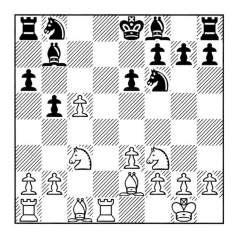

> ***Question:*** I take it that anyone who so cavalierly hands his
> opponent such trivially easy equality with the white pieces must
> have enormous faith in his technical skills in the endgame?

Answer: Correct! Kramnik, like Capablanca before him, is under the correct assumption that he can win even the most equal ending, and against a 2700+ rated opponent to boot! I watched this game live and just couldn't believe he managed to win from nothing. Then again, I would remind you of the QGA Kramnik-Kasparov from previous chapter (Game 43). Black shouldn't expect an easy draw if Kasparov had monumental difficulties in making one too. Basically, if you play this way as White, you refuse to enter the zoo of opening theory, weed out the dead ends and narrow them down to a few easily digestible ideas and plans. The play becomes more intuitive and less mathematical.
11...⟐xc5 12 ⟐d2!

> ***Question:*** Why retreat an already developed knight?

Answer: Multipurpose:

1. White transfers his knight to b3 to eye Black's most vulnerable squares: c5 and a5.

2. White clears the path for f2-f3 and e3-e4, seizing central space and taking control over d5.

12...0-0 13 ♘b3 ♗b4 14 ♗d2 ♘bd7 15 a3 ♘c5!

Tomashevsky very cleverly hopes to eliminate the b3-knight. 15...♗e7 16 ♘a5 is good for White.

16 ♘c1!

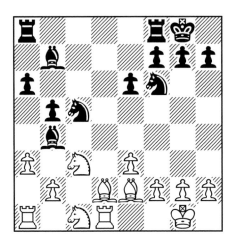

Not only avoiding the swap, but ensuring the bishop pair as well.

16...♗xc3 17 ♗xc3 ♖fc8 18 ♗d4 ♗d5! 19 f3 ♗c4!

Principle: *Eliminate the opponent's bishop pair if possible.*

20 ♔f2 ♗xe2 21 ♔xe2 ♘d5 22 ♖d2 f6 23 ♗xc5

> **Question:** Why give away his only imbalance advantage?

Answer: Because it wasn't an advantage. Black's powerful c5-knight was every bit as strong as White's bishop. Tomashevsky has defended well, and yet I still prefer White, due to his centralized king.

23...♖xc5 24 ♘d3 ♖c7 25 a4! bxa4 26 ♖xa4

Now Black's a-pawn is microscopically weaker than its white counterpart on b2.

26...♔f7 27 ♖a5!

Intending ♘c5.

27...♖aa7?!

27...♖c6 was better.

28 ♘c5 ♘b4 29 ♖d6!

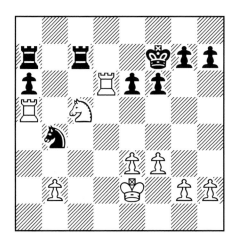

Kramnik continues to make progress.

29...♖c8 30 f4!

Planning to push forward on the kingside eventually, while also leaving his king an escape hatch on f3 in case Black infiltrates with a rook to c2.

30...♖ac7 31 ♘xe6 ♖c2+ 32 ♔f3 ♖xb2 33 ♘d4 ♖c7 34 ♖b6!

Threat: ♖axa6! – the a-pawn is a goner.

34...♘d3!

> **Question:** Why give away his a-pawn?

Answer: He decides that 34...♖a7?! 35 g4! is just too passive and so correctly hands over the pawn.

35 ♖xb2 ♘xb2 36 ♖xa6

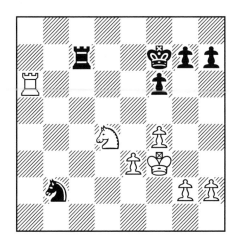

The new landscape: four versus three, all on the same side, with a rook and knight each – impossibly hard to win for White. Yet Kramnik does just that against a near-world class player.

36...♘c4 37 g4 ♘d2+ 38 ♔e2 ♘e4 39 h4 ♖b7

He isn't really threatening to play to b2, since his own second rank must be defended.

40 g5 ♔g6 41 ♔f3 ♖e7 42 h5+?!

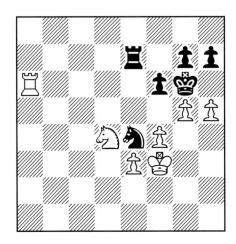

Kramnik gets fancy when he doesn't have to. He mistakenly rejects the line 42 ♖e6! ♖xe6 43 f5+! ♔h5 44 fxe6 ♘d6 45 gxf6 gxf6 46 ♔f4 ♔g6 47 ♘f5!! ♘e8 48 e4, when Black can barely move and is busted.

42...♔xh5 43 ♘f5 ♘d2+ 44 ♔e2 ♖d7 45 gxf6 gxf6 46 ♖xf6

The computer points out the amazing line 46 ♘d6 ♔g4!! 47 ♔xd2 ♔f3 48 f5 h5!, when Black's surging h-pawn allows him to draw, despite White's full extra piece.

46...♔g4 47 ♘h6+ ♔g3 48 ♖f8 ♘e4 49 ♖g8+ ♔h3 50 ♘g4!

Intending ♘f2+. If White can remove the knights, the rook and pawn ending is a win for him.

50...♔h4 51 ♘e5 ♖a7 52 ♘f3+ ♔h5 53 ♔d3 ♘f2+ 54 ♔d4 ♖a4+ 55 ♔d5 ♖a5+ 56 ♔e6 ♘g4 57 e4 ♖a6+ 58 ♔e7 ♖a7+ 59 ♔d6

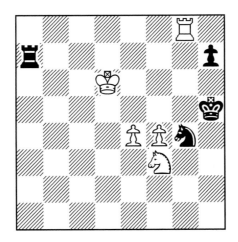

Exercise (combination alert): This one is mindbendingly difficult.
Black missed a stalemating trick which draws.

59...♖a6+

Answer: It would be unfair to hand Tomashevsky a "?!" mark for this move, since, to draw, he had to find the inhumanly difficult 59...♘f6! 60 ♖g5+ ♔h6 61 ♔e5 and now the impossible 61...♘xe4!! 62 ♔xe4 ♖a4+, when White's king has no place to hide and, no matter how he squirms, it's a draw. For example, 63 ♔e5 (or 63 ♔f5 ♖xf4+! 64 ♔xf4 stalemate!) 63...♖e4+! (do you remember the mentally-challenged, sheltered innocent, Chauncey Gardiner who could do no wrong? – the Peter Sellers character from the movie *Being There* reminds us of Black's rook, who is apparently protected by unseen forces despite his obliviousness to the dangers all around him) 64 ♔d5 ♖xf4 65 ♖g3 is drawn.

60 ♔c7 h6 61 e5 ♘f6! 62 ♖d8 ♔g4 63 ♘d4 ♖a7+ 64 ♔d6 ♘e4+ 65 ♔d5 ♘c3+ 66 ♔c4 ♔xf4 67 e6 ♖c7+ 68 ♔d3 ♔e5?

Instead, 68...♘a4! still easily holds the draw, as the internal politics continue to thwart and make powerless Black's dreams of promotion.

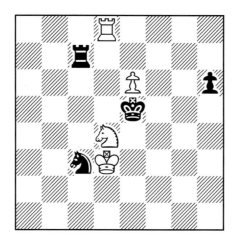

Externally, Black's drawing plan looks solid. But if we go deeper and examine the fringes, nooks and crags we spot a problem, like a ring of mould around the circumference of a cheese wheel.

> **Exercise (combination alert):** Black, on the threshold
> of a draw, stumbled and allowed Kramnik to win.
> How did White accomplish the goal to score the full point?

Answer: Step 1: Lure Black's knight to d5.

69 ♖d7! ♘d5

After 69...♖c8 70 e7 ♘d5 71 ♘c6+! ♔e6 72 ♖xd5! both rook and knight hang, yet Black is unable to digest either piece.

Step 2: Overload. White's last move short-circuits the defensive line. Black's cats continue to misbehave, so Kramnik emerges with the dreaded, disciplinary spray-bottle.

70 e7! ♖c3+ 71 ♔d2 ♖c8

Step 3: Overload again! Reinforce e7. Black's rook, whose eyes had yet to adjust to the dark, fails to spot the lurking intruder on c6.

72 ♘c6+!

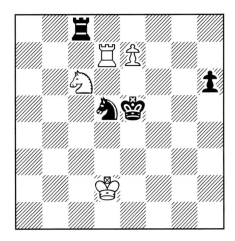

72...♔e6

Step 4: Removal of the defender.

73 ♖xd5! ♖xc6!

By far his best practical chance – but not against Kramnik!

73...♔xd5 74 ♘d8! would be Step 5: Interference. The knight's eyes are searchlights which illuminate the pawn's path to e8.

74 e8♕+

The queen, new in the neighbourhood, just nods and smiles in lieu of "hello!"

74...♔xd5

We arrive at the dreaded queen versus rook ending, not so easy to win.

Question: Can Black actually hold the draw?

Answer: Against someone like Kramnik there is no chance to achieve a draw. But from a practical standpoint, the rook holds the draw all the time when the participants are lower rated. In fact, I believe there was a GM vs. GM game played in the last few years (I don't recall the names) where GM (y) was left red-faced when he reached the 50-move mark without checkmating or winning GM (z)'s remaining rook! Once I had the rook side and, if memory serves, my lucky bugger of an opponent won my rook 48 moves later, just two moves short of the draw.

75 ♔d3 ♖e6 76 ♕b5+ ♔d6 77 ♔d4

Of course the first goal is to narrow the confines of Black's king.

77...♔e7 78 ♕f5! ♖f6 79 ♕h7+ ♔f8!?

Tomashevsky goes for a sixth rank fortress strategy. The computers say this is okay. The alternative would be to remain central and play 79...♔e6.

80 ♔e5 ♖a6

Divide and conquer, like slices on a pizza!

81 ♕b7 ♖g6 82 ♕h7 ♖a6 83 ♕d3! 1-0

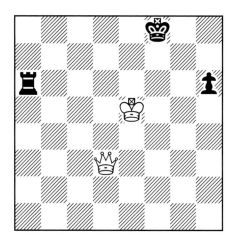

Admittedly anti-climatic. Tomashevsky either flagged, or just decided to save energy and resign now.

> ***Question:*** How does White proceed? His king is cut off from the sixth rank.

Answer: This is one of those endings which is really hard to explain. There seems to be no logical step-by-step path to achieve the goal, yet the people who know how to mate with king and queen are unable to explain how they did it! It reminds me of an Oscar Wilde quip: "Nothing worth learning can ever be taught."

Let's allow *Houdini* to show us the technique. Keep in mind there are myriad ways of how both Black and White may proceed: 83 ♕d3! ♖a7 84 ♕d6+ ♔g7 85 ♔e6 ♔h7 86 ♕d3+ ♔g8 87 ♕g6+ ♖g7 88 ♕xh6 ♖e7+! (circumstances get awkward for the murderer; the body he dumped in the lake earlier now bobs to the surface in a state of decay on e7, yet still remains clearly identifiable. Do you think computers dream? Watch out for stalemate cheapos!) 89 ♔d6 (Nyet! No stalemate for you today, buddy! The circuitous route via the back streets and alleys becomes necessary, since a direct path to Black's king is unavailable) 89...♖g7 90 ♕f6 ♔h7 91 ♕h4+ ♔g8 92 ♔e6 ♖g6+ 93 ♔f5 ♖g7 94 ♕c4+ ♔h7 95 ♕d4! ♖f7+ 96 ♔e6 ♔g8 97 ♕d5! (everyone agrees: the most nauseating aspect of young lovers is when they complete each others' sentences – White's king and queen are just such an obnoxious couple; meanwhile, Black's king and rook look like a couple out to dinner, only to finalize their upcoming divorce) 97...♖g7 98 ♔f6+ ♔h7 99 ♕h1+ ♔g8 100 ♕h5 ♖g1 101 ♕e8+ ♔h7 102 ♕e4+ ♔h8 103 ♕a8+ ♔h7 104 ♕a7+ picks off the rook. Black's king seethes with unfulfilled, impotent dreams of vengeance, as he is forced to pay homage to the woman who murdered his family.

Index of Openings

Figures refer to page numbers. Bold type indicates that Kramnik had the black pieces.

Benoni Defence	190, **382**
Caro-Kann Defence	54
Catalan Opening	**133**, 149, 249
Dutch Defence	128
English Opening	184, **316**, 341
Four Knights Game	12, 140, **387**
French Defence	243
Grünfeld Defence	346
Italian Game	355
King's Indian Defence	76, 90, 198, 264, 330, **392**
Nimzo-Indian Defence	113, **203**, **211**, **217**, 224, 323, **350**, 364
Petroff's Defence	**64**
Queen's Gambit Accepted	155, 168, 293, 397
Queen's Gambit Declined	56, 282
Queen's Indian Defence	44
Réti Opening	310
Ruy Lopez	**102**, 121, **163**, **238**, **302**
Scotch Game	**69**
Semi-Slav Defence	27, **31**, **38**, 95, 258, 377
Sicilian Defence	**21**, 50, **176**, 269, **276**, **287**
Slav Defence	84, 230

Index of Opponents

Figures refer to page numbers. Bold type indicates that Kramnik had the black pieces.

Adams.Mi	224
Akopian	95
Alekseev	190
Anand	168, 249, 323
Aronian	12, 121, 140
Brodsky	**21**
Bruzon	56
Carlsen.Ma	**133**, **211**
Chumachenko	269
Ehlvest	27
Gelfand	**38**
Giri	76
Gustafsson	**392**
Grischuk	264
Hodgson.Ju	84
Howell.D	**238**
Hracek	**163**
Kamsky	**382**
Kasparov	**31**, 90, **102**, 155, 293
Krasenkow	355
Leko	258, **302**, **316**, 54
Lputian	282
Morozevich	**203**, 230
Naiditsch	**64**, 184
Nakamura	128
Polgar.J	44, 113
Polgar.Zso	**276**
Ponomariov	**176**
Radjabov	243
Rozentalis	**287**

Shaked	**217**
Shirov	**69**, 310
Short	**387**
Svidler	149
Timman	341
Tomashevsky	397
Topalov	198, **350**, 377
Van Wely	50, 330, 346
Zhang Zhong	364

The following are some sample pages
from another great **move by move** book:

Cyrus Lakdawala

Capablanca
move by move

EVERYMAN CHESS

ISBN: 9781857446982 – 368 pages

Alekhine's tournament book *New York 1927* is one of the most mean-spirited and intellectually dishonest chess books ever written. The Russian, who quite obviously grappled with deep jealousy issues when it came to all things Capa, spouts venom throughout the book on his favourite target. Examples of the hate-speak:

1. "In the endgame, he (Capablanca) is not to be feared by a first-class master."

2. "It's unbelievable how self-consciously and weakly Marshall always plays against Capablanca!"

3. "Only then did it finally become clear to me how exaggerated were the general shouts of praise with which the quality of his performance in New York (1927) were greeted."

4. "...his self-confidence grew in the extreme, indeed turned into self-idolization." Well, okay, I admit criticism number 4 was possibly true!

Trust me. The entire book is like this! The tournament was played only a few months before their world championship match, and Alekhine was anxious to show Capa just who was boss. Well, as it turned out, Capa was boss and chairman of the board. He skated to a crushing victory 3½ points ahead of his nearest rival – Alekhine. In their personal games, they drew three, but Alekhine's single loss to Capa turned out to be one of the most humiliating of his life.

1 d4 ♘f6 2 c4 e6 3 ♘f3 b6

Capablanca successfully played the Queen's Indian at a time when few even knew what it was, essentially a hypermodern concept of controlling the centre via the wings.

4 g3 ♗b7 5 ♗g2 c5!?

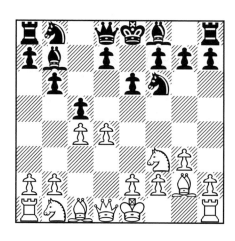

Inviting a Benoni hybrid, but not such a good way of entering one. 5...♗e7 is the more common route today.

6 d5!

Alekhine takes up the challenge "to avoid a draw", he says in the tournament book. 6 0-0 cxd4 7 ♕xd4 is the Hedgehog formation.

6...exd5

Question: Doesn't this just drop a pawn for White?

Answer: No. Please see White's next move.

7 ♘h4

The pin regains the lost pawn. 7 ♘g5 has been tried a few times: 7...♘e4 8 ♘xe4 dxe4 9 ♘c3 f5 10 ♗f4 ♕f6 11 0-0 and White's development lead compensated for the missing pawn, E.Kengis-M.Womacka, Baden-Baden 1990.

7...g6 8 ♘c3 ♗g7 9 0-0 0-0 10 ♗f4

This natural but weak move allows Black to equalize. Instead, 10 ♗g5! gives White an excellent Benoni. If Black tries 10...h6? then 11 ♗xf6 ♕xf6 (11...♗xf6? is met by the shocking 12 ♘xg6!, winning on the spot) 12 ♘xd5! ♗xd5 13 ♕xd5 ♘c6 14 ♕xd7 ♖ac8 15 ♖ad1! sees White emerge a pawn ahead in all variations (the threat is ♖d6!), J.Fedorowicz-V.Mezentsev, San Francisco 2007; while 10...♕c8 11 cxd5 gives White a much better version of the game continuation.

10...d6

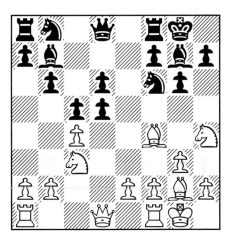

11 cxd5

Question: Isn't this just a bad Benoni for Black too, whose light-squared bishop hits a pawn wall on d5.

Answer: Black looks okay here. Keep in mind, White's knight went off for a jaunt on h4, so he lost time as well. Annotators often say a position is "equal". Perhaps a distinction should be made between equality and equity. In this dynamically balanced position, Black has equity.

> **Question:** Why can't White keep recapturing on d5 with pieces, with the intention of hammering away on Black's backward d6-pawn?

Answer: Your idea is playable and perhaps safer than the one Alekhine went for, but in most Benoni structures, Black gets counterplay against this plan. In this case Black looks fine after 11 ♘xd5 ♘xd5 12 ♗xd5 ♗xd5 13 ♕xd5 ♘a6 14 ♕d2 ♕e7 15 ♖ad1 (15 ♗xd6 is met by 15...♖fd8) 15...♖ad8, when White would be foolish to take on d6.

11...♘h5

To take the pressure off d6.

12 ♗d2 ♘d7 13 f4?!

Correctly criticized by Alekhine who gives 13 e4, threatening ♘f5. Now instead of Alekhine's 13...♘hf6, Black can try the more enterprising 13...♖e8!, and if White follows through with Alekhine's planned 14 ♘f5, Black doesn't look too bothered after 14...gxf5 15 ♕xh5 fxe4 16 ♘xe4 ♘f6 with equity!

13...a6 14 ♗f3?!

I hate that feeling when you sense something is amiss but you still choose to ignore the misgivings. Alekhine writes: "A totally weak move after which the game is hard to save. Losing time, only to place one's own piece on a worse square in order to force an opponent's to a better one."

14...♘hf6 15 a4 c4!

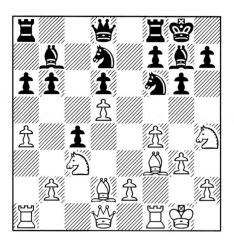

Very strong now that White no longer has easy access to ♘d4 and ♘c6. Black vacates c5 for his knight.

Question: Isn't it going too far giving your hero an exclamation
mark for this rather obvious Benoni plan?

Answer: The plan is obvious *today*, mainly because of games like this one. Don't take such
plans for granted. Someone first invented them. You and I are just copycats. At that time it
was a novel idea, so the exclam is for the creativity behind it.

16 ♗e3

Question: This move looks incorrect. Why did Alekhine block his e-pawn?

Answer: I think Alekhine was worried about the line 16 e4 b5. The queen check on b6
indirectly protects the not-so-loose b5-pawn.

16...♕c7 17 g4?!

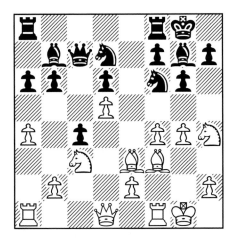

Thus begins the attack which never was. Alekhine says he just went for it since he
considered his position strategically busted anyway.

Question: Is this ferocity or simply desperation? Is White really lost
here to the point where he must begin such a desperate attack?

Answer: I'm not sure. A famished tiger views everyone else as food. Perhaps the move is a
sign of both ferocity and desperation. Let's try a calmer strategic approach, say 17 b4,
before Black locks things down with ...♘c5: 17...cxb3 18 ♕xb3 ♖ac8 19 ♗d4 ♕c4 20 ♕d1
♘e8! 21 ♗xg7 ♘xg7 22 ♘e4 f5! (White can't touch the d6-pawn) 23 ♘g5 ♘c5. Clearly
White stands worse here too, but perhaps not as bad as what happens after his lash-out
move.

17...♘c5 18 g5 ♘fd7 19 f5!?

The pawn lunges forward with a cry of outrage. White, hoping to brazen it out, gains more real estate without purposeful destiny. In so doing he leaves a gaping hole on e5, similar to the aftermath of a pulled tooth.

19...♖fe8 20 ♗f4 ♗e5

Before he gets shut out with f5-f6.

21 ♗g4 ♘b3 22 fxg6 hxg6 23 ♖b1

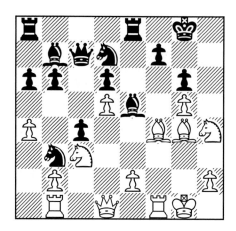

Exercise (critical decision): Black can play 23...♗xc3 24 bxc3 ♕c5+
which picks off White's d5-pawn. Would you give up your
precious dark-squared Benoni bishop for White's central pawn?

Answer: It's not even close. White collapses after the swap.

23...♗xc3!

Question: Really? Giving away his dark squares?

Answer: Principle: Counter in the centre when attacked on the wing. It was a good decision. White can't easily exploit the dark squares since his pawn on g5 gums up the works.

24 bxc3 ♕c5+

The counterattack begins in earnest. Black's queen watches her rival on g1 with cold eyes.

25 e3 ♘e5 26 ♗f3

26 ♗e2 ♗xd5 is also completely hopeless.

26...♘d3 27 ♔h1 ♗xd5 28 ♖xb3 ♘xf4

Question: Are there other ways for Black to win?

Answer: As Elizabeth Barrett Browning wrote: "Let me count the ways." Another win lies in 28...cxb3 29 ♕xd3 ♗c4 30 ♕d1 ♗xf1.

29 ♖b1 ♖xe3

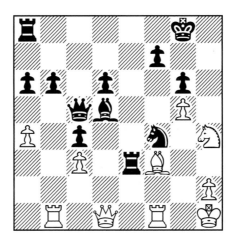

The "attack" descends into a murky, troubled dream and White's deranged forces talk to themselves, as if addressing the air. The rest is a bloodbath. Alekhine claims he was in too much time pressure to know to resign. More tournament book hogwash. The true reason, of course, was that Alekhine simply couldn't muster the courage to stick his hand out and resign to his hated rival.

30 ♘g2 ♖xf3 31 ♖xf3 ♘xg2 32 ♔xg2 ♖e8 33 ♔f1 ♗xf3 34 ♕xf3 ♕xg5 35 ♖e1 ♖xe1+ 36 ♔xe1 ♕g1+ 37 ♔d2 ♕xh2+ 38 ♔c1

The castaway on the deserted island watches glumly as his rescue ship recedes into the horizon.

38...♕e5 39 ♔b2 ♔g7 40 ♕f2 b5 41 ♕b6 bxa4 42 ♕xa6 ♕e2+ 0-1

Such losses between rivals leave deep scars within the mind. Alekhine paid Capa a very rare compliment at this point: "I feel ashamed of this game, but readily admit that my opponent took impeccable advantage of my errors." Resentment is futile in the face of elemental calamity!

> ## Game 21
> ### A.Alekhine-J.R.Capablanca
> 22nd matchgame, Buenos Aires 1927
> *Queen's Gambit Declined*

1 d4 ♘f6 2 c4 e6 3 ♘c3 d5 4 ♗g5 ♘bd7 5 e3 ♗e7 6 ♘f3 0-0 7 ♖c1 c6 8 ♗d3 dxc4 9 ♗xc4 ♘d5 10 ♗xe7 ♕xe7